Horace Tabor

Horace Tabor. *State Historical Society of Colorado.*

Horace Tabor

His Life and the Legend

Duane A. Smith

UNIVERSITY PRESS OF COLORADO

© 1989 by the University Press of Colorado

Published by the University Press of Colorado
5589 Arapahoe Avenue, Suite 206C
Boulder, Colorado 80303

The University Press of Colorado is a cooperative publishing enterprise supported, in part, by Adams State College, Colorado State University, Fort Lewis College, Mesa State College, Metropolitan State College of Denver, University of Colorado, University of Northern Colorado, University of Southern Colorado, and Western State College of Colorado.

The paper used in this publication meets the minimum requirements of the American National Standard for Information Sciences—Permanence of Paper for Printed Library Materials. ANSI Z39.48-1992

Library of Congress Cataloging-in-Publication Data

Smith, Duane A.
    Horace Tabor: His Life and the Legend

Originally published: Colorado Associated University Press, 1973.
        1. Tabor, Horace Austin Warner, 1830–1899. 2. Pioneer—Colorado—Biography.
3. Industrialists—Colorado—Biography. 4. Colorado—Lieutenant-governors—
Biography. I. Title.

F781.T322S63   1989   328.73'092   [B]   89-24878
ISBN 0-87081-206-8

10 9 8 7 6 5 4 3 2

FOR GAY

CONTENTS

Preface   vii

Prologue: The Legendary Tabor   ix

I. SEARCH FOR THE PROMISED LAND, 1855–1877

1. Time of Testing   3
2. Fifty-Niner Miner   15
3. Quiet Years   36

II. SUMMER'S PROSPERITY, 1877–1880

4. Bonanza   59
5. The Political Itch   79
6. Leadville's Son Becomes Denver's Patron   93
7. Sowing the Wind   109
8. Reaping the Whirlwind   127
9. Colorado's Entrepreneur   149

III. DISILLUSIONMENT OF SUCCESS, 1881–1889

10. "A Union Grand of Capital and Labor"   171
11. To Aspen and Beyond   190
12. The Great Senate Race   207
13. For the Love of Baby Doe   225
14. The Tabors at Home   246
15. Eroding Empire   259

IV. TWILIGHT OF A LEGEND, 1889–1899

16. So Fleet the Works   281
17. Back to the Earth Again   301
18. Measurement of a Man   316

Notes   325

Bibliography   369

Index   389

Map   396

HORACE TABOR'S
COLORADO

SCALE
0 10 20 30 40 50

● Town Where Tabor Lived

PREFACE

Oro City, December 27, 1876. Is a very shrewd businessman and not liable to lose money, has a good chance to make money as he has no competition. Estimated worth say $15,000.

THIS R. G. Dun report fairly and accurately described the pre-Leadville and bonanza Horace Tabor. An 1859er who had spent nearly two decades following the will-o-the-wisp Colorado mining frontier, Tabor was then living and working in out-of-the-way Oro City, near where Leadville would be one day.

Soon thereafter came the Little Pittsburg silver strike, and Tabor's fortune took flight. Very quickly, Colorado — and the rest of the nation — was hearing about Horace Tabor. "Denver's lucky star was on high when Governor Tabor decided to spend his fortune here," praised the *Denver Tribune* (September 7, 1881). The *Leadville Daily Herald* (July 8, 1882) also understood his contribution: "Colorado has produced fortunes for many men, but no man who has met with success has so freely made investments in this state, as has Governor Tabor."

The events that followed that amazing silver discovery on Fryer Hill, May 1878 unfolded like a classic Greek tragedy. Tabor weathered them all, and his name has resounded through the succeeding decades. No other Coloradan of his generation is so well remembered, nor does anyone else so typify the tempo of this legendary mining era. While the others — Henry Teller, David Moffat, Jerome Chaffee, Edward Wolcott — have faded in memory, Tabor is still alive, thanks in no small measure to that epoch-capturing opera, *The Ballad of Baby Doe.*

He is perhaps remembered for all the wrong reasons — the love triangle, the divorce, the decline and collapse — rather than for the faith, the optimism, and the investments that built Colorado. Even more regrettable is the fabrication that became fact; as far as can be ascertained, he never told Baby Doe to "hang onto the Matchless." Her later life — and death — these are catalyst enough for the legend, without adding a 1938-concocted story that seems unlikely ever to die.

Colorado historiography has evolved notably since the late 1960s, when I first researched the Tabors, but Horace's stature has not diminished. Caught up in the Tabor mystique, I have never abandoned the search for new information; he pops up almost everywhere that mining took hold. Even in areas where he did not go, his reputation and success pushed others forward in their search. His era is gone; mining now lingers as a mere shadow of its former substance. Be that as it may, Horace Tabor's story speaks to today's Coloradans, and to all who enjoy history, as clearly as it did a century ago when mining reigned supreme and opportunity beckoned over the silver mountain and into the next valley.

Duane A. Smith
May 1989

PROLOGUE

THE LEGENDARY TABOR

THE trans-Mississippi frontier has proven to be fertile ground for the raising of legendary figures, from Davy Crockett at the Alamo to the turn-of-the-century train robbers Butch Cassidy and The Sundance Kid. Each wave of settlement which spilled across the Mississippi left behind its own pool of men and women who walked larger than life on a vast land which seemed to demand such giants. The mining frontier, beckoning with the possibility of instant success and great wealth, naturally had a generous share of such individuals, better known today for what they are thought to have done than for what they actually accomplished.

Although other mining areas got an earlier start, Colorado emerged as the greatest of the western mining regions in the latter half of the nineteenth century. A cornucopia of mineral riches was locked in its mountain depths.

Of this state's mining men, none was better known in his own day, nor did any become more legendary, than Horace Austin Warner Tabor. Tabor's career symbolized all the vicissitudes of mining, politics, and business by which the growth of Colorado was to be measured; his experiences were thus the stuff of legend.

The legendary Tabor emerged, not — as the reader might imagine — after his death, but during his lifetime. Two Horace Tabors rose to prominence, one real and the other half-real. They easily intermingled so many times in their own day that they became harder and harder to distinguish as the years passed.

Many people contributed to the creation of one Tabor or the other, and some to both, further muddying the waters. In his lifetime Tabor was a subject for journalist-biographers by the score, many of whose accounts were blatantly false and contrived to fit a preconceived image. Almost all writers who came to Colorado in the late 1870s and early 1880s felt obligated to give some comment about him. A few, such as Leadville newspaperman R. G. Dill, Denverite Frank Hall, and mining reporter Frank Fossett, knew Tabor and his activities for some period of time and did a good job of describing what they observed. The same may not be said of most other contemporaries; they reported elaborate stories without bothering to do any research or talk with people who might have known the facts. In general, Colorado journalism of the period bore a highly personal stamp: editors and publishers reported their opinions and biases right along with the news. Unwary researchers have gone astray then and since.

At the height of Tabor's career, two of the best newspaper satirists were active in Colorado. They had a field day with Tabor and his activities. In Ouray, Dave Day of the *Solid Muldoon* kept his sharp pen pricking in Tabor's hide for over a decade. He was bettered only by Eugene Field, then an editor of the *Denver Tribune*, and the same man who later won fame as a children's poet. The stories these two concocted for their readers' enjoyment were accepted by others as gospel truth often enough to cloud Tabor's reputation well into the twentieth century.

Tales of his rags-to-riches career surfaced as early as the 1870s. Each new chapter was magnified or distorted by embellishments. Stories of his extravagances titillated newspaper readers in the parlors of fine Denver homes and the smoky saloons of the mining camps. The scandals that tainted some of his activities provided juicy fodder for armies of rumor-mongers and careless writers. On top of this, Tabor was of course the subject of the usual myths and fabrications about the wealthy, their lives, and their actions.

The legends have proved enduring, nearly always colorful, seldom authenticated, and only rarely trustworthy. The Tabor of legend was more fiction than fact, and his ghost might justly bemoan the poor treatment he received at the hands of twentieth-century biographers.

David Karsner, in his *Silver Dollar* (first published in 1932), carefully nourished the myths and compounded the inaccuracies, never letting history stand in the way of his story. Lewis Gandy's *The Tabors* (1934) evidences more interest and research, but, like all writers prior to the 1950s, Gandy did not have access to the Tabor papers, which severely limited his research. Nearly every book about Colorado or the Rocky Mountains mentions Tabor in some context, generally sordid sensationalism. The cleverly-written and ill-researched worst are Lucius Beebe's *Big Spenders* (1966) and Phyllis Dorset's *The New Eldorado* (1970).

Numerous pamphlets about his life have appeared in the past two decades, which generally add little of note and too frequently serve only to perpetuate old or coin new legends. Written primarily for the tourist trade, they capitalize on the sensational. Edgar McMachen wrote the best, *The Tabor Story* (1951); Caroline Bancroft has been the most prolific. Of the same genre, although a book, is Gordon Hall's *The Two Lives of Baby Doe* (1962), which lacks originality and depth and is laced with hearsay.

The Tabor story even entered the musical field, in the shape of the opera, *The Ballad of Baby Doe* by John Latouche and Douglas Moore, which premiered at Colorado's Central City Opera House in July 1956. Admittedly not completely accurate historically, it succeeded in catching the spirit of the times and the character of the man better than many of the so-called biographers of Tabor over the past ninety years.

A major biographical problem certainly has been that research materials have not been readily available until the 1960s. Even then, their use required time, effort, and a knowledge of various topics which too few writers were willing to acquire. Yet another problem for the biographer is simply that Horace Tabor himself was not the simple individual so often portrayed. A complex man, involved in so many diverse activities, cannot be neatly categorized.

Horace Tabor deserves a better place in history than has been accorded him to date. His accomplishments in politics, in building up Colorado, and in advancing mining were such that they need to be clarified and analyzed, if only to produce a clearer understanding of the state and its development during Tabor's era.

Today it is virtually impossible to catch the physical feeling of the era in which Tabor lived, except perhaps at Leadville. Here, situated on the slopes of hills draining down to the Arkansas River and surrounded by mountains over which towers Mount Elbert, Colorado's highest, in the town that Tabor knew so well, there still stand buildings where he worked and played; on the nearby hills are the ruins of mines he once developed into some of the greatest in the United States.

We must now go back to a time before super-highways crossed the plains and mountains, before a century of development raped the land. Back to a time when, as Tabor sings in the opening act of *The Ballad of Baby Doe*, opportunity beckoned beyond the horizon:

> I came this way from Massachusetts
> Through the Kansas Territory
> Pick and shovel in my hand
> Belly full of gin and glory.[1]

I.
SEARCH FOR THE
PROMISED LAND
1855-1877

CHAPTER 1

TIME OF TESTING

"Kansas cannot be a slave State!"
Herald of Freedom, April 7, 1855

ON AN extremely cold March morning in 1855, the first spring party of the New England Emigrant Aid Company arrived in the raw little Kansas town of Lawrence. Four inches of snow covered the ground, whipped by a wind blowing unhampered across the prairie and around the hastily-built wooden houses and stores. So many came in this group that not enough lodging was available, and a few suffered no small discomfort. Those who could not find shelter moved on to seek a farm site elsewhere. It was not a pleasant introduction to Kansas frontier life for the party of 192 men, women, and children, which had left Boston on the thirteenth.[1]

Among the party was a twenty-four-year-old stonecutter, who hailed from Holland, Vermont. Like the others, Horace Tabor came West to seek his fortune. Standing slightly over five feet ten inches, he was tall for that time; long used to hard work, he had a well filled out and muscular frame. In the prime of life, Tabor left the east — where steady employment but no spectacular career might be his — for the frontier. There anything seemed possible for a man of good health and fortitude who was willing to work hard and had his share of good luck. He had come not to pursue his occupation of stonecutter, but to try his skill at farming the fertile Kansas prairie.

The year 1855, however, was no ordinary one in the history of the westward movement, for Kansas was not simply open territory for fortune seekers and those wishing to start life anew. Kansas was aflame with political struggle. Kansas had to be saved from the slaveholders or the abolitionists, the choice depending upon one's political persuasion. The westward advance was now hopelessly mixed with the question of slavery extension into federal territories. Had it not been for this circumstance, Tabor and his party would not have been sent West so willingly by the Aid Company, nor would this organization have been so active in establishing towns, Lawrence and Topeka, and sponsoring the voice of "Free Soil" (the abolitionist slogan), the outspoken *Herald of Freedom*.

Tabor arrived on this potentially explosive scene with unrecorded views on the pressing issue, although years later he commented, "My politics were free soil. I have always been against slavery." Shortly before his death in 1899, he had occasion to write the *Denver Times* concerning his attitude toward the Negro. At that time he recalled an experience in Kansas back in 1857 or 1858, when he had given his only pistol to a slave fleeing the South.[2] The story may be apocryphal, since Tabor had not referred to it earlier and at that particular moment was wooing the local Negro vote.

No radical in any case, he turned his attention to the immediate goal of securing a farm and preparing it for summer crops. He picked the great central valley of the Kansas River, just below its junction with the Big Blue River, somewhat out of the mainstream of settlement. For many years previous this region had been viewed as part of the Great American Desert, fit only for nomadic Indians. The westward drive, as if by a miracle, changed all that; the "desert's" fertile soil and salubrious climate were now praised: a traveler passing through just before Tabor arrived noted the rolling landscape, the frequent groves of trees, and the soil's "deep rich loam."[3] Horace finally settled near the infant community of Zeandale, a few miles outside of Manhattan and well outside the immediate theater of conflict brewing in eastern Kansas.

Virtually a wilderness area, Zeandale had scarcely been settled when Tabor arrived in April 1855. As crude as it was, it offered more promise than did his home in northern Vermont. Born on November 26, 1830, in the county of Orleans, near the little village of Holland, Horace was a typical rural American youth. He had performed chores, worked long hours about the farm, and received from the local public school what was considered a good common-school education. The Tabor family, not particularly large for that day, had, in addition to Horace, two boys and a girl. The daughter Emily eventually married and moved to Kansas, where she reenters the story, and John would follow his brother to Colorado. Rural Vermont offered no opportunity for an ambitious lad, and he left home at nineteen to make his way in the world, yielding to a wanderlust that would eventually lead him to Kansas. In the meantime he learned the stonecutter's trade and practiced his skill in Massachusetts and Maine. Some of his early ingrained traits he maintained all his life, being described as late as 1879 as a Vermonter in "figure, speech, and temper of mind."

Out here, though, it was his farming skill that would stand him in good stead. He secured 160 acres by preemption and later, by borrowing, purchased another 320 acres. Much needed to be done — the land had to be cleared, a cabin built, crops planted, and the harvest gathered. Tabor's first crop was enough to get him through the winter, a harsh winter that was long remembered by settlers in Kansas. Throughout late December and January, the thermometer in Lawrence sank below zero and cold weather gripped the countryside. According to a local historian of Zeandale, the temperature dipped on occasion to thirty-one below and up to three feet of snow covered the ground. A neighbor recalled seeing Tabor walking home one winter day with a coffee mill under one arm. Replying to an inquiry about his health during the freezing weather, Tabor said, "You needn't worry about Horace Tabor ever starving while he has plenty of corn and a coffee mill to grind it in."[4]

By 1856, Kansas had been divided into two camps, each

with its own quota of partisans and each supporting its own territorial government, which claimed to control the whole Territory. Tabor's interest in politics had been passing, although warm enough to secure his nomination and election to the Free Soil House of Representatives from the Sixth District. It had been bitterly cold on the January 1856 election day, and there is no record of his casting his vote. Years later he pointed out how unusual it was to be chosen after such a short residence, then explained, "I was always prominent in the fight."[5] His prominence must have been hidden under a bushel basket, for no record of it has appeared. Nevertheless, the young legislator traveled to Topeka in March to take up his first official duties.

Topeka, the Free Soil capital, had changed since Tabor's visit a year before, when he had first gone to Zeandale, stone and brick buildings now rising among their wooden neighbors. Apprehension permeated the settlement, because already the so-called Wakarusa War had threatened to bring about open warfare. Tabor had taken no part in this, nor had anyone from his area. The *Herald of Freedom* was correct in calling the western parts somewhat remote from the center of the political strife. But still Tabor had come to Topeka, over poor roads, now snow and mud-packed, to be there in time for opening roll call on the afternoon of March 4.

Coming as he did from a relatively insignificant area, at first he only watched and listened, taking no part in the debates. Not until March 6 did the House journal mention him, and then only because he had been appointed to a committee on public institutions. On the following Monday, Tabor moved for a minor amendment related to printing material and was pleased when the other members concurred. The same day, he and all the legislators were invited to a special party given by the ladies of Topeka. The world of politics and society provided the member from isolated Zeandale a pleasant change from his normal routine.

On Friday, March 14, Tabor arose for his maiden parliamentary speech, offering the following resolution:

6

"Resolved that we request the codifying committee to take into consideration the importance of a law prohibiting hogs from running at large in the State of Kansas." He had put his finger on a sensitive issue, and the *Herald of Freedom* commented on it in a blistering editorial on April 19, 1856, entitled "Hogs vs. the People." They opposed the idea of corralling hogs, and so had the House previously, when Tabor's resolution had been ruled out of order. Two days later, on March 16, the House went into recess until July 4.[6]

Tabor went home to plow his fields, plant his crops, and take care of his homestead, while the country debated what was happening in Kansas. Threats and some violence marred that spring and early summer, making Kansas the emotional issue of the day. Against this background, he returned to Topeka, where the session was to open at twelve o'clock on July 4. Western Kansas still was not threatened and, as one traveler observed, politics were discussed a good deal but "Missouri is some distance off."[7] Missouri, as both Tabor and the traveler knew, was the nearest pro-slavery southern stronghold.

Topeka, Tabor found, was in an uproar; hostility toward the federal government because of its lack of support for Free State plans smoldered just beneath the surface. It flared into the open when President Franklin Pierce was burned in effigy. The House met at the appointed time, only to be dispersed by federal troops commanded by Colonel (and later Union General) Edwin V. Sumner. An intensely dramatic scene occurred. Sumner and his dragoons, supported by artillery, advanced on the meeting hall, ringed by hostile Free Staters. With great efficiency and dispatch, Sumner carried out his "painful duty." No violence ensued; the Free Staters gave three cheers for the legislature and Topeka constitution, followed by three "deep and loud" groans for Pierce, startling the already nervous horses of the troops. Tabor called the dispersal a "great outrage"; nothing that he could see in their legislative acts warranted such reaction by the United States. Pierce, he thought, wanted Kansas to be a slave state and adopted this method to break the Free State cause and save the Territory for the South.[8] Politics was thus brought home to him as never before, and he returned to Zeandale to tell his agitated constituents what had happened. Farming seemed dull after Topeka on that July 4.

As summer waned into fall, Pierce finally found a governor who could control the Kansas situation, six-foot-five-inch John Geary, whose height was matched by his ability and energy. Vigorous use of federal troops, plus disbanding of local militia, ended the more violent acts of pillage. No evidence suggests that Tabor was involved in any local Kansas events during those months. He next appeared at Topeka for the legislative session opening January 6, 1857. More active now than earlier, he spoke out on several issues and, significantly, was appointed a member of the committee to prepare a memorial to Congress stating "our grievances" and asking for admission into the Union.

While it was a signal honor to be selected as one of the committee's three members, the majority responsibility for drafting the report seems to have fallen on chairman James Blood, a lawyer. Instructed to report at an early date, the committee did so the very next day, lending credence to the idea that much of the memorial was already prepared and required only formal acknowledgment. The memorial presented familiar arguments, giving a straightforward recitation of the Free State cause. It was sent on to Congress, where nothing came of it. The Topeka House, on reassembling, found itself without a quorum and promptly recessed until June.[9]

Thanks to Geary's actions and the obvious numerical superiority of the Free Staters, the Kansas situation stabilized rapidly that winter and spring. Under such circumstances, the Topeka government became obsolete and a hindrance to the final solution of the question of who would control the Territory. The extra-legal child of expediency could be conveniently forgotten, the quicker the better. Horace Tabor was always a minor figure at the Topeka meetings, emerging into the limelight only briefly in that January 1857 session. He gained needed experience in parliamentary procedure and in the art of frontier politics and government which would stand him in good stead in the years to come. As the years passed, he reflected with pleasure and a sense of honor upon the turbulent days of his earlier years, when he had stood against slavery in Kansas. And in truth, it had taken courage to express one's views as a member of a legislature threatened by nearby enemies.

Still, that final January session in 1857 could not have passed rapidly enough for the youthful Zeandale delegate, for he was impatient to be off. His eyes and heart were fixed, not on Topeka, but upon Maine and his bride-to-be, Augusta Pierce. Absence had not cooled the love of these two, and Tabor was on his way back to be married.

What stories the Kansas veteran must have had to beguile his future in-laws and friends on the long winter evenings! Engaged for two years while Tabor homesteaded, the couple was finally married on the last day of January. His twenty-three-year-old wife was a New Englander to the core, dignified, industrious, and modest, although her spelling indicates only an ordinary education. There are no early portraits, but her later pictures show that she must not have been unattractive before two decades on the frontier took their toll. Though small of frame, Augusta had the personality to adapt to frontier conditions, and she worked loyally with her husband in their search for the fortune he knew was beckoning them. For nearly a month they remained in Augusta, Maine. Then they left for Kansas — a tiring, slow railroad trip, followed by a more pleasant boat ride up the Missouri River.

Some doubt exists as to exactly how the newlyweds reached central Kansas. Years later, Augusta remembered they landed in Kansas City, purchased a yoke of oxen and a wagon, loaded it with seed and farming tools, and went overland. But Kansas historian Albert Greene, writing about early navigation on the Kansas River, states that the Tabors came to Lawrence on the steamer *Lightfoot*; his account is based on the story of a passenger on the boat.[10] Until further evidence appears, Augusta's version will have to stand, although Tabor, with his bent for adventure, would have liked to take such a trip. Yet if they had, certainly Augusta should have remembered that novel way to reach Lawrence.

Whatever way they reached their destination, Augusta was in for a shock when she first looked about her new home. Desolation, the prairie winds, an entrapping loneliness, dominated the scene. A small solitary cabin, which for the past two years had served as Horace's bachelor lodgings, awaited her, a cabin whose appearance had not been helped by being vacant for several months:

> I sat down upon the trunk and cried; I had not been deceived in coming to this place. I knew perfectly well that the country was new, that there were no sawmills near, and no money in the territory. But I was homesick and could not conceal it from those about me.[11]

She more than mastered the situation. Quickly the cabin was cleaned and old issues of the *New York Tribune* pasted on the bare log walls, doubling as utilitarian wallpaper and as reading material to ease the shortage of that commodity on the frontier. While Augusta made their cabin more homelike, Horace began farming in earnest. Often she joined him in the fields after completing her house chores, but despite their combined efforts, the crop failed for lack of rain that first summer.

To secure money, Augusta reports that Tabor went to nearby Fort Riley to work as a stonemason, although post records fail to confirm this. Meanwhile, she boarded some of the nearby bachelors who fancied home cooking. Living alone was not to her liking but she was equal to the occasion. Their efforts somehow got them through the winter. In spite of such trials, the country around them was growing and looked less like a frontier. Zeandale managed the organization of a Congregational Church in 1858, and a school was started the next year. Kansas City and Lawrence both were expanding, and even neighboring Manhattan had made a start with twenty-seven dwellings and three stores.[12] It was a good land with which to grow.

The year 1858 proved a better one for the Tabors. In fact, they had an abundant harvest, but so did all their neighbors and the bottom dropped out of the market. Fate seemed against them in Kansas. To add to their domestic responsibilities, Augusta and Horace had become the parents of a young son, Maxey. Tabor's auspicious beginning and fond hope of wealth appear to have disintegrated before the harsh realities of frontier life and agriculture. Two seasons passed, and the family fortune looked no better than it had upon arrival. His experience in Kansas, Tabor later reminisced, "offered me little inducement to remain there."[13] They had persevered and worked diligently; with Augusta taking in boarders and selling butter and eggs, they had been able to keep going. But was this the life they really wanted?

Rumors reached Zeandale of a prospect which intrigued Tabor no end; gold had been found farther west. Such stories were not new; he had hardly settled in Kansas when the *Herald of Freedom* announced, on May 26 and June 2, 1855, that gold had been discovered at the headwaters of the Arkansas River. These rumors proved false. Now in the summer of 1858 the stories of gold were revived, and newspapers as far away as California were taking note. Gold had been found in the Pike's Peak region on Cherry Creek; even the conservative *New York Times* said so. On February 21, 1859, the *Times* editorially announced that there was no longer room for doubt that gold had been discovered, the rush awaited only the coming of spring. In the intervening months a hot debate ensued as to whether this was rumor or fact.[14] Anticipation gripped the Midwest and, despite denials, evidence mounted and hopes soared. A depression had settled over the region in the late 1850s, affecting not only the Tabors but thousands like them in cities and on farms. These people were willing to gamble one summer to see if rewards matched expectations. Only the winter season held them back; as soon as feasible they would be off to Pike's Peak, guided by one of the numerous guidebooks that had appeared, as if by magic, to answer the needs of the time.

For the Tabors in Zeandale such rumors posed questions not easily answered. Should they go West, sacrificing a season of farming, in hopes of gaining wealth? Should Tabor go, leaving his wife and son, or should continued effort be made for success here? If they read the *Herald of Freedom*, and they certainly had access to some newspaper, the answer would have seemed easy to reach. Letters from Cherry Creek diggings left no doubt about the richness of the discovery; without question, according to reports, it would equal the very best of California as soon as spring arrived. Men were making eight to ten dollars a day, money Tabor could not begin to make as a farmer or stonecutter. Letters appeared praising the climate and terrain, even though none of the writers had as yet experienced a real Rocky Mountain winter nor inspected the soil along the river bottoms. Careful instructions were printed concerning the best route to reach the gold fields, what to bring, and what dangers might be encountered. It was noted that one should treat the Indians courteously, but not too familiarly, and should an Indian "deliberately insult you knock him down." April was the best time to start, when the grass would better sustain the animals. A few pessimistic letters warned of hardship, and one even dared to state that gold had not yet been found in sufficient quantities, and that no one was averaging more than two or three dollars per day.[15]

Tabor, like thousands of others, weighed the pros and cons and decided to go. He had a mortgage on his farm, and saw no quicker way to retire it than in the gold fields. This came to be, in Horace's thinking, the primary motive for going West.

> I came out here for the purpose of mining, because we knew nothing of this country except as a mining country. . . . I came for the express purpose of trying to make money enough out here to redeem that land. . . . At that time I really had no other idea, except to redeem that land.[16]

Worrying about the mortgage and how to meet the payments after the past seasons provided the rationale for the trip. After four years, Tabor had only forty to sixty acres under cultivation, some stock, and a small house to show for his efforts.[17] How alluring the wealth of Cherry Creek was to a man in such a situation! Plans were made by Horace and Augusta and final preparations were undertaken for the journey across the plains. Augusta was not well, but this did not alter her resolve to go with her husband, even though Horace told her she might return to Maine.

They started for Colorado in early April, leaving their farm, which was rented and which Tabor continued to own at least through the 1880s. Either in the 1850s or later he had acquired some lots in Lawrence, which he kept also, though they remained undeveloped as late as 1887.[18] Tabor's career in Kansas had been typical of many others; his fortunes, while not outstanding, would probably have improved had he decided to stay. Unlike a miner, a farmer could not expect instant wealth, only a gradual accumulation, as the whole region developed and markets appeared. Tabor would not wait.

As the Tabor party moved West, unknown to them, news of significant gold discoveries finally reached Denver. Until the spring of 1859 there had been no real basis for the Pike's Peak gold rush. To be sure, some gold had been discovered, but the amount multiplied in the telling. Then, in the winter of 1858–59, three important discoveries were made at the future sites of Central City, Idaho Springs, and Gold Hill.

Many who started out for Pike's Peak turned back, damning it all as a hoax upon hearing of the high prices at the mines and the relatively small returns from the hard labor involved. Others decided to change direction and go on to California. One such fifty-niner, who started in March from Michigan, wrote in his diary his progressive discouragement over Pike's Peak. By May, far out on the Platte River route, he and his friends were encountering returning men who said the mines were a humbug, "and we were fools to go any further." Others they saw were reduced to begging food as they struggled to return home; he continued to meet "hundreds of emigrants camped, arguing and quarrelling" about what to do. He finally decided to go on West and bypassed the Colorado turnoff.[19] All in all, an estimated hundred thousand started, and approximately fifty thousand kept their resolve and at least reached Denver.

The journey was difficult for all who undertook it. The Tabors, joined by their good friend Nathaniel Maxey, went by the logical Republican River route, which passed near them, perhaps reasoning it to be shorter than the others. If life on the farm had been hard, crossing the plains was much more strenuous. Dust, wind, Indian danger, and the tedious miles frustrated them all. Augusta gathered buffalo chips to serve as fuel to cook what game the men were able to kill.

> This weary work fell to the women, for the men had enough to do in taking care of the teams, and in 'making' and 'breaking' the camp. The Indians followed us all the time, and though friendly, were continually begging and stealing . . .
>
> I was weak and feeble, having suffered all the time that I lived in Kansas with ague. My weight was only ninety pounds.

Sunday was a day of rest, although Augusta had reasonable doubts as to the use of the term, because the men hunted while she stayed to wash clothes and guard the camp. Maxey was teething and suffering from "fever and ague," thus adding to the burdens of this poor woman, who already served as cook and laundress for the whole party.[20] The road was not always well marked, since the Tabor party was one of the first. Some groups had started from midwestern states as early as February, only to find themselves on the plains before the grass could provide enough feed for their animals.

Although they could not appreciate it at the time, the Tabors were part of one of the great gold rushes in American history. They had become fifty-niners and begun carving out their own niche in history.

CHAPTER 2

FIFTY-NINER MINER

Silver runs in ledges and gold is where you find it.
Mining proverb

DENVER, less than a year old, loomed as a rough-hewn yet rewarding sight to those who chose to follow the golden dreams of fifty-nine. It was really two little settlements, Denver and Auraria, defiantly facing each other across the rushing waters of Cherry Creek. Horace Greeley came West and described what he saw through the eyes of an urbane Easterner. The architecture, he noted, was striking, "cottonwood logs cut from the adjacent bottom of the Platte, roughly hewed on the upper and under sides, chinked with billets of split cottonwood on the inner, and with mud on the outer sides . . . " Wooden floors were conspicuously absent, though Greeley did find one, and he also noted the luxurious accommodations offered the traveler:

> The Denver House, which is the Astor House of the gold region, has walls of logs, a floor of earth, with windows and roof of rather flimsy cotton sheeting, while every guest is allowed as good a bed as his blankets will make. The charges are no higher than at the Astor and other first-class hotels, except for liquor — twenty-five cents a drink for dubious whisky.[1]

The youthful city booster William Byers, editor and proprietor of the only newspaper, wrote of his community that it had about 150 houses with five stores, two hotels, two bakeries, two saloons, and one printing office. Proudly, he observed that sawed lumber was taking the place of logs and that frame buildings were rising rapidly.[2]

But Augusta remembered Denver as having only a few log cabins and eleven pioneer women. The Tabors stayed a week, recuperating from the rigors of the trip and learning first-hand of the discoveries in the mountains to the west. Tabor's knowledge of mining must have been scanty, for nowhere in his previous experience could he have acquired the skill of prospecting or panning. He listened with great interest to the stories of those who came down from the mines, as well as to the tales of those who, yet to go, were nonetheless eager to disseminate their meager knowledge to any who would listen.

Mining was what Tabor had come to do, so he loaded his young wife and son into the wagon and pushed on to the place that was to become Golden, Colorado. Here, with supreme confidence in his wife's pioneering abilities, and because his footsore cattle could go no farther, Horace left his family and went on to look for his bonanza. For weeks Augusta waited patiently, the silence broken only by those who passed the camp on their way to the Gregory (Central City) or Payne's Bar (Idaho Springs) diggings. Years later this episode was still fresh in her memory, "nothing there but just myself and our team, silence reigned around; not a soul but me and my baby, and I was a weakly woman, not nearly so strong as I am now."[3]

Finally her husband returned, having selected his claim at Payne's Bar. They set out for Gregory's diggings, then on to Russell's, and finally to their destination. The last segment proved the worst, according to Augusta, taking three weeks because "[we] had to make our road as we went. We would only make about three miles a day; a wagon had never been there before." Eventually, the goal was reached, probably around the middle of August, and Augusta received her first taste of life in a Colorado mining camp. The tents, lean-tos, and other assorted shelters probably did not much impress her as a community.

Now Tabor had finally reached the diggings, and only hard work stood between him and the fortune he had been seeking since he came West four years before. He quickly learned the elementary skills needed for a placer mining operation. A pick, a shovel, and a pan were his tools, and a strong back and eager desire provided the power. Youth was on his side — he was twenty-nine years old, had suffered no known serious illnesses, and was blessed with youth's unbounded optimism. This optimism was to carry him through years of disappointment. Further, he had an asset which many fifty-niners lacked — a wife who accompanied him, faithfully sharing his trials without shirking. Augusta might have felt that her health was not good, but the climate seemed to improve it, and she had a strong constitution.

Horace went prospecting and mining, while Augusta tended the home and provided extra income by selling her tasty baked goods to miners eager for home-cooked food after enduring a bachelor's fare for months. So successful was this working combination that enough money was made to pay the debt on the farm left behind in Kansas and to tide them over the first Colorado winter. Summer, meanwhile, quickly drifted into fall, for the Tabors had arrived late at the diggings. Before the first snows, Tabor found what he considered a profitable claim. Then the snow fell. "Old-timers" questioned whether a woman should try to winter in the mountains, especially with a small child. The concerned Tabor listened, pondered the tales of dreadful snowslides, and decided to take his family back to Denver, where better shelter could be found than a log cabin with a tent roof.[4]

Upon returning to the site, he found that his claim had been jumped, a misfortune for which he had no recourse within the vague mining law of the day, because he simply had not done the required monthly assessment work. Legally, if not morally, he had abandoned his claim. "There was no law in those days," sorrowfully noted Augusta. Horace learned from this setback; he would be more cautious the next time. Whether he had been deliberately deceived with tales of hard winters and driven out of Payne's Bar will never be known, but he never returned to mine in that district again, turning instead to newer discoveries.

Dejected, Tabor went back to Denver, a sadder but wiser man. Still, he had acquired some knowledge of mining methods and an idea of what to search for in prospecting. His family had survived the trip across the plains and a season at the mines, so, all in all, he was fortunate. He had money, though not as much as some; still, he was richer than many unfortunates who had long since returned to the States, disgusted at the "humbug" called Pike's Peak. Like others who stayed, Tabor derided these "gobacks" and "pilgrims" and remained convinced that a great new day would dawn in 1860.

The Tabors now settled in a rented room over a store for their first extended stay in Denver. Denver had changed in the short period of their absence; now it had absorbed Auraria. Like other frontier mining communities, Denver grew astonishingly in its first year, optimism and expectation leading many to plunge where normally they might have held back. Real estate values went up with demand; brick buildings were appearing, lending an air of permanence. A school had started, a circulating library of fifty volumes had opened, two theaters provided entertainment, and a local brewery provided refreshment.[5] Horace took it all in, for the first time relishing the excitement of a growing mining community, excitement little Payne's Bar could not offer.

It proved a restless winter for the young miner, who was still seeking a golden fortune. While Augusta stayed in Denver, providing a home for Maxey and taking in boarders to supplement the money earned earlier, her husband went back into the mountains. Part of his time that winter was apparently spent near Pike's Peak, where he joined others in promoting a new town, Colorado City. Town promotion, an age-old frontier activity, was not new to him, since he had observed it in Kansas; this time, however, he was one of the instigators, dreaming that someday this town would

be the state capital. Taking time only to construct the first
house on the site, Tabor rushed back to Denver to try to
convince others to move to this future mercantile and political
center. Only disappointment awaited him, because Denver
was full of similar plans: rumors of new discoveries, new
towns, and better opportunities swirled around the feverish
settlement like the wind-driven snow in the streets. No one
could afford to ignore them, since one never knew which
might hold the key to the new bonanza. "Come to the Tarryall
mines." "No, go to the Blue River." "Invest your money
in St. Vrain." "Bradford is the best place for settlement."
So it went.[6] Unfortunately, Tabor's Colorado City had no
vision of buckets of gold to offer, and it could not successfully
compete. Finally, in February, despite a general lack of interest
in his project, Horace and Augusta again packed their goods,
and the faithful oxen pulled the wagon and family down
to Colorado City.

On arrival, Augusta found only a few log houses. The
promoters promptly gave her several lots for no reason other
than that she was the first lady there. Tabor weighed the
future of the town and came to the correct conclusion that
his fortune lay in the mountains; having come West for gold,
he would seek it again in the spring. Others decided that
the site had a future; it did grow some, and several promotional articles were placed in Byers's *Rocky Mountain News*
praising Colorado City as "situated on the direct road to South
Park and the Arkansas River gold fields." But the promoters
were wrong and Tabor was right, for, as Augusta observed,
Colorado City was never much until the coming of the Denver
and Rio Grande railroad and the establishment of Colorado
Springs nearby. Horace simply stated it "never amounted
to anything."[7]

Stories and rumors of gold in South Park now bore fruit.
Tabor turned his face westward, moving up the wagon road
over Ute pass into the park, one of the three large, high valleys
of the Colorado Rockies. Their journey probably began in
early March and they were joined by Nathaniel Maxey and

Samuel P. Kellogg. Over the pass they struggled, pulling and pushing their wagon slowly across a trail previously used only by Indians and a few whites. The way was so steep that often at night they could look back and see the smoke from the dying fire of their previous campsite. Using pine trees for brakes they would carefully roll the wagon down the slopes. Even finding a level place to sleep presented problems. On reaching the park, the little party set out in search of an earlier group they had heard was somewhere ahead. Despite the beautiful setting and a sunset which Tabor still remembered years later, their situation was not promising. After several days of searching they found a faint trail that eventually brought them to the Arkansas River, high and fast in the spring runoff. Trying to ford it proved treacherous and the wagon had to be unloaded to get it safely across. A wet, cold day passed before everything was securely on the opposite bank.

Without word of other parties or knowledge of the actual location of the gold discoveries, the little group turned up the Arkansas and, after a difficult journey, reached the future site of Granite on Cache Creek. Here they stopped, rested, and turned to prospecting. Tabor whipsawed some fallen trees to make a rough sluice box, and even Augusta set to work mining. The gold was there, though mixed with heavy black sand which could not be separated by panning, and they had no quicksilver. Quicksilver would have solved their problem, for it has a natural affinity for gold, separating it easily from the almost equally heavy black sand which hampered the Tabor party. Augusta worked by the hour, first trying to pick out the larger pieces of gold, then using a magnet in an attempt to attract the iron-permeated sand. The method worked, though not as well as she had hoped, the gold being too fine — a pennyweight might be a full day's reward. After four weeks, only exhaustion and very little pay resulted from the efforts expended. Later, others with proper equipment would make a small fortune at Granite.

At this depressing time a man reached their camp, telling

of a discovery at California Gulch farther up the Arkansas. Here, for the first time, was concrete news which promised the diggings they sought. Without regret, they abandoned their discouraging claims and moved on, now heartened by the anticipation of immediate rewards.

On May 8, the party arrived in California Gulch, with its panoramic view of the upper Arkansas Valley. Augusta's "always very enterprising Mr. Tabor" put aside scenic contemplations and hurriedly went in search of a claim. His wife proved quite a celebrity, being the first woman to reach the district. With the added attraction of her young son, she was particularly welcome in California Gulch's masculine world. The men, in honor of the occasion, built her a log cabin in two days, and the Tabors moved into their new home. The hard-working oxen now paid the supreme sacrifice, since they were the only available source of meat.[8]

This new bonanza at which the Tabors arrived was richer by far than anything they had found previously, or so its discoverers claimed. While Horace's party had been laboring up Ute Pass and into South Park, Denverites heard rumors of $4.50 a pan "dirt," then of $20.00 to $25.00 per day on the Arkansas River. "Should this prove true, 'What a Stampede' when the snow goes off," wrote local businessman William Bradford. What a stampede, indeed! March passed, then April, and finally May before rumor could be confirmed; by then the rush was on, and only the fainthearted still had doubts that California in 1849 was about to be replayed and surpassed.

A discrepancy has existed from 1860 regarding the actual date of discovery. But it was some time after April 12 when a prospecting party reached the gulch and, despite deep snow, worked their way up it, and finally found "color" (gold) in their pans, after digging holes through the snow to reach the creek bed. Whether a member of the party, Abe Lee, actually exclaimed that he had all of California in his pan is, of course, questionable. So the story goes, and the site was christened California Gulch. News soon leaked, and men

21

from Kelley's diggings, some twenty miles away, abandoned their less-promising sites to hurry to the new discovery. Following the established pattern, a miners' meeting was called to set down laws for the formation of a mining district, in particular to stop the absentee ownership which had so plagued Gregory's diggings the season before. Working miners would have the best chance here.[9] At this point, the Tabors appeared; prospects seemed better than anything Horace had seen. Men already were venturing into nearby gulches and finding color, although at the moment it was "small potatoes," only three to five cents a pan.

By the end of May, a local correspondent of the *Rocky Mountain News*, Lewis Dow, informed his readers that people were constantly coming in and that a camp was appearing, with blacksmith, shoemakers, attorneys, and merchants. Prices, he moaned, were nearly double those in Denver, due to the scarcity of provisions, and he warned latecomers to go elsewhere, as most of the claims were taken. Tabor had finally had some luck in arriving at California Gulch early. Many who failed to heed Dow's warning found themselves not so fortunate.

The experience acquired in the Payne's Bar misfortunes of fifty-nine now paid dividends to Horace, because this also was a placer gold area. The tiring work of digging and the endless washing of sand and gravel were things he had done before. He had acquired the skill needed to swirl water around in a slightly-tipped pan, washing out the lighter waste material and leaving the heavier free gold. Claims were filed above and below the original discovery site; Tabor's best strike occurred above, and he washed out from five to seven thousand dollars that summer. The abandonment of Kansas at last appeared to be a wise move, though more fortunate neighbors reportedly made even more, some as much as sixty thousand dollars. Although he prospected elsewhere without success, Horace was not bothered, since he had made a substantial amount. Augusta, meanwhile, supplemented their income by taking in boarders. As she said, "There were so many men who could not cook and did not like men's cooking, and would insist upon boarding where there was a woman and they would board there all they could."[10] Around the hard-working couple the days passed swiftly, the green of summer fading to the aspen yellow of fall.

This was the first real mining rush they had ever seen, as thousands of "oldtimers" and newcomers alike crowded into the new El Dorado. Prices of claims soared; one reportedly sold for ten thousand dollars. Soon companies replaced individuals, and a good day's earnings ran from one hundred to one thousand dollars, depending on location and equipment. In August, the federal census taker reached sprawling California Gulch. He somehow missed the Tabors in his report, which showed this to be a predominantly masculine world, with fewer than forty women and girls.[11] How many people there were at the peak will never be known; the wilder estimates reached twenty thousand, but seven to ten thousand would be nearer the truth.

Augusta took interest in the development of this settlement, finally named Oro City, which grew haphazardly up and down the gulch; it was no New England town, but it held promise. She frowned upon the saloon, gambling houses, and red-light district which materialized; the miners, however, welcomed the "gay gamblers and the frail sisterhood." Eventually, Augusta came to understand and adjust to, if not approve of, this sordid aspect of the mining frontier. Her friendships with neighboring women ameliorated the isolation which had been her lot so much of the time since leaving Maine, as did the arrival of the mail, bringing with it letters and newspapers. Apparently on an informal basis, she became postmaster of the upper part of the gulch, where they resided, passing out the deliveries of the infrequent and costly mail service.

At the peak of the rush, of course, a reverse reaction set in, and the Tabors watched as the disappointed turned back. Rich as it was, California Gulch simply did not have enough paying claims for all who came. By August the fever-

23

like pitch of the gold-hunting mania subsided. Culture was still on the upswing, though. A traveling Methodist minister appeared, preaching to a large congregation and organizing a Sunday school before departing. Augusta certainly approved of such improvements, which meant that Oro City was becoming "civilized." Its growth had followed no pattern, except that the business houses — saloons, general stores, and blacksmiths among others — were clustered in one section, giving "a respectable show," as one writer said. But civilization had its drawbacks. Man had markedly changed the site in the one season he had been there. The gulch lay stripped and ripped open for miles in and about the Tabor home, and the once-clear water now had turned to liquid mud by the time it reached the Arkansas River. In the haste to get wood, the nearby hills had been denuded of trees, and every place was littered — bottles, boxes, cans, broken shovels, and around the cabins whatever the occupants discarded.

As the nights grew cooler, many left, including Augusta and Maxey. Horace had managed to accumulate enough money that summer to send them back to Maine for a winter visit. It was more than a pleasure trip, however, because Augusta carried money with her to buy supplies to open a store the next spring.[12] When Horace observed the profits that could be made by shrewd businessmen, the Tabors decided to branch out into the mercantile business. Because he had one of the few gold scales in Oro City, he had been called upon to weigh the gold found nearby. This activity, together with the boarding of miners and the delivery of mail, gave them their start; it would be a simple matter just to add supplies. Augusta and Horace had hit upon the scheme that would keep them prosperous for the next decade and a half.

By mid-November mining came to a halt, cold weather and then snow ending placer operations. Fresh excitement was temporarily generated with the claimed discovery of silver, but nothing appeared to come of it. Horace and those others who remained turned to a new interest, politics and the formation of "Jefferson Territory." Tension mounting back in the States over the 1860 election and secession threats had far less impact in isolated Oro City, which heard of these events a week or two after they had occurred. The failure of the federal government to provide territorial status, plus the natural frontier inclination to form such an entity, stimulated organization of an extralegal territory. Legislative districts were created and members elected for the November term. Chosen from California Gulch's upper district was one "Mr. Taber," who "may be known by his pugilistic appearance." When the session opened in Denver, H. W. Tabor and three others were appointed to a committee to memorialize Congress. Horace had been this route before. If his previous Topeka experience had been frustrating, it was worse in the Jefferson territorial legislature. The session lasted until December 14, even moving its locale to Golden before the House adjourned *sine die*, without accomplishing anything.[13] Hounded on all sides by increasing opposition, Jefferson Territory never had a chance, and it ended its precarious existence in May 1861 at the arrival of William Gilpin, newly-appointed Colorado territorial governor. Horace's second political experience proved less profitable than the first.

Otherwise 1860 had been a good year for Horace and his wife, each helping to make it successful. Back in Maine, Augusta held her listeners enthralled as she described for them the mysteries of the "wild west." In Oro City Horace passed the last months of winter anxiously awaiting the coming mining season. Algernon Weston, better known simply as A. S. Weston, wintered at Oro City and came to know Tabor. He left behind some letters describing the conditions. "We have been well and doing as well as could be expected for winter. Of course we have taken out but little money from the mines on account of the cold weather but have been preparing for a successful spring's work."[14] Still, when he wrote in April, he forecast nearly a month's passage before the ground could be "washed." "Mining," he concluded, "is uncertain business."

Augusta returned that spring, and the Tabor store opened under her management, while Horace continued his mining ventures. His attention turned to Iowa Gulch, some two miles south, where he and a party of men had worked as early as the previous November. They finally uncovered a rich deposit in April.[15] Hopes were high, only to be dashed when it proved to be only a small pocket. For a while though, it was front-page news, as more districts were organized and even a town platted, Lake City. People continued to head for Oro City. One was Wolfe Londoner, who would cross the Tabors' path many times; he wrote that people lived in tents and wagons.[16] It was something like 1860 again, except that the rewards were not there and the returns from each day's long hours were less. California Gulch had passed its peak as a placer camp.

Many just moved on — such was the transitory nature of the mining frontier — but the Tabors had more to ponder. Their various interests were returning a small profit. To move would mean seeking another promising location. Yet such a place now appeared, not too far away. To the "dull times" and "general gloom" of Oro City came word of a locale just northeast across the Mosquito Range, where gold had been discovered. It offered both placer and quartz mining, the latter promising to be more permanent. The rush started in June, and a new camp with "a bright and promising future" emerged. The ballyhoo surrounding it was similar to what Horace had seen the previous year, and included giving the place the grandiose name of Lauret City, a common ploy to conjure visions of grandeur.[17]

Tabor faced a hard choice in leaving a paying claim, albeit in declining California Gulch, to follow the golden goddess to another untried digging. The lure of mining now was obviously in his blood, for he packed his furniture, supplies, and merchandise, and migrated. The Tabors left with more money than they had come with, Augusta commenting, "we had acquired what we considered quite a little fortune, about $7,000 in money." They were no longer poor and would not be again, moving now in the respectable upper social class of mining camp society.[18] Despite the newfound wealth, no thought was given to returning to Kansas; the Tabors had come to Colorado to stay.

The next seven years were passed at Lauret, which became better known as Buckskin Joe, after one of the pioneer miners of the place. Postmaster Tabor announced the name change officially in February 1866. Initial prospecting had been done in 1859, though the real opening came a year later when the quartz mines especially gained attention. The Phillips was the most famous mine; it kept this camp going for several years. Second territorial governor John Evans praised the district in 1862 as the "most extensive and probably richest mining country in the Territory."[19] For a while it was the "liveliest little burg" in the southern mines, one enthusiastic visitor proclaiming that it "had more respectable families, nice folks" than any other mountain town "save Nevadaville and Central City." Augusta was pleased, and she realized the camp had better prospects than Oro. When the Tabors came, it had a theater and, for a short time in 1862, its own newspaper, the *Western Mountaineer*, which folded because of Democratic leanings and a too-small population. A sporting reputation as a "fast city" did not endear it to Augusta. However, the much-loved Methodist minister, the Rev. John Dyer, visited the camp frequently, providing a spiritual uplift in this materialistic environment. A drifting miner, William Dutt, lived there for a few weeks in the summer of 1862 and wrote his impressions to his sister. His disappointment proved prophetic. He liked little of what he saw, an "awful looking country," where he would not care to remain very long; its unattractiveness was compounded by a cold climate:

> I am spending a very lonesome time here. . . . Times are dull and every thing quiet and a great many idle men just now. I have seen more idle men lounging about this place in a few short weeks than I have ever before seen at one time. Work and money is equally scarce . . .[20]

Tabor had much less success mining than he had had

back in California Gulch, but his business did considerably better. Coming soon after the initial rush, he stayed seven years, until the camp was virtually deserted. His unpretentious and sparsely stocked general store, as one person remembered it, was in the front of the cabin he built for a home. He sold a variety of supplies, from groceries to mining equipment. Unlike other storekeepers, Horace willingly offered credit, gaining a reputation as a "miners' sutler" who was willing to assist poor prospectors when in need. This help quite often was in the form of a grubstake, that is, furnishing supplies in return for a share of whatever, if anything, was discovered.[21] This established a pattern that he continued for years, without marked success.

For the greater part of his stay, Tabor served as postmaster; he was appointed in June 1863 and his successor was named five years later, to the month. This position proved a boon to business, since the post office was in the store. Augusta helped both in the store and in running the post office, although there is no official record that she ever served as acting postmaster. Tabor's infrequent trips to Denver for business passed almost unnoticed by history, except for an occasional item in the paper about his staying in this or that hotel. There was no reason to notice him particularly; he was only one of many on similar business from the mountain towns. For a short period, Horace served as superintendent of schools in Park County, resigning in late 1866 or 1867. What special qualifications he might have had are unknown, but he had received as good an education as most and a better one than many of his contemporaries. Perhaps his standing in the community, more than anything else, secured the position for him. Apparently, school affairs throughout the Territory were chaotic during the entire decade. Horace Hall, superintendent of education and later president of the University of Colorado, commented that it was no uncommon thing for funds to be misappropriated by county and district officers. No record of misconduct, or hint of any, by Tabor exists. He was, however, apparently lax in filing his annual reports, required by law: in 1867 only two counties had sent theirs in to the Territorial school superintendent; Park County was not included.[22]

Even though Buckskin Joe served as the county seat until Fairplay surpassed it in population and gained the honor, Tabor's participation in politics was light. His interest, however, continued. His attention now focused on the war, and he and Augusta followed the Union cause, as the battle reports appeared in the *Rocky Mountain News*. For the Tabors and other Buckskinites, 1862 proved to be an exciting political year, because the Democratic leanings of their *Mountaineer* stirred up a hornet's nest of pro-Union sentiment. Furthermore, the recruiting officers' activity drove home the impact of the war as nothing else could this far from the battle scene. Statistics became much more meaningful when one knew someone in service. Although there was little real need to worry, Horace remembered his very grave apprehension of "what was going to happen to us," if Confederate General Sterling Price had been successful in conquering Missouri for the South. While Tabor did not join the army, an inaction he later regretted, he did remain active in the Republican party, renamed Union for the war's duration. He confessed that he had "almost nothing to do at that time."[23] Not choosing to join the Colorado Volunteers, Tabor could have helped to secure a Union victory only symbolically by contributing to the Sanitary Commission or buying war bonds. Whether the Tabors did either is unknown.

Even if Tabor was not one of the "boys in blue," he *was* a fifty-niner. Throughout his life he was proud of this distinction. As early as 1866 he was elected a vice-president of the Pioneer Association from Park County. Tabor did not make it to Denver for the meetings; possibly he wore on special occasions the uniform adopted by the association — a black felt hat, red flannel shirt, and black pants, completed with a silver 59er badge.[24]

"They are considered well to do here and they certainly are thrifty like the down eastern Yankees." Thus did Samuel

Leach, mail carrier to Buckskin Joe, describe his friends, the Tabors. Leach came to know them well in 1862–63, when they were still fairly young. Horace was in his early thirties and Augusta was in her late twenties. Leach liked their son Maxey as well, who was now sitting up in a high chair and eating the same food as his parents. Large for his age and observant, he toddled around in clothes made by his mother from old flour, sugar, and salt sacks. Augusta, whom Leach considered thriftier than her husband, let nothing go to waste when it could be advantageously used. Nothing about Augusta received more praise from Leach than her cooking: "It has spoiled me eating so often at the Tabors. I am becoming finicky." In one letter to his brother George, he relished the thought of a pot of salt pork and beans prepared by her, just as he liked them, without molasses or other condiments.

Despite the short growing season and high altitude, Augusta was determined to supplement their diet with home-grown vegetables. Men scoffed, but the resolute woman countered, pointing out that vegetables were raised in the Alps and Apennines, so she saw "no reason why they cannot be raised here." Horace was put to work clearing and spading the ground, while a seed order was sent to Illinois for lettuce, carrots, onions, radishes, turnips, beets, and potatoes. Seeds were planted in boxes in the house, and by May 1863 the garden was started. Regrettably, no further Leach letters survive, but if willpower and determination could triumph, Augusta harvested at least some of her crops that year. To supplement their diet further, the Tabors owned pigs, chickens, and two cows, whose milk was drunk or churned into butter. In all, they became as nearly self-contained an economic unit as could be found on the mining frontier.

Augusta tended the store, looked after the mail, kept boarders, and made a profit at it all. She had time not only to sew clothes for Maxey, but also to make shirts and socks for Horace and soap for the family's use. Leach shrewdly observed, "the men like her pretty well although she is a driver."

A driver she was, and Horace apparently profited from

the driving. He knew it, and told Leach, "[I have] to be prodded just like the ox they drove across the plains." Leach understood and even sympathized. "I can well see why he plans for three months in the year for vacation, for existence as it is now leaves no room for leisure. It is not a restful place to spend the Sabbath." He also observed that Tabor never made fun of Augusta's efforts or interfered at all; he did not, in fact, do anything around the house on his own, although he generally helped out when called upon. Such testimony clearly supports the long-held contention that it was Augusta who made the difference in the quiet years of the 1860s and 1870s.

"Very good natured," and "full of fun," Horace had to take a day off every now and then. Once, when going fishing, he stopped to pick up Leach. Unable to go this time, his sometime companion Leach wondered what Tabor expected to catch so early in May. "Nothing at all, [I'm] merely going for the sake of going fishing," he laughed, and went off in his lumbering fashion, "pitching along in his high boots." At night, after sorting the mail, Leach and Tabor played cards, and Augusta joined them, belying her often sober New England image. Tabor spent most of his own working hours, except when needed in the post office, mining.

Leach spent one Sunday in March 1863 with the Tabors. The discussion turned to the future and their plans for it. "Sam, twenty years from now I shall have enough money to take things easy three months in each year and live comfortably at hotels in New York or Washington." Augusta promptly spoke out and said she had no such thoughts. Both of them, she thought, ought to work and save as long as they were able to do so to make sure they would have enough to carry them through the lean years of old age. One comment led to another and soon Leach found himself in the middle of a domestic spat, in which he had the good sense to keep his mouth shut. So did Tabor, after a few minutes, and Augusta let off some of the frustrations of life with Horace and of the frontier before she was through scolding. Tabor liked his leisure too well to suit her, taking too much time off for his fishing, hunting, and card-playing. The sharp tongue continued to rake him, any protest being futile; Horace did not exert himself as fully as he might have, she claimed, and was too easy-going in business. If she had not looked out for him and the family finances, they would not have possessed a dollar in the world.

Eventually the atmosphere cleared, and Leach concluded, "But I like them both very much, each of them has fine qualities and they are good company." Tabor must have become used to such outbursts and shrugged them off with few second thoughts. Augusta could not change her man, but she loved him in spite of his faults.

Regardless of who was responsible, the Tabors, Leach estimated, had accumulated almost twenty thousand dollars since 1859. This figure probably reflected the inflated values of some claims or mines, for it seems impossible they could have acquired this much so soon after leaving Oro City. Their farm in Riley County, Kansas, was rented and returned them "a good sum." Augusta even planned to go home in the summer of 1863, if all went well. The Tabors' prosperity continued, and they planned to make their fortune in Colorado, hoping to return to New England in their old age to enjoy it.[25] They were not alone in this desire; many who came West shared a like dream of finding a fortune, then going back East to enjoy it among the refinements and comfort of that more settled land.

Leach's letters are the only first-hand knowledge of the Tabors at that time presently known to exist. One other miner who knew the Tabors in the sixties supported Leach's statements in an interview many years later. To Nathan Hurd, Augusta was "an angel of mercy," whose infinite kindness of heart and acts of benevolence were legion. Tabor, too, he thought, had a kind heart, a much better man than he was later accredited.[26]

A final comment on Augusta's role comes from Augusta herself. Women were conspicuous on the masculine mining frontier; they were in short supply and in great demand. Thinking of this some years later, Augusta wrote,

Really the women did more in the early days than the men. There was so much for them to do, the sick to take care of. I have had so many unfortunate men shot by accident, brought to my cabin to take care of.[27]

After the days of Dutt, Dyer, and Leach, the fortunes of Buckskin Joe waned and the Tabors' with them. Prosperity of a sort lasted until the fall of 1863, with the Phillips Mine continuing to lead all others in production.[28] Still the Tabors remained. They had no other choice since no new mining discoveries tempted them elsewhere.

Buckskin Joe's plight reflected fairly that of the entire Territory, as mining slid into the doldrums during the Civil War. The surface placer ore bodies were exhausted and the easily-milled quartz gold found near the surface of the mines was gone. Deep mining took equipment, money, engineering, and mining skill not readily available in Colorado at that time. The refractory character of the ore made it extremely difficult to mill; crude stamp mills lost much of the gold down the creek or on the dump. Nor did Colorado attract much Eastern investment, at least not as much as was needed.[29] Optimism remained high. Too high, thought a special correspondent to the *New York Times*, who disgustedly observed, on February 16, 1866, that provisions were still very expensive and labor could not be had without an outlay which would discourage a "states' man."

Lack of opportunity characterized most of the Territory. The census of 1870 showed a population increase of only 5,000, making the total 39,864. The astute observer, Frank Fossett, however, noted that during the decade some 100,000 people had sojourned within the Territory.[30] Some mining districts were abandoned; others, like Buckskin, retrenched, just barely hanging on. Pessimists cashed in their chips and scurried back to the States. After all, other mining districts, such as California and Nevada, had shown more wealth and growth during the first decade than languishing Colorado.

Colorado had also passed through a frenzy of stock selling. Stock in the mines was sold mostly to Easterners, who purchased fancy, if untried, equipment, built elaborate buildings, and hired "experts and professors" to run the mines and mills. The Territory seemed to be literally infested with charlatans and their gadgets. The inevitable collapse hurt Colorado's mining reputation and left behind only a heritage of useless monuments scattered around the mountains. Horace witnessed one such dubious transaction at Buckskin Joe in 1866, a little later than most. The Excelsior Lode was sold to the Colorado Gold Mining Company of Philadelphia, which hired Professor Alfred DuBois to supervise operation. After some $450,000 had been expended in machinery, on the mine, and in a large mill, the long-awaited principal run netted about $4.50 in gold. This company's operations, plus local expenditures, temporarily revived Buckskin Joe; then came the suspension, and the temporary "lively" boom died, Fossett believing its demise killed the town.[31]

Tabor, meanwhile, operated his mines with marginal success. By 1868 he seems to have concentrated his efforts on a placer claim which he owned in partnership with several others. This involved the construction of a 1,500-foot flume to bring enough water to the site. Although taking out a reported thirty dollars a day per man, Tabor could not have thought too much of the venture, for he sold his interest for three hundred dollars. Reminiscing with a fellow owner later, he could not even remember the price he received for it. "[Isaac] Ware, whatever became of that mine we had in Buckskin Joe?" Ware replied that he had sold his interest for eighteen thousand dollars in 1894. "The Devil you say," concluded Horace after being reminded of what he had taken for his share; he put it aside with the comment that he had too many irons in the fire to remember all his business transactions.[32]

The revival of Buckskin Joe in 1866 kept the Tabors there longer than they might have stayed otherwise. Bayard Taylor, who visited it in late June or early July of that year, wrote that it seemed larger and more active than its near neighbors and probably numbered between three and four hundred people. The camp showed no apparent signs of decay. He noted that it had modestly eschewed attaching "city" to its name, which "in Colorado is quite an honorable distinction." A well-known traveler, writer, and lecturer, Taylor was on a tour of Colorado and gave a lecture at Buckskin. Since he was the most distinguished person to visit the camp in years, it is not hard to imagine Augusta and Horace among the audience of nearly one hundred which gathered in the evening to hear him. Taylor characterized the populace as "for the most part men of education and natural refinement, and their hospitality is a favor in a double sense."[33] Augusta would have enjoyed his comment and might have read it, since his letters appeared in the *New York Times* and later in book form.

With the collapse of the Excelsior Lode speculation, the handwriting was on the wall and Horace read enough to look elsewhere. What he saw was neither inviting nor encouraging. Silver had been found at Georgetown and several other locations; however, methods of smelting and practical experience with the ore were still lacking. The older gold camps, such as Central City, offered no special incentives. But across the Mosquito Range, quartz mining had started in California Gulch. It appeared that this offered the best opportunity, in a region the Tabors were intimately familiar with, so they turned their faces back to the site of their early prosperity. Sometime in the late spring of 1868, they recrossed the range and resettled themselves at Oro City.[34]

Older now, their young boy grown from a baby, Augusta and Horace were making their third major change of base since leaving Kansas. The lure of better prospects had beckoned them once more. The pattern was familiar to Augusta, as she started again to set up housekeeping and helped open the Tabor general store. They abandoned Buckskin none too soon, for the next year a visitor noted the dilapidation of what once passed for homes. Only twenty-five or thirty men still resided there, not a single family. The traveler peeped into windows and wandered through the "old town," for such places held a sort of fascination with all the ruins of a "city, rusting and rotting, neglected."[35]

CHAPTER 3

THE QUIET YEARS

Altogether, this vast area [Lake County] of all sorts of mineral, grazing and farming, and timber lands, belongs mostly to future explorers and settlers . . .

Wallihan, *Rocky Mountain Directory*, (1870)

IT WAS back to Oro City, not, however, back to the placer riches of 1860. Gold was still being taken from California Gulch, the hopes centering this time on the Printer Boy Lode, located near the head of the gulch.

The bonanza surfaced none too soon for the destiny of the area. Since the Tabors had left, the fortunes of California Gulch had been dwindling steadily, even consolidation and hydraulic mining failing to rally them. The placer deposits were declining, and other mining discoveries were simultaneously beckoning. The Montana gold fields lured many away during the Colorado mining doldrums of the mid-sixties. Bayard Taylor visited Oro City as well as Buckskin Joe during his 1866 tour. His first impression was negative — the place "did not promise much" — yet he observed that one should not judge Colorado camps by their outside appearance. It was July 4, and no one was working. That evening he gave his lecture, which was concluded by an Independence Day ball attended by all the ladies of the upper Arkansas Valley — "hardly a baker's dozen." Taylor traveled on, but with a more favorable opinion, for he had been royally entertained within the limits of available resources. Mining, he commented, was still profitable in the gulch, and the hope for the future lay in the lode mines, which had been discovered but not worked as yet.[1]

The Colorado historian Orando Hollister, writing the next year, painted a dismal picture of the gulch. Relics of its former life littered the almost-deserted site: tin cans, worn-out shovels, half-buried sluices, old clothes, broken furniture, and rubbish of every description. Hollister, too, felt that future prosperity depended on the development of lode or quartz mines. Bluntly and truthfully, Hollister wrote that nothing was more deceptive or ephemeral than the feverish prosperity of a placer mining country. The same year, Louis Simonin, touring Colorado, far from his native France, met a discouraged California Gulcher who told him Oro City was virtually deserted and that the placers would soon be exhausted, thus ending the last faded hopes of the miners.[2]

Altogether this would not have been a cheering prospect for the Tabors, and if it had not been for the sudden prominence of the Printer Boy and the encouragement it gave of finding other similar mines, Horace would have been foolish to recross the mountains. By June 1868 the family was reestablished in Oro City, waiting anew for the whim of chance to present them with their fortune.

The familiar pattern once more resumed: the store opened, boarders came, miners were grubstaked, and Horace became postmaster and express agent. His appointment was dated November 30, though he apparently served from July 1, and he continued in this capacity until he moved in 1877. The salary was not excessive — $155 a year in 1868–1870 and $220 in 1872–1874. Even this small amount was not paid entirely, forcing Horace to file a claim later to get his money. Postmaster Tabor had to handle two deliveries per week, yet with the limited number of people in his area the load could not have been too burdensome.[3] The real financial remuneration came from having customers come to the store to pick up their mail. And the congenial postmaster enjoyed the chance it brought to converse with friends when they stopped by.

Other than having to fill out a few government forms and place an occasional notice in the paper, Tabor's duties were strictly limited to the sending and receiving of mail and gold shipments. It was the latter that provided a few moments of Western excitement. Twice, gold shipments were stolen after leaving Oro City, although not by masked robbers holding up the carriers in the best tradition. Each time, packets containing gold simply disappeared.

The first robbery involved the disappearance of two registered letter packages on June 21, 1869, before they reached Granite, the next stop on the mail line. Oro City was the end of the route. Postmaster Tabor immediately started searching for the missing letter packages, because they held gold; one was his own, containing sixty-five ounces on their way to the Colorado National Bank in Denver. On the second day, June 23, he and a small posse found the two packages; both were opened and the gold was missing. Suspicion immediately pointed to the carrier, Henry Farnum, since, as the *Rocky Mountain News* noted on June 26, both postmasters (of Granite and Oro) "are most reliable and responsible." A bit damning for Farnum's cause, the gold was uncovered in his stable. Tabor promptly filed a complaint against Farnum, charging him with "unlawfully and feloniously stealing" letters from the United States mail. A year later he was a principal prosecution witness in Farnum's Denver trial. He testified that he had locked the mail sack and that the next man to have a key to open it was the Granite postmaster; then he recounted the events of the search and finally identified the recovered gold. After Farnum was found guilty, his lawyers promptly asked for a new trial, and the case dragged on without further testimony from Tabor.

Hardly had the excitement died down when trouble struck again. The second robbery proved much harder to solve. On this occasion Tabor placed five registered letters containing gold dust and nuggets in a package and sent them to Denver on July 21, 1871. The package reached Fairplay, where it simply disappeared, much to Tabor's distress, for he had personally sent about a thousand dollars in gold to the First National Bank. On receiving word of the disappearance Horace frantically rushed to Fairplay, where he identified some of the stolen papers, minus the gold, and hastily concluded that the deputy postmaster was the guilty party. No Sherlock Holmes, Horace misread the evidence and fell for planted clues, temporarily adding only confusion to the mystery. Finally, in October, a detective was called in and found the thief, William Beery.

Again Tabor was subpoenaed as a star witness for the prosecution, this time facing a tenacious cross-examination by Beery's lawyer. The evidence against Beery pivoted on the identification of the package and the gold, some of which had been recovered. Tabor stoutly maintained his identification of both was correct and, upon being asked if he had a good memory, replied "pretty fair." The crux of the case rested with the gold, and here the lawyer questioned the witness closely; but Horace stood his ground. "I can identify gold — any person can that has handled it. There was a piece that I brought in the day before, noticed that I found the same piece there . . . I never saw two pieces alike. Don't think there could be. Never saw an instance to my knowledge." Eventually he received full payment for the gold lost, compensating him somewhat for the anxious moments spent trying to solve this robbery and recover his property.[4]

Augusta, in her short description of her experiences later, entitled "Cabin Life," recalled one method Tabor used to foil any potential robbers.

> I have been taken along as body-guard a great many times when Mr. Tabor was going to Denver with treasure, because he thought he would not be so liable to be attacked. I have carried gold on my person many a time. He would buy all the gold that he could and would carry ·it down ourselves rather than trust the Express . . . I had the gold in buckskins, then put in gunny bags, then laid on the horse and then my saddle put on over the blanket, and bring it out that way. There would be nothing visible but the saddle. If anyone came along they would rather search him than me.

The resourceful Augusta had long since overcome the physical ailments she complained of in Kansas and early Colorado, for the trip to Denver was taxing.

> There were some miles that we could not ride our horses on account of the wind it blew so fiercely. We had to have our clothes tied on firmly. In some places it was so steep we had to hang on to our horses tails, it was all the horses could do to get up.[5]

The Tabors' main business continued to be the store, and it must have profited to the point of their being able to hire a clerk, so they wouldn't have to close it when they went to Denver with the gold. Here, too, Augusta was an important help to her husband. She and Horace apparently argued over how soon Maxey should be put to work, Augusta getting the best of it, and Maxey went to school. "I told him I would go into the store and do all the boy could do." She did that and more, for "he found I was a better hand at keeping the books than he was." Talented in this direction, Augusta took over posting the returns for the mail and proudly recalled that in seven years only one paper had been sent back for correction.[6]

Business in a mining camp was a day-to-day proposition, especially in one such as Oro City, which languished in the backwash of Colorado mining until 1877. The excitement of the Printer Boy flared briefly and passed — Oro City settled down to the placid existence of a declining mining region. Tabor's store did not have a large stock, nor was the volume of trade large, but this was a family-run operation with only minimal overhead. The competition seldom exceeded one other store, Tabor generally having the community to himself. He also had the advantage of being one of the old-timers and an established merchant.

He operated what was referred to as a general store, as ubiquitous on the mining frontier as the saloon. The familiar staples were stocked: flour, coffee, salt, beans, sugar, and dried fruits, supplemented by butter, eggs, salted and fresh meats, and vegetables in season. The miners' favorite, oysters, and a few other canned goods graced the shelves. Along one wall could be found boots, shoes, ready-made clothes, bolts of cloth, needles, thread, and possibly a few bonnets for the ladies. Miners' pans, shovels, picks, rope, and assorted other items needed for mining completed this department. A few patent medicines and drugs rounded out the stock. Probably at Christmas a small selection of toys brightened the scene. One corner of the crowded log store served as post office, and the back rooms were the Tabors' home. It might seem logical now, with her added responsibilities, that Augusta would no longer take in boarders, though with her ambition it seems likely that she still found time to do it.

Credit kept the business afloat. Even though he might not have wanted to extend it (which seems doubtful), Tabor was forced to do so. Mining did not provide a steady income for his customers, and they had to transact much of their business on the credit principle. If they paid, then Tabor had helped his neighbors continue mining; if they did not or could not, he simply lost the amount of the loan.

Tabor's methods of operation are revealed in his purchases from the wholesalers in Denver. Only a few records remain which tell of Tabor's paying off the balance of this or that account. The records show that he ordered 25,000 lbs. of goods from Denver in the fall of 1870 to carry him through the winter, picking this time because freight rates were lower than they would be later. The records testify to Tabor's sound business acumen in another sense. A Denver merchant inquired of him if he would sell some local flour in his store. Tabor responded that he could not give him the price desired, because his customers preferred another brand and he had to keep it or they would buy elsewhere. "I have no objections to your selling in this market and if I had it could make no difference of course." Concluding, he said that he would try to sell some of the flour, "if you wish," but "you would have yours sold one dollar less to insure a sale." The records also illustrate the problem of collection. Tabor sent one of his customer's promissory notes to Denver, either for collection or to pay for one of his own business debts.[7]

Isolation in the mountains meant that Oro City prices were not cut drastically by the coming of the railroad to Colorado. The building of the Denver and Rio Grande helped some; however, Oro City had no hope of ever being directly connected by rail with the outside world so long as mining languished in its present condition. Tabor overcame this isolation as best he could by trying to have his goods shipped in at the lowest possible freight rate. Still the prices at Oro City ranged far·above Denver's, and each added cost simply cut deeper into the small mining profits. For example, in July 1872, flour selling at twelve dollars per hundredweight in Tabor's store was selling for five to seven dollars in Denver. Rio coffee sold at thirty-five cents and sugar at twenty-two cents per pound, higher than the Denver prices of twenty-seven to thirty cents and fourteen to eighteen cents. Eggs at Oro City sold for fifty cents a dozen, compared to thirty to thirty-five cents in Denver. Only one item reversed this trend, potatoes, which were a bargain in Oro at four cents a pound, a penny lower than in the big city. The difference probably is explained by the fact that Denver offered new potatoes, which customarily sold for a higher price.[8]

For Tabor, life generally drifted by easily in the 1870s, although a prominent Denver merchant remarked:

> He is an honest man, and will pay his bills when he can; but what business can he do in Lake County? There isn't enough business there to keep a cat alive, and in protection to myself I have limited his account to fifty dollars.[9]

Nevertheless, Tabor's position grew, materially and in personal prestige. Without question he was Oro's most prominent merchant and one "of the best citizens of the county." His confidence in California Gulch seldom if ever wavered. Like merchants in other camps, he did all he could to boost his home and its mines. As early as June 18, 1868, the *Rocky Mountain News* reported he had come down to Denver with "some very rich" gold quartz samples, plus some fifty ounces of placer gold. In an item that must have warmed Tabor's heart, the paper commented, "All they want there to revive the flush times of 1861 is a swarming, working population."

In the years that followed, Tabor entered mineral exhibits at the territorial fairs, wrote letters, and brought more samples to newspaper offices to keep the name of Oro City and California Gulch before the investors and the general public. He stood to gain as much as anybody — and more than most — if prosperity reappeared, because his store would boom and his local mining investments would become more valuable.

Always alert to new business opportunities, Tabor opened a second store at Malta, near the mouth of California Gulch, when mining started to revive in the mid-1870s. Here some stamp mills were erected, and a small community was established. Although some confusion exists concerning it, Tabor possibly had a branch store in lower California Gulch before he opened the one at Malta.[10] For the moment, Horace's business sense proved accurate and he tapped all the major consumer markets in his limited area.

The credit which Tabor provided to his customers and the grubstakes he gave to prospectors and miners helped keep the district alive, even if they were a source of anxiety for the Tabors and a drain on their capital. A default by one of his large debtors could be a serious setback for the entire business.

In 1872 one J. P. Green secured a contract to cut and supply ties for the Atchison, Topeka and Santa Fe railroad, which at the time was rapidly nearing the Colorado line. The ties were to be floated down the Arkansas River to Fort Dodge, where easy transportation awaited them to the railway right-of-way. This was an ambitious program, for which Green hired a hundred men. He ran up a heavy supply bill with Tabor, and then found the task more than his resources and ability could master. Tabor, realizing Green could not make a success of his plan, became genuinely alarmed because of the money owed him. To protect himself he took the contract from Green, or, as another story states, Green simply left, and Tabor undertook the job, hoping to recover the debt.

Horace hired a large group of men, only to have winter set in before the contract could be fulfilled, forcing postponement of the project until the next year. He worked with the men, leaving Augusta to tend the store while he struggled to get the logs down the river. Augusta held up her end of the business, though not without some worry. "We had a good deal of money to take care of, we had the only safe in the country and had to keep everybody's treasures in that safe, and I was a little afraid for the five months he was gone from home."

Rather than recovering his money, Tabor found himself spending more, with the contract deadline approaching. To his dismay the annual spring runoff, on which he counted so heavily to float the logs, proved low after a light winter snowfall. Instead of water transportation, he had to use hired teams to get the logs out to meet the deadline or risk losing everything. The contract conditions were fulfilled, though the costs skyrocketed way beyond Green's estimates and Tabor's fears. Not only were there wages and the extra cost of teams, but there was also the steady expense for food, as his crew would eat "an ox at one meal and more too." Tabor was financially overextended, despite all that Augusta did to send money from the store.[11]

More than five months of labor and endless worrying produced no profit. In fact, it had taken almost all of Tabor's abilities just to break even and avoid losing his original investment and loans. While he could have accepted his initial losses, it would have been most uncharacteristic of him, because he believed that success rewarded the adventuresome. Augusta stated that her husband had friends guarantee the project's completion by signing forfeiture bonds, payable if he did not fulfill it. "He was a man who would not allow his bondsmen to pay,"[12] she proudly noted. It is impossible to overestimate the importance of Augusta's help in carrying out this project.

Notwithstanding events like the Green affair, Tabor prospered in the 1870s. While it is impossible to state his wealth accurately, it is abundantly clear that the Tabors were not poor at Oro City. In the 1870 census records, Tabor's wealth was given as five thousand dollars in real estate and five thousand in personal property, making him the most substantial merchant or miner in the whole camp. A historian of the day estimated it at thirty-five thousand dollars by 1878.[13] They were a respectable upper middle-class family and would have been so in any Colorado mining camp of that time.

Oro City, Tabor's home and the center of his business activities, prospered anew soon after he returned. The camp, by common consent, simply moved two and a half miles up the gulch to reestablish itself near the Printer Boy mine; the exact date of the move is unknown, but was most probably 1868, the year of the great excitement. Horace Tabor, notoriously weak about dates, later said it occurred in 1871, which seems improbable. He also said that he moved the post office, and the name Oro City just naturally followed,[14] which seems logical.

Situated in a lovely little meadow, surrounded by low rolling hills, except where a stream cut through each end, the second Oro City was esthetically a marked improvement over the formless, wandering site of old. Very little of note occurred here. The camp's best year was 1868, then it slipped, stabilized, and finally headed down an endless road of decline. Horace, in a private letter, revealingly wrote in 1870, "Very dull and many leave." Trout fishing in the neighborhood continued good, gladdening fisherman Tabor's heart.

Here the Tabors entered middle age and their boy grew to manhood. Oro, in the meantime, never amounted to much as a Colorado mining community, never successfully emerging from the backwater of the mining frontier. Horace and Augusta, watching camps surpass it in wealth and population, persisted in their determination to remain, perhaps retaining the abiding hope that the great days of 1860 would return. Far from Denver and with nothing happening to arouse interest, Oro City and the activities of its leading family passed unrecorded as the seventies winged by. The best description left of the camp comes from the 1870 census, which was taken by William Beery (presumably the same man involved in the mail theft the next year).

Oro City had just finished digging out from a severe winter, which deposited over nine feet of snow, when Beery arrived in June to take the census. What he found was typical of a Colorado camp of Oro City's size and condition. Males predominated among the 251 people who lived there. Augusta had the companionship of twenty-five other married women; there was only one single woman over fifteen. At one time earlier there had been so few women that Horace tried to hire a companion to keep his wife company. Twenty-two families had children living, producing a low average of 2.8 children per family. The population was relatively young, with only ten people over fifty years and fifty-four under fifteen. The median age was roughly 30.5. They came from all over the world, England and Ireland topping the list. Augusta found ten other Maine natives, a much higher figure than usual for the mining West. Except for Virginia, the South was poorly represented, with New York and Ohio leading the states in sending native sons and daughters to faraway Oro City.

The Tabors were by far the wealthiest residents, which reflected as much the generally poor financial condition of the rest of the community as their own means. Slightly older than average, they were still the youngest of the small business and professional class, numbering two physicians, one saloon keeper, the hotel owner, and themselves. It was an overwhelmingly white settlement, with only one colored person reported. Although no one listed teaching as an occupation, twenty-eight children had gone to school during the previous year. One hundred and twenty-five dwellings of all shapes, sizes, and descriptions were occupied, the miner's shack dominating the scene. This was Oro City, as William Beery statistically portrayed it and the Tabors saw it in June 1870.[15]

Tabor, as the prominent merchant and wealthiest citizen of Oro, helped guide its destiny with the steady hand of one who had been a fifty-niner, calling upon a decade of business and mining experience to justify his decisions. The English poet and author, Charles Kingsley, who would later contribute some memorable lines to the Tabor story, saw the respect even then given these pioneers. "The fifty-niners, as they proudly call themselves, are looked on with a kind of respectful admiration by the younger Coloradans, as the little pioneer aristocracy of the territory . . ."[16] For the moment, if the Tabors were poor country cousins compared to some of the more influential Denver and Central City fifty-niners, their distinction was not thereby diminished.

In July 1870 a traveling correspondent for the *Rocky Mountain News* visited Oro City, calling it once "very prosperous," now showing marked signs of falling to decay. Little change came in the following years. Two stores were listed in 1872, one in upper and one in lower California Gulch, both owned by Tabor. School sessions opened and closed; however, if Maxey was a typical product, the students acquired only the most rudimentary type of "book learning." Maxey, though, did receive enough education to clerk in his father's store and assist him in other ways. The coming of the Hayden survey party in 1873 provided some excitement, when it camped near the mouth of the gulch. Postmaster Tabor was busier than usual handling the expedition's mail, which had been forwarded to his office. By 1874, if not earlier, Oro City could boast of an IOOF Lodge; if Horace joined, he made no mention of it. A traveling preacher continued to supply religion, supplemented by a local Sunday school.[17] Slumbering and forgotten, Oro City waited.

As befitted his position as one of Lake County's leading citizens, Tabor again entered politics. Lake County, then much larger, encompassing present Lake and Chaffee and part of Gunnison counties, languished behind the rest of Colorado development. Though a large county, it had only a small population, estimated at 800 in 1875. A dozen Colorado towns had larger populations, and politically Lake County was of small importance. Politics, though, were hotly contested in this mining area. Republican Tabor started with little advantage, because the county voters generally supported the Democratic party.

The "Old Man," as Tabor was affectionately called, was elected county treasurer, serving from 1876 to 1880. Ever an alert businessman, he traded in county warrants, an activity, noted Charles Thomas, a long-time friend and political rival, in which a county treasurer has "a sort of an inside track." Tabor's duties were not heavy, and he appointed his son as deputy treasurer. This form of nepotism apparently was condoned by the voters, for Maxey did more and more of the work after his father's financial and mining responsibilities took the bulk of his time.[18]

By entering into the political arena Tabor opened himself to attack by unscrupulous opponents. Though not personally vulnerable, he still had to face the barbs. In February of 1876 there was a movement to annex Lake County to Park County for judicial purposes, and for some reason now lost the Canon City *Avalanche* published a sarcastic tirade against Horace, entitled "Domestic Tragedy in Lake County." It charged Tabor with being jealous of Augusta and cruel to her, resulting in her elopement with Ward Maxey of Fairplay. This was so blatantly false that Tabor did not deign to answer it; one of his friends did, though.

This stalwart friend denounced all particulars and angrily attacked the diatribe as a "humbug and malicious falsehood," a "hellish plot," now frustrated. The writer noted that he had met both Tabors at a wedding in Granite four days after the tragedy supposedly had occurred. The *Avalanche* had gone to press without "full and reliable particulars," but need not be sorry about it, since, like "all other slanders uttered against the good citizens of Lake County, there was nothing to it." He ended his letter by praising Horace as one of the best citizens of the county, prominent as a merchant, postmaster, and county treasurer, and insisting that his "counterpart and better half" was not known to love "any one better than her husband."[19] Nothing came of this isolated incident, and the Tabors possibly had a good laugh over it. Colorado politics could be rough, with no holds barred, not even one's family being immune to attack, as Tabor found out.

Tabor the businessman and Tabor the politician was still

Tabor the miner. The first and last were hard to separate. While concentrating on merchandising, Tabor never completely gave up mining or his interest in it. In his own words:

> I have always had people out prospecting. Lots of folks thought that the Little Pittsburg was my first venture but I had been at that same business for twenty years. There is hardly a time that I have not had men out prospecting. I would furnish them a stake for a share. I was always assisting the prospector one way or another, mostly in the substantials of life; something to eat; that was the all important thing.

A friend who knew him in the 1870s observed that no "sober, industrious" man ever asked for a grubstake and was refused. Though such activities did not produce a high average of returns, it took only one bonanza to erase hundreds of failures. Again Tabor said, "All that I was making in my merchandise business, I put into prospecting; all the profits went into prospecting and the first great result was the Little Pittsburg." By the late 1870s, Tabor's business books had thousands of dollars of unpaid accounts, which he simply consigned to "profit and loss," never expecting nor even attempting to collect.[20]

It was discouraging to have such a low grubstaking batting average, but Tabor stayed with it, accepting his misfortunes without complaining. On his own he prospected without noticeable success. "I walked a thousand times over Fryer hill and never thought it worth while to stick a pick into it." And there, ironically, at that spot, he was within a few feet of more wealth than he ever dreamed of or anticipated finding. An anonymous writer, signing himself only as H in a letter to the *Rocky Mountain News*, July 21, 1872, referred to California Gulch: "I think this county the richest in latent mineral wealth, and the most isolated and inaccessible region now known." This individual summed up the problems facing Tabor and others who hadn't lost faith in the region. A railroad might have helped, but few outside of California Gulch wanted to invest money to build one, when there were so many more lucrative markets available.

The rich Printer Boy had started the 1868 rush, and it

proved easy to work, especially during the early years when great masses of almost pure gold were taken out. Unfortunately, although active prospecting vigorously resumed, no further mines as rich were found. The deeper the Printer Boy went, however, the more costly mining became, water finally becoming so troublesome that the mine was temporarily abandoned due to lack of proper machinery to pump it out. R. G. Dill described California Gulch as most desolate in appearance, with deserted and dismantled cabins and claims stretching from Oro all the way down the gulch. Six months of the year the district was practically isolated from the rest of the world by storms and snow, while the country was so barren and worthless as to be hardly worth thinking of; in fact, "nobody thought much about it."[21] The only redeeming feature Dill saw in this despised region was the thoughtful, intelligent men who had abiding faith in its greatness. One wonders whether they would have been considered so thoughtful had the future turned out differently.

As soon as he arrived, Horace began dealing in claims, accruing no great profits. Such prospects as the Fourth of July, the Pilot, Great Eastern, Ten Forty, and Buck Eye lodes passed through his hands, in partnership with others, and made nobody rich. Even Augusta occasionally appeared as a partner. He gained a little experience from each, but Tabor sought something more concrete.

Tabor and the rest of the Oroites remained, while conditions grew progressively worse with the decline of the Printer Boy, the one major producing mine. Notwithstanding their isolation, Lake County and Oro City merited summaries by Rossiter Raymond's agents in the monumental government mining reports of the 1870s. Out of these volumes comes a clear picture of the times and problems Tabor faced. Despite the 1868 quartz boom, placer mining predominated throughout the decade and into the 1870s. In the 1871 report it was conservatively estimated that, since the discovery of gold, California Gulch had yielded $2.5 million, the annual yield steadily declining. The number of men working the claims dropped to around sixty and even dipped into the fifties. In 1871 placer operations were curtailed by lack of water, the winter snowfall having been too light. The next year, both lode and placer operations were carried on briskly, with the latter showing deposits paying five dollars a day. This was followed by another fair year, although few placer claims were worked steadily. A short water supply and an unusually early winter hampered work in 1874, most of the old ground now being considered worked out. Lake County ranked a poor fifth that year among the mining areas of the state, although, as Raymond admitted, it was hard to arrive at definite figures. By 1875, the reports centered on quartz mining, with gold, silver, nickel, and cobalt ores mentioned as having been found.

For Tabor the quartz mining in upper California Gulch offered the first prolonged opportunity to study deep mining. The Printer Boy main shaft was down more than three hundred feet by 1874, and had levels drifting on the vein at various intervals along the shaft. This was a good example for him to examine, for as Raymond reported, "The excellence and durability of the work on the surface, combined with the safety and neatness with which the mine is timbered, and the manner in which the mine is being opened, are very flattering to the skill of the managers." The Printer Boy proved very pockety, with, on one occasion, a panful of dirt yielding 132 ounces of gold. In 1873, it produced steadily, yielding about nine thousand dollars per month and a collection of leaf gold from it was exhibited at the territorial fair.[22] Unfortunately, every time abundant water appeared for placer operations, the quartz mines flooded.

The ore mined in the Printer Boy and other smaller mines was easy to mill by first crushing and then working it through some form of amalgamation where quicksilver separated the gold. Free gold was finally produced after retorting out the quicksilver. Except for the large amounts of ore and the stamps used to crush the rock, the process was similar to that used by Horace and Augusta back in 1860–1861, when they separated gold from the heavy black sand at the bottom of their pan or sluice box. Malta, the site of Tabor's second store, became the milling center for the gold mines. Some of the mining companies early put up their own stamp mills, with varying results and savings of gold, which was the key factor in any operation. A few independent small operators still used the old method of an *arastre* to crush the ore. This simply involved crushing the ore by dragging a rock over it repeatedly, not an advanced milling technique.

Despite both placer and quartz mining, California Gulch failed to live up to the optimistic forecasts of the prophets of 1860. Its elusive fortune seemed always to belong to the future. The same could be said for the whole Territory. The 1860s had not been noticeably advantageous for Colorado mining, and the early 1870s, though better, were no match for the boom of Nevada's Comstock. Yet men refused to lose the optimism characteristic of the mining frontier. Territorial Governor Samuel Elbert, for instance, wrote in 1873:

> Whilst old and established mines have continued to lay their wealth at our feet, the preparation for new and extensive mining operations in districts both old and new, are far greater than at any former period, and not only show established faith in the richness of our mines, but augmented vitality in mining, as a permanent and remunerative industry.[23]

The hope of the future lay with silver, not gold, and the greatness was near at hand by the time the governor wrote. Georgetown and Silver Plume already were turning out silver in increasing quantities, as was Caribou to the north of them. Lake County lay slumbering, but already rumblings were heard which would change not only Tabor's life but the entire history of Colorado.

Silver had been rumored early in California Gulch, and the weekly *Rocky Mountain News* of October 10, 1860, called it a virtual "silver lode mania" with scores of lodes discovered and "most everybody" having a piece of rock in his pocket to illustrate the richness of his find. The silver mania died as it had lived, fleetingly. The inexperience of the men involved had misled them, for silver was not found in the native state, as they claimed to have discovered it. Silver lodes were said to have been uncovered throughout much of the then-mined mountains, but nothing came of them, for neither skill nor smelting methods were available in Colorado to handle complex silver ore. Not until the mid-1860s were permanent silver mines opened, and several years would yet pass before silver could be profitably worked.

Traditionally, the discovery of silver at California Gulch is credited to two men, William Stevens and Alvinus Wood, who came there in 1874 to construct a ditch to work placer claims they had purchased. They, like the multitude of miners before them, found operations hampered by a heavy black mineral which proved difficult to separate from the gold. Unlike the others, Stevens and Wood were decidedly curious as to the character of that black rock. Tradition, attributing no initiative to those who came before, awards these two credit for testing it and finding it to be carbonate of lead, rich in silver. Keeping their secret, they moved to secure title to some of the surrounding quartz claims, meanwhile working their own. Not until 1876 did the information leak of the discovery of silver. But Frank Fossett wrote, "As to who were the original discoverers or first locators of the carbonates the writer does not pretend to decide."[24]

Fossett was right, because the discovery of silver antedated Stevens and Wood. A letter in the *Rocky Mountain News* on July 21, 1872, described a silver lode near Oro City with "prospects remarkably rich, and something handsome is expected to come of it." The same paper in November, 1873 reported a meeting of prominent local citizens to discuss the need to build a smelter to handle silver ores. Money was always the obstacle, and it was decided to sell $100 shares to reach the $20,000 thought necessary. The reporter listed four mines showing silver, though he said he felt this step would not have been necessary were it not for the reluctance of capitalists to invest. The project, despite encouraging early share sales, never materialized. Even more significant, the record book of the Oro City Territorial Assay Office, from the very first entry, September 8, 1873, lists samples with silver content, a few with a high percentage. Nor were the returns limited to just a few claims. For example, in September 1873 seven different mines showed silver ore, and the following June the number jumped to twelve.[25] Rossiter Raymond's report, which appeared in 1875, discussed the silver and gold veins in the Upper Arkansas district. His conclusion, "as yet there is no market for silver ore," concisely summarized the major problem.[26] The nearest mills were too far away to allow much but extremely high-grade ore to be shipped via the slow and expensive wagons or even more expensive mules.

It must have been common knowledge to the residents of Oro City, and certainly to its storekeeper-miner-grubstaker, that silver existed, the question being only where the richest sites were. Tabor did not run a sample of ore through the Territorial Assay Office under his name until March 16, 1876, and there is only a cryptic note that Tabor paid the cost, no mention of the mine or ore breakdown. Other previous samples might have been his, but he is not named. The same is true for 1877–1878, when Horace was obviously interested in silver mining; however, there is no mention of his name in the book. The only mine for which Tabor had ore tested was the Dyer, and during the spring and summer of 1876 he had five samples run, one showing very good high-grade ore.[27]

The Dyer never proved to be a significant property for Tabor, although it was called "a remarkable mine, one of the best producers of high-grade ores in the camp." He purchased half of it from the Rev. John Dyer, whose son had owned it before he was assassinated in Granite during a Lake County political row. Tabor never owned it completely, and it was one of the first mines he later sold to Eastern investors.[28] Located near the head of Iowa Gulch, where Tabor had had such high hopes back in 1860–1861, the Dyer passed through his hands, probably before he and his partner really had an opportunity to work it thoroughly. Other mines required much more of his attention and gave him a much larger return.

The year 1876 marked the beginning of the rush for silver. The *Engineering and Mining Journal*, March 17, 1877, reported that production the previous year in Lake County had been almost eighty thousand dollars in gold and over twenty-one thousand in silver. The Malta works were now in operation, limping more than striding, but offering the home smelting market long needed. Oro City, as it dug out from under the winter's accumulation of snow in the long-awaited, unseasonably late spring of 1877, stood on the threshold of its greatest years. Despite the weather, prospecting started early and reports of rich new discoveries spread throughout Colorado.

II.
SUMMER'S PROSPERITY
1877–1880

CHAPTER 4

BONANZA

"We have a marvelous camp here and a very stirring town."
Tabor to Henry Teller, May 29, 1878

THE spring of 1877 rekindled once more for the Tabors the excitement of 1859, 1860, 1861, and 1868, the intoxication of a mining rush, with all the long-deferred dreams of wealth. Augusta again packed their belongings and they left Oro, which Horace correctly gauged not to be the camp of the future; they moved slightly over two and a half miles down the gulch and a little northward to what was a yet unnamed infant settlement, soon to be called Leadville. Youth had forsaken the Tabors — eighteen years on the Colorado mining frontier had seen to that — but Horace, at least, displayed the 1859 enthusiasm. This move, so short a distance in mileage, represented a lifetime in its implications.

Arriving in July, they opened their store, the second in Leadville, Charles Mater having beaten them by several weeks, and the familiar routine was resumed. Not willing to sever completely the ties to the old home in Oro, Tabor left Maxey, nearly out of his teens now, to run the family store and serve as assistant postmaster. By retaining some ties, Tabor protected all bets, just in case the assumption prompting his move proved wrong. It did not. Oro, so long persistent, soon was bypassed in wealth, population, and fame; it slipped into the background, never to attain the pinnacle Tabor once had hoped it might.[1]

A little more cautious now than earlier, when he had abandoned everything in the scramble for gold, Horace timed his arrival to coincide with the opportune moment for getting himself in on the ground floor, a prime necessity for a merchant who planned to tap a developing mining rush. He was hardly settled before a budding rush started.

R. G. Dill wrote that from July the population increased with extraordinary rapidity. By fall there were perhaps a thousand people in the camp, most from nearby mining districts. Silver was there in the surrounding hills, though not many of the miners had had experience with it. Men scurried around and over hills and gullies searching for likely mineral outcroppings or simply a profitable-looking spot to sink a test shaft. By the end of the year, both the conservative *Engineering and Mining Journal* and the excitable *Rocky Mountain News* were picturing a great future for Leadville. A correspondent of the former wrote that a visit to the noted camp could not fail to impress one with the belief that its prosperity was assured. The New Year would be greater yet. "Meanwhile the mines already found and opened are themselves and alone of worth and extent enough to build up a large community." The *News* called it the state's friskiest camp and without hesitation proclaimed that by next summer Leadville promised to be by far the liveliest and one of the largest mining towns in the West.[2] Tabor's luck was certainly changing, even if only a portion of these predictions materialized. In one short move he jumped from the backwash of mining into a flood; here, as never before, were opportunities begging to be tapped.

With a well-established reputation as a merchant and miner's friend, Tabor settled into an easy routine as one of the leading citizens from the day he arrived. Men came to his store to purchase supplies, pick up their mail, and discuss prospects with the genial host, who paid close attention to their reports. He grubstaked heavily without outstanding success, but he never gave up hope or lost faith. The camp, meanwhile, grew around the base of Carbonate Hill, the site of the important discoveries. Other merchants set up shop; Horace would not have this camp to himself as he had had Oro City. Finally, those heralds of a camp's prosperity, gamblers and prostitutes, appeared. Crowded stagecoaches strained to meet the demands of impatient patrons who scrambled to see this new wonder for themselves. Many visitors inquired at Tabor's convenient store, the owner for the first time basking in the attention accorded a minor celebrity. A reporter for the New York *Mining Record* asked him about the district's prospects, and he replied that lead had to go up a cent or two, then all would be happy.[3] Unknowingly, he put his finger on a fact that would be as significant to Leadville's history as the price of silver. The fortunes of this camp were to be hitched to two minerals, not just the more lucrative silver.

Tabor's store, located on Chestnut Street, grew with the camp, soon surpassing any he had operated previously. Printed stationery letterheads, advertising Tabor as a dealer in wines, groceries, provisions, liquors, miners' supplies, tobaccos, and cigars showed his affluence; an earlier heading had been more modest, reading simply "H. A. W. Tabor, general provisions and outfitting store." Initially, he listed his other stores at Oro City and Malta, but by March, 1878, those names were deleted. By then Tabor's conservatism in continuing the other stores had been overcome by the flush of Leadville's prosperity. He boldly advertised: "If you want anything from a small size needle to a large sized elephant come and see me, for I positively declare I will not be undersold. Call and satisfy yourselves." They did call, and as a result of the expanded business, eighty-five thousand pounds of freight were received in one day the next June; most of it was sold within a week. The business often grossed as high as a thousand dollars a day that summer, a remarkable transformation in one year.[4] In a letter to the *Denver Tribune*, June 12, an enthusiastic Leadvilleite described the "wide-awake and energetic" local merchants as being busy days, nights, and Sundays supplying the large demands of the camp. Prices were high as a result of the freight rates and the rapidly expanding market, which gave the merchants a bonanza rivaling that of the mineral treasure house being unlocked around their community. At long last, profits flooded into the Tabor safe.

Well established by the end of 1877, he and Augusta, who no longer had to take in boarders to supplement their scanty income, found themselves in the first rank of Leadville society. A delightful story, perhaps apocryphal, has been preserved of how Augusta and two friends planned to brighten the first Leadville Christmas. Deciding to raise money to purchase toys for all the children, they found the stores not very well stocked, forcing them to improvise but not daunting their Christmas spirit. Everyone who could donated money, and enough was given for a community-wide party, where the children and all who came received some gift.[5]

For the men more serious plans were afoot, a movement to organize a municipal government. Many camps got along fine without one, primarily the small ones such as Oro City. Leadville, with its future assured, certainly would need the steadying hand of city fathers to guide its destiny, or so argued the progovernment faction. Horace naturally found himself in the midst of the controversy, for besides his mercantile position, he was still Lake County treasurer and acting post-master.

On January 10, 1878, Tabor and four others were appointed commissioners and election judges to "perfect a town organization." A lively debate ensued over what to name the settlement; some sources give Tabor credit for suggesting Leadville, but others disagree. It matters little who promoted the name; the significant fact is that it won over such rivals as "Agassiz," "Carbonateville," and "Harrison." Drafting the incorporation papers, publication of the election notices, and other activities took the rest of the month. Right up to election day, February 4, Horace busily labored in the town's behalf. Fortunately for those running for office, the incorporation won a landslide victory, thereby launching the municipal government.[6] Those elected in February served until April 3, when the first regular municipal election was scheduled.

Elected and subsequently reelected mayor, Tabor gained yet another responsibility, as well as a distinct honor; his neighbors had shown their respect for him and confidence in him. In both of these elections, he ran on a nonpartisan platform. Local party politics did not make an appearance until 1879. The new city fathers faced a situation which might have overwhelmed less determined men. Organizing a government was only one part of a complex job, which included wrestling with innumerable problems associated with mining communities and the general urban situation, finding an equitable tax system, and, finally, providing needed public services. Only the perceptive or the fortunate avoided the pitfalls that awaited every decision made or question left unanswered.

The government hierarchy consisted of the mayor, a board of trustees, and various civil officers, such as town attorney, clerk, treasurer, and marshal. As presiding officer at the board meetings, Tabor was supposed to vote only to break ties, but during the last half of his term he voted regularly on all issues. City ordinance further specified that he preserve the meeting's decorum and order, appoint all standing committees, and chair the important Board of Health. In the general running of city government, the mayor was charged with seeing that all ordinances were strictly enforced, that revenue was promptly collected, and that municipal government was "properly, justly and economically" administered. As mayor, Horace signed all licenses, contracts, and city warrants and "from time to time" made reports to the trustees. For all this responsibility the council, during Tabor's administration, voted the mayor the princely sum of $3,000;[7] when compared to what other mayors of the time received, this was indeed generous remuneration.

The mayor's first problem was to stabilize the rapid turnover in high positions in his administration. This crisis reflected no inability to cooperate with Tabor, merely the rapidly changing conditions in Leadville, with people coming

63

and going, finding better paying positions or turning to mining. The situation, which was tolerable during the short term from February to April, became during the full year a virtual officeholders' musical chairs. Two new trustees were selected, and the police magistrate's bench had to be filled twice. One town marshal was killed, and the original street commissioner and the clerk and recorder resigned. In each case, Tabor faithfully appointed replacements. The town treasurer quit toward the end of the year, leaving no time for a new appointment. In all, only the town attorney, surveyor, jailer, and two trustees served the full term with Tabor.[8]

As the initial Leadville government, Tabor's administration passed ordinance after ordinance relating to the routine matters of government and operation. The city was divided into wards, certain streets were renamed, and a numbering system was devised for homes and business buildings. Each city official's duties were delimited, a wise move which gave substance to initial sketchy directions. Ordinances defining misdemeanors and regulating streets, sidewalks, animals running at large, and other similar urban problems came into being; even more important, a fire department was organized and fire prevention regulations placed on the books. To produce revenue, a business license fee system was initiated, a technique common to mining communities, eventually becoming a main revenue pillar for the treasury. As early as the second trustees' meeting, February 28, a saloon license of $200 had been approved. With such a transient population and a rapidly changing real estate valuation, Mayor Tabor and his council felt they had to resort to this expedient. A ten-mill tax assessment was even passed, which produced very little at first. Though these ordinances would be later amended or repealed, a start had been made, a framework established.

One of the worries that clearly prompted the organization of Leadville's government had been the threat of lawlessness. "Our well known and popular merchant H. A. W. Tabor was chosen for mayor; . . . the board is a good one . . . and henceforth law and order will be strictly enforced," a satisfied resident wrote to the *Denver Tribune* of March 3, 1878. The initial steps in this direction were to let a contract for a city jail and to hire a marshal. In April, Tabor appointed George O'Conner, who was killed before the month was out. A hurriedly called trustees' meeting gave the marshal's position to Martin Duggan, and Tabor authorized the offering of a $250 reward for the arrest of O'Conner's murderer, who had fled. Much to Leadville's relief, the incident did not augur a reign of terror. The aggressive Duggan, an Irishman who had been in Colorado eighteen years, meanwhile survived his term, despite a controversy aroused by his assaulting a local barkeeper, which forced the trustees to hold a hearing. Although he took no formal action, on the city attorney's advice, Mayor Tabor admonished Duggan to be more careful in the future and to set a good example for the entire police force. The force needed some kind of example — one of the constables was arrested for attempting to rob a woman, a charge he vehemently denied. Charges of police brutality emerged at the same time, marring Tabor's closing weeks as mayor. This prompted one newspaper to editorialize that the police force should be made up of sober, clear-headed men who were capable of understanding the law and enforcing it.[9]

A less sensational but more crucial issue, water — for sanitation, drinking, and fire-fighting — became a prime consideration for Mayor Tabor and his trustees. By mid-1878 the use of wells and water from nearby streams proved inadequate and dangerous, as pollutants from mining operations and rapidly multiplying privies threatened all who drank it. Saloons and John Barleycorn helped the less-inhibited avoid such perils; ironically, cold water could be deadlier than whisky.

Fire, that dreaded scourge of the mining camps, lurked in the minds of worried Leadvilleites as a hideous potential visitor. It was readily apparent what would happen to the hastily-built wooden structures now drying in the sun and wind. A careless match or spark could start a major conflagration, as the insurance companies knew when they established higher than average rates. Here again, the issue's urgency brought it to the attention of the trustees in February 1878, when they passed an ordinance regulating the use of stove pipes, then followed with other restraints. Only an adequate water system offered a concrete measure of safety. When municipal efforts in this direction were checked by financial impotence, private capital was sought to alleviate the perilous conditions. A concerned Tabor called a special election, in which a majority of the votes granted the Leadville Water Company the right to build and operate a water works.[10] By the end of Tabor's term it was virtually completed, and Leadville's problems eased, Tabor meanwhile receiving plaudits as the chief promoter.

The need for sanitation precautions hung like a millstone around the city fathers' necks; they accomplished very little, even though the problem was pointed out repeatedly by the local press. Americans at Leadville were no different from those elsewhere — they littered and tossed garbage with reckless abandon, compounding the disorder by having great numbers of animals stabled and roaming in and around town. Hotels, boarding houses, and restaurants added their share, piling food scraps and trash in alleys behind their establishments or in vacant lots. Failure to properly construct outhouses and cesspools contributed to the stench. All these together produced a serious threat to health, as well as offending the beholder and his olfactory nerve. The summer sun brought out the worst by activating the manure and vegetable rubbish, which winter cold had mercifully frozen. Flies and rats swarmed to the banquet. Over it all hung the noxious smoke pouring from the smelters. As the spring of 1879 approached, Tabor and the trustees bestirred themselves and managed to clean up some of the main thoroughfares. After some hesitation, a committee was appointed to buy a garbage cart and horse, only to report back that it had made no headway. The trustees foolishly let the matter rest, failing to confront the basic problem of trash collection or enforcement of sanitation ordinances, which remained dead letters on the books. Money was needed, more than either the voters or administration seemed willing to provide. The lack of initiative cannot be condoned, although it can perhaps be placed in better perspective when one realizes that older, established towns did no better.

Of a positive nature, Tabor's government opened Harrison Avenue, the main thoroughfare of the "cloud city." Tabor's guiding hand is evident here, for he served as president of the Leadville Improvement Company, which accomplished the feat. A census, taken in late 1878 or early 1879 under the direction of the trustees, found over five thousand people living within the city limits. Indefatigable civic booster-promoter Mayor Tabor also saw his camp go from a third- to a second-class incorporated city.[11]

During his tenure such diverse local firsts were achieved as sending a telegraphed greeting to Denver's mayor on the completion of the telegraph line between Colorado's front ranking communities, and the raising of a local military company. The mayor also called a special meeting to take some step toward solving the pauper problem, which surfaced even in booming Leadville. The disturbed trustees, after discussing cost and responsibility, came to a revealing decision: the paupers would be housed in the town jail and the county would have to pay the actual cost of care and feeding. Tabor continued to sell various sundries to the city and no one raised the conflict-of-interest issue, at least not openly.

Leadville grew, under Mayor Tabor's benevolent guidance, from a collection of cabins into a booming mining camp on the verge of becoming a town. Frame houses replaced shanties, which in turn gave way to brick buildings, as the camp took on the appearance of permanence. Horace himself, as befit his position and wealth, had a frame house built — no more log cabins for Augusta. The business district, too, took on new respectability and size. Almost before a man became adjusted to old businesses, new firms opened, as increased wealth demanded a larger variety of goods than the general store could provide. Clothing stores, boot and shoe stores, meat markets, drugstores, tailor shops, and bakeries opened. Fresh vegetables, meat, and fruit replaced their dried and salted counterparts to tempt the housewife and the men "batching" on their own. For those, probably not many, who wanted to take a break from the relentless pursuit of wealth, the nearby streams and lakes were a "trout haven." For those not devotees of such sport, game and fish were provided by others for the Leadville market. In February, Leadville's first newspaper, the *Reveille*, was published (with a prominent Tabor advertisement), under the editorship of Richard Allen, who had moved there from Fairplay. The excitement and interest in the first edition almost rivaled that of a new discovery, resulting in a grand raffle auctioning the first copy. Always alert to opportunity, Tabor promptly invested money in the worthwhile enterprise.

The "fair but frail" and their gambling friends, sensing correctly that in this masculine world of easy money their services would be much in demand, flocked to Leadville in numbers Augusta had never seen before. The few adventuresome girls there the previous autumn were joined by a host of their sisters, who formed the nucleus of Leadville's red-light district. The church ventured in to save the faltering, visiting ministers appeared early, then Sunday School classes, and finally a sanctuary and bell, which, when it rang for the first time, is supposed to have caused one miner to exclaim, "I'll be darned if Jesus Christ hasn't come to Leadville, too."

Throughout the summer and fall of 1878 the camp grew by leaps and bounds. Every day, and especially on Sunday, the business district hummed with activity, people crowding the sidewalks, the streets congested with freight and ore wagons. Throughout the community, construction struggled to keep pace with demand — an impossibility. Store rooms rented for fifty to one hundred and fifty dollars per month, depending on location, and were often hard to come by at any price. Small two-room log cabins rented for twenty-five to thirty-five dollars. Paint! There was no time to dress up the buildings, so Leadville presented a decidedly naked appearance to the visitor.

Lawyers rushed to Leadville in increasing numbers, until, as one wag put it, you could not throw a club across Chestnut Avenue without hitting two or three of them. Still they came. Services of the sharp and shrewd were in great demand when heated litigation broke out over the rich and not-so rich mining claims on Fryer and Carbonate Hills. Probably to the children's dismay, schools opened, and Leadville took on a settled appearance, all considered, at least in the proud eyes of its own residents.[12] The wilderness was gone; civilization had triumphed.

The "civilization" that emerged proved unreceptive to the Chinese. One who boldly ventured in found himself quickly ushered off, for Leadville offered no congenial atmosphere for the Oriental. Other minority groups, not so roughly handled, were allowed to come and go.

The excitement, the abounding optimism, the frontier spirit blended into life, was a never-to-be-forgotten experience, and even Tabor, who had been this route before, was caught up in the spirit like any newcomer. Carlyle Davis, long-time Leadville newspaperman, described it in this manner: the effect of everybody having so much money, so suddenly, made them spend it freely, and at the most exorbitant prices for everything. Another called it, "all a wild hurrah and speculation." Perhaps the feeling can never be expressed adequately in prose, but one woman, writing about her Leadville youth just at the end of the boom period, came very close to conveying it. "There is something intangible, felt and experienced in an inexplainable way, connected with life in a boom mining camp. That certain something got into my blood at that time and will never leave me. Everything was an adventure."[13]

Visitors were overwhelmed; they called Leadville "roaring," "the magic city," a "fast place," a "glorious camp," and a "marvel" that amazed, surprised, titillated, and baffled them in turn, almost as if it were a zoo, with the locals replacing exotic animals as the main attraction. Helen Hunt Jackson, the most noted 1878 visitor, wrote her impressions for readers of the *Atlantic Monthly*. What she observed in the residential district were freshly-hacked stumps, litter, plain log cabins, unpainted board shanties, tents, or various combinations of the three — not very inspiring home architecture. The business district was something else; here the town pulsated. Over business and residential sections alike poured smoke from reduction works, contaminating the air with a "lurid column of almost rainbow tints." She saw the drama of new fortunes being made, interviewed women for the feminine view, then boarded the stage and returned home.[14]

Not everyone was happy with Leadville's sudden dominance, particularly other Colorado camps, since it lured residents away by the score from older communities. All of them suffered, for none was so rich nor so promising as Leadville in the magic year of 1878. People came from the old regions, such as Central City and Georgetown, from newer camps, and even from districts just recently opened, Lake City, for instance. No immunity protected any of them; bitter comments spewed forth: "It is our candid opinion that had all the boys who went over there from this county [Clear Creek], and sunk holes on the carbonate belt, done the same amount of work here, their general average of receipts would have been greater."[15] The "boys" were not listening, and simply ignored such editorial opinions. Booming Leadville's aspirations of becoming the county seat of Lake County were now fulfilled.

This was Leadville of 1878, Tabor's Leadville — a booming, sprawling community on the verge of instant cityhood. Colorado had never seen its like before and this was only 1878; 1879 promised even greater wonders.

Postmaster Tabor, his official appointment dated from February 19, 1878, faced problems of a magnitude his experience had never before encountered. Governmental bureaucracy ground slowly even then, thus his office continued to rate fourth class, with his salary based upon the sale of stamps. Out of his own pocket Horace ran the post office for the year, employing a steadily larger staff to handle the mail swamping his office in a volume second only to Denver's. Each morning long lines greeted the opening of the doors, as men anxiously awaited letters from home or from business associates. Some pressure mounted to move the site from Tabor's location to another end of town. A worried Tabor wrote Senator Henry Teller, "Therefore if you should be asked to move the office and make [a] new appointment of PM please do nothing until you give me an opportunity to be heard. . . ." Concluding, he emphasized that he felt the office was in the right place and had the support of "far better men" than the opposition.[16] Whatever caused the dissatisfaction, the postmastership by the end of the year palled on Tabor, and he resigned.

Tabor the merchant also terminated his active career. A new building had materialized, but business failed to hold the attraction that had once sustained him. Profits mounted, but they were small when compared to his mines, nor was the prosaic merchant's life appealing when measured against the bonanza excitement of mining. Either in late October or early November he sold out, turning his full attention to mining ventures.

Mining had definitely captured Horace's attention, increasingly monopolizing his time since his Leadville arrival. At first the old story had repeated itself, and he had failed to find the right combination, resulting in small returns. Then two nondescript prospectors came to his store asking for a grubstake, Tabor to receive one-third of anything they found. Although George Hook and August Rische displayed little experience with Leadville ores, the ever-generous merchant had staked many before them with similarly unpromising credentials, and now he tried his luck once more. On or about April 20, 1878, the agreement was concluded, and the two prospectors set out, turning their attention to Fryer Hill, where George Fryer had just found the New Discovery, opening up the richest bonanza in the area. From this point on, the story becomes confused, even in accounts given by the participants. The sequence apparently went like this: they found a spot which appeared promising and staked a claim. By coincidence (some would call it luck), Hook and Rische picked the one spot on Fryer Hill where the mineral came closest to the surface. After digging down twenty-six or twenty-seven feet, they hit a vein of extremely rich silver carbonate ore. With this strike, Tabor's fortune took wing. The best contemporary statement was that of Rische, who testified under oath six months later that they started sinking the shaft April 22 and on May 1 discovered the Little Pittsburg vein.[17]

Around this discovery many legends have grown up, the most persistent being that Tabor included a jug of whisky in the grubstake. The story goes that, after finding a comfortable spot, Hook and Rische sat down to indulge and, being satisfied, decided that right where they were was the perfect spot to dig. Variations on this theme have flourished, the account depending on how the writer tended to embellish it. Not one of the men involved, and all were interviewed, mentioned the whisky, which under the circumstances might be understandable, though not logical, considering their personalities. Nor did the early accounts in the press in 1878 relate the tale that way, and certainly it would have made good reading. At least one person, Carlyle Davis, who knew all the participants, called the story ridiculous, and Rische flatly denied it.[18] Legends die hard, however, and this one became a part of the Tabor myth.

The Little Pittsburg paid from the "grass roots," accelerating the stampede to stake out claims on Fryer Hill. By July the Little Pittsburg and the New Discovery were each turning out seventy-five tons of rich ore per week. Such production brought potential buyers racing to the three partners' doors; despite offers reportedly as high as a hundred and seventy-five thousand dollars, they refused to sell. Thousands of dollars went into their pockets, and boundless reserves awaited development in a mine now valued at a million dollars. The

Little Pittsburg gave Horace the wealth he had so long sought. To protect the property the owners applied for a federal mining patent — none too soon.

Such wealth attracted unscrupulous individuals, who would have liked a share in the bonanza, and one group which had a good claim. Tabor, Hook, and Rische found themselves in court defending their interests against the claims of the Winnemuck, the first of the controversial mining cases in which Horace was to become entangled. Hook and Rische, in locating the Little Pittsburg, had claimed part of the older and apparently barren Winnemuck lode. The owners of the latter, encouraged by their neighbor's discovery, sank their own shaft, striking ore at 150 feet. Both parties now claimed the other was mining their ore; the Winnemuck, to enforce its claim, posted armed guards, which Tabor countered by going to court and attaching their ore to stop its sale. The case was sent to Denver for a hearing before Judge Thomas Bowen. Meanwhile a series of sweeping moves completely changed the Fryer Hill picture.

The key question was that of who owned the nearby New Discovery, prompting a series of complicated maneuvers. George Fryer and Josiah Eads had discovered it on April 4, the latter selling his interest a month later to William Borden. Borden, a mineralogist from Rhode Island, provided the money and skill for development of the mine, until he sold out in October to a group which in turn conveyed title to the Winnemuck interests, who now flanked the Little Pittsburg on both sides. Tabor realized he was in serious trouble; if the Winnemuck owners purchased Fryer's remaining half-interest, they would own older titles flanking his property, measurably strengthening their case.

Tabor and Rische, in the meantime, had been making their own strategic counter moves. In late September, they bought out Hook for $90,000 or $98,000, depending on which source one reads. Hook retired to live off his good fortune. In the same transaction they also purchased his share of the Dives, a small claim next to the Little Pittsburg. Money was no particular worry, since their mine was producing a reported $8,000 daily average. At this point, suave Senator Jerome Chaffee, banker, politician, and one of Colorado's premiere mining speculators, purchased Fryer's share of the New Discovery for $50,000 and then accepted Tabor and Rische's offer of $125,000 for his interest — a cool profit of 150 percent in only a few weeks — one story had it happening all in one day.

Sighing with relief, Tabor and Rische staved off trouble by securing control of half of the New Discovery, only to face a series of time-consuming, costly court cases if they hoped to clear their title. Lawyers, not mine owners, reaped the biggest rewards from this situation. The Little Pittsburg, meanwhile, did better and better. Lou Leonard, the slightly built twenty-one-year-old bookkeeper Tabor had brought in from Denver to work in his store, reported that the mine was the "biggest thing" on the continent, working fifty men and taking out over $10,000 a day. A severe pneumonia attack, a hazard of Leadville's elevation, forced Leonard to Denver to recuperate, where he became a prime newspaper source of doings on Fryer Hill. Chaffee, regretting his error of selling out, purchased Rische's share of the Dives, New Discovery, and Little Pittsburg for $262,500 or, as Rische claimed, $265,000; Horace gained in this shifting of partners an experienced and clever ally in his struggle with the Winnemuck. Chaffee probably knew the intrigues of the game as well as any man, having been speculating in Colorado mines since the 1860s. Further, he had as a friend and partner the Denver banker David Moffat, who represented an important source of money and influence. Not as experienced in mining as Chaffee, Moffat, having caught the mining fever, was involved with him in working and selling the then well-known Caribou Mine.

Apparently under Chaffee's steady hand, a compromise was finally reached, resolving the Little Pittsburg-Winnemuck conflict. The solution, consolidation of all claims, which required agreement on a just and equitable distribution of spoils, took several weeks. The Little Pittsburg, Winnemuck, Dives, and New Discovery were consolidated under the title of Little Pittsburg Consolidated Mining Company, with Tabor and Chaffee retaining 73 percent of the stock. Later in 1879 Chaffee, Tabor, and Moffat purchased the 27 percent minority shares and gained control of the entire operation.[19]

The Little Pittsburg people would have relished gaining control of the Little Chief, which lay between their mine and the New Discovery. When their overtures came to naught, they took the owners to court and asked for a writ-of-injunction to stop further mining, arguing that the Little Chief was working the New Discovery vein. This involved the highly technical question of direction of veins and the right of following a vein across sidelines. The court ruled against them on the grounds that, in the case of Fryer Hill "claims must be bounded at all depths by vertical planes."[20] Thus their hope of adding this mine to the consolidation went aglimmering.

Tabor's faith in the Little Pittsburg paid off handsomely, even when the money it cost him to carry on the fight against the Winnemuck is considered. That astute observer Frank Fossett estimated that the mine produced $375,000 up to the middle of November, and another source stated that less than $100,000 had been expended through the end of the year to operate it. It was a good mine, with every prospect of getting better. Said Charles Hill, superintendent of the consolidated company, when asked to give an estimate of the property's wealth, "If we tell the truth people won't believe us, and we don't want to lie about it."[21] More to the point, the *Denver Tribune* noted on November 23, "This mine within five months has made two poor men rich and promises to make two rich men vastly richer, and as yet it is not a twentieth part prospected or a quarter exhausted as prospected."

When all the trouble was over, Horace had come out of his first big mining undertaking and conflict virtually unscathed. Seizing the opportunity when presented, he aggressively developed the Little Pittsburg, successfully (with the help of others) checked the attempt to wrest it from him, and by the close of 1878 had gained invaluable experience and allies for further mining ventures. The Little Pittsburg had been mined conservatively, with no speculative intentions, and money was reinvested in the property, which had become one of the best equipped and timbered mines on Fryer Hill. For a man whose previous experience had been limited to small-time operations, this was a commendable record.

Tabor's cup overflowed in 1878; after the Little Pittsburg, he turned to the undeveloped Chrysolite. Located at the north end of the New Discovery, it had been found by William "Chicken Bill" Lovell, a lovable sort of rogue. Having little success, through lack of ambition or capital, Lovell decided to sell his claim to the "Croesus of Colorado," who was known to be in the market for such merchandise. Detrimental to his plans was the fact that the shaft had not struck ore-bearing rock; however, neither dismayed nor thwarted, "Chicken Bill" borrowed ore from the Little Pittsburg and "salted" the Chrysolite. Tabor purchased a quarter-interest in it for $900. Horace had not been fooled; at least he later chose to remember it that way. "I did not buy it on that account. I believed the man 'salted' it but the 'salt' part did not count with me. I bought it exclusively on account of its location . . ."[22]

Tabor's estimate of potential worth proved much more accurate than Chicken Bill's. After sinking the shaft another twenty-plus feet, his miners hit a second bonanza to accompany the Little Pittsburg. Tabor's fortunate co-owners included the well-known Chicago merchant, Marshall Field. The Chrysolite, while not producing as well as the Little Pittsburg, showed ore yielding 187 ounces of silver per ton, with so much high-grade in sight by the end of 1878 that even the most pessimistic must have been convinced that Horace had done it again. He needed no convincing, and $50,000 went to buy the nearby and promising Little Eva, and $15,000 for the Eaton, both of which merged into the Chrysolite group.[23] In buying these claims adjoining his original property, the increasingly cagey Tabor was wise, since they gave him a stronger hand and prevented lawsuits, even if the initial cost was high. The Little Pittsburg lessons were paying dividends.

He now looked elsewhere, and purchased the Belle of Colorado on Iron Hill and also the Lime Mine, adding to his growing number of Leadville properties. Advancing further afield, he invested in some lodes at the new camp of Alpine, causing a flurry of excitement, yet failing to find another Little Pittsburg. And Tabor money went far down into the little-developed San Juan country to purchase an interest in the Dolly Varden.

Iron and Carbonate Hills had made Leadville famous, only to be superseded in the public eye by Fryer Hill and its rich mines. Tabor and his partners, well on their way to controlling the entire hill, moved to buy out the "small fry" and consolidate their two major mines. The editor of the *Pueblo Chieftain* thought the hill should be renamed "Tabor's Sinai." The *Reveille*, back in the spring, had forecast, "we confidently predict that the close of the year 1878 will bring to light a bonanza of mineral wealth in Lake County compared with which the celebrated mines of Utah and Nevada will sink into comparative insignificance."[24] And it was coming to pass.

As befitted his new eminence, Tabor became one of the prime movers in the plan to establish a club room and mining exchange. The plans, reflecting the atmosphere of grandeur which gripped silver-struck Leadville, included the purchase of the "most elegant residence in the city" convenient to the business district and fitting it up with a restaurant, bar, billiard room, and exchange where residents and visitors alike could meet and discuss their mining transactions. Nothing could be too grand for the new mining entrepreneur and his friends, who suddenly had become the elite of Colorado's greatest silver camp.

Tabor's first year in Leadville had been unlike anything he had ever experienced. Exhilarated, though not without trials, he admitted, "I never knew a man as busy as I was in Leadville at that time." Even with the assistance of Lou Leonard and his other employees, his time was fully occupied from morning until (sometimes) midnight. An amazed visitor corroborated Tabor's own statement about his workload, "the [amount] of business he transacts every day is simply astonishing."[25]

The sudden appearance of wealth proved a mixed blessing for the Tabórs. The bond which had held them together, forged in the common struggle for survival on the Colorado mining frontier, now was weakening. The nagging, driving Augusta, whom Leach had observed and Horace tolerated, seemed anachronistic in their present circumstances. Horace, aglow with new possibilities, forsook the conservative ways of his wife; one or the other would have to modify his style to avoid an inevitable clash.

In accordance with his stature and activities, Tabor received accolades from his fellow citizens. A Leadville miss wrote a poem in his honor that fall, which failed to become one of America's great literary pieces, but which nonetheless expressed what his town thought of him. One of the stanzas follows:

> He is an honor to our fair young mining town,
> He ranks among the first of high renown
> And to the honor he hath a legal right;
> In aiding the poor miner he took great delight.[26]

The "Father of Leadville" had finally found the promised land of his youthful dreams, after a twenty-two-year struggle on the Trans-Mississippi frontier.

CHAPTER 5

THE POLITICAL ITCH

"The *News* and *Democrat* must retract manfully or
I shall commence suit at once . . . "
Tabor to William Hamill, August 22, 1878

OTHER honors besides his neighbors' admiration and a poem came Horace's way in 1878. His quarter-century interest in politics had certainly not diminished; it was only natural now, with his increasing wealth and position in Lake County, for Tabor to shift his view from county to state politics.

His debut was innocuous enough, consisting of his taking time out from the Little Pittsburg developments to appear as delegate from Lake County to the Republican State Central Committee meeting in Denver in mid-June. The budding mining entrepreneur pushed vigorously, to no avail, to have the size of the county's delegation to the state convention increased. This seemed only fair to him and his Leadville neighbors, but the rest of the party was as yet unwilling to recognize the changing situation. After selecting Denver as the party convention site, the one-day caucus adjourned. Behind the scenes the Republican leadership listened with interest to Horace's enthusiastic promise of a Republican victory in Lake County that fall. Despite an unwillingness to grant extra delegates, they longed to capture the county and were more than willing to give attention to any promises from its wealthiest resident to produce votes.[1] Thus began his first venture into top-level state politics.

Within a month, trial balloons were being sent up from Leadville proposing Tabor for lieutenant governor. His friends, it was rumored, planned to present his name; although the undeclared candidate chose to remain silent, it is hard to imagine his not being pleased and well aware of what was occurring. Tabor continued his mining ventures, which represented money in the bank, a factor which could not be overlooked in Republican party finances. The *Denver Tribune*, July 25, thought the connection was obvious: "Another very productive property, and one likely to make a candidate for Lieutenant Governor, is the Little Pittsburgh [sic] . . . "

The days were rapidly slipping away if Tabor planned to make a serious bid for elective office, because the party convention was to be in early August. Tabor would have to take advantage of the political conjuncture. The Republican party had come to Colorado in 1859 and had been greatly strengthened in subsequent years by its success nationally in electing presidents, who in turn passed out Territorial patronage to loyal party workers. This should have entrenched the party in an almost unbeatable position; instead it led to local leaders' fighting among themselves over "loaves and fishes" and (before 1876) the issue of statehood.

Colorado had become a state in 1876, and this opened new vistas for the Republicans, who rose to the occasion by winning a majority in the legislature, which rewarded Chaffee and his one-time rival, Central City's Henry Teller, by electing them to senatorships. Tabor's new mining partner, Senator Chaffee, joined by ex-Governor John Evans, led the Denver group, whose power was contested by a coalition of the mountain towns and any allies they could secure.

No rookie, Tabor realized that Denver and Arapahoe counties, as the most populous areas, carried the greatest political weight. Black Hawk and Central City, once the state's premiere mining camps, were a distant second. Denver and the mountain towns generally shared the major offices, with the other parts of the state given a few to appease their local voters. The tightly-knit party leadership was headed by Chaffee, the controlling party spirit and leader in the statehood fight for longer than anyone else. Shrewd, calculating, and able, this fifty-three-year-old native New Yorker could make or break any aspirations Tabor might have. Indeed, he could lay claim to being the most influential Colorado Republican politician and statesman of his era.

Chaffee's younger senatorial colleague and fellow New Yorker, Henry Teller, had opposed him back in the 1860s, but reached political accord with him in the early 1870s. The persistent Teller, possessed of an intelligent and logical mind, would have a very large role to play in Colorado history, despite being somewhat puritanical in outlook and retiring by nature. Together now they dominated the party, symbolizing the marriage of Denver and the mountain areas.

Only slightly less important was Georgetown's genial, pug-nosed William Hamill, the "consummate politician." Mining man and speculator, he had turned to politics with a driving ambition for high position that was scarcely concealed. The youngest of this triumvirate, he had been chosen chairman of the Republican State Central Committee, and loomed as most important for Tabor's aspirations. Behind these three were a host of others — some younger men on the rise, such as Teller's brother Willard and the two Wolcotts, Henry and Ed — ready to back one candidate or another, depending on who might offer the best aid to their own careers.

A newcomer to Colorado, Frederick Pitkin, had emerged by that summer as the leading candidate for governor. Arriving in 1874 to see if the climate would benefit his seemingly terminal case of consumption, Pitkin was a living, walking testimonial to the beneficial effect of Colorado's clear, dry atmosphere. This much-admired Connecticut-born lawyer's rise in party politics had been as fast as his medical recovery.[2]

Up in his Leadville offices, Tabor pondered these facts, and added to them one other — the ace up the aspiring politician's sleeve — the sudden emergence of Leadville. The historian and politician, Frank Hall, who knew this period first-hand, wrote that from 1879 into 1882–1883 this community was the dominating influence upon state politics.[3] Already the impact of population, wealth, and a new crop of mining millionaires was starting to make itself felt.

Horace, or someone speaking for him, finally consented to allowing his name to be advanced, and the Tabor boomlet came out into the open on July 22, when the Lake County Republican convention recommended its favorite son for lieutenant governor. With only two weeks to the state convention, the tempo immediately picked up. Tabor's campaign centered on his popularity in Colorado's fastest growing town and county and his contributions as Leadville's mayor and principal benefactor. In a letter obviously timed for the opening of the convention the next day, on August 7, a dedicated supporter eulogized Horace for his energy in promoting Leadville, his long residence in Colorado, and his help to miners; it ended by proclaiming him the most popular candidate in the interior of the state.

Tabor did not go to the state convention as an official member of the county delegation, either through modesty or the realization that it would be better to remain detached from the give-and-take of the meeting. Establishing an informal campaign headquarters, the candidate for the first time bowed in the political spotlight, as he warmly greeted numerous callers.

The convention opened, and Lake County proudly placed its leading citizen in nomination, with a "feeling of pleasure and confidence" in the man who "possesses ability and represents the many interests of Lake County" and whose nomination would do justice to his section, to the party, and to Colorado. Gilpin, Boulder, and Custer County speakers rose to second. With the flowery rhetoric out of the way, an informal ballot showed Tabor running strongly in front of his nearest rival. From then on there was little question of his victory, and he won easily on the first formal ballot, his nomination being then made unanimous.[4] The recently-announced candidate's initial try for party nomination had succeeded more easily than he had any right to expect.

No deep analysis is needed. Tabor was available, an attractive candidate, and a faithful party worker. Of course, many a man has lost with just those qualifications. R. G. Dill adds that Tabor was selected as a representative of Lake County, which at the time was estimated to poll not less than one-third of the entire state vote. Tabor, it was hoped, could carry that county. An enemy of Tabor's within the party put forward still another reason for Tabor's victory. This was Ed Wolcott, who charged that Tabor's nomination was simply a swap between the party with position and Tabor with money: "to its lasting disgrace," said Wolcott, "the party traded one for the other."[5] In Tabor's case availability, residence, and finances overwhelmed other candidates whose claims to the nomination were just as good, if not better.

Frederick Pitkin headed the slate, and energetic and impulsive James Belford, the "red-headed rooster" from Central City and former Territorial Supreme Court justice, was selected to run for the House of Representatives.

Not yet much of a speaker, Tabor wisely refrained from anything more than a very brief thank you to the convention and a promise to deliver a Republican majority from his area. The immediate problem confronting his campaign workers was one of getting their candidate more widely known; in August 1878, Tabor's name was not yet a Colorado household word. A campaign biography was published, stressing, as those things typically do, virtues, popularity, history, and character. Republican papers jumped on the bandwagon, lauding Tabor as a man of the people, a miner, and a man of nerve, force, and excellent administrative ability.[6]

The convention had done its work well in balancing the ticket — Pitkin from Ouray, Tabor from Lake, and other candidates from Arapahoe, Gilpin, Weld, Larimer, Pueblo, and El Paso counties — thereby appealing to the north and the south, the mountains, and Denver. The geographic and economic divisions tended to overlap, representing the pressure groups within the party. For Republican unity such a balance continued to be essential, since the state's southern portion wished to have a senator from that area but had no one ready for the position. Thus it had to be pacified with appropriate sops.

Senator Chaffee's term was up, and the Republicans needed to capture control of the legislature again in order to elect a Republican senator. For this, they needed money. The Democrats had picked William Loveland, a director of the Union Pacific railroad and the new owner of the *Rocky Mountain News* (now a Democratic sledgehammer), for governor. Their campaign chest was well stocked, but Republican Party Chairman Hamill was hampered by a shortage of funds, making Tabor's wealth even more vital to the party.[7] Tabor went home well satisfied; not only had he triumphed, he had met most of the leading state Republicans, contacts that would be significant in years ahead.

Leaving Denver on August 10 with his county delegation, Horace arrived at Leadville, in obvious good spirits, to be warmly received by a crowd of well-wishers and the local band. Sounding more like a politician every day, he spoke briefly. "I cannot find words to express my gratitude for the token of respect and also for your endorsement of my nomination. I am so much a part and parcel of Colorado that whatever is for her interest is for mine. I hold that if a man takes an office, great or small, he owes his constituents all his efforts." The assembled faithful responded to such platitudes with three ringing cheers, after which Tabor departed for home and Augusta. Local Republicans promptly notified Hamill that they would go to work at once to organize.[8]

Not much in the way of campaigning was planned for Tabor by Hamill; his inexperience in public speaking and the lesser significance of his office argued against an active campaign. What was needed was keeping Lake County in line, which, despite his June optimism, still appeared to be an unknown factor. The large influx of population since then had changed the camp's complexion, and there had been no election to test party strength. Tabor and his fellow workers had plenty to do here for the next few months; Hamill no doubt envisioned that Horace would go quietly about the job of enlisting support. Fate intervened, and Tabor suddenly became a prime issue and a controversial candidate, as the

Democrats ended all worry about his name not becoming known.

R. G. Dill, who wrote the standard state political history of this era and took part in much of what occurred, called the 1878 campaign, without exaggeration, one of the fiercest, "most productive of vituperation and general nastiness," that he had ever witnessed. Tabor had not even returned to Leadville before Loveland and the *News* opened up on him with both barrels. Tabor replied on his arrival, "When nominated for an important office it is a sure thing that any man will be slandered and abused, but all I have to say to the opposition is 'go ahead!' " They took him literally, leaving nothing untouched in a no-holds-barred personality smear. The sometimes humorous, decidedly vicious and dirty attack which followed hurt Tabor deeply.

The *News* commenced the battle on August 10, as he was leaving Denver, with the accusation that the nomination had been dictated by one of two motives: to cultivate friendly relations with "our sister territory Utah" or the desire to find a new political depository in place of the traditional First National Bank of Denver, Chaffee and Moffat's bailiwick. "Either of these motives will explain the nomination of a shambling, illiterate boor for the second place on the Republican ticket in preference to men of sterling character, and defined principles . . . " For the reader who might have been mystified by the reference to Utah, the *News* elaborated in the next issue. "Was Tabor entirely off with the old love before he was on with the new? Two souls with but a single thought: two wives that love as one."

The same day Loveland's editor hit upon a different theme. "If both of Tabor's wives should take the stump, aided by his hundred chinamen, what a red-hot canvass they would make!" How did Tabor make his fortune? By importing cheap Chinese labor to "the exclusion of the pioneer miners."

According to the paper, Tabor's soliloquy following such lurid disclosures became:

How happy I'd be with either dear charmer
were t'other dear charmer away.

One supposed exposé then raced on the heels of another, with the *News* carrying the banner. When Senator Chaffee returned to Colorado to campaign, it pictured him urging Horace, "that sentimental child of love," to take the stump to counteract the growing dismay and demoralization on every side. The newspaper grew rapturous over what a Tabor appearance might be like: what a jolly entertainment it would be to mingle Tabor's variety show with one of Belford's spiritual seances [Belford took his lumps over supposed infidelity]. Then Loveland's writers imagined what might happen if Tabor happened to become governor. Why the antechamber of the executive office would become a variety house where "The can-can will be given with modern improvements and a bewitching danseuse will be imported from the Parisian comique . . . " Wearied state officials would be soothed by delights "rivaling the glories of Mohammet's paradise."[9]

This relentless slander aroused the ire of Horace, his friends, and the entire party. Something needed to be done and done quickly before irrevocable damage occurred. Outlying town newspapers picked up Loveland's charges and reprinted them for readers who could not distinguish fact from fabrication. Could the accusations that he violated Victorian morality and family sanctity sink his campaign? Tabor's opening response simply was to deny the stories as incredible. "I have lived in what is now Colorado, for a little over nineteen years, and I think if I had had more than one wife — which I haven't — you would have found it out before now." Friendly Republican papers leapt to his defense, demanding evidence of bigamy, proof of Loveland's charges. None came forth. They fought with satire, countering the *News*'s insinuation of Mormonism and infidelity going hand in hand in Republican politics by charging that Loveland could not be expected to grasp the well-known fact that every Mormon in Utah or elsewhere was a Democrat. One Boulder paper calmly warned Loveland about conducting a style of political campaign that would not win in Colorado. Still, there was no retracting or letting up on the Tabor issue.

Some charges fell by the wayside. Tabor, an old fifty-niner, was no pilgrim or Johnny-come-lately. Nor had he brought any Chinese into Leadville. One indignant Tabor supporter offered one hundred dollars to any Democrat in Lake County who would say over his signature that Tabor ever brought Chinese into the county.[10] No takers appeared.

Still the damning charge of polygamy would not rest, making titillating reading for the gossipy types and good saloon conversation over a glass of beer. A Lake County sympathy backlash in Tabor's favor provided some consolation. In a letter to Hamill, the county chairman observed, "We mean 'business' up here, and intend to carry this county if among the possibilities. The groundless attacks of the 'News' and 'Democrat' upon Mr. Tabor will do us good here." The Leadville *Reveille* blasted the character and nature of the *News* and said its slurs fell stillborn, gratifying only the perverse, depraved, and corrupt tastes of its editors.[11]

Tabor remained stubbornly silent, believing this to be the best immediate defense against such obvious falsehoods, for fear that anything he said might be misconstrued. Augusta, too, remained quiet, hurt by these accusations, perhaps wondering if it was all really worthwhile. Horace stayed home and worked hard to capture Lake County for the entire ticket. A few letters written to Hamill about varied topics still exist from this period. Enough canvas to cover a wigwam-shaped frame to hold fifteen hundred people was needed for a rally. With the wigwam finally completed, Tabor ordered campaign song sheets and fifty Chinese lanterns with candidates' names on them, then watched with interest when the wigwam served as the site for Leadville's campaign highlight — a debate between the two major candidates for Congress, Belford and Democrat Thomas Patterson. For over three hours, the two debated before an estimated crowd of three thousand, the overflow standing outside. Through all the stress and bitterness Tabor kept his composure and optimistically wrote his state chairman, "everything looks lovely." The secretary of the county Republican club told Hamill that they needed more money to pay canvassers and other expenses, because the building of the wigwam had swallowed up all the funds they could raise at present. Other people sent Chairman Hamill letters stating that "Tabor is carrying everything before him and with him"; even Democrats were swinging across party lines to vote for him.[12] Considering its anti-Tabor stand, the *News* on August 30 printed an interesting story: when Republican rowdies seized control of the stage at a Democratic rally, Tabor had come and asked them to withdraw peacefully, much to his credit, the paper said.

With the campaign swinging into the last weeks of September, the alert Hamill warned all counties to organize paid registration and canvassing committees. The strictest economy must be observed, yet they were to prevent illegal Democratic voters from stuffing the ballot box and see that every registered Republican voted. A horse-and-wagon committee was even to be established to provide transportation to the voting places.[13] Thoroughly organized, Hamill predicted, the party would win.

All was not going well for poor Horace, because the *News* continued its barrage of attacks unabated. It accused him, perhaps truthfully, of purchasing eighty barrels of beer for the Leadville campaign, though there was nothing particularly scandalous about such actions during this period. More important, considering Hamill's need for money, was Loveland's claim that Tabor reneged on a promised donation of $20,000 to the hard-pressed campaign chest. And returning to the old topic, the *News* editorialized on "Elder Tabor's lament" and "disclosed" Tabor's motto, "Kiss and never tell."[14]

The repeated insinuation and name-calling finally proved too much for the beleaguered candidate, who resorted to his ultimate weapon — a libel suit. For weeks such a course had been hinted at, if Loveland did not reform; Loveland's open refusal had been matched by stony silence from Leadville. So outspoken did the *News* become that it actually played on the theme, warning Tabor to save his money. Finally, indignation could be held back no longer, Tabor demanding in an open letter to Loveland that an "immediate and unconditional retraction" be given all charges of his having two wives. The defiant reply, the aforementioned editorial on "Elder Tabor's Lament," ended all hope of compromise; Tabor launched a $30,000 libel suit, exactly the figure Loveland paid for the paper and plant. Loveland refused to be cowed. He wrote that Tabor's objection in the suit to being described as a shambling boor was well taken and evidently resulted from a typographical error.[15] Here, indeed, was he due the widest latitude of indignation. With this sarcastic concession, Loveland dismissed the suit.

The *News* then temporarily shifted its attention to Belford, accusing him of making an "insulting proposal to a young lady." Whether the switch resulted from the suit or just public saturation and craving for a new sensation cannot be determined. But as the race entered its last hectic days, the *News* again returned to its favorite subject. A humorous jab at Tabor's continual refusal (so the *News* claimed) to contribute to the party highlighted the initial blast. As bad as Tabor was, the paper further intoned, he at least was no shylock or dealer in "cutthroat mortgages," as was Pitkin. Loveland attacked the Republican Denver *Tribune* and *Times*, with justification in the *Times*'s case, for neglecting Tabor's campaign. Near the campaign's end, the *News* pictured Hamill busily arranging to swap off Tabor, the "Leadville chicken" being too heavy a load to carry without some compensating advantages.

Loveland's attack began to bear fruit, but fortunately not as he intended. Tabor's friends rallied to his support, as did more and more miners, who viewed the attack as against one of their own.[16]

Despite the best effort of the Democrats, the Republican press confidently predicted victory as election day neared. Chaffee reportedly offered to bet $10,000 on the Republicans; no Democrats offered to cover it. The *News*, the night before the election, took one last swing at Republican "mormonism, infidelity, and cutthroat mortgages," then retired. On election day, October 2, the *Tribune*, sensing victory in the early voting, headlined: "GLORY! The Republicans of Colorado May Rejoice To-Day. The Broom is Not So New, But it Sweeps Clean." Even with a few reputed last-minute Democratic shenanigans, Lake County backed its favorite son. He polled 49.8 percent to his nearest competitor's 42.8 percent. He ran strongly in Arapahoe, winning by 400 votes, thus capturing the big county. Horace carried five of the six key counties: Lake, Arapahoe, Gilpin, Boulder, and Clear Creek, losing only Democratic Las Animas. His margin of victory lay with these. Elsewhere, he rolled up a two-to-one majority in El Paso and did well in the mountain counties, except in southwestern Colorado, where he was narrowly defeated. With the exception of El Paso and Weld Counties, Tabor lost in the less-populated and agricultural eastern part of the state. In Lake, Clear Creek, Jefferson, Larimer, Gilpin, and Park counties, he ran ahead of his running mate, Pitkin. In the others he ran behind the rest of the ticket, perhaps reflecting to a degree the result of the Democratic press's slashing attack. His total vote, 13,891, while some 400 less than Pitkin's, still gave him a comfortable 1,900 lead over his opponent, Thomas Field.[17]

No ray of hope brightened the Democratic camp following the Republican sweep. The *News* was quiet for several days, then entitled its comments, "Small Consolation," and continued, "Pitkin and Tabor run side by side all over the state. Now what does that prove? Will some of the republican moralists please tackle the problem."[18] The outcome had significant results, even if Loveland chose to ignore them. First, the Democratic party dropped into a secondary role, where it stayed for the next decade. If any question of whether Colorado could be counted a Republican state had existed, this now was convincingly answered. Second, Tabor had emerged as a political figure and power in the Republican party. The editor of the *Boulder County News* concluded on October 4 that the best lesson was the stinging rebuke administered to the vulgar style of political journalism. If such a lesson had been learned, it was soon forgotten.

The bitter campaign left no outward scars, although its influence may be reflected in Tabor's later hard evaluation of politics: "I always took an interest in politics; always will probably, either to help somebody that I want to help or oppose somebody that I want to pound down. . . . " Twice now Tabor's personal life had been maliciously maligned over some political issue. His role in the campaign had been important, if not overwhelming. Without question, he contributed monetarily to the campaign, undoubtedly not as much as hoped; how much is not known, although the *Denver Times* on September 17 jokingly said that he contributed five or ten dollars just to please the *News*. While his prestige and power had helped secure Lake County, his victory in Denver resulted from the well-oiled Republican machine, not from personal achievement. Out of it all, the new lieutenant governor emerged as the champion of mining and miners. "Not a politician, not a seeker for office," but a miner in a commonwealth where "over half the people are miners," proclaimed a devoted follower.[19] For one rapidly becoming the state's richest capitalist, this was a rare image he managed to convey.

Tabor moved into the periphery of political power, rather than its center. Colorado politics pivoted on personalities, not issues; within minutes, it seemed, after a campaign started, issues went by the board. Only a continual attack by the Republican press on third-party Greenback ideas kept any semblance of issues before the electorate. At the end, Tabor had not placed himself solidly in the Chaffee-Teller orbit or in the camp of opposition within the party. Perhaps still unsure of himself, he played a cautious, fence-straddling game. What effect this would have on any future hopes only time would tell.

Still unresolved was the libel case, and the apology Horace so ardently desired had not been forthcoming. Finally it came, months after the campaign concluded. In April 1879 the proceedings of the suit were withdrawn, and the *News* expressed "its profound regret that it was ever made the medium of their [Tabor attacks] dissemination." Eating crow, the paper labeled his domestic and business relations unblemished and called Tabor a "gentleman of honor, integrity, ability and worth," and an upright citizen.[20] Why Loveland took this particular means to attack Tabor is unknown. He undoubtedly exaggerated, yet in view of subsequent events, it seems hard to believe he made up such charges from whole cloth. Perhaps rumors of less than domestic tranquility at the Tabor home flitted about, although Augusta and Horace maintained a proper appearance. What basis the *News* may have had has been lost.

What a grand year 1878 had been for Tabor, even considering the harassment of the late campaign! He looked about with satisfaction and saw a wonderful field of opportunity opening, leading to unknown horizons. No standing pat with present gains for a poker player like Tabor. The gamble appeared worth taking, and the stakes were high.

Horace Tabor, c. 1883. *Library of Congress.*

Oro City was Tabor's home until 1877. This shows the camp in 1873. *State Historical Society of Colorado.*

Augusta L. Tabor. *State Historical Society of Colorado.*

Elizabeth Tabor. *Denver Public Library Western Collection.*

Nathaniel Maxey Tabor. *State Historical Society of Colorado.*

Lou Leonard, Tabor's trusted lieutenant and
mine manager.

The start of Tabor's fortune was here, the Little Pittsburg Mine. *State Historical Society of Colorado*.

Matchless Mine, Leadville, Tabor's best-run and most productive in the 1880s.

Tabor Opera House, Leadville, the epitome of this camp's cultural aspirations. *Henry E. Huntington Library.*

Chestnut St., Leadville's first commercial district. *State Historical Society of Colorado.*

CHAPTER 6

LEADVILLE'S SON BECOMES DENVER'S PATRON

"Mr. Tabor is a gentleman to whom Denver
should extend a hearty welcome. We
need him and more like him here."
Denver Tribune, Feb. 2, 1879

A S 1878 closed, Tabor prepared to return to Denver to
assume his duties as lieutenant governor. Actually his
tasks in this office were light, almost a sinecure, where
a "useless figurehead" might be safely deposited. For the
more ambitious it served as a launching point for loftier goals,
particularly by increasing one's circle of friends and construc-
tively using what prestige the position possessed. Tabor's
cronies confidently predicted he would fill the office with
honor and astuteness; others, not so sure, adopted a wait-
and-see attitude. First, he had to resolve the problem of securing living quarters; that proved easy, thanks to Chaffee, who,
being in Washington, graciously offered his private suite of
rooms in the Evans block.

The Denver to which Tabor came was caught up in the
excitement of a senatorial contest, resulting from Chaffee's
decision the previous June not to seek a second term because
of failing health. Privately Chaffee wrote to Teller:

> I never felt better over any act of my life than that of retiring
> from politics. I am perfectly willing anybody else shall occupy
> all the places in government. I want none of them. There

is no dignity practiced in the Senate, nothing but a scramble
for the floor.

He predicted there would doubtless be a scramble for his
place, not that he cared; "I am sick of it, really, disgusted
with it and this gives me a good opportunity to get out."[1]

Instead of a scramble, Nathaniel P. Hill shot to the front
and maintained his position. This cultured and conservative
former college professor had helped solve the knotty problems
involving the smelting of Colorado's refractory gold ore and
had established the state's most advanced smelter at Black
Hawk. Though not an adept politician, he carefully set about
to secure the senate seat, wisely backing Hamill for party
chairman and supporting the 1878 campaign with a $2,000
contribution. Hamill returned the favor by supporting Hill's
bid. Astute and opportunistic Edward Wolcott, who had
helped promote the alliance by bringing Hill and Hamill
together, promptly hitched his political fortunes to theirs.

Despite Chaffee's public statement and private sentiments, many of his supporters were reluctant to see him
leave public life and indiscreetly pressed his claims. These
indiscretions displeased Hill mightily, but they did not alter
his front-running position. Unfortunately for him, his campaign never aroused much enthusiasm in the Teller-Chaffee
camp, the former, in fact, giving subtle support to the Chaffee
boom. Since June, when he wrote the previously quoted letter,
Chaffee had returned to better health and had had a change
of heart about resigning. The rejuvenated Chaffee, aided and
abetted by his friends, entered the race, while Hill fumed
about this stab in the back. After all, both Chaffee and Teller
had given a pledge to support Hill, who added fuel to the
fire by publishing a letter Chaffee had written promising not
to interfere or run. Out of it all flared a party feud, which
left Chaffee and Hill extremely embittered; Hill especially
nursed hard feelings for years.

Frank Hall cursed the greed for the senatorship (considered the top political plum in Colorado) as the "bane of
our political system." The craze which hit every time a seat

was up for election affected almost all Colorado politicians and was not improved by the caucus system, which allowed the party in control of the legislature to select in private who would be chosen. To Hall the caucus system was a sister evil.[2]

Numerous pitfalls faced Tabor, should he not play his cards carefully; since he hoped to seek higher office, he could ill afford to offend either side. The Democratic *Rocky Mountain News*, trying to sow further seeds of dissension, deepened Horace's troubles by editorially pushing him for the vacancy. This amazingly hypocritical reversal can only be comprehended as an attempt to weaken an opponent and deepen party cleavage. Temporary editorial embarrassment could be suffered if the end were achieved. Suddenly, as if a real swell had developed, the *News* published letters and the paper cried, "Whoop 'em up for Tabor." All this proved too much for the *Denver Tribune*, which sarcastically commented that, if given a few chunks of high-grade ore from the bonanza king, the *News* might be less clamorous. When asked about the struggle and his sudden candidacy, Tabor sounded like a politician, taking the astute way out by changing the subject "with great ease."[3]

On a bright, pleasant January 15, Horace put aside such worries, as he rode in a short inaugural parade; then with the rest of the new administration, he took office. As lieutenant governor, he served as president of the senate, having a vote only in case of a tie. Expressing a hope to preside with fairness to all parties and to have the assistance of all senators, Horace assumed his duties. His first one was to preside over the official election of the new senator.

The suspense of the choice dissolved quickly before a Hill phalanx, which did not crumble despite pressure on it and elected its man in four ballots. Tabor received not a vote and could not have seriously considered himself a candidate. He must have chuckled over the *News*'s audacity, because his libel case was still pending at the time. Despite pronouncements of party unity, little of it was evident at the moment; the ill-fated Hill neither forgot nor forgave those who turned against him. The relationship between Colorado's senior and junior senators, Teller and Hill, was strained, needless to say. For years afterward, the ill feelings generated in the fight raked the party.[4]

Presiding over Hill's official election, Tabor later remembered, was the most significant thing he did; "In regard to my experiences as Lieutenant Governor, there was nothing of especial interest." This session lasted until February 9, and the attendance record of the president was very good; he chaired twenty of twenty-three meetings. A reporter viewing one of these sessions remarked that the unusually "early" 9:00 A.M. opening caught the chaplain unaware and absent, saw half the members present looking disgusted, and found the president himself looking sleepy. Much to the amazement of his enemies and the delight of his friends, Tabor earned praise as presiding officer. Such adjectives as "prompt," "proficient," "intelligent," "tactful," and "judicious" were used to describe his efforts. Under his benign presidency, the senate passed a myriad of routine measures, concerning such things as branding and herding stock, defining responsibilities of sheriffs, and memorializing Congress for establishment of a military post in southeastern Colorado.[5]

Such relatively light duties gave Horace plenty of time to investigate Denver and its potentialities; he used it judiciously. First he purchased the Henry C. Brown home on Broadway, considered one of the finest in the West, for $40,000. Augusta had never basked in such affluence; her husband soothed her uneasiness by pointing out that the financing of such endeavors was no worry with money flowing in from the Leadville mines. Nor was cost spared to furnish the home. There on the night of February 7, Augusta and Horace bowed into the social whirl by sponsoring one of the highlights of the season, a grand reception in their new home. Denver and all Colorado's political elite turned out, and the congenial host responded with the best to wine, dine, and entertain them. The evening passed pleasantly, and featured dancing, a special wine room, and an elegant table brimming with food. The whole house sparkled with lights and gaily arranged flowers. Augusta, in a velvet-trimmed black silk dress, graciously presided over the affair.[6]

Her thoughts on the occasion were not recorded, unfortunately, yet she, more than anyone else, realized how far they had come in less than two years from their Oro City cabin. As if to show the stark contrast, her husband later that year presented her with $100,000 and the promise that any gift she desired would be hers, if she only expressed the wish — jewelry, clothes, anything befitting the wife of the state's leading mining man and lieutenant governor. Augusta, restrained by her New England upbringing, was appalled by such extravagances. This industrious, simple woman, who enjoyed housework and gardening, seemed out of place in the new merry-go-round of affluence.

If Horace ever stopped to consider his wife's feelings in these matters, he quickly put such thoughts aside as he looked around Denver, that endless world of opportunity. He briefly considered Pueblo as a prime source of investment, then abandoned that idea to invest in the town that he accurately sensed would become the state metropolis.[7] Not yet in such an exalted position, Denver had still come a long way since the Tabors' first visit twenty years before.

After a slow decade during the 1860s, which saw Denver's population increase by only thirty people over the 1860 census, the 1870s produced a remarkable spurt: from 4,756 to more than 35,000. Old landmarks disappeared, replaced by brick structures, as a substantial business district and railroad yards emerged where once log cabins and freight wagons had predominated. The catalyst for even faster growth came with Leadville's silver. Such leading citizens as Moffat, Chaffee, and ex-Governor John Routt hurried to 'the camp to make fortunes, while others, who did less well, still returned home with money. Soon Denver felt the surging impact of the Carbonate Camp of Leadville and its silver millions, and by 1879 was on the threshold of emerging as the greatest city of the

Rockies. Prosperity was everywhere, with the community growing, construction pushed to the limit and still unable to keep pace with demand, and a mining empire opening at her doorstep.

With one eye on expanding Denver and the other on Leadville, Tabor in 1879 entered into a near-orgy of expansion. Before the year was out he had constructed an opera house, purchased more mines, incorporated a gas company, served as president of two telephone companies, invested heavily in Leadville's *Reveille*, and purchased large amouts of stock in the powerful First National Bank of Denver. He was rumored to have even greater plans in mind. The details of these transactions need not concern us at the moment, yet the scope of his plunging certainly revealed a new vein of his personality. When queried by a reporter about his being "too heavily loaded" with investments, confident Horace replied:

> And I attend to all of my business myself. I have a sort of
> an idea that Tabor's business can better be managed by Tabor
> himself than by anybody else. I have made numerous invest-
> ments and I think, in time, that I will be able to secure a
> fortune, but I intend looking after all of my business myself,
> and I have never yet felt that I needed the aid of any other
> than Tabor.[8]

In Denver he started conservatively, yet optimistically, with one of the soundest investments he ever made — the purchase of stock in the First National Bank. A direct descendant of Denver's original private mint — Clark, Gruber & Co. — the First National had been organized in the spring of 1865 by, among others, three men who played important roles in Tabor's life: Moffat, Chaffee, and Eben Smith, the astute mining engineer whom Tabor would call upon on several occasions. It had grown to become Colorado's strongest financial institution, with resources of over $1 million in January 1879. Tabor purchased ten shares of capital stock in the bank from Moffat for $1,000 and was elected to the board of directors, which included his two mining partners, Moffat and Chaffee, the former the bank's cashier and the latter its president. The purchase of 880 shares from Chaffee in September brought Tabor's holdings to 44 percent of the total, at this time the largest single amount held by any individual. At the next annual stockholders' meeting in January 1880, Tabor continued on the board and was elected to the vice-presidency. According to the bank's board minutes, the vice-president received $300 per month; whether Tabor collected it is open to question. Never active in bank affairs, he proved not overly conscientious about attending meetings. The next year he chaired the meeting that reelected him to the vice-presidency, a position which carried with it automatic election to the board. Reflecting the sudden influx of wealth from Colorado's mining regions, the bank's resources jumped to $2,407,552 by March 1882.[9] Nothing more clearly showed Tabor's new position in Colorado and his business acumen than his election to the board of directors of this prestigious institution.

The First National Bank served as his headquarters for a while. There he transacted many of his mining deals and laid the plans for his Denver investments, which helped change that city's history. Rumors, meanwhile, flew about town, claiming inside information on some exciting project he was just about ready to undertake.

Tabor's name was becoming as important as his money. Who should appear as president of the recently-incorporated Colorado Edison Telephone Company but Horace? And his knowledge of that recent invention was limited indeed. Who but Horace was approached to sponsor a hose company, and then liberally provided funds for uniforms and equipment? The members responded promptly by naming themselves the Tabor Hose Company No. 5. Civic-minded Tabor also offered a fifty-dollar purse for the best fruit display at the 1879 state fair, showing that his farming instinct had not completely disappeared.

But Leadville, not Denver, hosted the expansiveness of his first investments in 1879. Although he had now moved to Denver, Tabor still spent much time in his old home, maintaining a comfortable apartment and office there. It was here that he got his first real taste of banking, not so foreign a field to Tabor as it might seem, since his store's safe had long served as a depository for gold, and his scales weighed the amount shipped or sold. A simple form of banking it was, to be sure, but all that had been needed in Buckskin Joe or Oro City. Such primitive methods did not long suffice for Leadville, and several banks had opened in 1878, including the Bank of Leadville. Horace was president, son Maxey was on the board of directors, Little Pittsburg codiscoverer Rische was vice-president, and George R. Fisher was cashier. Fisher had the only practical skill in conventional banking, in Philadelphia and Denver, and ran the institution, while the others reveled in the glory of their new title of bankers. Public faith in the bank, boosted by the knowledge that the wealth of the Little Pittsburg and the status of its incorporators stood behind it, was shown by a thriving business at the end of 1878.

Such a prosperous firm could not stay long in its original cramped quarters. The president solved the problem by building a handsome brick structure on one of Leadville's busiest intersections, Harrison and Chestnut. On the second floor were his private offices. Fisher had just nicely settled in when, on a February morning, a portion of the wall next to him collapsed; luckily, he escaped serious injury. Blamed on frozen cement which had subsequently thawed, the damage was repaired and proved to be the only setback the Bank of Leadville suffered in 1879. Deposits received in 1880 reached $61 million and the bank stood on firm ground as one of Leadville's soundest.[10] Tabor did not pay much attention to the bank, what with his multitude of interests; anyway, banking was too sedate to sustain his continued attention.

Elsewhere in town, he adventurously invested his Fryer Hill money. The telephone arrived here, as in Denver, in 1879, with Tabor the president of the Telephone Exchange. By fall the system was in working order, lines criss-crossing town and reaching out to the surrounding mines; then came connections with Denver. The next year Tabor helped incorporate and served as president of the Leadville Telephone Company, a reorganization of the older Exchange. The newest Bell instruments were installed, giving the elated community one of the best telephone systems in the country. Despite such improvement, the system's newness and related problems hampered operations, keeping the company from operating on a dividend-paying basis for years. Regrettably, the altitude and winter weather forced abandonment of the Denver connections via Mosquito Pass, forcing Leadville to return to more prosaic Western Union ties. Horace received much-deserved praise for his enterprise and public spirit in supporting this endeavor.[11] It is hard to imagine how it could have survived the first years without his financial backing. Again, as in the case of the bank, Tabor wisely brought experienced partners into the company.

To brighten night-shrouded Leadville, Tabor and others formed what became the Leadville Illuminating Gas Company. Contracts for the $75,000 worth of gas lines were let in the spring, and by November operations began. President Tabor decreed that such problems as hauling coal by wagon from Pueblo would not be permitted to interfere with progress, as the firm lighted both streets and private homes. The initial system proved faulty, and in 1880 another $40,000 was spent for repairs to improve it, producing, said the local press, a gas far superior to that manufactured in Denver. Customers received bills every two months, "to be promptly paid," according to company policy. This efficiency paid off; the concern became one of the town's lucrative businesses, even though its patrons risked a certain danger — they were repeatedly warned to shut off gas if a leak was discovered, open the windows and doors (a chilling midwinter experience), and notify the company.

Despite its importance to the community, the company initially had a difficult time trying to sell bonds. Tabor and William Bush, previously proprietor of Central City's famed Teller House, ended by buying the bonds at less than face value. Tabor had met Bush during the 1878 campaign, and a strong friendship had developed. Later, the Leadville Illuminating sued Tabor for what they claimed had been unfair advantage taken of them in the bond sale. Tabor won the case. The company eventually owed Tabor an additional $74,000 for property purchased and money loaned.[12]

Several attempts were made to organize a streetcar company to offer service to and from the mines and along the main streets, none being successful. Tabor, with his banking partner Fisher, served as director of one, the Leadville Omnibus and Toll-Road Company. It went into operation with only about half of its stock subscribed, and then found that daily business averaged a less-than-lucrative fifteen dollars.

No one moved more decisively than Horace to provide needed fire protection, both in his capacity as mayor and as a private citizen. As a large property owner, he undoubtedly was partly motivated by self-interest, but his actions also reflected his altruistic public spirit. Eventually, Leadville would secure a paid professional fire department; initially, though, volunteer units answered the call, the original fire company being the Harrison Hook and Ladder, with Tabor as a charter member. These social as well as utilitarian organizations needed money for hose, trucks, buckets, ladders, uniforms, and other necessities. In Leadville, as in Denver, Tabor generously stepped forward with funds. To spur initiative, Tabor had offered a carriage to the first organized hose company. The response had been almost immediate and forthwith an "elegant hose carriage and mountings" were presented. In gratitude the donor was elected a life member, and the company acquired his name, Tabor Hose Company No. 1, organized in February 1879. Tabor, in return, took an active interest and served as company president for the next three years.

Though he did not actually fight fires, there were other rewards for Tabor — the social affairs and banquets he frequently attended. A toast to "the health of Lieutenant-

Governor H. A. W. Tabor, which was drunk midst round after round of applause," crowned one jovial affair. The recipient responded, "happily complimenting the excellence of the Leadville Fire Brigade," and pledging his future support to all "enterprises inaugurated for the benefit of the City and her citizens." Such sentiment, known to all as more than mere oratorical gesture, was heartily applauded and justly so. On another occasion, the Tabor Hose boys had "outdone themselves" arranging a parade, complete with band and torches, in honor of their benefactor. Such demonstrations reflected the genuine esteem in which Tabor was held during these early years. He responded with a further outpouring of his wealth. In July 1880, for example, he headed the sub-scription list with a five-hundred-dollar donation to send the "fire laddies" to the state tournament, where their record the previous year had been "brilliant, if not successful."[13] Competition was keen between volunteer fire companies to see which one was the fastest in racing to a fire plug and getting water flowing through the hose. Practical and also sporting, these contests appealed to the late nineteenth-century American. Horace, whose liking for athletics must have been none too deep, still enjoyed these races, more than likely placing a few side bets on his Tabor Hose. Tabor's company became one of the best in the state and did yeoman service in Leadville for a number of years. Still, his enterprising appetite was unsatiated, pushing him to help organize still another hose company, named after his friend Bush. His role here was neither so prominent nor so lasting.

An equal source of Leadville pride was its military com-panies. These, too, were primarily social organizations that gave the volunteers a chance to display their uniforms, although some served a more practical purpose, being affiliated with the Colorado National Guard. Again the gener-ous lieutenant governor opened his purse, providing $10,000 to uniform and equip a company originally known as the Tabor Highland Guards, then the Tabor Guards, and finally the Tabor Light Cavalry. Though nothing was organized until

August 1879, the idea had been considered since the previous March, when Pitkin had suggested the need for some military organization in Leadville. At that time there had been unfounded rumors of a possible bread riot, and the anxious governor thought this a prudent way of avoiding serious trouble. After the initial expense, Tabor had continued to donate money to the company, as he expressed it, for "putting the boys in good shape." The "boys" responded with honor guards, receptions, and balls, plus innumerable toasts drunk to Tabor's continued good health and prosperity. Holding no official rank in this particular unit, he was given the honorary title of general.[14]

Besides such public contributions, Tabor privately gave to charities, churches, and individuals. Dill concluded that it would be impossible to list the "private benefactions of Gov. Tabor," for he was one of those "who do good by stealth and blush to find it fame."[15] The entrepreneur had more than just a business outlook.

As the town's most prominent man, even if not now a resident, Tabor was the one from whom reporters naturally sought information about the community. In one interview for the *Denver Tribune*, March 12, 1879, he gave some sound advice to those seeking to rush into mining before considering all consequences:

> Yes, I think it [the future] will be better than at present. You see we can't accommodate everybody at Leadville, and men can't prospect much now, hence if they are coming it will be well for them to postpone the time at least until the middle of May. They will then have a better chance to do something, and will not run so many risks. I would not advise outsiders to come in before the middle of May.

On responding to a question about law and order, Tabor, still mayor, proudly answered, "We do keep good order. The majority of the people are law-abiding, and our police regulars are good. We allow but very limited latitude to the rascals."

What Mayor Tabor said and what was actually happening

differed slightly; still he may be forgiven for a slight exaggeration. It was not easy to live in Denver as lieutenant governor and try to serve as mayor of Leadville. This dual role produced an intriguing legal question concerning his right to continue in the latter office, but he did not resign, stepping down only when his term was up in April 1879.

When in Leadville for a meeting, increasingly rare in 1879, Tabor presided at the board of trustees meetings. Typical of those he sat through was the one of February 26, 1879, which had on the agenda petitions regarding special policemen, a railroad right-of-way, approval of a plat for a new addition, the question of who would run the chain gang, city incorporation, and a general review of police affairs (resulting in the decision to forbid the use of intoxicating liquors by on-duty members).

Everything Tabor's Leadville administration did required money, which was difficult to obtain through taxation; eventually, it ended in the red after being unable to cover the running expenses of $20,795.42 for the year ending April 1, 1879. While saloon licenses brought in over $7,000 and police court fines another $1,800, a deficit of $11,300 existed in outstanding warrants when Tabor left office.[16] He also dumped another problem on the lap of the incoming administration — lawlessness. Leadville had grown too quickly, had too much easy money floating about, and offered far too many temptations for the riff-raff to resist. It was difficult to secure good men to patrol the community at the salary offered. In truth, Leadville was sitting on a powder keg as Tabor stepped down. He got out just in time; the Leadville *Daily Chronicle* of May 9 headlined the local news: "HELL LET LOOSE, the Bloodiest Night in Leadville's Calendar."

The administration's failure to curb this problem blotted its record, which had been very good, though not exceptional, otherwise. Everything that it did or failed to do must be weighed against the problems faced. It is doubtful that anyone else could have done much better; governing a mining camp was a thankless task, especially one in Leadville's state of expansion. Demonstrating his sense of responsibility and interest, Tabor had attended fifty-nine of seventy-seven sessions, and possibly more (attendance was not kept at several sessions). This amazingly large number of sessions showed the magnitude of problems faced. Most of the meetings were specially called.

Just before Horace left office, a resident signing himself Cass wrote the *Denver Tribune* that the mayor had been an excellent executive officer who had a well-managed police force and a diligent and active city administration. R. G. Dill commented that Tabor brought form and order out of rudimentary chaos, put the wheels of conservative progress in motion, and left his successor a city government organized and functioning, with such services as paved streets and gas and water works if "not perfected at least well under way."[17] Tabor could not have hoped to accomplish much more than that in fourteen months.

Banking, gas lights, telephones, fire and military protection — Leadville had them all, thanks to Tabor's initiative and money, in addition to his work in the city government. Tabor had proven a true benefactor to the camp from which his fortune sprang. One void remained, and Horace moved swiftly to fill it: Leadville lacked a first-class entertainment house, so he built the Tabor Opera House, the capstone of his projects.

Leadville's populace could view many theatricals and variety shows that aroused the miners' passions and advertised the wares of the chorus, yet nowhere in the town could a man take his wife and children to a respectable theater. By 1879, with wives and families appearing in ever-increasing numbers, the demand grew for better-grade entertainment. Receipts in some of the lower-class establishments reached a reported twelve hundred dollars per night, offering hope that a family-type theater would be able to pay its way. Such dual motives excited Leadville's foremost citizen, and another project was born.

The site chosen was next to Leadville's finest hotel, the Clarendon, on Harrison Avenue, owned and operated by

William Bush. The Clarendon had opened lavishly with a sumptuous Victorian banquet that included lobster, fish, chicken, eight varieties of meats, six vegetables, six desserts, and an abundance of other tempting morsels. Leadville had come of culinary age with the Clarendon, locals claiming it rivaled even New York's finest. Tabor wanted his opera house to be the finest as well, and it was.

When the three-story Tabor Opera House opened on a cold, crisp November 20, 1879, it ranked as Leadville's "most beautiful brick structure," and even the chronically critical had to be impressed with the interior. Walking up the grand staircase the visitor entered the main auditorium, decorated in red, white, gold, and sky blue. Gas lights, which marked the debut of the Leadville Illuminating Gas Company, glowed warmly in brightly polished new fixtures. Upon reaching his seat, the patron sat down on a comfortable chair upholstered in scarlet plush. Another flight of stairs took him to the dress circle and gallery on the building's third floor. Private boxes could be reached from the main floor. The attention of the nearly nine hundred people who crowded in, including standees, was immediately caught by the freshly painted drop curtain with its glorious mountain scene framing a rather incongruous old castle with a stream running by. The owner had a penchant for such idyllic scenes.

On that grand opening evening, a double bill, headlined by "The Serious Family," was presented by the well-known Jack Langrishe company to launch the festivities. Proud Tabor was there, as was Bush, who leased the building. On the second floor front, the lieutenant governor had luxurious offices, replacing those in the bank. Eventually, a covered passageway was constructed between the Clarendon and the Tabor Opera House to better accommodate the guests.

For the first season Langrishe entertained the customers, as he had been doing in Colorado almost since the Pike's Peak rush. No more popular man could have been found to typify the Western theater. Langrishe well deserved the title of "Colorado's favorite actor."

Slightly remodeled the next year, the Opera House went

on to reign as Leadville's best. Some of the camp's roughness seemed to vanish with its opening and with the quality of the performances given; Leadville was gaining urban respectability. The editor of the *Democrat* felt obliged to give the patrons a hint, however, that each chair had a hat rack fastened under the seat so that hats would not have to be held or placed on the floor. Tabor enjoyed visiting his theater when in Leadville, an occasion which the local press liked to commemorate with appropriate grateful remarks about its founder.[18]

Leadville came of age in another sense as well; its stock exchange finally attained sound footing, after a tenuous start in 1878. Under the guiding hand of Tabor and others, it was officially incorporated in May 1879, the first meetings having been held in April. To his collection of offices Horace added that of president and member of the board of directors. Throughout the summer it was an active institution, with sessions being held every evening at the Clarendon; then it closed for the season. When it was resurrected the next year under the same auspices, Tabor (holding the same offices) presided over the first meeting and was picked to serve on the committee to draft a constitution. Exchange seats cost $500, limiting those who participated. Principally, it reflected the price fluctuations of New York and could not stand independently. Despite ups and downs, the exchange managed to survive, Tabor using it occasionally for some stock speculations and sales, but it could never hope to continue as a permanent institution.[19] Tabor and his friends found it more convenient to work through Denver or New York. But the fact that Leadville sought to establish an exchange revealed the mining community's high aspirations. Tabor's aspirations had also taken wing in 1879, as shown by the multitude of investments now carrying the Tabor name.

CHAPTER 7

SOWING THE WIND

"But to no other king than Carbonate,
are we expected to bow."
Leadville Democrat, Jan. 1,1880

LEADVILLE'S and Tabor's high aspirations were not unjustified, not in the flush of mining prosperity of 1879. Like his town, Tabor glided serenely into the summer of his prosperity, wealth sitting easily on his shoulders, money flowing freely through his hands. On paper he had become a millionaire; basing fortunes on the worth of mines, however, is at best tenuous. Never one to sit idly counting his fortune and admiring newly-won prominence, Horace moved swiftly to reinvest his profits in mining as well as business, literally, in the biblical admonition, sowing the wind.

Never expecting each investment to return a profit — Tabor knew mining better than that — he realized that one Little Pittsburg offset many failures. This philosophy charted his mining destiny.

On Fryer Hill the riches from the Little Pittsburg continued to roll into Tabor's coffers. The late winter of 1878–1879 had been used to retimber the greatly-expanded underground workings, thereby fortifying the walls against the anticipated pressure of the spring runoff. About half of the two hundred to two hundred and fifty miners employed worked on the Little Pittsburg itself, the rest on the consolidated properties. A January dividend of $100,000, followed by February's

$125,000, clearly established this property as Leadville's most valuable. Mining reporter Frank Fossett estimated the consolidated company's profits from mid-November 1878 through May 5, 1879 to have been $519,321.[1]

James Hague, well-known and respected mining engineer, examining the property for a client in April, gave the clearest professional report available by a person not involved in the company. His employer was particularly interested in ore in sight and further ore-bearing areas. He wished to have an "absolute result of an exhaustive examination," even preparing a code to be used to report significant findings via telegraph.

Of the three mines, "At the present moment the most important . . . having regard to ore in sight and productive capacity, is the New Discovery." Most of the work had been done on the claim's east side, which appeared to Hague to be the most valuable, and he "hardly expected" the west side to equal it. He observed that the present ore-bearing ground had been developed entirely since the consolidation. While the Winnemuck might produce in the future, at the moment it offered practically nothing "in resources to measure." The old owners had worked out the Little Pittsburg's upper and richer seam; while it was certainly in a better condition than the Winnemuck, its reserves could not "well be calculated." Neither of the last two was as systematically developed as the New Discovery, yet Hague judged that each had a considerable amount of ground likely to be productive. Confessing there were no means available to ascertain accurately the amount of ore mined before the consolidation, he produced for the period afterward some interesting statistics. The average value received per ton, $62.54, represented between 60 and 70 percent of the real value of silver in the ore when mined; the rest went for smelting, shipment, refining, and marketing of bullion. This yielded a total of $165,162 from the Little Pittsburg, $252,261 from the New Discovery, and only $18,605 from the Winnemuck through March 31.[2]

In a coded telegram April 16, Hague stated his conclusion: "There is now in actual sight three or by liberal estimate four hundred thousand dollars. Value of the mines on bedrock basis five hundred thousand dollars or considering future possibilities might be rated for a speculative market of one million." Hague's estimate was conservative advice that might have been taken by those who in 1879 were excitedly counting profits as they contemplated buying into the company.

A follow-up letter more specifically outlined Hague's views. The key was the New Discovery; if it produced up to its present estimated reserves of three hundred thousand dollars, then all would be well. The future was "exceedingly uncertain" and any prediction concerning it was simply a matter of conjecture. On the other hand, if all reserves bore out, taking into account all future possibilities, it would doubtless "raise the estimate of the value of the property to a figure considerably beyond that of the ore now in sight."[3]

The Little Pittsburg was indeed on the market, and Tabor and Chaffee were actively courting Eastern investors. Hague's client did not buy; even if he had made an offer based on Hague's examination, it would have been too low to match the plans of the Little Pittsburg Consolidated. Hague, given permission to examine the ledger books of the company, reported that to April 1 Tabor and Chaffee had been paid $101,349 each in dividends and the other partners less according to the amount of stock each owned.[4] Why entertain a bid of a paltry few hundred thousand, when bigger fish, in the several-million-dollar range, were almost begging to be hooked? Such a dividend-paying investment could not be allowed to slip away for mere peanuts. A coldly logical buyer might have questioned selling even at an inflated price, but rational thinking was a scarce commodity in Leadville in 1879.

In March, Tabor went East, visiting Chicago, Cleveland, Buffalo, and New York, everywhere eagerly sought after for first-hand information about Leadville mining. In Chicago he did not register as a hotel guest in order to avoid interviews with people clamoring for information; suddenly the once obscure Oro City storekeeper was in great demand, as investors leaped to grab a beam of his lucky star. Denver papers reported his reception with pride, since few Coloradans had ever been so well received in the East. The *New York Tribune*, somewhat naturally playing on the "rags-to-riches" theme and thereby promoting a legend, found Horace's attraction in the exemplary tale of how a poor Leadville man became a millionaire and lieutenant governor.[5] Such lionization amused Tabor, who nevertheless kept his wits about him and went about his business.

In Chicago he interviewed architect William Edbrooke about designing a building he had in mind for Denver. Edbrooke was prominent at the time for, among other achievements, designing the College of Notre Dame. The two discussed plans and reached an agreement, Tabor not bickering about the steep fee of $4,500 asked by the architect. Money was not his worry at the moment; a few thousand would not stand in his way. The two parted, Edbrooke to plan and Tabor to continue his tour, chuckling over rumors appearing in Denver about his intentions. As grandiose as they seemed to readers, they would not match what he planned. That could wait, mining matters could not.

On to Cleveland, where Horace talked to owners of the Alaska Mine, located near some Tabor properties in the San Juan mountains. Negotiations proved successful, and he and Rische purchased a half-interest in that property. Alaska stock, which had been a drug on the Cleveland market, suddenly came to life in the wake of Tabor's involvement.[6]

The main business at hand, though, was not the Alaska or hiring of architects, it was the tempting Little Pittsburg. Chaffee, now residing in the East, had been busy arousing interest, not a very hard job with the glowing press reports cascading out of Leadville, and Tabor came to reinforce him. The bait was glamorous, especially now that they had incorporated the Little Pittsburg for $20 million, with a capital stock of 200,000 shares at par value of $100. The amount raised many eyebrows; still, the *Engineering and Mining Journal* at least partially supported it as being merely nominal, a standard for measurement of its value, although the *Journal* regretted the adoption of such a large capitalization. What the editors warned their readers about was the relation of the shares' selling price to the standard.[7] The selling price then fluctuated in the $20 range. Such academic discussion did not worry Tabor, Chaffee, and Moffat, all members of the board of directors, which also included as window dressing some Eastern stockholders. To put increased emphasis on their Eastern outlook, they opened a branch office in New York City.

Leadville mines suddenly blossomed into one of the easiest available methods to increase one's fortune, more lucrative than the railroads and other stocks so sought after by affluent Easterners. Without too much difficulty Chaffee found, with the able assistance of several New Yorkers, a group of wealthy potential investors who planned a grand excursion to visit the Little Pittsburg before they invested in its stocks or increased their present holdings. The rigors of the four-day trip were softened by a private railroad car stocked with wine, liquor, and the best delicacies money could buy. While enjoying the pleasant, relaxed atmosphere, they could discuss the prospects of the company with its directors, including Moffat and Tabor. They stayed in Denver only three hours; such was their haste to see the enticing silver treasure, which had been so attractively painted for them. One intended purpose of the trip, it should be noted, was to show that mining was being carried on in an honest and intelligent manner, the idea being to help Easterners feel more confident about investing money. California and Nevada stock promotions had given the industry a black eye and had scared away potential investors. Crowed the *Rocky Mountain News*, "Their high position cannot but be of advantage to our mining interest when they return, and it will be a great help in placing other stocks on the New York market."

The nationally known mining engineer, Rossiter

Raymond, one of the editors of the *Engineering and Mining Journal*, came with the party to examine the mine from a professional standpoint. Members of the New York Stock Exchange, prominent bankers, investors, and at least one newspaperman, Charles Dow, made up the remainder of the party.

Advance publicity stirred these tourists to a heady antici-pation, matching — probably surpassing — the effect of Leadville's elevation. For a number of days the mines pro-duced ten thousand dollars daily and Moffat, more flamboyant than usual, promised to take out a hundred thousand in twenty-four hours should his guests desire to see such a wonder. Such faith by the owners conjured silver visions in the heads of these normally conservative businessmen. Even the mining journals were carried away, stating that if the in-vestigators pronounced a favorable judgment upon the Little Pittsburg, the company's stock would secure a popularity unequaled by any in this country.

The Little Pittsburg's directors asked no one to buy, just to examine; in fact, they would not even allow stock to be purchased until after the thorough investigation had been completed. Whetting the appetite and holding the prize just beyond reach accelerated the chase. The party toured the site and looked over the mines, gazing at the area where Tabor had taken out six hundred thousand dollars, with Horace there to tell them all about it, though stretching the amount just a little. The directors showed them ore valued at over a million dollars, which had been blocked out to mine, and then pointed out that only 3 percent of the actual property had been worked. Imaginations took wing. Carefully, the group examined the books and the detailed bookkeeping sys-tem, asking questions of the directors, superintendent, and others, who willingly answered with enthusiastic reports.

Finally, on the last day, Raymond, who had been working separately, gave his preliminary report, which proved to be the *piece de resistance*. According to Dow, the report was "ex-ceedingly satisfactory to the Little Pittsburg folks." This under-

stated it, to say the least, for Raymond claimed $2 million
of ore reserves in sight and favorable indications on the rest
of the property. He was ably supported by nationally known
California mining engineer Winfield Scott Keyes, who had
examined Fryer Hill in February for San Francisco clients and
called it the "biggest pot of money in the world." While the
more conservative Raymond would not commit himself that
far, the next day he told the party's members that at least
$2 million more was almost certain to be found in the New
Discovery's hitherto unexplored northwest corner. He
finished his presentation by describing his vein structure
theory, hardly an exciting topic to covetous buyers, who had
silver fortunes dancing in their eyes.

Seldom had potential mining investors been more skill-
fully brought to a fever pitch over stock sales. Tabor, Chaffee,
and Moffat finally announced that they would retain controlling interest in the company, graciously offering, however,
50,000 shares for sale at $20 each to those interested. If the
buyer purchased immediately, he could still receive the June
dividend, as the company planned to pay $100,000 monthly,
with enough reserves in sight to keep going at this rate for
three to four years. Fifty thousand shares disappeared in a
twinkling, and those unfortunates who did not buy then paid
$25 per share for another 30,000 shares which quickly
materialized as consolation. Most of the original amount had
been pledged before the examination was finished, so great
had been the enthusiasm. As far as Dow could learn, every
man in the party who had an option on shares closed it,
because the more a man knew about the mines the more
confidence he gained in them.[8] The farewell meeting turned
into a festive occasion, with the happy stockholders passing
a series of resolutions thanking Chaffee, Moffat, Tabor, and
the others for the courtesies shown the party. With the complete success of the venture assured, these Colorado financiers
must certainly have silently given their own thanks to the
buyers for their even greater generosity.

The company kept its promise throughout 1879,

altogether paying seven monthly dividends of $100,000 each and sweetening the cake with an extra one of twenty-five cents per share.[9] By the year's end the New York *Mining Record* was praising the company's highly favorable prospects and the able and honest management of its directors. Reflecting this record and public confidence, when the stock finally appeared on the New York exchange, opening at $29 in late October, it reached a high of $34 a share during a very active week's trading early in December. Englishmen, too, joined the rush when stock went on sale in London.

Such transactions could not escape legal entanglements. Some of the former owners of the Winnemuck asked for a receiver for the company, charging that their mine had not been properly developed and, therefore, that they had not received a just share of the profits. They alleged further that Chaffee had not been given the option to convey their property into the Little Pittsburg Consolidated. The plaintiffs finally withdrew their complaint after an out-of-court settlement, which, though not disclosed, was rumored to have included a handsome sum.[10] With this entanglement out of the way, operations proceeded smoothly.

The story circulated in early September that Moffat had purchased Tabor's stock for $1 million, thus gaining three-fourths of the stock for himself and Chaffee. According to this report, Tabor was paid two checks of $250,000 and the rest in government bonds. The rumor was confirmed in an interview with David Moffat, who, along with Chaffee, had purchased Tabor's one-third interest; only the method of payment differed from the story which appeared in the *Rocky Mountain News*. Horace wisely invested part of his money in First National Bank stock.[11]

Such phenomenal success with the Little Pittsburg encouraged Tabor to strive for greater heights. He and his partners controlled the other big mine, the Chrysolite, and it, too, was attractive to investors. With the main attention focused on the Little Pittsburg, the Chrysolite did not catch the public eye until the second half of the year. Once the action started, it moved steadily toward the same goal, if by a slightly different route. Consolidation came first, with Tabor and his associates, Marshall Field and John Borden, who already owned one-third of the neighboring Vulture, purchasing the rest, bringing it into the Chrysolite company. One small oversight cost them dearly before the consolidation was completed, a little triangle of ground between the Vulture and the Little Eva, which had been overlooked and not included in the original surveys. A warning by the *Engineering and Mining Journal*, back in April 1878, about sloppy surveying with likely results of dispute, fell on deaf ears; Horace and most others ignored it. Now he wished he had heeded. Opportunistic miners saw the mistake, claimed the plot, and successfully operated the two thousand square feet until their larger neighbor bought them out. By September, the Chrysolite was obviously for sale.

Intriguingly, both Hague and Raymond again entered the picture and examined this mine. Hague's report, based on a late August tour, showed that the Tabor-Field combination owned or controlled a group of claims, including those previously mentioned (Vulture, Eaton, and Little Eva), as well as the Kit Carson, All Right, Fairview, Carboniferous, Pandora, Solid Muldoon, and Colorado Chief, all lumped together under the Chrysolite name. In this combination the Chrysolite was the most valuable, yielding $242,939 from October 1878 into August 1879, while the Carboniferous and Vulture followed with $182,344 and $170,517, respectively.[12] The others yielded very little, and were added primarily to strengthen the main properties and prevent costly lawsuits from developing.

Raymond's report on the Chrysolite was more sketchy than that on the Little Pittsburg, though no less enthusiastic. Visiting the property some three months before Hague, he felt it must contain $4 or $5 millions' worth of ore, then added the strange (for a mining engineer) phrase, "*I believe* the property to be worth considerably more than five million dollars; but this figure is not based wholly upon personal knowledge."

Winfield Keyes exuberantly proclaimed, "the Chrysolite Silver Mining Company, in my opinion, stands without a rival amongst the silver-lead deposits of America." [13]

The result of all this examination produced the desired result when, on October 15, 1879, the Chrysolite Silver Mining Company completed the purchase. The prime mover in all of these shadowy dealings was apparently George Roberts, a mining speculator who worked his way from California in 1849 through Nevada's Comstock, and on to Leadville. He was a successful operator, a speculator's speculator. His first known appearance in Leadville had been back in February when he, Keyes, and others visited the town. Yale-educated, German trained, Keyes worked closely with Roberts and, undoubtedly, they visited the Chrysolite at this time. He then assumed some unspecified role in the operation, because Hague wrote in August, "I rec'd a letter from Roberts withdrawing his objections to my examining the Borden and Tabor [property]." Hague and Keyes then spent two days in the mine.

Roberts stayed behind the scenes completely, but canny Frank Fossett said he (Roberts) and unspecified others purchased the property and organized the company. He remained in the background for a very sound reason: his name was not particularly well respected in Eastern mining circles. New York's *Mining Record* described him a few months later as one who vended wares at inflated prices that gravely damaged the whole mining industry with Eastern people. Personally quite charming, Roberts displayed indomitable energy, experience, and coolness under pressure, all of which would have attracted him to Tabor. Lending credence to Fossett's statement was the fact that Winfield Keyes was at once appointed general manager of the new company, and later the main shaft was named Roberts.

The Chrysolite's capital value was somewhat more modest than the Little Pittsburg, set at a mere $10 million with 200,000 shares at par value (the capitalization divided by the number of shares), $50. The price was a reported

$2,778,000, a major percentage of it in stock.[14] In the sale Tabor received one-fourth of all the stock, which he continued to hold, while also serving as an officer. Interestingly, he also was listed as one of the company's organizers. He was reported to have purchased even more stock, thereby furnishing further proof to the conservative investors that he had faith in his own property.

Easterners quickly assumed at least nominal control by being appointed to various offices. Daniel Appleton of the book publishing firm became president; Arthur Sewall, later to run for vice-president on the Democratic ticket with William J. Bryan in 1896, was a trustee, as was Nevada senator John P. Jones. They were joined in a few months by Ulysses Grant, Jr., who had examined the Little Pittsburg with the other Easterners back in May and June. Lesser lights were also appointed, but the mine was actually supervised by a small group including Winfield Keyes as general manager, presumably Roberts, Tabor, and a few others on the scene.[15]

This time none of the ballyhoo that surrounded the Little Pittsburg promotion was resorted to. Leadville property was too well known, basking in the successful glow of that mine and other smaller operations as well. Again, the *Engineering and Mining Journal* endorsed the incorporation. Going further than previously, it claimed that the property had the advantage of being endorsed by two of the best authorities in the world as to the value of this class of mines, Keyes and Raymond. Further, it was governed by a strong board and had Keyes as manager. The investors' hopes were borne out by the end of the year, when two dividends of $200,000 each had been paid, and the stock ranged into the $30 class. The public, unable to purchase the original offering, all of it having been taken by subscription, soon got its chance and responded wholeheartedly, the limited shares available becoming a hot item.

These two mines made Tabor a national figure. Where once he could stride along unnoticed, now he was recognized on the street and pointed out to the uninitiated as Leadville's bonanza king. Leadville and Denver knew him well; New York and other Eastern cities were becoming better acquainted with him as he came and went on mining business. Profits continued to mount; it seemed that no matter where he placed his money, it multiplied. Trusting his judgment or mining sense, he purchased a score of mines throughout Colorado. Each time he did, more cautious investors responded, willing to trust his decision and wisdom. Newspaper editors particularly sang his praises, the editor of the Aspen *Rocky Mountain Sun* prophesying, "Governor Tabor arrived Friday and now a spirit of enterprise will be inaugurated." "Governor" was now the lieutenant governor's nickname. Another commented on Tabor and Rische's investing in the San Juan mountains: "doubtless this action will turn the attention of many capitalists to the region."[16] Where Tabor invested, his fame went also, opening new vistas for old-timers and newcomers alike.

Tabor held great hopes for his mines in the beautiful San Juan mountains. His investments there the previous year had been just a sampling; now he plunged with confidence born of Leadville success. His interest had been rapidly kindled by the promising Alaska Mine, located at the head of Poughkeepsie Gulch, midway between the two young mining camps of Silverton and Ouray. Situated in the Alaska Basin, surrounded on three sides by the jagged San Juans, it was one of the most sweepingly beautiful of all Tabor's mine sites.

The Alaska Mine, uncovered in 1874, failed initially to surmount the region's isolation plus the high altitude of the site (over twelve thousand feet). Not until 1878 did it and its slightly lower neighbors, the Red Rogers and Saxon, come into their own. The *Ouray Times*, with a large dose of local pride and self interest, claimed the Alaska was one of the best mines on the continent. The turning point came when a Cleveland group of capitalists managed to gain control of it and several other claims early in 1879 and capitalized the property for $2 million; at that moment the deepest shaft was only forty-five feet deep.

Tabor moved into the district in February by spending $55,000 of his Leadville riches on the Red Rogers and Saxon. His main interest continued to focus on the more promising Alaska, which he bought while in Cleveland in March. Following his Cleveland transactions, he sent his partner Rische hurrying from Denver to inspect their prize. Rische came back well pleased, stating that these were the richest mines in the state, although observing as an afterthought that the distance from the railroads was, of course, something of a drawback. When Tabor came home he happily consented to be interviewed concerning his new purchase: "My opinion is, since you ask it, that the mines are worth two million today; and they would bring it in any other section than the San Juan." Enthusiastically exaggerating, Horace predicted that the Alaska property "is worth nearly or about the same now, I suppose, as my interests in Leadville."[17] For this bargain he paid only $125,000. The San Juans gladly welcomed Tabor. When he visited there in July, the reception extended from Lake City westward, nor did the lieutenant governor hurt his image when he declared that "the San Juan was going to be the great mining center of Colorado in the future."

Soon the Tabor magic blanketed Poughkeepsie Gulch, the work force increased, shafts were sunk, and new machinery was brought in personally by Tabor on his July visit. The locals fully appreciated all their new neighbor accomplished, because already others had been induced to come where pathetically little capital had gone before. Not only mines interested Horace, but also possible sites for reduction works and new and better roads from his property to the existing works at Gladstone, a small camp just over the mountain from the Alaska. Here he located a mill site for future development.

Morgan Draper, a consulting engineer visiting Poughkeepsie Gulch, also grew ecstatic, saying its very rich ore "beggared description." As the winter season closed in, the twenty-five men employed at the Alaska were working

121

ore yielding a reported 300 to 1000 ounces of silver per ton. To supervise the operation Tabor sent his brother John out from Denver; Horace himself had no intention of enduring the cold, frosty months locked in the heart of the San Juans. Tabor's burst of activity aided not only mining but the entire local economy, since he bought timbers, mining supplies, grain for mules and horses, hired men for numerous jobs, and in one week purchased $1,833 worth of groceries for his miners' boarding house.

Shaft houses and other buildings went up, readying the property for winter and allowing John Tabor to keep the men working on all the mines throughout the remainder of the year.[18] As a mere sideshow, Horace incorporated the Betcher and Grand Central Mining Company to work two other San Juan properties by that name.

These investments and the San Juan tour had given Horace a much broader mining outlook. He came face to face with the interlocked problems of isolation and lack of transportation, which, despite his efforts, he was unable to resolve. Better local roads, new machinery, a larger working force — all helped develop the mines — but to no avail unless these other problems could be overcome. Peak production would never be achieved nor the real worth of the property shown until a solution was found. Only a handful of men had the courage, desire, and, most important, the resources to leap successfully into the underdeveloped San Juan. William Weston, one of the important early mine developers in this region, understood very well Tabor's contribution. Writing to the *Engineering and Mining Journal* on December 27, 1879, he credited him with starting the "ball rolling" by investing in the Alaska Consolidated: "where the big fish go, the small fry all follow," and he supposed more property changed hands in Poughkeepsie Gulch at big figures than in any other district in the San Juans.

During 1879 Tabor shrewdly acquired majority interest in the soon-to-be legendary Matchless Mine. Discovered in 1878, supposedly one of the wonders of Fryer Hill, it failed

to develop as did some of its neighbors. Potential, not production, thus caught Horace's imagination. Negotiations for the
property were concluded in late August and early September,
when Tabor paid over $87,000 for controlling interest. Later
he purchased the remaining interest for $30,000, becoming
sole owner. Although hindered by a lawsuit which hung over
the property, the new owner set to work exploring it. Instant
success did not reward his efforts; of the three shafts sunk,
only one showed any ore and water flooded the lower workings. Since it was situated on what local experts considered
unpromising ground, the Matchless never had been
adequately explored. Tabor's luck seemed to have pinched
out, at least with respect to the Matchless, for no silver had
been found; only an iron ore vein rewarded several months'
effort. This purchase gave Horace the largest interest on the
hill, outside of the consolidated mines in which he was a
major partner. Doubts raised about the worth of this latest
purchase didn't upset him; as he expressed it, the joy of
owning something without others sharing had its compensa-
tion, and profits would furnish him with "pin money — so
to speak."[19]

At the close of 1879, with his income in thousands per
week (if not per day), Tabor was still ready to "go his bottom
dollar" on Leadville and San Juan mines. His fortune and
his future appeared to reside here. Reflecting both his
increased experience and wealth, this no longer small-time
operator plunged wherever the risks seemed warranted and
sometimes on just a hunch, as in the Matchless. No obstacle
appeared too great to discourage him or certainly Tabor would
not have staked so much on his San Juan venture; without
transportation this district was apparently years away from
reaching its mining potential. Yet he boldly advanced, and
others came after him, speeding up settlement and increasing
attractiveness to railroad lines, which were sure to come to
tap this wealth.

Little or no consistency was displayed by Tabor in selecting this or that mining property. The Matchless, for one exam-

ple, personally interested him because of its potential, while the San Juan investments reflected Tabor's desire to invest in new mining areas. These mines, at least, were inspected by Tabor before he bought. Later New Mexican investments were based on a foolish reliance on other men's reports of their richness. He bought the Vulture Mine in Arizona on the basis of its reputation, in order to sell it. Likewise the Poorman Mine at Caribou was secured for quick sale, although producing regularly at the time. The Tam O'Shanter, near Ashcroft, was purchased after examination by Tabor-hired experts and the securing of a bond to work the property. Tabor and others used this bonding method to examine a mine thoroughly. In this case, he paid $5,000 and had ninety days to work the property before paying the remainder of the sale price or forfeiting the bond. The person who owned the bond could sell the mine as well, although under the same conditions as if he had purchased it. The Wheel of Fortune in Summit County was sheer speculation, based on high-grade ore at the "grass roots." The list could be extended throughout his multitude of investments with only one common thread — his aforementioned faith in mining and the realization that though not every mine would be a producer, it only took one rich property to erase many unproductive investments.

From humble beginnings, Horace had entered the realm of major mining speculation and finance, having for partners some of the most prestigious names in Colorado and men well known throughout the country. The once openly frank individual was changing, too, as he learned the techniques and rules of the game. Upon returning from his Eastern swing, Tabor had commented that capitalists there appeared pretty well informed as to Colorado values and standards. "But my interest in these men was not deep. I did not want any of their money to run my mines with for they are all capable of running themselves." Even then he was in the midst of the negotiations over the Little Pittsburg. He also proved very devious when Nevada's Senator Jones came to Denver, apparently discussing the sale of Leadville mines.[20] On his own Tabor probably would not have conceived the plans which led to the Little Pittsburg and Chrysolite companies. This took the hands of masters and he found many around him: Chaffee, Moffat, Roberts, and Jones, all of whom had prior experience. They came to quench their thirst in Leadville's abundance. For them Tabor, with an unsullied reputation and currently front page news, was a godsend. Not content to incorporate, the lieutenant governor also operated alone, adding a few techniques of his own and coming out a richer man. By confidently retaining his stock, Tabor showed he was not completely a speculator; at least on the surface, his partners did likewise.

In Eastern eyes one man alone symbolized Leadville's new-found bonanza. Not Chaffee nor Moffat, who already had wealth; nor men like Roberts, Jones, Field, and Keyes who came with the first rush; but Tabor, who had been there in the lean days and suddenly exemplified all that mining could do for the individual. *Harper's Weekly,* although calling him lieutenant governor of Nevada, a mistake somewhat understandable considering the geographic ignorance of not a few Eastern editors, said he presented a good illustration of what people do in that state who have suddenly acquired wealth. "Nothing could ever entice him into dissipation, or even mere luxury," the article forthrightly declared, and the sketch closed with a prediction that Tabor might someday appear in the Senate. *Leslie's Illustrated* added further misinformation, particularly concerning the Little Pittsburg discovery, which they placed "about five years ago," although giving a favorable report on the new millionaire. Leadville newspapers had a field day chronicling new Tabor stories as they appeared in the Eastern press. A single example will suffice. A Michigan paper claimed Tabor as a former citizen, now worth fifty million dollars, who, at the time he struck carbonates, was working for day wages as a stonecutter.[21]

Tabor, taking his notoriety in stride, continued investing money in Colorado mines. The year had been an excellent one for him, in mining his best, and everywhere he moved ahead. Leadville's silver wealth supported a multitude of his activities, from mining to theaters. No better summary of what had transpired since his wise move from Oro City could be given than the comment which appeared in the *New York Tribune*, July 7, 1879, discussing the mining frontier in general, Leadville in particular:

> Men pass here for what they are, and not for what they have, how they are dressed or where they were born. Nobody cares who a man's grandfather was or of what state he is native. No one can afford to treat another with contempt because he is unfortunate; the wheel may turn over and the poor man of today may become the millionaire of tomorrow.

CHAPTER 8

REAPING THE WHIRLWIND

"For they sow the wind, and they shall reap the whirlwind."
Hosea 8:7

LEADVILLE and Tabor by 1880 sat astride a wave of popularity and prosperity that looked virtually infinite. Investors almost stumbled over themselves seeking some mining scheme. Everything Tabor touched apparently turned to silver, with mines in bonanza or on the threshold; he dealt from a financial strength never rivaled before in Colorado.

Although he no longer had any direct connection with the Little Pittsburg, his name was still closely associated with it; he watched with interest this mine's operations. At first the Little Pittsburg did what its promoters had promised. By mid-January, $850,000 in dividends had gone into jubilant stockholders' pockets. Ore in sight was reportedly even more valuable, pushing stock prices into the $30 range, with predictions of $50 before the year was out. But the pleasant dreams of armchair mining men received a jolt in mid-February when the price suddenly dipped to $22, and 17,000 shares changed hands before it righted itself. Then during the week of February 15 the price fell to under $20, resulting in such a stampede of panicked sellers that by the second week of March stocks crashed to a sickening low of $7.50 per share.[1] The Little Pittsburg had broken; the glorious days of unbounded confidence in Leadville and Colorado silver mining vanished like a late spring snow.

Tabor and others wondered why, as did hundreds of

irate Eastern stockholders. Leadvilleites blamed New York capitalists, who "know no more about what they are buying than a boy five years old." Easterners blamed Western betrayal and some even hinted at Wall Street "bears," Colorado variety, trying to depress in order to buy cheaply. The editors of the *Leadville Democrat* concurred, recommending holding on to the stocks: "when you've got a good thing, keep it — keep it."[2] Further investigation, however, pointed a guilty finger at inside sources, particularly Tabor's two ex-partners, Chaffee and Moffat.

The New York *Mining Record* muckraked the mess with special tenacity, since its competitor's editor, Rossiter Raymond, had been intimately involved in the sale. It posed a series of editorial questions on March 13 which cut to the core of the matter. Had many of the leading stockholders sold out? Had Chaffee and certain others sold out without notifying their friends? Had Hague's report been suppressed? The *Mining Record* had no answers, stating only current rumors, but it hoped that the public learned that ex-senators, millionaires, bankers, and their associates were no better than their fellow men when it came to stock dealing.

Only insiders could answer, but silence greeted the inquiries. Finally, Moffat replied, charging the fault to the mine, not the management. Chaffee then consented to be interviewed. His comments unintentionally proved both enlightening and damning, opening many eyes. Informed early in 1880 that the bonanza ore pockets were fast being exhausted, Chaffee concluded the vein had pinched out. These reserves were the key to the Little Pittsburg's future. On advice that ore would last through June and, by then, new deposits would certainly be found, it was decided not to announce the actual situation for the sake of preventing a panic. A small pool of insiders was created to buy up stock to maintain the price. Chaffee flatly stated he was the "heaviest loser" in the crash, only to have the self-sacrificing stance demolished when it was disclosed that he and Moffat had sold 51,000 shares — over a quarter of the capital stock

— by March 5.[3] Further investigation revealed that on March 13 Chaffee telegraphed Moffat to sell out. Chaffee, completely on the defensive, lamely admitted he had done so because by then only two or three directors still held shares.

Partner Moffat also denied any wrongdoing, claiming he really knew nothing of mining and that this was his first stock operation. In fact, he had been grossly deceived by management, or so he announced.[4] The once boastful director retired under a barrage of criticism, since he was certainly no rookie in the game of mining speculation, not with the Caribou and Little Pittsburg sales behind him. Mining engineer Raymond defended his earlier position and again spoke optimistically about future ore reserves in the April 2 issue of the *Engineering and Mining Journal*. The investing public, however, had had enough of the Little Pittsburg and was not about to be reconverted by such optimism.

Rumors flew, denials countered accusations, and still the whole story failed to emerge. Despite the aspersions cast on the activities of his former partners and the fact that he was as much involved in the Little Pittsburg sale as any of them, Tabor nearly managed to escape blame. Fortunately for his reputation, he had sold out in time and to his partners, not on the stock market. The final payment for his shares had come due March 7; in the meantime Chaffee had had an option to buy the stock at any time, though Horace collected dividends until the last payment. Thus he took the frosting off the cake and was left with none of the crumbs. Such business sagacity was highly praised, and Tabor avoided the epithets of "gambler" and "speculator," now being bandied about so freely. Perhaps the image of the honest storekeeper who was not a calculating mining man worked in Tabor's favor, for the public had known him in this capacity for two years. Tabor, always very cautious in expressing an opinion on the Little Pittsburg, said when pressed that he doubted the mine was played out, yet he felt certain its reserves had been reduced. He rested his case with the statement that, since selling his stock, he had paid very little attention to the management of Little Pittsburg affairs.[5] Rumors said that he had purchased large quantities of stock at low prices, but Horace held only one hundred shares in April.

Although he was not directly involved in the Little Pittsburg collapse, Tabor's reputation suffered in the long-term evaluation. The crash came back to haunt him on several significant occasions. In Colorado eyes he had done no wrong; in Eastern eyes guilt by association branded him.

Chaffee, Moffat, and all others involved now withdrew with their profits, while the onus fell on Leadville and Colorado mining. Distrust describes the immediate reaction. Hague even had trouble selling his Chrysolite stock once the run started in February. Leadville booster R. G. Dill bemoaned the chill put on capital coming to the camp and on the spirit of mining enterprise; so did the Leadville newspapers. The state suffered as the prestige of its most famous district waned. Several years passed before the aftereffects of the Little Pittsburg fiasco wore off.[6]

Not everyone thought of it as a complete disaster. Outspoken Dave Day, for one, predicted from Ouray that it should serve to dampen excessive capitalization, which he called a "base fraud" that was paralyzing the mining industry. Others agreed, believing future operations would be conducted more conservatively and more in line with accepted business techniques. Business dealings of the gilded age being what they were, there was still left open a wide latitude of corruption for unscrupulous owners.[7]

It is hard to tell what caused the Little Pittsburg crash. Frank Fossett pointed out that several large blocks of mineral, counted as valuable reserves, had proven low grade and fatal to the company. The failure to continue finding rich lodes forced the management eventually to curtail production, creating a panic among the public, who had been told that years of dividends remained buried in the property. Dill went further, blaming poor management and operations. Combining all of these reasons with Chaffee's explanations produces a sketchy picture of the collapse.

The guilty parties, if any, are not so easily uncovered. The Eastern press was sure they were the directors, those on the inside, "those men most interested in its success." Jerome Chaffee and David Moffat, president and vice-president respectively, received the brunt of the blame. Even the *Leadville Democrat* felt that, in the public mind, the guilt of these two had been settled, and it was joined by other Colorado sources.[8]

Conviction, however, rested on circumstantial evidence, simply because other types of evidence were and still are unavailable. If either man left any papers, they have not been found. Previous mining dealings, their own testimony, and circumstantial evidence lend a great deal of credence to a guilty verdict. Both were involved at this same time, under similar circumstances, in selling the Caribou Mine to the respected Wall Street financier, Robert G. Dun. At a crucial time they withheld information, sold stock and got out, leaving the remaining Caribou 'and Little Pittsburg stockholders holding the bag. Also guilty were the parties that over-capitalized the Little Pittsburg at $20 million, instilling a false confidence in the buying public, and the general management which gutted the mine to provide those monthly dividends so dear to stockholders' hearts. Too much had been promised too soon, and what the directors planned when the rich ore pockets ran out is unfathomable.

The Little Pittsburg's role in the Tabor story now ended amid the whirlwind of the spring of 1880. Never again, despite optimistic predictions, would it bounce back to the 1879 heights. The mine was nearly played out. Chaffee, in his final report, proudly declared, "I venture to suggest that in the history of mining few companies have ever been able to make a better showing for their first year's operations, or have better prospects for the future." Right he was on the first count, wrong on the second, as the stock continued its dismal descent, falling to $1.95 by the year's end. For Horace it had been a valuable experience, gaining knowledge of large-scale mining and business methods. Playing his cards well, he withdrew at the right moment with the money he earned from ore, property, and stock sales — it became the basis of his fortune. The grubstake given to Hook and Rische on that April morning in 1878 could not have been turned to better advantage.

Leadville, stunned but not defeated, still had a number of producing mines, including the Chrysolite. The ever-optimistic *Rocky Mountain News* on May 21 proclaimed that Colorado was pleased with its prospects, since nothing could compare "with our wondrous carbonate fields"; they would last forever, "long after the present and next generation." Such spirit could not be crushed by one bad experience, even if it had involved the Little Pittsburg.

Tabor, meanwhile, continued his holdings in the Chrysolite, in April owning 73,000 shares of this mine, which was rated one of the best among Leadville's biggest producers. R. H. Stretch, a mining engineer, went even further, "There is no question that today the Chrysolite property is the finest silver mine in America." An examination found the property in excellent condition, both inside and out.[9]

The enthusiasm was ignited by the company's production during the early part of 1880 under Winfield Keyes's competent management, when the mine increased shipments and opened new ore pockets. Public confidence soared, the stock price jumping accordingly to $40 before leveling off at a more reasonable figure. The only problem had flared briefly in February, when the company decided to levy a small monthly assessment on the miners for doctors' fees (no innovation in Western mining) to provide medical service. A brief strike resulted, ending amiably enough, the management allowing the miners to vote on the issue, which they roundly defeated. Dividends flowed into the stockholders' coffers, the fourth one, coming in February, amounting to 2 percent, or $200,000, softening somewhat the blow to Eastern investors in the ill-fated Little Pittsburg.

The *Mining Record* expressed reservations about several developments within the company, particularly the money made by Roberts and his associates in the stock sale and their option to buy back half of the stock, within eight months of the sale. Tabor's role was questioned with reference to the amount he received for his "full paid" stock in the original sale. In the general aftermath of the Little Pittsburg collapse in March no answers came either from the company or from Tabor.[10] The *Record* went out of its way to calm its readers, stating specifically that the Chrysolite was a splendid property and no faith had been lost in it. So passed an early hint of dissatisfaction.

Under Keyes's hard-driving management, Chrysolite production reached $242,641 in March. The local press, desperate for something to remove the Little Pittsburg stigma, grew ecstatic. Rossiter Raymond again appeared with a report congratulating the company upon a bonanza, and a Leadville writer chimed in with the reassuring statement that the mine looked excellent.

Just when it looked as if the Chrysolite owners had nothing to fear, a slight hint of something amiss caused a panic in the edgy stockmarket and the stock sank to under $20. It rallied, but the *Engineering and Mining Journal* of April 17 called for capitalists, men willing to ride out minor storms, to buy mining stock, not the little speculators who jumped in and out with every rumor. Not until June, even with the setbacks, did the New York Stock Exchange record fewer than 10,000 shares sold per week, a very active market. The price stayed low, in the $13 to $20 range, an indication of uneasiness which was not improved when the company reduced its dividends by half. The whole Leadville mining market reverberated under the reduction. Comforting reports from Keyes rushed East about better ore than ever in sight; still the Chrysolite, the "key note of the market," appeared to be under another "bear" attack. One excited critic quickly pointed to the Little Pittsburg crowd. Before the situation could right itself, another rumor, that the company planned to suspend monthly payments in favor of quarterly, sank it further.[11]

Ill-timed and harmful, grumbled the *Mining Record* about Chrysolite management maneuvers. The worried editors advised investors not to panic, for "one or two summer showers do not cause a flood."[12] At this point, with the Chrysolite seemingly running down a well-traveled road, public attention suddenly shifted from it to the Leadville miners' strike, Colorado's first major labor trouble. The hard-pressed Chrysolite people gained a breathing spell.

Keyes, who had planned to take a vacation to visit his family in San Francisco, canceled the trip on the morning of May 26, when miners struck the Chrysolite. The simplest explanation called it an attempt by the workers to gain higher wages and prevent the discharge of some men. Such issues as a management ban on smoking in the mine along with a push for more work per shift added emotionalism, while the general disquiet of Leadville since the Little Pittsburg failure added fuel to the fire. The worry that the coming of the railroad would bring an abundance of workers, thereby depressing wages, or possibly causing an increase in the working hours at the same wage, with the same end result, also troubled the miners. The strike, when it came, was apparently unpremeditated. The men paraded to other mines and asked their coworkers to join them. At this point the Miners' Cooperative Union entered the struggle, adding support to the workers' cause. The following days produced numerous meetings, where opinions were clarified and demands were made upon the mine owners, who promptly rejected them. The situation continued peacefully, the strikers promising not to destroy property and both sides listening to the other, but neither would give an inch. Led by their gifted spokesman and leader, a short, stout, determined Irishman, Michael Mooney, the miners held firm. The *Democrat* moaned, "No calamity, save that of a general conflagration . . . could have been more disastrous to the vital interests of Leadville and this mining district . . ."[13] Its wise advice to each side to beware of consequences went unheeded, and both settled down to weather a long-drawn-out contest.

Keyes, meanwhile, lined the Chrysolite shaft house with heavy iron, hired armed guards, and continued to operate with nonstriking miners on eight-hour shifts and the old wage of three dollars per day. Rumors of violence prompted his protective actions, as rancor replaced earlier rapport. In an interview Keyes claimed the situation had become somewhat exasperating, and he was thinking seriously of closing the mine for the season unless an early solution was reached. The company simply could not afford to hire guards for an extended period, he and the New York directors agreed.[14] Shutting down in preference to suffering losses appeared to be a radical policy for this mine, which had produced more than enough to cover such added expenses. If the Chrysolite closed, others would probably follow; at the moment the threat seemed to be mostly bluff.

Behind the scenes the mine owners bided their time, Tabor staying especially calm, considering that all his Leadville mines, not just the Chrysolite, were threatened. Up to this time no evidence has appeared that he disagreed with any of the Chrysolite Company actions since the first of the year, or with the handling of the strike. As the strike continued, a small shipment of arms reached Leadville to strengthen the Tabor Guards in case of an emergency. Tabor himself stayed out of public view, while his guards eventually were pressed into patrolling the hills and guarding what nervous citizens considered the dangerous parts of town. Such precautions were deemed to be necessary, yet amazingly little pressure actually built up against the mine owners during the first ten days of the strike, early June passing quite peacefully.

As the strike dragged on, only the Chrysolite and Little Chief went to the expense of hiring armed guards; the rest simply suspended operations. Tabor's smaller properties followed the latter course. The lengthening strike deepened divisions between miners and owners. Keyes, spokesman for the owners along with George Daly, manager of the Little Chief, refused to concede. In the interval water flooded the lower levels of some mines and stock prices tumbled across the board. Still they waited. Tabor, in the meantime, blandly assured a reporter that the strike would be over by June 13.

In Denver, Governor Pitkin had been steadily informed of developments by his lieutenant governor and others. On June 11 Keyes left to confer with the governor, hardly reaching the capital before the break finally came. Certain Leadvilleites, taking the situation into their own hands, formed a citizens' executive committee to provide an adequate force of armed men to maintain peace. The committee, meeting in Tabor's private rooms, organized a parade, intending this demonstration to overawe the strikers and show the unanimous support of the people for the mine owners' side. Down the main streets came a brass band, local military companies, and mounted citizens, to meet an unexpected reaction. A near-riot ensued, as the marchers were jeered with "foul and abusive language" and greeted with a few missiles; supporters' cheers failed to drown out the opposition. Swinging into Harrison Avenue, the parade halted in front of the Tabor Opera House to hear a few encouraging words from its patron. Unfortunately, the entire speech was not preserved, but it is known that Horace, speaking from the balcony, defended the owners' position as open and aboveboard. Exhorting the populace to peace and quiet, he promised that miners desiring work would be protected, thereby eliciting cheers from his like-minded listeners. Not all of them approved, though, and hisses greeted his utterances throughout the brief address.[15] Times had changed; the friendly storekeeper of two years before stood there on the balcony of his opera house in the role of a capitalist trying to convince the workers that they should allow management to have its own way. Neither the parade nor Tabor's address had the desired effect.

Worried about the increasing threat of violence, the sheriff telegraphed Pitkin, requesting that the militia be sent and that martial law be declared. Pitkin, unsure of the situation, hesitated to take these ultimate steps, telegraphing Tabor, "Is any compromise possible? If so what character?" The citizens' committee reacted to this hesitation by sending Pitkin a telegram on June 13, stating that the law officers were unable to preserve order and protect property. Tabor's signature was the first of over one hundred which urged upon Pitkin the absolute necessity of immediate martial law. Telegrams, letters, and personal interviews reaching Denver from the scene finally tipped the scale. Frank Hall, the governor's private secretary, vividly recalled the strain of the moment. On signing the martial law proclamation Pitkin turned to those around him, "Gentlemen, please bear witness that I do this with extreme reluctance, but it seems to be the only solution of the difficulty, and I feel it must be done."[16] Pitkin's reluctance was understandable since, in suspending civil law in a labor dispute, he was setting a state precedent, and also leaving himself and his party open to criticism if the action proved unwarranted. And 1880 was an election year. The action by the governor, heartily endorsed by the owners, broke the back of the strike. The *Democrat* put out a special edition, in disgust announcing, "Leadville's humiliation is almost complete."

Throughout the next week, while Tabor was in town, saying little but letting his actions show his sentiments, he worked closely with the Colorado National Guard, as it garrisoned Leadville. His private rooms in the Tabor Opera House were converted into plush general headquarters, and he helped procure less fancy accommodations for troop barracks. Undoubtedly, Horace was relieved to see the troops, for a rumor was abroad that the Tabor Opera House would be burned.

The owners, now in complete control, laid down the rules that would be followed. The miners wanted an eight-hour schedule and a return to the old wage scale. Owners replied that from now on their right to regulate the affairs of their mines was absolute; they would rehire only those miners who had not taken an active part in the strike; in the case of the Robert E. Lee, two-thirds of the new crew were men not employed before the strike. By the fifteenth the crisis had passed and, at last, Private (sometimes journalistically advanced to Corporal) H. A. W. Tabor of the Colorado National Guard was marched into belated service. The owners, four days later, adopted a resolution thanking the local citizenry for their support and, on the twenty-second, the troops were withdrawn. The July 3 issue of the *Leadville Circular*, a mine owner-sponsored paper boosting Leadville, completely exonerated them. Imminent riot faced Leadville on June 12, the editor claimed. "But for the foresight of Governor Tabor and W. S. Keyes, who sent in hot haste for the Iron Guards and Chrysolite guards, it is hard to say what might have happened." They prevented trouble when the only regiment of the Colorado National Guard available at the time could not restrain the crowd during the parade. Years later, Tabor expressed regret for his actions in breaking this strike;[17] such incidentals did not worry him at the moment, because he and his fellow owners were riding high.

Almost immediately after the proclamation of martial law, the Democratic *Rocky Mountain News* jumped on Pitkin and others involved in this "most offensive and arrogant" denial of labor's rights. "It was not a necessity, neither was it justified under the circumstances." Law and order in Leadville, exclaimed the paper, consisted largely of the vigilance committee kind. The issue became a political football in 1880 and for a time afterward, as Pitkin stoutly defended his actions. Tabor meanwhile busied himself raising funds to help defray expenses apparently incurred by the citizens' committee during the strike, hoping that everyone would cheerfully contribute.[18] The state expenses ran to some nineteen thousand dollars for transporting and maintaining the troops. For the miners there was no victory. That fall, without an increase in wages, their hours in each shift were raised to ten; no cries of indignation were raised openly — so complete was their defeat.

The strike was over, the owners were triumphant, but Leadville had chalked up another black mark to add to that of the Little Pittsburg. Sensational stories, misrepresentation, and biased reporting did nothing to enhance the camp's or

the mines' prestige. The causes of this strange, almost sense-
less strike mystified contemporaries. Reliable R. G. Dill felt
they would never be fully understood. While a strike could
readily start over rumors, was that the case here? A recent
scholar of the strike feels it came about because of latent
fears and a toughening of the Chrysolite management in its
dealings with its workers. Yet he discounts what seems to
this author to be a very real possibility, that the strike actually
was fomented by management to gain its own ends. Such
a view was held by the press and other observers at the
time. As early as May 28, the *Democrat* printed a current rumor
that the Chrysolite management was behind the strike. Later,
the editor accused management of closing the mines, not
because of the strike, but simply because it was more profitable
to do so. Finally, the paper published a letter which called
this "half-hearted strike" merely stockjobbing to depress
stocks.[19] The *News* supported this position and went one step
further, placing the blame for what resulted, quite naturally,
on the Republican leadership.

The *Mining Record* in New York reported it was being
freely expressed that the strike came at a very opportune
time for the promoters, heavy holders, and other insiders
weary of staggering under a "load they could not possibly
carry much longer." Denver's *Inter-Ocean*, taking a similar
position, went even further, observing it was widely asserted
in Leadville, Denver, and elsewhere during the strike that
the Chrysolite's internal condition was at the bottom of the
trouble. Two Leadville residents who put their thoughts down
on paper said the same thing.[20] In light of what happened
to the Chrysolite, such speculation and hearsay cannot be
casually pushed aside.

The Little Pittsburg failure, the shaky Chrysolite position,
and now the strike made the public wary of Leadville investments. As the Eastern press picked up the discouraging
theme, the owners became edgy. Some policing had to be
done, warned the *Leadville Circular*, July 3; the time had passed
for selling doubtful holes for hundreds of thousands, either

in money or in stock. Easterners were not dupes. In order to sell mines now, paying mineral should be in sight and capitalization reasonable — an amount which could be paid off in four or five years. Sound advice!

To promote Leadville stocks, among others, Tabor had helped organize the American Mining Stock Exchange in New York City. Comprised of California men, including Roberts, his old friend Chaffee, and a few New Yorkers, it set out boldly to challenge the prestigious New York Stock Exchange. The exchange's ambitious purpose was to serve both as a broker and banker by stimulating investment in legitimate mining properties and by offering a trust company in connection with the exchange to lend money on good mining stock, banks being noticeably reluctant to do the same.

The scheme had hardly been discussed, when the *Mining Record* editorially opposed it. Seeing the fine hand of Roberts and other California speculators behind the endeavor, the editor instinctively reacted negatively. The New York Stock Exchange struck another blow by forbidding its members to deal in or with members of the rival exchange, thus crippling its activities. Despite such opposition, the new exchange got started in June 1880 with speeches and a special luncheon catered by Delmonico's. Tabor sat on the board of trustees. New York by 1880 was ready to replace San Francisco as the leading mining stock center, a natural development since Colorado had replaced Nevada as the leading mining state and it relied on Eastern investment. There were many, though, who honestly questioned whether New York was ready for two mining exchanges.

Starting slowly, the American Mining Stock Exchange dealt primarily with Leadville, Nevada, and California shares, the Chrysolite being a prominent item. Although the *Engineering and Mining Journal*, which did not share its competitor's sentiment, thought it made a very satisfactory showing, transactions apparently ended in mid-August,[21] possibly because of the worsening Leadville situation. Too many of the exchange's founders were deeply involved there for it to retain public trust for any length of time. Eventually, the remnants joined the old stock exchange. Tabor's enthusiasm for stock exchanges did not wane, even though he lost a little money in the establishment and operation of this latest venture.

Back in less glamorous Leadville, the Chrysolite languished in the strike's aftermath, passing over its June dividend. Strike-generated expenses were assumed to have caused this difficulty. When July came with no improvement, rumors revived concerning a weakness in the company's future prospects. Early in the month, encouraging prospect work revived weak public confidence only to have it dashed again by the rumored resignation of board members. The bellwether of stock value, the New York Stock Exchange, gave interesting readings on the Chrysolite. The number of shares sold increased steadily from 14,000 to 27,000 at mid-month, and the price dropped from $17.00 to $9.25. In such an unsettled atmosphere, nearly all the officers and directors suddenly took their vacations or otherwise disappeared from public view. Several subsequently resigned, new trustees being elected. Someone was selling shares, but just who could not be discovered. Tabor was a logical candidate since, as the *Commercial Bulletin* of New York observed on July 18, he was "really the arbitrater of value," if he chose to be, so far as the market was concerned.[22]

Horace was also being attacked from another flank: the Little Pittsburg disaster was being rehashed. Despite earlier denials, questions were being asked. Unsubstantiated Colorado and New York rumors further undermined public confidence. Was the Chrysolite gutted? Was the management incompetent? Was it not following the Little Pittsburg? Had not the quality of Chrysolite ore drastically diminished? Reassuring comments that the reason for the stock decline was another bear movement failed to restore faith.

Then came the crash. Seventy-four thousand shares were sold the week of July 18, and ninety thousand the next. The price held amazingly steady for a while, then collapsed to $6.75. Again the analyzers emerged. The mine was all right;

poor management and stock manipulation caused the break, which in turn demoralized the entire mining stock market. Pacific coast gamblers were responsible, they claimed, an idea somewhat consoling to New Yorkers who had lost heavily, though this recouped none of their losses.

The company retaliated by publishing an open letter refuting the rumors and trying to reassure the public that all was well within the organization. The events of the past two weeks were simply an attempt to break the price, the company disclosed; stockholders should not panic. Tabor confidently assured readers that he still owned the shares taken when the original sale had been made, thus ending speculation that he dumped his stock on the market. Strengthening his case, he pointed to his purchase of additional stock at $42.50 and more when the price dipped into the twenties. To a stockholder Horace asserted, "I spent a quarter of a day in our Chrysolite mines and I found them in excellent condition — *in fact, better than I had ever seen them.* We know of course, the property is of great value, but there is *beyond this certainty a reasonable hope of immensity.*"[23] Tabor was not the only one to be dragged forth to support the Chrysolite; Rossiter Raymond and W. S. Keyes, the "ablest silver mine manager in the country," were also called to its defense.

These encouraging statements had hardly dried in print before the company suspended dividends. The company's epitaph, concluded one observer, should read, "Died of misrepresentation, overcapitalization, extravagant management and consequent exhaustion."[24]

The Chrysolite continued to struggle on and, considering all the pressure, had a commendable August record, while the wolves growled at the door. On August 3, the harassed Keyes tendered his resignation as manager and a large number of men were discharged. His resignation was not crucial at the moment, since he had been away for a month on vacation and the mine had been run by an acting manager.

The last period of calm was shattered in the middle of September, when suddenly 115,000 shares were sold in a week, followed by two more weeks of over 100,000, resulting in a price break to $3.75. Critics now attacked from all sides. Prospect work had been sadly neglected, shouted some. Others said Eastern speculators had run the mine too long, or charged that the stock was being "beared" by some inside manipulators. It was even stated that the old villains, California promoters, were trying to ruin the management's reputation by spreading "unfounded and erroneous" rumors in order to rebuy control.[25] A few disenchanted investors with long memories pointed out that there never had been any reason from the first for the stock's high price, except unscrupulous methods of stockjobbing. These and other charges buried the beleaguered company.

The final outcome was the president's resignation and his replacement in October by Rossiter Raymond, who successfully and conservatively guided the Chrysolite fortunes for several subsequent years. Forcing out the president caused open warfare between the old guard of trustees and officers who had been in power most of 1880 and the new for control of the company; it ended abruptly with the election of a board of directors controlled by the latter, a new board, as a report read, which was "not only competent but honest."[26] Confidence in the new management was shown in the steadily climbing price of stock, back to nearly $7 per share by December. While the Chrysolite had not fallen so far as the Little Pittsburg, and its future was much brighter, it would never again be so prosperous or such a favorite of the mining stock crowd.

In his first annual report, Raymond reviewed the trials the company had suffered during the past year. Concisely, he listed what he thought caused the difficulties: obligations incurred in purchasing the property, the attempt to maintain large monthly dividends without sufficient development or working capital, the expenses due to the strike, fluctuation in the mine's output, and borrowing money in advance of actual realization of earnings, which left a total debt of $400,000. Rumors that the company could not repay this money had brought it to the brink of disaster, necessitating an arrangement whereby creditors accepted pro rata payments from mine earnings. A special investigating committee of the board received reports from various individuals involved with the mine, most of which proved contradictory, offering no guidance to conditions at Leadville. The new management thus was going ahead almost in the dark, moaned Raymond, though still determined to save the property and put it back on a dividend-paying basis. This project was just nicely started when a fire broke out in the mine, seriously curtailing mining for months.[27] Up to this time, it would hardly seem that this $10 million corporation, barely a year old, had been properly operated.

Tabor's role in all these events remains cloudy. A large stockholder, whose name still gave confidence and lent an air of glamor, he remained in the background throughout. He was on the board until ousted along with the rest of the old guard in November. One source claims he "unloaded" his stock in August; he definitely sold some, but he still held a great deal. In a Tabor exposé the next spring, the *Mining Record* speculated that he sold 45,000 shares at $7, which indicated he had been active in the market either sometime in August or after November. According to Colorado sources, a major factor in the Chrysolite's decline had been an attempt by unidentified California-Comstock sharpers (presumably Roberts) to fleece Tabor out of his fortune. While this certainly could have been a highly probable factor, it was only one of many. A Tabor defender felt that Horace had learned a lesson from all of this — not to be caught in any more doubtful stock operations.[28]

Tabor was not the only one affected by the dealings of the illusive Roberts; at least two Eastern journals blamed the man and his friends for the whole Chrysolite debacle. Roberts had parlayed several mines into stock promotions by methods similar to those involved in the Chrysolite, then beared and bulled the stock while staying out of the limelight. His fine hand, or that of someone who had learned his lessons from the master, certainly stirred up the Chrysolite trouble. Among things that he was known to have done were to push for quarterly dividends, to consolidate all the claims, and to keep enough stock to be considered a "prominent" manager of the company. An unidentified man, "well known in mining circles," said at the end of 1881 in a newspaper interview that Roberts operated principally on the Chrysolite and Little Chief in Colorado. This anonymous Roberts admirer said there were few more capable men in the country; Roberts, he felt, knew how to influence prominent people and knew the value of the press in selling mines. Few others openly praised him.

As Raymond said, the company became heavily indebted while trying to pay promised dividends and found it could not go both ways at once. Some of this debt, $250,000, was owed Tabor from the transfer of the Vulture Mine into the consolidation, a sum eventually paid him in August. A large part of the debt had been foolishly incurred on ore yet to be mined in order to meet the last dividend, so that the public would not lose confidence in the stock. Upon assuming complete control, Raymond, in his journal, quite correctly placed the full blame on the old management and, referring to the gaseous condition in some of the mine levels, quipped, "Formerly, the mine was all right, and it was the management that suffered from gas. Now the management has been ventilated and purified, and the gas has taken to the mine."[29]

Leadville's year of troubles ended with the Chrysolite's collapse. Mine, district, state, and personal reputations suffered serious, in some cases irrevocable, damage. Instead of being one of the wonders of the age, the Little Pittsburg lay gutted and the Chrysolite was being called, "this notorious Colorado mine."[30] Leadville mines dragged on the market, investors shying away. Capital and labor had pulled apart openly now, and while Leadville still ranked as number one, that certain spark which separates a booming, youthful town from one slipping into middle age flickered out.

The Little Pittsburg and Chrysolite failures followed a similar pattern of pitfalls: overly high capitalization, too much concentration on monthly dividend payments, and exploitative mining. Failure to explore and find new reserves led to decline in production and passing over a dividend, which resulted in starting a chain reaction in both cases. Chronologically, the pattern was startlingly similar: the Little Pittsburg appeared first and fell first, within a year; the Chrysolite came on in the fall of 1879 and broke in the late summer of 1880. Each blazed brightly for a time, faded, and finally ceased profitable production, while Eastern stockholders watched in disbelief. The strike was the only major difference.

If the Chrysolite management instigated the strike in an attempt to sell out from under, as suggested, the tactic was unsuccessful, since only about thirty thousand shares changed hands during the period. If, on the other hand, it was simply an attempt to give management an excuse to avoid paying a dividend and buy some time, it worked briefly. The trustees misjudged the situation, however, if they thought this would be enough to stabilize public confidence.

Moffat and Chaffee came out of the 1880 whirlwind much damaged in reputation, while Roberts only added some dubious laurels to his already shady reputation as a mining speculator. Two of the age's leading mining men, Raymond and Keyes, were burned as well. Raymond's judgment, especially, may be questioned when weighed against his contemporary Hague's report on the Little Pittsburg. Keyes, blamed for the Chrysolite failure, weakly retorted that he only obeyed orders, sometimes in protest. With his previous Comstock experience he might have protested more strongly; he also stands tainted by association, having come in with Roberts, highly recommended by the California group. Both of these engineers rebounded with vigor, going on to further fame in their professions, so neither was permanently injured by the Leadville fiasco. One has to feel a little sorry for the board members of both companies, who often enough were simply window dressing, pawns for the speculators behind them. Their reputations suffered as well, perhaps forcing them to investigate more carefully the next board they agreed to serve on.

Tabor's reputation, while damaged, was less seriously affected than Chaffee's or Moffat's. He had not been hurt by the Little Pittsburg, except indirectly, and his Chrysolite activities had not been primarily responsible for its collapse. At the end he still retained stock, thus suffering a paper loss, along with the rest of the stockholders. All was not lost however. Horace received $275,000 in dividends from the Chrysolite. The honest merchant-miner image of 1878 was nevertheless tarnished by his association with the two properties. Three years later, Tabor was hauled into court by disgruntled Chrysolite stockholders and sued for $10 million, the plaintiffs filing suit on the grounds that the stock purchased in 1879 had been sold with the "design and intention" of defrauding the purchasers.[31] While this was only one of several similar cases against others involved, it showed what had happened to Tabor's reputation. Nothing came of the proceedings.

The strike illuminated a new element in Tabor's character — the capitalist determined to protect his investment against labor's threat. Horace, no longer the always-ready grubstaker and friend of all, had become a millionaire whose relationship with the men in the mine altered as the gulf between them widened. The absentee owner replaced the congenial neighbor. Though he perhaps wanted to retain the old camaraderies, it was now impossible for the men to look upon him in the same way that Hook and Rische had done.

Aside from the Chrysolite and Little Pittsburg, Tabor was busy elsewhere in mining during hectic 1880. He toyed with the Bull-Domingo Mine near Silver Cliff, which had long been under a cloud of bitter litigation. At one time he, Chaffee, and Pitkin were announced as buyers, then within a few weeks it was announced that a New York party had purchased it, no mention being made of the first three. Tabor was lucky he did not buy, because the sale promptly was tied up in court, although he unfortunately acquired stock in the company.[32]

Such misadventures did not dampen his enthusiasm for the mining game. To his growing Leadville collection he added the Excelsior Mine on Carbonate Hill. Just at the start of 1880 he acquired part of an apparently insignificant lode, notable primarily because of its unusual (even for a mining claim) name, the Lickscumdidrick. Horace lived to regret this purchase, because the Lickscumdidrick, supposedly well marked, involved him in six lawsuits during the decade. It overlapped all of its neighbors. Of more importance, he later purchased a percentage of the May Queen and Union Emma. The former became part of the Hibernia Mine, and the latter, after Tabor worked it in 1881, was sold and eventually incorporated into the famous Robert E. Lee Mining Company.[33]

The year 1880, once so promising, harvested the bitter and the sweet for Tabor and Leadville. Leadville mines prospered as never before, only to suffer damage from speculation and the strike. The dividends, cash received from sales, and the value of stock increased Tabor's wealth many times over. Yet over the rosy panorama hovered a cloud of uncertainty and doubt raised by his involvement in speculation and shady mining practices. Possibly his great faith in Leadville simply betrayed him; it is equally possible that he entirely approved of what happened and simply went along to reap whatever profits could be harvested. Evidence was mounting to support the latter conclusion, yet the final returns were not in.

CHAPTER 9

COLORADO'S ENTREPRENEUR

"... the judgment he [Tabor] has displayed in making
mining and real estate investments have convinced all
doubters that he is not merely a child of fortune but
also has business capacity of highest order."
Rocky Mountain News March 18, 1880

WHILE Tabor was suffering through the agonizing developments in Leadville in 1880, his investments were
spreading throughout Colorado, gaining for him increasing acclaim as the state's number one entrepreneur. Denver especially received the largesse of his silver millions, as the
pattern of the previous year continued, with Tabor investing
in a multitude of areas.

His principal effort, completed in 1880, would be construction of the "Tabor Block," the popular name for the
building plans which Edbrooke had drawn and presented
to Horace the previous year. Much to the dismay of Denver
contractors, Edbrooke and Tabor tapped a Chicago man,
Charles Cook, to build it. The stated contract price was
$102,500, with Tabor paying all freight charges on material
shipped to Denver. Soon shipments arrived from all over
the country: cut stonework produced by Illinois State Peniten-
tiary convicts, sandstone from Ohio, boilers from St. Louis,
pipe from Pueblo, and, from still other places, plate glass,
internal finishing wood, iron columns and gridwork, lumber,
more stone, and an elevator.

Before the building was finished, rooms were being

149

snapped up by anxious merchants who wanted a location in Denver's newest and most modern business block. Those who had hoped for a fancy hotel or opera house to grace the city were temporarily disappointed. Wisely, Tabor chose to invest in something that would pay a steady return.

Initial local disappointment over going outside for an architect, contractor, and materials was partially dispelled when Tabor purchased goods and hired men from within the community, and the city's most expensive and architecturally handsome building inched upward. No cost proved too great for Tabor, and when it was completed, he could justifiably be proud of his Tabor Block. Five stories high, it dominated the posh Larimer Street business district; a grilled iron front dressed the first floor, stonework covered the rest. A fancy fenced roof line, topped by fourteen little towers, completed the decor, impressing one viewer, "as though it was intended to last for all time to come."[1]

As the Block neared completion, the *Rocky Mountain News* gave its readers a verbal guided tour. "A noble monument of enterprise, faith and pluck," wrote the captivated reporter, "massive, yet elegant in design, containing the most modern conveniences that safety permits and experience approved." The elevator, one of the "most elegant and comfortable" found in the country, caught his attention, as did the large, airy, well-lighted offices, each with plate glass windows. The Tabor Block made a substantial contribution to Denver's business district, setting the standard for much that would follow.

Horace gained a sound investment, for, when fully rented, the Tabor Block returned a steady income; it also represented collateral in case he needed to borrow money. Now Tabor's vision soared to something much finer, more exciting than a mere business building — an opera house. Not just any opera house; it would have to be the finest money could build — a Tabor Grand Opera House. Grander than Leadville's, it would be a landmark for Denver, a fitting monument to Tabor.

With the purchase of lots on the corner of Sixteenth and

Curtis in March, the scheme was set in motion. Tabor hired Edbrooke as architect. Jealousy reared its head in Leadville, where a newspaper scathingly commented, "It is to be hoped that Denver's agony on this subject is now over, as Leadville has supplied the capital for this enterprise." When interviewed about his plans, Tabor assured reporters that it would be a credit to the city, but he "had yet adopted no definite plans." With Edbrooke, he went East that spring to inspect theaters and gather ideas for their own creation. Having confidence in his architect, Tabor allowed him to handle construction funds. His confidence was well placed. Edbrooke, in his late thirties, was at the peak of his career. With the approval of the plans, construction started.[2]

Denverites waited expectantly, peeking occasionally at the work, watching a rumor grow to reality. The opera house slowly rose, Tabor and Edbrooke heightening the suspense by withholding the complete plans and design. Plans for a January 1, 1881, opening date had to be discarded when construction proved too slow even to approach it.

The Tabor Block built and an opera house being constructed would be enough for almost any man for one year, but not for Tabor, who displayed an increasingly rash boldness in his operations. It was rumored that he would build a hotel, which, according to William Bush, would be seven stories high. These plans never got beyond the paper stage, though Tabor did invest in Denver's finest, the Windsor. The magnificent Windsor (Dill said nothing west of the Missouri River was its equal) had opened in June 1880, built primarily by English investors. Maxey and Bush, who had both come to Denver, gained a long-term lease on it. Just how much of Horace's money was involved is not known; he seems, however, to have been a major stockholder.[3]

Maxey had been holding a less important position within his father's operations since Leadville, perhaps reflecting a desire on Maxey's part to do something on his own. It is more probable that he sided with his mother in a quarrel which was splitting the family. For years, it seems, Horace and Augusta had not been too congenial, as she tried to curb some of his habits. As far back as their visits with Leach, this nagging was obvious. The coming of wealth only accentuated some of these faults, by giving Horace the money to indulge as he desired. Augusta did not approve of his excesses, and she appeared with him or involved herself in his affairs less and less. Yet the situation was tolerated, as such situations often are by married couples for the sake of keeping the family together. This was true then as now. Money, fame, and travel gave Tabor the opportunity to let his eyes wander, and what he saw were young and pretty girls willing to make a fuss over him, something his wife could not or would not do. She knew Horace well and in her way loved him, or she would not have put up with as much as she did. Older, less attractive, possessed of a sharper tongue, Augusta offered no physical attraction or comfort. Frigid, unbending, she drifted out of his life, while he quite understandably sought love elsewhere, and found it, to his satisfaction.

Tabor's ever-loyal sister Emily shed light on the way this had all come about, when she consoled her brother:

> I do not blame you for leaving her. You could not bear her fretting and complaining any longer. I saw enough when I was in Denver, never satisfied with one thing you did or one thing you got for her, whether house, carriage, diamonds or anything you did ever pleased her. I have gotten tired of her letters of complaints to me and have not written her for sometime.

And leave her he had, Augusta testifying later in court that he moved out in July 1880, giving her their home, which he occasionally visited during the remaining months of 1880. Poor Augusta failed to grasp where the trouble had rested; in her mind she had been "a true, faithful and loving wife, forgiving of her husband's faults and shortcomings, aiding and assisting him in their common business and sedulously striving to make their home and family pleasant, comfortable and happy."[4]

Tabor spent much of the year traveling to Leadville and back East, taking an apartment in the Windsor while in Denver. Augusta certainly was anxious to buy into this business, which she did in December, perhaps to keep an eye on her errant husband. The Tabor matrimonial problems were now somewhat in the open, raising speculation in Denver as to what would happen next.

Plenty of things occupied Tabor's attention besides his troubles with Augusta, and possibly he felt relieved that he left an eroding home situation for the freedom of bachelorhood. Lavishly, he invested in numerous projects, including enough newspapers to entitle him to be one of Colorado's ranking newspapermen.

Tabor's earliest newspaper activities had centered in Leadville, where he owned controlling interest in the *Reveille*. Despite its pioneer status, supplemented by the Tabor bankroll, it became the victim of strong competition and more newsy rivals. Last-minute attempts by the *Reveille* editor to find new resources proved fruitless, and his final edition appeared on January 8, 1880. For some time prior to its demise, the *Reveille* had been operating in the red, and Horace, simply tiring of putting more money into the venture, merged it with the *Leadville Daily Herald*. The *Democrat* wrote that Tabor had withdrawn to stop further expense, although it placed no blame on him personally for the failure. Despite the fact that the town had at least nine other daily and weekly papers at the moment, the editors of the *Democrat* felt that there was room for more because "no better index to business prosperity" than newspapers existed, if bright, newsy, and enterprising.

The *Herald* proved a much sounder investment. This staunch Republican paper, edited by R. G. Dill, made its initial bow in October 1879, and with the *Reveille* merger Tabor gained $1,550 worth of *Herald* stock. All was smooth sailing until 1882, when Dill and other stockholders opposed Tabor's political ambitions, resulting in a complete shakeup of the ownership.

While a stockholder in the *Herald*, Tabor partially owned and helped establish the short-lived *Leadville Evening Times*. William Bush, president of the company, hired George Wanless as editor and business manager. Though not present when the contract had been drawn, Horace later talked with Wanless, verbally agreeing to the terms. New equipment came from Chicago, and the paper, Republican in politics, sailed proudly forth in February, only to flounder and sink. Its credentials had been sound enough, even a rival admitting it covered the local news well. A strong aroma of partisan politics clung to the *Times*, particularly evidenced by the advancement of some of its stockholders. By June, Wanless, his salary over five hundred dollars in arrears, had had enough and resigned. A new editor, trying to get the owners together, found to his discouragement that they did not care anything about their own business; he certainly did not, and thereupon closed the paper. Wanless, meantime, unable to collect his salary, took the owners to court, testifying that Tabor had promised to pay whatever the court decided was his share. According to Wanless, Tabor admitted that he himself had not given the paper much attention and had allowed arrangements to be made by Bush.[5]

Thus Tabor chalked another newspaper loss up to experience. Frontier journalism was a risky business at best, especially in a community where strong rivals held a commanding lead over any brash newcomer. His success not having been too great, Tabor praised the *Leadville Circular*: "Parties desiring reliable reports on mines and prospects in this State cannot do better than to employ the Leadville Circular Company." Such sentiments were also shared by Keyes and Daly, all three thereby returning a favor to the paper which had staunchly defended their actions during the strike. Whether Horace backed such sentiments with investment is unknown.

Futher west, Tabor underwrote the *Elk Mountain Bonanza*, located in Gothic in Gunnison County. He had no better luck with the *Bonanza* than with his earlier efforts; it ceased publication in March 1881,[6] although for a different reason. The camp was simply not large enough to support even a weekly paper. The newspaper business in itself, however, was only part of his growing interest in the newly-opened Gunnison country.

South of Gothic, at the county seat in Gunnison, Tabor was president of the Bank of Gunnison, one of the first established on the western slope of the Colorado Rockies. Opening with the town in 1880, the bank got off to a fine start, and a year later Horace increased his holdings in it. As with Leadville banking, he did not directly enter into bank affairs; the business was operated by the cashier, Samuel Gill. Reorganized as the Iron National Bank in June 1883, with Gill as president and Tabor and Moffat as directors, it eventually merged with the First National Bank to become Gunnison's soundest banking house. Augusta held shares in it until her death. Horace pulled out before that. He also acted as a silent partner in the Bank of Crested Butte, located in the camp of the same name.[7] As a result of his holdings in Denver, Leadville, Gunnison, and Crested Butte, Horace emerged as one of the state's leading bankers.

Tabor's investments in the Gunnison region also reflected his never-ending interest in investing and promoting new mining districts. His investments in Gunnison, which became the principal town of the county, show that he correctly judged the present situation in relation to the future. It was not easy, for as one resident sadly wrote, "Gunnison is a tough place, now full of strangers of the worst type. Railroad men and all sorts, I carry my pistol in my hand ready for use, if I go to town after dark."[8] In three major Colorado mining districts which opened during this period, Aspen-Ashcroft, San Juan, and the Gunnison country, Tabor seized opportunity when offered, doing much to chart the course of development, and equally important, to advertise and promote the regions when they desperately needed it.

From the Gunnison country to Chicago was a far jump. Tabor made it, money and all. His interest in that city went back to his dealings in Leadville mines with Marshall Field and other Chicagoans. Visiting the metropolis on several occasions, he realized that bustling Chicago, like Denver, was growing, its railroads tapping the beef, pork, and consumer markets of the agricultural Midwest. It represented virgin territory for a man of Tabor's means, if he had the wisdom and luck to invest correctly. Tempted, Horace examined and invested.

Impressed with the idea that putting money into Chicago real estate was a safe and judicious investment, he purchased property in south Chicago and made typically grandiose plans for its development. Rumors abounded that he paid $1 million for it, but were mere fabrications, newspaper speculations. They made interesting reading, though, and helped confirm the legend building around Tabor. His biggest investment — and the earlier one might have been in some way connected with it — was in the Calumet and Chicago Canal and Dock Company, made sometime during the period of 1880–1882. A speculative venture to build a new harbor and industrial complex plus real estate promotion, the company's stock value would increase as construction moved along, because of increasing the value of land it owned, thereby enriching Tabor. The enterprise had been organized back in 1869 to build a canal between the Calumet River and either the south branch of the Chicago River or the Illinois and Michigan Canal, but had not progressed to match expectations. The warehouses, docks, and other buildings still existed only on the drafting board. Unfortunately, developments in the 1880s did not unfold favorably, and Marshall Field commented to Horace, "I hold some and while I do not care to increase my holdings would not sell at the price [they] would now bring." Another on-the-spot advisor revealingly wrote him the same year, 1883, ". . . their sales have fallen off this year wonderfully. There are absolutely no sales of stock and nothing bid for it."[9] Despite such discouraging reports, Tabor hung onto his share and awaited a different turn of events.

His speculations were not limited to land; Tabor plunged

into the stock market with as much enthusiasm as he did into mines. The Comstock, although now several years past its peak as a silver producer, caught his fancy. Forty thousand dollars went into shares of the Sierra Nevada, Union Consolidated, and Mexican mines. More money went to purchase shares of Nevada's State Line and Colorado's Robinson mines, both George Roberts ventures. Horace's friend Bush claimed to have "entered into arrangements" with the Robinson Mine managers to gain inside information. Bush's inside information cost Tabor almost $16,000 in stock losses, Bush promising to make up half of it. These transactions were conducted through brokers, and, regrettably, no records remain as to overall success or failure. The only isolated evidence is a note to Tabor from S. V. White & Co., stating his stock losses amounted to $50,438. What was involved, and whether these were real or paper losses is unclear.

Through Ortell & Co., stock brokers, Tabor speculated in corn, wheat, and pork futures, investing $80,000, which he sadly admitted he never got back. Dealing through Chicago and New York boards, Tabor and Bush, in partnership, speculated on grain options, repeatedly changing options, with Horace underwriting the effort. When this particular operation ended he came out about $10,000 ahead.[10]

These are but examples from a very shadowy realm of Tabor's finances — stock speculation. Undoubtedly, he was very active in this area during the early 1880s, with what results one cannot say. Speculating with the recklessness that had infiltrated his business transactions, he purchased with gay abandon, using sums which would have awed other men. In this game Horace rated as a neophyte, consequently suffering his share of beatings. Except when in New York or Chicago, he was compelled to work through others, with a time lapse which might have helped but more often hindered. When he worked through a respectable brokerage house which could advise him, the time factor was not so serious. Otherwise, Horace generally stood to lose.

Back in Denver and Leadville it was more fun to dream

about new projects than to worry about stock losses, which could be covered with silver ore. Leadville no longer served as a center of investment, but Horace helped incorporate the Evergreen Lakes and Mineral Springs Company to develop property and promote recreational facilities and the "propagation and culture of fish." The whole project was mere speculation compared to his previous endeavors. Nothing came of a rumor that he would build a Leadville business block, and by 1882 Tabor's attention was so entirely focused elsewhere that he appointed Charles Rowell, a lawyer and also a Vermont native, his general Leadville agent. Denver finally triumphed in the rivalry for his money. His natural inclination always favored the new, the expanding, the untested — a carryover perhaps from his earlier mining days. Leadville, by the 1880s, held none of these attractions for a businessman.

Building railroads into Leadville, however, was a different matter, a subject which had long fascinated the lieutenant governor, whose wealth now allowed him to dabble in it. As a mine owner, he also knew that the coming of the rails meant an increase in mining and a decrease in mining costs.

Without question Leadville needed a railroad; almost two years had passed since the discovery of the Little Pittsburg and still the camp had not secured a rail connection. Not that railroads were not making the effort; while other Western towns had to bow and scrape to the iron idol, two companies, the Denver and Rio Grande and the Santa Fe, were fighting each other over access to the Royal Gorge to see who would be the first to reach the carbonate camp. The Rio Grande won, a victory that did not necessarily please all Leadvilleites, since they did not care to have their town bound "hand and foot to Denver." Competition was still vital, since only then would there be a good chance to avoid the monopoly stranglehold of a single line. Tabor and others formed the Pueblo, Canon City, and Leadville Railroad Company, with himself and Bush on the board of directors, while the struggle between the two major lines over the right-of-way went on. The company was a bluff, and dissolved once the legal conflict between the two major lines ended. Tabor, meanwhile, sided initially with the Rio Grande in its struggles, criticizing the judge who presided over proceedings involving the two lines for being dilatory in his actions. Placing his prestige on the line in an attempt to hurry the city council into granting the company the right-of-way into town, he went to a special meeting to advocate its cause. He failed. Though calling the council's inaction scandalous, Horace need not have worried, for the coming of a railroad was too momentous an occasion to be long hindered by city fathers.[11]

Even while backing the Denver and Rio Grande, Tabor still was interested in other railroad ventures. He helped to organize the Leadville, Ten Mile, and Breckenridge, a project which went no further than securing a right-of-way, promptly conveyed to the Rio Grande. A more ambitious plan was the Leadville and Great Eastern Broadgauge Railroad, to which he subscribed $5,000, as did some others. As the name implied, this would be standard gauge, as opposed to the narrow-gauge Denver and Rio Grande. Despite a prestigious board of directors, including Horace, ambitious ideas of connecting with Santa Fe, and a completion date set for the fall of 1880, the road failed to materialize.[12] Possibly these projects were simply an attempt to force the Rio Grande into a more favorable relationship or to make money by forcing that line to buy out the drawing-board competition before it became real. Two other companies proved just as illusory, the Leadville Mining Railroad and the Lake County Steam and Horse Railway, with Horace as president. The former included that inveterate railroad promoter and political rival, William Loveland, plus Winfield Keyes, among the incorporators.

Of a similar nature, although this time coming out of Denver with tracks actually laid, was the Denver, Utah and Pacific Railroad, in which Horace invested. Although he served as president, joined by Bush, Henry Wolcott, and a group of New York investors on the board of directors, this line was primarily David Moffat's baby. The tracks reached the nearby Mitchell coal fields, and plans raced ahead for crossing the mountains. Tabor had gone on to other things before this road amounted to much.

In Denver itself he headed a company to provide cheap local transportation, sorely needed in the mushrooming city. Under the name of the Denver City Chariot Omnibus Company, Tabor proposed to put a line of horse-drawn chariot omnibuses (extremely popular in the East, according to reports) with a nickel fare into service on the major streets; they would also be available for use on special public occasions. Supplementing the already-established streetcar lines, the omnibuses would go where the others did not. Denver residents waited eagerly for such a modern improvement — and waited and waited. Some six months after the original announcement and four months after the date the line planned to be in business, the public could still only wait. The *Rocky Mountain News* explained that the delay resulted from an Eastern lawsuit against the coach's patent holder, which finally had been settled, and four coaches now were being built for Denver. The four chariots arrived, were placed in service, and the nickels were collected, not in rewarding amounts, unfortunately. By July 1881, the company had been completely reorganized and Horace was out,[13] because he wished to be.

Such transportation refinements remained unknown in the more isolated sections of Colorado, meaning that the stagecoach reigned supreme in these places until the railroad's arrival. In far-off Durango, a Denver and Rio Grande nurtured town, stage lines served as feeders into the San Juan mining camps. On a trip to the new community in late 1880 or early 1881, Horace acquired an interest in the Pioneer Stage and Express Company, in partnership with former Leadville stage owner Perley Wasson, the original owner. Stages ran into Parrott City, Fort Lewis, Silverton, and Rico. The company soon found itself involved in three lawsuits, mainly attempts to sue Horace because of his wealth. One case involved an employee's attempt to collect claimed back pay; Tabor won it. The other two were dismissed. But these troubles, together with the railroad competition to Silverton and the undoubtedly small returns on the stage run, discouraged him. Within a year he sold out his share in the company now called H. A. W. Tabor Pioneer Stage and Express Line. His one experience with staging thus ended.[14]

Tabor's transportation investments, if not always sound, were certainly varied. And it is only with hindsight that one can say he gambled recklessly in this area. At the time, any one of these companies could have matured into an extremely profitable business, because others had been started and prospered with even less backing. Tabor's did not succeed, but that was the gamble anyone took and he knew it. No needless tears were shed. He never did give up his interest, particularly in railroads.

Tabor had faith that his investments eventually would return a profit, or that some at least would make more than enough money to cover a few losses. He played the game zestfully. His shotgun pattern of investment put him into diverse occupations at the slightest whim. Augusta's nagging about plunging had never curbed this. Horace was hitched to an expanding vision of greatness, unchecked by reality's reins.

The investments made in 1879–1880 ran from the financially sound First National Bank stock and the Tabor Block to pure speculation in companies whose claims were based only on their stockholders' names. Tabor stayed with some of them too long, plunging much too much good money after bad. His shotgun approach too frequently left the outcome to chance, his investments having spread far beyond anything one individual could steadily watch. How he became interested in any given endeavor remains a mystery; but he certainly attracted promoters in swarms.

Except for his few sound investments and the promising future of the Tabor Grand Opera House, most of his ventures lost money. Undaunted, he pushed on, spreading himself too thin, leaving his investment empire vulnerable. He pushed on in politics as well, the two merging in his desire for newspapers, a prime ingredient for any politician's plans.

Tabor's maverick stand within the Republican party,

together with his finances and his political base in Lake and Arapahoe counties, made him a party force to be reckoned with, one that all factions might woo. Still, he needed to maintain his touch on the local level if he hoped to make any headway on the state level, where the glittering prizes awaited. More than one Colorado politician had sunk in the quicksand of local partisan fights; Horace knew he would have to be wary.

No longer living in Leadville, Tabor remained a political power there. But his influence was being steadily eroded, and he failed to realize it immediately. For any drive on the state scene he needed Lake County's support, so he remained interested in what once had been his private fief. His opposition was gaining — boldly with the *Democrat* founded by his political foe, William Loveland, and subtly on the precinct level. In 1880, in a city election, Tabor reluctantly found himself drawn into the fray, only to find that absentee political bosses can burn their fingers more quickly than resident ones.

Bush toyed with the idea of running for mayor, which was one reason for the founding of the *Evening Times*; his boom broke and the nomination went to another. Three parties entered the race, the *Democrat* charging that the Bush and Tabor "gang" backed the workingman's Independent Party to draw votes away from the Democrats. Accusations of nefarious schemes, involving contracts, bribes, illegal profits, payoffs, prostitutes and a "war upon poor men in behalf of the rich," drifted through town. Tabor, went the opposition refrain, did not "dirty his hands" with such activities, working through his lieutenants to "buy what cattle he needs to carry his points."

Evidently, he did not buy enough, because the Democrats captured Leadville, with Loveland's paper gleefully noting that Tabor's money and his personal appeals and letters had produced nothing, merely stimulating the Democrats to extraordinary exertions. Without question, the election proved embarrassing to Tabor and weakened him. His prestige had been on the line to hold the state's second largest community.

Ouray's Dave Day, knifing Tabor's political ineptitude, pictured Pitkin prostrate with grief, admitting that had Tabor "written two or three more letters to his influential friends in the carbonate camp the straight Republican ticket wouldn't have received a d---- vote."[15]

Nothing that happened on the local level in Colorado during the 1880s was too surprising. Too many leaders and both major parties stooped to bribery, vote registration fraud, arm twisting, and any other method to achieve the desired result. Tabor's specific activities are unknown, but it is likely that the *Democrat*'s indictments were not too wide of the mark.

State Republican leadership jockeyed for position in the upcoming presidential nominations, while Horace wallowed deeper in the Leadville morass. Ex-president Grant, making a strong bid for a third term, despite the scandals of his first two, was opposed by Maine's James G. Blaine, early the Colorado favorite. Grant's supporters, ably led by John Routt, turned the tide, gained momentum, and threatened to sweep the state convention. Sensing that the split weakened the party and his own future chances, Tabor wrote an open letter to the press supporting the idea of unpledged convention delegates, "free to exercise a wise and statesmanlike discretion." At the same time, the lieutenant governor confided that he would willingly support either the "Plumed Knight or the Silent Soldier." Grant forces immediately challenged Tabor's neutrality, branding him a Blaine man; it all proved academic when they swept the state convention in May, and Horace received another slap when Lake County selected Grant delegates. Whether he did favor Blaine is unknown; he might simply have felt the need for support after the Leadville debacle and decided to join the Wolcott-Hamill group which backed Blaine. Tabor's hopes of going to the national convention went aglimmering. Routt, Republican state chairman, led the Colorado delegation, only to be hurt at home by the eventual failure of the Grant drive.[16] Horace played his cards much more shrewdly this time than at Leadville, pocketing a few political IOUs for later repayment. His score in picking winning candidates, however, remained perfect: zero.

Republicans could hardly turn around before it was time to select the state ticket. For some time Tabor had expressed a desire to step down. He had had all the honors the office could bestow, and now he wanted something more concrete. Also, the Democratic press was making it rather hot for him over his role in the strike and the declaration of martial law. With the 1878 campaign still fresh in his mind, and having just left his wife, he did not relish the idea of a replay.

A Tabor-for-Governor boomlet died in January, sponsored as it was more by the Democratic press than by the "old Man's" loyal backers. Lake County selected him as delegate-at-large to the state convention, which met at Leadville. Both parties congregated there, demonstrating the town's prominence in 1880 despite its problems. Putting aside any thought of the governor's chair, Tabor gave a "very pointed and handsome" nominating speech for Pitkin, who had decided to run again. Party harmony, restored since last year's senate fight, held together during the convention and the campaign.

Not a candidate, Tabor remained behind the scenes, but not far enough for the *Rocky Mountain News*, which accused him and several other bonanza kings of subscribing $12,000 to support a German-language paper, probably the *Colorado Journal*, to win the German vote. The Leadville strike question would not die, nor would Democratic resentment of Tabor's money; thus he became a minor campaign issue, nothing like 1878. The Democrats failed to find enough issues or stir up the electorate, and again they went down to defeat.[17]

Tabor could at last retire from office to devote his full time and acumen to his business interests. According to Frank Hall, the decision not to become a candidate again was both "distinct and unchangeable." Still, he and a coterie of bonanza kings were considered likely to have their eyes on the senate race two years hence. Marking time till January, Tabor's whole course suddenly veered when the lieutenant governor-elect was mortally wounded by a guard at his own mine. Thirty-two-year-old George Robinson, owner of the Robinson Mine and chief citizen of the camp of the same name in Summit County, had probably been tapped for the office for the same reason Horace had been: money. A dispute over mining claims led to the tragic accident, opening the question of who would be lieutenant governor. The state constitution did not provide an answer.

In the East when the Robinson tragedy occurred, Horace returned to find himself the center of controversy. Personally much grieved at the untimely death of his young colleague, Tabor was embroiled in a politically explosive situation. He had to watch the state senate nomination for president pro-tem, because, if he chose not to serve, the man whom the senate nominated probably would. Henry Wolcott, backed by the Hamill-Wolcott-Hill faction, and Lake County's A. S. Weston, long a friend of Tabor's, jockeyed for the position. From his headquarters in the Windsor, Tabor lobbied for Weston, spurring rumors of a deal and needlessly arousing the Wolcott faction, which eventually won.

Horace then played his trump card, announcing his decision to remain as lieutenant governor, blocking the ambitious Wolcott. Tabor's hand now forced, he drifted back into the Teller camp, while the Wolcott and Teller factions fell to bickering, trying to get legislative committee appointments. With Pitkin's inauguration on the eleventh, the question was still not finally decided. Tabor told the senate that afternoon that competent legal authorities could find no legal successor, so he would remain. The tempest finally died, despite threats by a bitter Wolcott to take the matter to court, and Horace served for the next two years.[18]

Just prior to this January session, Tabor for the first time became acting governor while Pitkin was absent from the state. Routine duties filled his week: commissioning notaries public, sending and receiving several requisitions for criminals, and pardoning one man. Matters of importance were filed away to await the governor's return. During the three periods he assumed the duties of acting governor, Horace was particularly energetic in pardoning. Generally his actions were highly commended by the press, although the *Democrat* grumbled that he was too tender-hearted, allowing sentiment to override better judgment. Michael Logan, convicted of rape, was pardoned because Tabor was convinced the woman involved was neither "chaste and pure" nor virtuous. "Virtue, the brightest and most sacred jewel in a woman's soul, is not lost or destroyed by force," moralized Horace in the best Victorian manner. On a more serious case, Andrew Bigger's death sentence was commuted to life imprisonment at hard labor for a murder committed while marshal of Ophir. Twice reprieved at the last moment, Bigger was most relieved and, according to the *Solid Muldoon*, remarked, "Well, it is damn lucky for me that consumption took Pitkin south." Editor Day, no fan of either Pitkin or Tabor, railed, "prostitution, backed by sufficient manhood to defy public opinion, is far preferable to a combination of moral cowardice and total depravity." In his last period as acting governor, Tabor also shortened the sentence of another convicted murderer, John Steele, because new evidence strongly suggested his innocence; he also pardoned a forger after receiving a petition from some of Denver's leading merchants stating that the man was "weak minded."[19]

In each case he weighed the facts presented, read the accompanying petitions, then made judgment, showing a fair, compassionate nature. His conscientious work received praise. Apart from these cases, he handled only routine matters. His longest term as acting governor was September 2–30, 1881. The only sad note during this gay month in Denver was the death of President James A. Garfield, in observance of which Tabor issued a special proclamation and chaired a commemorative meeting. His most active time as governor was during two weeks in December 1882, when he issued four pardons.[20] He had done well, much better than many suspected he could. Colorado need not have felt embarrassed to have this mining man in political office or executive position. Although the opportunities for constructive work had been severely circumscribed by his temporary position, he moved with vigor where he could.

As president of the senate during the 1881 session, Tabor slipped noticeably from his 1879 record. He chaired fewer than half the sessions, leaving the duties to his political foe, Henry Wolcott. Wolcott also served as acting governor through half of November 1882, when both Tabor and Pitkin were out of the state — small crumbs for a man of Henry's drive.

Tabor's popularity grew during his two terms, reflecting his competent handling of the office and its duties, few Coloradans doubting that he had shown the capacity for the position. The lieutenant governor's political stock of course was not hurt by the building of his two opera houses, the Tabor Block, and his sponsorship of numerous civic events. Even the failures of the Little Pittsburg and Chrysolite were looked upon in some quarters as a positive good, since those high-flying Easterners had been bested by local mining men.

III.
DISILLUSIONMENT
OF SUCCESS
1881-1889

CHAPTER 10

"A UNION GRAND OF CAPITAL AND LABOR"

*"Let no one call Colorado a barren waste,
or speak of it as a wild, rocky place."*
Rocky Mountain News, September 6, 1881

I N 1881 Horace Tabor found his cup was full to overflowing. He had weathered the 1880 Leadville troubles, his political prestige was growing, his banks were strong, his mines were producing and more were being added, his business investments were promising, the Tabor Block was rented, and best of all, his Tabor Grand Opera House was rising. Proudly, Denver newspapers noted that it was the most costly building for its size on the continent, predicting that when completed it would be a "Thespian Temple worthy of any city in the world."

To make it one of the strongest and safest buildings known, Tabor ordered that no effort be spared. Supplies came by the carload: first, the outside timbers, stone and iron, then the inside furnishings. Cost was no obstacle in the search for materials to make this a place worthy of Denver and its benefactor. His old partner, Marshall Field, sent one shipment of carpets, tapestry, silk plush, and chairs totaling $15,714. Other cars brought in mirrors, handcrafted woodwork, a piano, kettle drums, various fixtures, an iron safe, and whole carloads of items to fulfill Tabor's dream.

Tabor watched and enjoyed the construction of his latest

creation. Already the second-richest man on Denver's tax rolls, he steadily moved toward the number one spot. In his own way, Horace described his motives to his friend, Judge Wilbur Stone. As Stone remembered, they were inside the building and Tabor was sitting on some framework:

> I am going to have it just as nice and beautiful as I can have it, for money. I do not intend to cut anything short, for want of money, but you are very much mistaken if you think I am building this other than as a business enterprise; the public may look at it in that way, but I can say to you that I am building this for myself, to make money. From one standpoint, a selfish interest; that is to say, I know that it is going to make money for me. If it makes money, I can make twice as much out of this opera house block, having this opera house in it and I have other property that it will help.[1]

In spite of the best efforts to insure safety on the project, one serious accident marred the construction. The north wall collapsed in mid-January 1881; sidewalk speculation that the whole structure was unsafe and liable to come tumbling down speedily followed. Denver's mayor promptly appointed a committee of competent men to investigate, which reported back that the building was safe and substantial and placed the blame for the collapse on vibrations caused by gusty winds. This resulted in a $5,000 loss, but only temporarily stopped construction; repairs were made.

Then came the long-expected announcement: the $850,000 opera block would open in September. William Bush, now working with Tabor as informal opera house business manager, signed the well-known Emma Abbott Company for the opening attraction. At the height of her career, the petite, pretty, and newsworthy Emma Abbott perfectly complemented the grand occasion. As the memorable day approached, the Denver press chronicled the special arrangements for the opulent opening. Reduced rates were given by all railroads running into the city, with excursion trains scheduled from the nearby mountain and plains towns. The chief of police, anticipating a rush, made specific arrangements for the evening: all carriages were to come by way of Curtis Street, head down toward Arapahoe and Lawrence, and after the opera pick up patrons and owners by reversing the order. The management, too, made arrangements to handle the expected crowd and keep gate-crashers out. The precautions were so well enforced that when Tabor and Edbrooke appeared on opening night, it was reported they were stopped by the guard at the outer door for not having tickets. Only after Horace clearly identified himself were they allowed in. Mutterings about high-priced tickets brought this press retort: "Save money, buy a ticket, it's expensive to run an opera and Denver's pride should be touched in this matter to see that a good house is present every night."

Proper dress for such a momentous occasion worried Denverites. The society editor of the *Rocky Mountain News* advised that, certainly, if one wished to appear in the most elegant style, nothing would be against it, though the opera house was not built for the select few, but for the people. Therefore, let Denver look no further for the correct dress than the "man who owns the magnificent structure," as he "passes up and down our streets in attire as plain as that he used to wear before he struck it rich." Let them copy in this respect Colorado's unassuming son. Denver's new beau monde appeared in coat and tails, not, however, sewn with gold thread or with buttons of "solitaire diamonds of the first water," as the fun-loving staff of the *Denver Tribune* imagined.

Tabor enjoyed a moment of popularity unmatched by any other Coloradan up to that time. As the "red letter day," the "greatest in the history of Denver," neared, no tribute seemed too grand to bestow upon him; indeed, it was commented that if he had run for senator, the office would have been given to him by acclamation. The *Tribune* crowed that Denver, thanks to the opera house, was well on its way to becoming the handsomest city in the union. For that, they said, Tabor deserved distinct recognition for his public spirit.[2]

The Tabor Grand Opera House opened on the evening of September 5, not quite finished, but far enough along to awe the first-nighters. Magnificent in concept and construction, it was the finest opera house between the Midwest and Pacific Coast, one of the best in the United States.

A persistent drizzle throughout the afternoon and evening failed to deter the "immense audience," which filled every seat. A large number of camp chairs were crowded into the parquet to take care of the overflow. Much to everyone's delight, Emma Abbott, in honor of the occasion, opened with the mad scene from *Lucia di Lammermoor*. Immediately following her performance, the drop curtain went up, and Tabor was asked to come forward. Horace chose this night, because of the separation from Augusta, not to occupy his private box on the left side of the stage, even though it had been most "elaborately and tastefully trimmed with flowers" and fronted with a floral design spelling his name. Nevertheless, Tabor was in attendance and proceeded to the stage amid "vociferous applause" that echoed throughout the house; then he stopped and bowed. Looking uncomfortable in his formal attire, as a reporter observed, or perhaps just nervous, Horace stood while his career was briefly reviewed, gracious tributes paid him, and a special poem read to honor the occasion. On this, his special evening, he was presented with an autograph album and a golden watch fob symbolizing his rise from miner to owner of the Tabor Grand, "as an appreciation of the love which you have bestowed upon Denver and her people." Modestly, the acting governor briefly answered:

> It is sixteen months since I commenced the building of this opera house. At that time I looked Denver carefully over with its people and here found a town at the base of the Rocky Mountains — a city of 30,000 or 40,000 inhabitants: the finest city, I think, of its population on the American continent. I said if Denver is to have an opera house it should be worthy of the city. Here is the opera house, I shall leave it to your judgment if I have done my duty in this respect [applause]. Here is this beautiful album and fob chain — as beautiful as can be. I shall prize them every hour I live. I shall prize them not for their price value, but for the spirit in which they are given.[3]

With applause ringing, Tabor stepped back and the evening was concluded with the scheduled production of "Maritana."

One shadow marred the evening's splendor, the hauntingly empty Tabor box. Horace took the bows alone that evening; Augusta was nowhere to be seen. Not that she had wanted it this way — she pleaded in a poignant letter to be allowed to go with him to this performance:

> Believe me that none will be more proud of it than your *broken hearted wife*. Will you not take me there and by so doing stop the gossip that is busy with *our* affairs?
>
> God knows that I am truely sorry for our estrangment and will humble myself in the dust at your feet if you will only return. Whatever I said to you was done in the heat of passion and you know the awful condition I was in when it was said. Pity I beseech you and forgive me and let us bury the past and commence anew and my life shall be devoted to you forever. Your loveing wife.[4]

Despite this soul-exposing plea, with the poor spelling showing the strain of the moment, Tabor showed no forgiveness, nor could he grant her wish. Separation no longer satisfied him, he was pushing for divorce. Certainly as early as January 25, 1881, Augusta and Horace had had a face-to-face confrontation in Leadville about the matter, with no results. Tabor then turned to Bush for help, only to have negotiations stymied by Augusta's demand for alimony, apparently half of Tabor's fortune. Although advising Tabor that a divorce scandal might ruin his political career, Bush continued throughout the year, at his friend's insistence, to try to pressure Augusta into agreement.[5] She steadfastly refused. Her letter to her husband showed her continued love, despite all the anguish suffered on his account in the past months.

For the time being Tabor could put aside his domestic troubles, as he read the congratulations which continued to pour in for days. "PERFECTION!" headlined one article. "It will remain a monument to Denver enterprise for many years to come and a monument of which anyone might be proud." Even churches, which often opposed the theater, rose to praise, the minister of the First Baptist Church stating in his sermon that money in the hands of such men as Horace Tabor was most wisely bestowed. The warmest thanks and gratitude of the public, he concluded, should be given to this generous benefactor.[6]

Already legends surrounding the building and its owner were growing, mostly traceable to the facile pen of the *Tribune*'s Eugene Field, later to be famed as poet of children's verse. This fun-loving journalist's whimsical wit makes comments in his paper suspect, unless they can be verified by other sources. Field never tired of playing practical jokes, which included writing poems and attributing them to other people, or fabricating news stories and printing them as the truth. Coming to Denver as associate editor only a month before the opera opened, he stayed for two years, during the heyday of Tabor's influence. Horace, among many others, felt the prick of his pen, his wit's rapier thrust.

Stories by Field about Tabor are legion, but a couple will serve as examples with regard to the Tabor Grand. The story of Horace's replacing the portrait of Shakespeare in the opera house with one of his own, asking "What the hell has he ever done for Colorado?" is attributable to Field. So is the report in the *Tribune* that when two newsboys were looking at Tabor's and Abbott's pictures on the *News*'s front page, a third little fellow appeared, thinking they were looking at the *Police Gazette*. On seeing the pictures, he innocently exclaimed, "Golly, when are they going to be hung?"[7] Celebrating the opening in a short poem, Field flashed the brilliance that later would make him renowned. Part of it went,

> The opera house — a union grand
> of capital and labor —
> Long will the stately structure stand
> A monument to Tabor!
>
> For many a year and many a year
> Our folks will have the habit
> Of lauding that illustrious pair,
> Tabor and Emma Abbott.

One feature of the Tabor Grand Opera House caught everyone's attention — the drop curtain with its portrayal of the ruins of an ancient temple. Those curious enough to examine it found at the bottom these lines by Charles Kingsley from his poem "Old and New":

> So fleet the works of men back to the earth again;
> Ancient and holy things fade like a dream.

It is barely possible that Tabor had indeed met Kingsley when the latter was in Colorado Springs recuperating from a severe cold in the summer of 1874, or during an earlier visit. Whether Horace had only read these lines somewhere or was given a book containing them remains a matter of conjecture.[8] For whatever reason, the lines were placed on the curtain and have been considered prophetic in the Tabor story. Nothing of the sort was intended in 1881.

The grand event was over; the excitement, however, continued on through the Abbott Company's two-week stay. One theatergoer wrote years later, "*Martha* was the opera I saw; it made a strong impression for some of its refrains are still familiar in my mind." The *News* and *Tribune* debated the merits of the performances, but it was a one-sided affair, as Field stuck pin after pin into his rival, as he had done in the newsboy story. Actually, Emma and her company had given Denver some of the most professional musical performances the town had had the pleasure of hearing. For the first two weeks the opera house cleared a profit of over seven thousand dollars.[9] Tabor's wishes were coming true.

With the completion of the opera house, Tabor's major Denver construction was finished. In less than two years he had added two outstanding architectural achievements to Denver's paltry number. For a decade they ranked as primary attractions, being a must for the visitor to see. The opera house remained the focal point of Denver's theatrical world and a leading cultural center. Horace moved his offices there. The Tabor Opera House block emerged as a premier business location, one of the first to pull away, even though slightly, from the Larimer Street axis, which had dominated until now.

He had earned all the toasts and accolades that were showered upon him. In a materialistic sense the accomplishments were great, but no more so than the faith and confidence he had placed in Denver, which encouraged others to match his example. Of all the mining millionaires Tabor was the first, and the leading one, to reinvest his fortune at home. He had shown the way, and a grateful public responded with its tributes to a man who symbolized the lure and the promise that was the mining frontier.

Denver applauded, too, when, in an 1881 state election to fulfill a constitutional requirement to choose the capital officially, Tabor swung his prestige behind the city. Joining a host of well-known Coloradans, including John Evans, William Byers, William Loveland, and Henry Wolcott, Horace worked hard on a committee to secure the honor for Denver, showing he could forget political rivalries to work with erstwhile opponents. The results proved both gratifying and logical, as Denver won in a landslide.

Denver could also be proud of its new stock exchange, which Horace enthusiastically helped promote. In January and February 1881 a series of meetings were held in the Windsor Hotel to organize the Denver Stock Exchange. Tabor, with his Leadville and New York experience, chaired some of the sessions and strongly urged upon the assembled financiers the necessity of such an organization. In order to set the concern in operation, $50,000 had to be subscribed, the optimistic officers feeling it could be raised within thirty days after the first call was made. Anticipating great benefits for the city and state, the firm opened its stock board, waiting anxiously for outside money to grab those tempting Colorado stocks. But it did not happen that way, and a hint of trouble appeared when the president resigned. As vice-president and member of the board of directors, Tabor replaced him, with Bush taking his old position. Even with the wealth of the Colorado mining men behind it, the Denver Exchange did not survive, for reasons similar to the Leadville failure. Easterners still continued to prefer their own institutions. In April

1882 Tabor suggested that Colorado companies form a pool, register their stock like Eastern companies, and designate a Denver bank as their depository.[10] The Denver Exchange passed into history, as much a victim of the New York Stock Exchange as the other two with which Tabor had been associated.

On paper a stock exchange was a superb idea; in practice it took a group of active bidders and sellers to keep it going. Denver had plenty of the latter, far too few of the former. In addition, as Colorado mines passed into out-of-state ownership, fewer mining shares were available to be offered by local sources. Then, there was the reputation that some Colorado mining men had acquired, which was not likely to stimulate confidence. Horace and others might have hoped otherwise, but experience had shown that Colorado just could not support its own exchange.

As Tabor enlarged his business empire, he continued his search for new and profitable mines, realizing his financial base was anchored securely to mining. Unrestrained now by Augusta, he purchased mines with abandon, surpassing the previous decade. One may quibble over whether his actions were idiotic or shrewd, but Augusta's anguished protest in *The Ballad of Baby Doe*, "Lord-a-mighty, no! He wants to buy *another* mine: The man's idiotic," is not far from the truth.

Dollars flowed out and some returned with a profit, while Tabor, standing at the apex of his mining career, was being described as the boldest mining operator in the states. Buying established mines, and gambling on untested properties, he plunged ahead. His Chrysolite stock returned dividends as Raymond's skill revived it. Tabor's interest waned, even to the point of purchasing another man's claims against the property and taking the company to court for $15,000, then settling for $6,000.[11]

The Robert E. Lee had flashed brilliantly into Leadville prominence in January 1880, yielding $118,500 in twenty-four hours, a year before Tabor entered the picture as a stockholder.

179

By then the Lee had been gutted by strenuous production, and Tabor got in too late to make a big killing. Similarly, he owned part of the Big Chief, located on Carbonate Hill, hanging onto his interest throughout the decade without noticeable success. Nor did the Glass-Pendery Consolidated Mining Company, of which he was president, add to his fortune.[12]

The Matchless, however, rewarded his endeavors, providing him with a fortune instead of merely "pin money," a silver bonanza just in time to tide him over the building of the Tabor Grand. Under his old assistant Lou Leonard's direction, development work pushed ahead, every foot seemingly solid silver. The scoffing of 1879 turned to praise within months. By August 1880, when the Matchless hit an early peak, even Tabor was astonished, recovering his poise long enough to pronounce it worth $2 million.

At year's end, with production just starting to climb, he was receiving a monthly profit of $25,000. Unlike some of the other operations with which he was connected, Tabor chose to operate the Matchless fairly conservatively with a small labor force, or, as the *Leadville Daily Herald* said, "This mine is Governor Tabor's pet, and he does not choose to overwork it." Extremely rich specimens were found in this property, including one twelve-pound lump of almost solid horn and native silver, and ore that assayed over eleven thousand ounces of silver per ton. Leonard received a great deal of commendation for his management. One of the youngest mine managers in Colorado, only in his mid-twenties, Leonard was an extremely likable, active young man, popular in Leadville and with his boss. More than that, he was regarded as a most reliable and shrewd businessman.

With the Matchless doing so famously, Horace found himself in court to defend his ownership, as claimants appeared like wolves circling an intended victim. The case gave Leonard and Tabor's lawyer Lewis C. Rockwell plenty of headaches in collecting affidavits and evidence and warding off encroachers. The trouble came from neighboring mines, the Dolphin and Big Pittsburg. Lou, writing to Rockwell, exclaimed that he planned "to give them a benefit you bet," if they broke into Matchless ground, and he hoped Rockwell would obtain an injunction to stop any attempts to do that. Rockwell quickly shot back, "You don't want to kill any of them under any circumstances, but you want to put every imaginable obstruction in their way." The cost of the proceedings proved worthwhile, as Tabor finally settled the claim to his satisfaction.[13]

If 1880 and 1881 were good years for the Matchless, 1882 was a vintage one. By the end of January the mine had produced about $1.5 million, ranking it now as Tabor's best producer; in March alone it netted him a profit of $82,000. Although production at this level could not be maintained, it did not decline drastically that year. The property became one of Leadville's showcases and the Society of Mining Engineers toured it while in Colorado in August 1882.[14] Realizing Leonard's worth, Horace involved him in other projects; consequently, he spent less time with the Matchless. Like the mine, Leonard was one of Tabor's assets. The Matchless indeed lived up to its name.

On the other hand, the vaunted San Juan mines failed to develop as expected. The winter of 1879–1880, for which Tabor had worked so hard to prepare, proved him a prophet by producing snow levels at six feet, topped by what were charitably described as "many huge drifts." John Tabor kept work going throughout the winter on the Alaska, Saxon, and Red Rogers mines despite such handicaps, and on through spring and summer, only to be disappointed in the meager results. Frederick Amelung, a mining engineer who visited the mines in August, put his finger on the problem — the ore occurred in irregular pockets and chimneys with no regular pay streak. In addition, water forced the Saxon's closing. A shipment of rich ore went to Lake City to be worked, emphasizing once more the lack of a nearby mill. Isolation hampered the entire region, and finally even Horace conceded he was stumped. His properties were not worked that winter nor reopened the next summer, causing consternation in the San Juans because he had been considered the herald of prosperity. One irate local called it a freeze-out against the San Juan for some imagined grudge; then charged that blundering work under incompetent management last season should not cause Tabor to injure the whole region by refusing to continue development.[15]

Yesterday's savior, today's whipping boy, Tabor had run the gamut. Without question he was well within reason not to push development at a moment when isolation permitted him to ship only high-grade ore profitably, when poor transportation resulted in high costs, and ore occurred only in scattered pockets. Tabor would wait for the coming of the railroad; the San Juan boosters would just have to stew a while. The charges against John Tabor's management may have had some substance. He was just learning the profession, but such ingratitude was hardly called for. In spite of its relative failure as a producer, the Alaska Mine did contribute something; it gave its name to a mineral found there — Alaskite.

As he diversified, the selection of his mine managers was particularly important, for on their skill, knowledge, and experience rested Tabor's success or failure. Early in his career and later during the 1890s, he directed his own operations, but not in the flush of his prosperity. The men he picked displayed varied backgrounds. Lou Leonard, who managed so many of his mines, had no previous mining experience; nonetheless he developed into one of the best that Horace employed. John Tabor supervised mines for his brother for years without any apparent prior experience, while A. V. Bohn had some experience before joining Tabor. Tabor also employed experienced mining men such as Eben Smith, Oliver Harker, and Cyrus Gribble. On his main Mexican venture, he selected apparently skilled Mexican managers and a personal friend, A. S. Weston, to oversee the operation. Some of the companies Tabor was associated with employed nationally-known men such as Winfield Keyes, but Tabor's responsibility in their selection is unknown. No firm conclusion can be drawn as to what standards Tabor might have used in choosing his managers; wherever he could, he picked men he personally knew.

If the Chrysolite represented the past and the Matchless the present, then the Henriett and the Maid of Erin symbolized the future of Tabor's Leadville mines. Both seemed valuable from evidence of early exploration, but neither had been fully developed; the Maid was hampered by a lawsuit between it and the neighboring Vanderbilt, resulting in only assessment work being done. Tabor and the two others who owned the property watched as money was drained off to the lawyers faster than it was returned by the ore.

The Henriett reached mineral in January 1881, to the great satisfaction of its owners, including Tabor, Moffat, Chaffee, and the "Mr. Republican" of his day, Maine's Senator James G. Blaine. Once opened, the Henriett proved a consistent, if not spectacular, performer. Exploration work, carried into 1882, exposed a large body of ore. Such attractive possibilities proved tempting to English investors, guided by the diplomatic hand of Moffat, who went to Europe and found purchasers for $1.5 million, negotiating in both Paris and London. Mining experts examined it and pronounced the mine valuable, and so, after two months of talks, the Henriett Mining and Smelting Company, Limited, took over control. Tabor and Moffat, showing commendable faith, retained the bulk of their share in stock — at least half of the sale had been stock, not cash. Despite warnings that this was the same group which guided the "notorious Pittsburg swindle," the English company seemed well pleased with their purchase and promptly declared a 2 percent dividend.[16]

While almost all of Tabor's mining sales involved acceptance of some stock in lieu of cash, as the years went by he accepted more stock and less cash, especially in disposing of marginal mines. The widely publicized sales involving hundreds of thousands, or even a million, dollars failed to net Horace the amount the casual reader might suspect. The stock's worth depended on intangibles at the time of the transaction and actually added little hard cash to Tabor's liquid assets.

The Scooper Mine near Leadville embroiled him in some controversy in Philadelphia, the city of brotherly love. Tabor, while visiting there, was served with a writ charging him with swindling the Philadelphia owners, who were unhappy because the ore had petered out after the sale. Horace wriggled out from under this one on a technicality, although Maxey was really the culprit, having bonded and sold the mine. On being interviewed, his father shrugged it off with the comment that, if there was a fault anywhere, "it is the fault of God and of nature for not putting more silver in it. That is all I can say." Such homilies neither soothed feelings nor salvaged profits. But this was tranquility compared to the Hibernia tempest.

No mine led Horace into more trouble than his connection with the Hibernia; the *Mining Record* published a series of muckraking articles and editorials exposing his methods and "double dealings." The Hibernia Consolidated, made up of the Hibernia, May Queen, and Surprise claims, broke into prominence in the summer of 1880. Stock soon appeared on the market, boosted by strategically timed stories of the mine's wealth and a prompt declaration of dividends. Such good reports, plus dividends and an upswing in the stock price, whetted the public's appetite, reaffirming Barnum's maxim that a sucker is born every minute.

President Tabor placed James C. Langhorne, a "very clever gentleman and competent manager," in charge of actual operation, together with a few others of Chrysolite notoriety. Continued encouraging reports aroused the *Mining Record*, which sensed another Leadville stock speculation. In March 1881 it began an exposé of Tabor's Hibernia "manipulations," relentlessly pursuing the prey for two months, discomfiting Horace and further tarnishing his reputation.

The *Mining Record* struck with a blast, accusing Tabor of misleading Easterners with respect to the Hibernia's true condition, then unloading his stock. When the stock price did break, adding fuel to the fire, Tabor's position was undermined by some Colorado papers boasting that he was having fun with the boys, avenging whatever loss he suffered on the Chrysolite. The *Mining Record* promptly seized this as further evidence of Horace's speculation: "For the life of us, we are unable to perceive how Governor Tabor can have 'rubbed out a black mark or two given him by the Chrysolite,' by successfully unloading upon other people his stock in the Hibernia at a profit and above its intrinsic worth." The journal openly charged Tabor with having sold stock while making statements calculated to deceive the public.

Broadening the attack, the editorial guns were turned on that Colorado threesome rapidly becoming infamous in mining circles, Chaffee, Moffat, and Tabor. Using the Henriett, which the editors felt would go the way of those other mines, as a jumping-off point, they noted that these three had been singularly successful in selling stock to great personal advantage, while the companies ceased to be profitable to the shareholders. A compromise between the Matchless and Hibernia over disputed land looked suspicious. Had it not all been done for Tabor's benefit? Certainly this was not a safe precedent to establish without some outside referees, "But all is grist to the mill of Governor Tabor." Finally tiring of the game, they took one last blast, entitled "Accountability of Mine Mis-management"; while not mentioning their favorite whipping boy directly, the editors made it obvious to anyone who had read the *Mining Record*'s past issues whom they had in mind.[17]

Tabor's friends rallied to his defense, particularly the *Leadville Daily Herald*, which had the double duty of defending the town's present weakened reputation and that of one of the paper's owners. The facts, it said, simply did not justify such a conclusion; this enterprise "is a legitimate one" and worthy of confidence. Tabor spoke out, too; he had gone into the transaction in good faith, invested heavily, and while the mine had not yet met expectations, he still had confidence. "Charges of dishonesty or fraud have no foundation."

Still the price of the Hibernia skidded alarmingly, falling in three weeks from $1.60 to .50 per share. This surprised everybody, wrote the *Herald*, although it should not have caused all the howling against the management in the Eastern press. Rebutting the critics, at the annual meeting in May the stockholders reelected the old management while the *Mining Record* watched, frustrated by its inability to stop Tabor. Not even Leadville sources really knew what was happening on the inside.

Then two strange episodes complicated further this already puzzling case. First, the directors passed a resolution closing the mine to everyone not working there, including the Colorado directors. Second, on June 15, the Eastern directors, feeling confident, declared the sixth dividend of $30,000, only to have Tabor openly recommend it be rescinded because the money was not available. He announced the Hibernia was not doing well enough to pay a dividend, only to have the directors threaten to resign if it were not paid. The *Mining Record* pointed out, "Vulgar success in unscrupulous things is very apt [to] make men dizzy." Not so, defended the *Leadville Democrat*, saying that Tabor was acting honestly in not paying a fraudulent dividend. At this point, Tabor brought in his trusted lieutenant, Lou Leonard, to manage the mine after Langhorne resigned. This expedient naturally aroused the *Mining Record* further, but the Hibernia's day had passed. Leonard was faced with the unenviable task of stopping operation when no new ore deposits were uncovered, and the company subsequently foundered, $15,000 in debt. The mine, noted the *Herald* in December, was thoroughly played out; the directors were considering leasing it.[18] Another $20,000 had to be borrowed from the First National Bank of Denver to pay off miners' liens on the property to prevent its being sold at a sheriff's sale. Leonard ended the month with a surplus of $70, and all work stopped.

The reader of 1881, perusing the accounts, would have to make his own choice as to what to believe among the accusations, defenses, and counteraccusations concerning

Tabor. The decision would not have been easy then, nor is it now. Without question, the mine was played out as the result of some very exploitative operations, of which Tabor and the other directors were guilty. Nor can the practice of borrowing money on expected ore value to pay a dividend, as had been done the previous June, be condoned. In Tabor's defense it should be noted that he had been in the East, not Leadville, at the time. On the superintendent's recommendation of ore in sight, he approved and helped secure a loan of $15,000; upon arriving in Denver, however, he learned that the mine was in no condition to pay a dividend. Between the announcement and the actual rescinding, large amounts of stock were sold. Supporting his position, Horace responded that he "acted in good faith, relying entirely upon statements made to him that the latest advice from the mine warranted the declaration of the dividend."

On the charge of shady practices Tabor has to stand circumstantially convicted; too many people bragged that he was getting even on the Hibernia sale for the Chrysolite misfortunes for this accusation to be completely untrue. An unidentified mining man observed that the Hibernia "was a comparatively small matter, but it was pretty well done." But there is not quite enough evidence to convict him of the *Mining Record*'s charge of bulling and bearing the stocks. The deposed Hibernia superintendent, Langhorne, testified that he, Bush, and Tabor had a business agreement. For 10 percent of the profits the other two made on stock transactions, Langhorne told them when he thought it was expedient to buy or sell in relation to what was happening in the mine, a correspondence stealthfully carried on by cypher.[19] This speaks poorly for Tabor's fiduciary relationship to other shareholders, showing also an unfair and unwise use of inside information for purely personal ends.

Last-minute attempts by New York stockholders to redeem the property failed, and it was seized by the sheriff in January and purchased by Tabor's Leadville agent in March for the exact figure of the note held against it by the First

National Bank. The *Mining Record* and *Herald* again crossed editorial swords, reviving old arguments though shedding no new light. New York stockholders, determined not to lose their property, reorganized under a new name and redeemed the mine within six months, severing Tabor's relation with it.[20] To be sure, many questions went unanswered and remain so to this day.

Tabor's handling of the Hibernia produced serious doubts about his concept of legitimate business practices and the responsibilities of officers to stockholders. The lessons learned from the master mining speculators in the Chrysolite and Little Pittsburg sales were bearing fruit; clearly Horace was no sport of circumstance. In fairness, it should be noted that these practices were not exclusive to Colorado or Tabor and his friends; self-serving, irresponsible entrepreneurs were to be found in many Western mining operations.

While involved with these bigger mines, Tabor continually pressed his search for additional bonanzas, investing in a whole series of little mines, whose only fame rests on that of their owner. For a while in 1880 he hired prospectors to search in his behalf, only to find few rewards, so he gave up this novel approach and went back to buying or bonding already discovered mines. In Leadville he bought the Iron, Breece, Del Monte Consolidated and Denver City Consolidated; elsewhere, the Columbia Mine below Breckenridge, the Augusta Mine near Gunnison, and a placer operation close to Granite on Cache Creek came under Tabor ownership or stockholding. At Granite he came back to where he had camped two decades before and had failed to recover the powder-fine gold. The Como Iron, Coal and Land Company placed Tabor at its head and made Moffat its treasurer, although the former owned only 341 out of 10,000 shares. Great hopes did not produce great profits from the company property, located some nine miles from Como in South Park. Coal, iron, silver, gold — it was all the same to Colorado's mining king.

A report that Tabor had purchased part of the Delaware

Mine opposite the small mining camp of Decatur caused a neighboring company to issue a prospectus stressing that Tabor's Delaware vein without doubt passed through their ground. At Grand Mountain, near Leadville, Horace bought some prospect holes; "his theory is that from good prospect holes big mines grow." He was wrong this time, however. In the Ten Mile region, located north of Leadville in Summit County, the Wheel of Fortune became partly his, but he never had time to work this marginal property. When a boom flashed in Boulder County's Jamestown, Tabor was there angling for prospective mines.[21] Everywhere, it seemed, Tabor's money rushed to seek the elusive bonanza. Hardly a district opened where he did not venture; to the uninitiated a new Colorado mining district did not seem to have any tangible future without Tabor. The projects that did not pan out he simply ignored, turning instead to others.

CHAPTER 11

TO ASPEN AND BEYOND

*"Mining is thought by many a lottery. I do not so
consider it; it is a legitimate business."*
Horace Tabor, January 1892

OF THE discoveries during the same period as Leadville,
only Aspen eventually came to rival the "queen" seriously as a silver producing region. Tabor waded into this
relatively undeveloped district in the early 1880s, at first ten-
tatively, then plunging. As in the San Juans, which now
receded into second place, Tabor was determined to get in
on the ground floor. His first small undertakings, bonding
the Silver Bell in 1880 and buying an interest in the Silver Star
and Chloride Mines, apparently failed to meet expectations.
A promotional town company, the Leadville and Roaring
Fork Mining and Prospecting Company, also caught his attention; he became a director, and the company responded
by naming part of the site Tabor Square. Though Roaring
Fork proved to be a dud, Tabor's other interests grew and
prospered, especially his big catch, the Tam O'Shanter.

Located above Ashcroft, Aspen's threatening rival, it was
composed of several claims, including the Montezuma, the
whole taking its name from the hero of Robert Burns's poem.
For $100,000 the property could be purchased; a bargain was
struck, following examinations by Tabor and mining experts:
$5,000 down and the rest to be paid after ninety days, if
the property proved worthy. Work was begun immediately
to beat the deadline; a rich ore vein was uncovered and the

high-grade rushed to Leadville to be smelted. This clinched the deal in September 1881. Again, as in the San Juan, Horace found mining in a new district problem-filled. In a failing attempt to lure the Denver and Rio Grande to Ashcroft, Tabor offered to contract his mine to ship fifty tons of ore every weekday for the first six months. The bemused lieutenant governor observed, "Well they do not get such offers as that every day, and were so astonished that they had to take time to consider it." Before winter set in, bunk houses and other structures had been put up and plans laid to build a smelter in the spring.[1] Tabor and his co-owners, Chaffee, Bush, and others from Leadville and Denver were satisfied.

News of this wondrous mine appeared at the same time as the opening of the Tabor Grand Opera House, and when asked about it by a *Tribune* reporter, Horace laughingly claimed, "I'm afraid to go and look at this big vein. Everybody who's been up there has come back crazy."

Down Slate Mountain, some four miles from the mines, was the burgeoning little camp of Ashcroft, which even possessed a weekly newspaper. Stimulated by the sale and the new owner's projected plans, it came alive. Soon all the standard ingredients appeared: saloons, stores, hotels, post office, and the ever-present scramble for choice building sites. Horace had seen it all before, but now he was the great benefactor; on his mine rested the success of this settlement. To jump ahead of the story slightly, as the summer of 1882 raced by, the boom reached its zenith. Money from his miners' paychecks kept the local economy lively. The "Mining Wonder of the West," one exuberant promoter called Ashcroft, although even he had to admit that mining was costly there, the winter snows retarding operations into July.[2]

Everything was progressing famously. When the noted Leadville smelter man, James B. Grant, had been induced to join with Tabor to build an Ashcroft smelter, the value of the Tam O'Shanter skyrocketed, one-twelfth interest being sold for $50,000. To facilitate reaching the mine Horace planned to start construction on a road in the spring of 1882.

He expected, said the *Denver Tribune*, to create something of a sensation that year with his Tam O'Shanter.

A sensation was created, but not the type Tabor would have wished — his mine was caught in the most costly litigation he had yet faced. The trouble erupted in January 1882, when a mob of angry miners gave Samuel Bruckman ten minutes to leave Ashcroft. The victim of this outrage was a Leadville mining and real estate broker. He claimed he had grubstaked the discoverers and had not been given his third share, and promptly took the sellers to court. The $95,000 payment to complete the purchase was placed in escrow, enjoined by Tabor, in the Bank of Leadville to await the court's verdict on the title. As litigation dragged on, Tabor understandably became reluctant to invest large sums in the property, and the sweeping benefits planned for Ashcroft temporarily went aglimmering.

The original discoverers, James F. Chaney and Nicholas Atkinson, muddied the waters even further by filing a suit charging Bruckman with working in collusion with Tabor to enable them both to get the mine and keep the money. These plaintiffs now decided they wanted the Tam O'Shanter back. Both sides promptly filed cross-complaints, with the astonished Tabor insisting he was justified in protecting himself by enjoining the money and was not involved with Bruckman. Tabor won the first round regarding the money, but the primary issue of ownership was turned over to a court-appointed referee, Willard Teller, brother of the senator and a noted lawyer. Not until December 1882 did he hand down his decision, giving Horace the rights to the property and supporting his position by declaring that no evidence of fraud existed.

This failed to satisfy Atkinson, for one, who decided to appeal. Tabor, he argued, wanted to compel "us boys to take little or nothing," because he knew "we were poor and he was rich and powerful." The case dragged on until 1888, when the Colorado Supreme Court decided for Tabor against Atkinson. In the meantime the Bank of Leadville failed and

the $95,000 was lost. A last-gasp suit was based on the conten-
tion that since the money had been lost, Atkinson had never
been paid; he therefore, sued to recover his rightful property.[3]

But in the meantime Horace, hesitating to work the Tam
O'Shanter at full capacity, continued exploration, promising
to move ahead vigorously in the near future. Ashcroft, disappointed at the turn of events, still continued to support the
lieutenant governor and gave him an enthusiastic welcome
when he visited the camp in August 1882. The proposed
mill fell victim to the lawsuit, and ore had to be shipped
to Crested Butte, a costly expedient. Tabor hired Eben Smith,
one of Colorado's most skilled mining men, as his superintendent and sent Lou Leonard over on at least one occasion
that fall. As winter closed in, Smith pushed developments,
amid glowing reports from all sides about his efforts and
the Tam O'Shanter's future prospects.[4]

Colorado's mining king looked beyond the state for
investments and readily found them, for wherever he went
he attracted attention and found someone ready to sell. Far
down in isolated southeastern Nevada, near Pioche, Tabor
headed the Day Silver Mining Company, owners of the mine
of the same name, originally called the Jack Rabbit. An exceedingly rich surface pocket got this property off to a flying start,
only to have the stock collapse to 10 cents a share on the
San Francisco Stock Exchange. Sometime in the early 1880s,
probably 1881, Tabor's group, a San Francisco-based corporation, gained control of it, a mine no longer in good ore. Mining
in the whole state was in the doldrums, as the governor
reported, "Much of this [mineral wealth] lies dormant for
lack of capital and transportation facilities."[5] Horace's skill
and luck wove no special magic in this part of Nevada, nor
did they produce any financial returns, even though mining
at the Day continued spasmodically for the rest of the decade.

He operated on a larger scale in New Mexico, a territory
long known to have mineral deposits, though it lagged behind
its neighbors. Ignorance of mineral riches was the reason,
wrote Governor Lew Wallace, while a successor thought more

prospecting needed to be done and more reduction works constructed. "Mining men feel confident, and I concur with them, that in a very few years New Mexico will stand in the front rank for mineral productions." [6] Tabor agreed, turning his attention to the Territory's southern part at Lake Valley, which came into its own as a mining district in 1881–1882. Near the mines a collection of buildings, scattered across the sparsely vegetated desert floor, surrounded by low rolling hills, signaled a community's start — a bleak setting, not enhanced by the continued Apache menace. The coming of the railroad spurred development, which was spearheaded by the Sierra Grande Mining Company. Unfortunately, it was another George D. Roberts speculation. Tabor joined John E. Wurtzebach, German-born metallurgist and mine owner from Denver, in constructing a sampling works for Roberts's mine. Although Wurtzebach and Tabor were supposed to have the exclusive privilege of purchasing ores, Roberts backed out, which resulted in Tabor and Wurtzebach suing for $100,000 damages, based on the contention that $25,000 had been lost in constructing the works. The case was settled out of court two years later. Embarrassingly, Tabor owned stock in the Sierra Company.

Such an inauspicious start failed to dampen Tabor's enthusiasm. He traveled to New Mexico for the opening of the sampling works and took the opportunity to examine the area, promptly bonding the Iron King and purchasing controlling interest in the Montezuma Mine near Las Vegas. In September 1882 Lou Leonard and his young wife came down to visit these and Tabor's newest mines, the recently-bonded Solitaire and St. Clair, located northwest of Lake Valley, near Hillsboro. A second Comstock, "only richer," proclaimed a telegram to Denver. Horace modestly remarked in his imperturbable manner, "Yes it looks as though I was going to make a strike." To further his interests he purchased shares in the Solid Silver Mining Company. The Solitaire and St. Clair remained the most promising; despite some trouble over title, Tabor and his partner in this venture, Wurtzebach, gained control.

A strange silence fell over his operations in 1883, with no mention of new discoveries or working of his New Mexico mines reaching the papers. By 1884 he obviously was no longer operating the properties, because he had a lawyer trying to evict squatters from them. Not particularly enamored with his assignment, the lawyer wrote Tabor, "If you can imagine anything more miserable than sitting in Lake Valley waiting for a paper I can't." [7]

Tabor's New Mexico ventures failed — and failed miserably. The reason was not too hard to uncover. Two visitors to his Solitaire and St. Clair mines had come away with the same opinion: pockets of rich silver ore had been found on the surface, but there was no indication of a permanent vein. One concluded that it had been worked out and was "not worth twenty-five cents." Apparently, Tabor had not found any ore after he took over. To complicate the picture further, the district's ore proved hard to smelt, and throughout these years there was no smelter available to handle it. [8] Tabor certainly must have examined these properties and been deceived by surface indications; beyond this he had relied too much on other men's opinions. For an experienced mining man this showed poor judgment. It should be remembered, however, that the gambling nature which characterized Horace's activities here had paid off handsomely before; he could not be faulted for having tried. In another speculative Wurtzebach-inspired New Mexico venture, Tabor was one of the directors of the Los Cerrillos Mining Reduction Company, which was supposed to have operated out of Santa Fe in the Los Cerrillos district. What, if anything, came of it is unknown.

Tabor's Nevada and New Mexico investments pivoted on mines which had shown paying ore from the "grass roots." The Day, Solitaire, and St. Clair, all pocket rather than vein mines, could produce sudden bonanzas, seldom a steady income. Too much barren rock separated ore pockets, and the mining costs did not lessen as Tabor probed farther. The gamble on this type of mine was decidedly greater than with the Matchless, for example, which followed a generally pronounced vein. Tabor's misfortune was entering into the game after the best-paying ore had been removed, and, of the three, only the Day had had much development connected with it. The Leadville tactic, inducing outside capital to invest in marginal mines, had been neatly reversed, Horace this time holding the bag.

Mexico caught Tabor's eye for the first of several investments that kept him involved there for the next fifteen years. Under the guidance of Porfirio Diaz, Mexico had become an enticing area for American mining investors, with its low taxes and liberal mining laws. The northern Mexican states of Sonora and Chihuahua, and the long narrow Sinaloa bordering the Gulf of California, emerged as early favorites. Tabor chose none of these but went to the more southerly state of Michoacan for his initial plunge. The *Mining Record* strongly opposed Americans turning south when such excellent opportunities still beckoned at home; in an editorial on July 2, 1881, the editors protested heatedly against "essaying any wild casts of the net for fortune among the mountains of Mexico." Americans refused to heed, going into Mexico in steadily increasing numbers throughout the 1880s.

Tabor's tentative venture was without question strictly a promotional effort, gambling on undeveloped mines and claims under the name of Michoacan Syndicate. Within forty miles of Morelia, the state's capital, the Syndicate merged thirty gold and silver "mines," all productive, or so proclaimed a promotional pamphlet, which also promised dividends in the near future. Mining engineer William Denton, who had spent twenty-five years in Mexico, presented the scheme to Mexican and American investors and these optimistic forecasts were based primarily on his reports. The fascinating lure of Mexico's already famed mineral wealth, combined with Denton's statement that these rich properties had just barely been opened, was supposed to lead potential investors to the conclusion that riches were theirs by merely buying stock.

An impressive group of men (probably mere window dressing) was included in the prospectus. Tabor was president; other officers were Massachusetts's Benjamin F. Butler; Thomas Jordan, editor of the *Mining Record*; Louis Janin, well-known mining engineer; John P. Jones, Nevada senator; and other American businessmen, plus a group of prominent Mexicans. On the surface it all looked sound, and the Syndicate, with headquarters at New York and Morelia, set out to attract money by issuing extremely promising reports during the winter of 1881–1882. Large shipments of machinery were forwarded and back came exultant reports of high assay returns.[9] When spring came, reports stopped, and nothing more was heard of the Michoacan Syndicate.

Several things may have happened. For one thing, there were few takers. Conceivably, the public had not been so gullible following the Little Pittsburg, Chrysolite, and Hibernia debacles, for there were men associated with these in the Syndicate who were becoming notorious in mining circles. Moreover, Americans were not yet ready to invest in Mexican mines, since they were certainly unknown commodities on the market. Additionally, the United States, after several prosperous years, slipped into a slight recession and the money market tightened. Without question, the organizers found that returns would not justify the expense of their own continued operations; rather than spending more, they simply dropped the whole project. Tabor probably was not overly active in this scheme and again was useful for his name as well as his money. How much he might have lost is problematical, but certainly less than in New Mexico. By associating himself with this and other similar enterprises, Horace unwisely continued undermining his reputation, whether he chose to recognize it or not. The opportunity to be involved in such a grand undertaking with well-known people was apparently irresistible. Back in Oro City days he could not have imagined such opportunities unfolding for him, even in his wildest dreams.

Mining anywhere could not succeed without its twin allies, cheap and reliable transportation and reduction works, a fact that had been repeatedly driven home to Tabor since the early seventies. With his investing appetite unsatiated, Horace leaped into the smelting industry in 1879 with John Wurtzebach and others, organizing the Smelters' Supply Company in the carbonate camp. This proved much too tame; the next year Horace incorporated the Tabor Milling Company and set about to build a mill at Leadville, a stamp mill, since the camp already had an abundance of smelters. He selected Peter McCann, an experienced Georgetown millman, to take charge of it; he was joined by the knowledgeable smelter owners, James Grant, Edward Eddy, and William James as partners. With his usual abandon Tabor pulled out all the stops, sending McCann to Chicago for equipment, selecting a site on the Carbonate Hill slope facing California Gulch, and letting his building contracts. The idea of the mill was sound enough: to treat low-grade silver ore and especially gold, which was still being mined in the area. The old smelters were not equipped to handle it. The mill opened in November 1880, launched auspiciously with contracts from the Matchless and Robert E. Lee.[10]

Once started, daily routine replaced enthusiasm. The Tabor Mill also found itself up against ruthless competition, not only from local smelters but also from those in Pueblo, Denver, and even Utah, which offered special advantages to offset added transportation costs. Samuel Emmons observed in his famous Leadville study that ore-buying there was somewhat different from the practice in other camps, in that ore was purchased outright from the mines for cash, with deductions made for loss of silver and treatment cost. This meant that McCann, as superintendent, needed to be as economical as possible and a sharp buyer in order to survive, since his operation was one of the smaller ones.

The Tabor Mill, though soundly constructed and having first-class machinery, never challenged its bigger, established rivals in production, ranking eleventh out of sixteen Leadville mills at the end of 1881. Tabor was not one to give up even when his partners did. In July 1882, McCann and two others sold out to Tabor, who now owned three-fourths of the business. The new manager Tabor brought in changed the process somewhat and added new equipment. By the close of the year the mill had shipped $280,000 worth of bullion, far behind the leader's $2.3 million, and had lost $31,000 besides. The whole operation ended in May 1883, when the mill burned, never to be rebuilt. The loss, felt the *Leadville Daily Herald*, was a serious one, since there was now no stamp mill in the area. Tabor disagreed, withdrawing completely from the Leadville smelter business. The Tabor Mill failed simply because only a small minority of the ore could be worked better by stamps, not enough to make it profitable. The mill's original $100,000 cost, divided among the partners, had been supplemented by the running expenses and further modifications of machinery, so Tabor had come out in the red.

Other problems had been mounting for the mill as well, particularly over water rights in California Gulch; four other smelting companies had taken the Tabor company to court over water appropriations. The case was pending at the time of the fire. And McCann sued Tabor to collect money he alleged was due him.[11]

Once he got started in the milling business, however, rumors proved self-generating concerning future plans. The press had him building mills at Gladstone and Rico in the San Juans; he considered one at Aspen; and he seriously intended to build an Ashcroft mill when the Tam O'Shanter troubles intervened.

He also helped incorporate the Tabor Mine Company, along with his perpetual partner Bush, Drake DeKay, who had been in on the Chrysolite and Michoacan adventures, and a few others. After buying maps and pamphlets for advertising and fancy stock certificates to sell, the company offered its shares, apparently having in mind raising money and then having the company buy claims in Lake County. The project faltered when sales proved few and the price quickly dipped to only one dollar and stayed there. By September 1881, transactions in Tabor Mine Company stock reached zero, never rallying.[12] It is not inconceivable that the prospectors hired to search for promising claims were somehow tied into this company.

The history of the virtually stillborn Tabor Mine Company epitomized the majority of Tabor's frustrating mining investments during these years — all looked good on paper, only to prove blanks in the mining lottery. Deficits drained the Tabor fortune, raising doubts as to how long it could continue to underwrite his plunging if another bonanza were not uncovered. There is little to explain his actions rationally, except his oft-stated belief that another Little Pittsburg would appear somewhere among his many investments. Encountering for the first time the problems of absentee, out-of-state ownership, previously experienced only from the other side of the fence, Horace found himself trapped, too gullibly and enthusiastically taking the always so freely offered advice. It was hard to recognize the businessman who could proudly say back in 1879, "I attend to all of my business myself." By 1882, everywhere one looked, Tabor speculated wildly, displaying magnificently a flaw in his character that his modest circumstances and Augusta had perhaps kept suppressed. For the time being nothing seemed serious, and Tabor certainly was not worried.

He helped promote the National Mining and Industrial Exposition to display to the United States and the world the minerals and mines of the Rocky Mountain region, especially Colorado. Long considered an excellent way to advertise resources, such exhibits had brought awards to Colorado from the 1867 Paris Exposition and the great Centennial Exposition of 1876 at Philadelphia. Now, rather than going elsewhere, Denver would have its turn.

H. D. Perky, former Nebraska lawyer and recently arrived Coloradan, suggested the idea as early as 1880 to Denver businessmen, finding Tabor and William Loveland most receptive. From the idea's conception two themes emerged: to advertise the entire region, thus overcoming the "prevailing ignorance everywhere," while focusing attention on the sponsoring city, with its central location in the Rocky Mountains. Tabor headed the association organized to direct planning and operation, but the attempt to raise funds in 1881 failed to generate needed public enthusiasm, forcing postponement until 1882.[13]

The Mining and Industrial Exposition Association, as it was called, learned from that premature start, carefully planning its new campaign. With Tabor again president, Loveland as treasurer, and Perky as general manager, a drive was launched to convince the public of the many benefits that would accrue, including removing erroneous impressions, stimulating interest, and introducing capital to investment opportunities. A pamphlet boldly set August 1 for the opening date and advertised classifications of exhibits, covering a broad spectrum from mineralogy to household goods, from art to machinery, and one "catch-all" miscellaneous department.

Something like this was needed in Colorado to help restore confidence in mining after the disastrous year 1880 at Leadville. Very quickly the local press rallied to support the project, assuring publicity. Next, the association's directors purchased forty acres of land on South Broadway for $25,000, for a building site. As the *Tribune* asked on February 8, "But who is to furnish the money?" This had been carefully planned, too; a canvassing committee launched a citywide drive, after dividing Denver into special districts for this purpose. The results were gratifying; $30,000 came in during the first few days and after several weeks the total reached $75,000. Among the big contributors were the Union Pacific ($10,000) and the Denver and Rio Grande ($5,000), both standing to profit from increased tourist travel. Although Tabor and Loveland had reached only part of their intended goal of $200,000, they entered the second phase with renewed confidence. Representatives were sent to all Colorado counties, nearby states and territories, and to New York to sell bonds or solicit outright contributions.

Tabor's favorite architect, William Edbrooke, prepared several sketches for buildings: detailed plans, bids, and the awarding of the contract for $145,000 followed in rapid order. Bond sales, meanwhile, made rapid strides in Colorado and the East, though not without some grumbling. The editor of the *Park County Bulletin*, for example, did not see why his county should be asked to contribute $20,000 for Denver's benefit. Why, the editor mused, had not Denver's wealthy patrons oversubscribed, if it were such a good thing?[14] Tabor had caught the vision, starting with a $10,000 pledge and soon investing over $30,000; Loveland was not far behind.

The first significant public display of progress came on May 2, with the laying of the cornerstone, Horace presiding. Dignitaries, including Pitkin, Loveland, and ex-governors Routt and Evans, joined the festivities, which were highlighted by a parade and appropriate orations. Following the day of congratulations, serious work started on the building; according to plans, it had to be ready to receive exhibits on July 15. The association published its rules and regulations, stating that it would not charge for space or award premiums, as this had "been so freely condemned" at other exhibitions. On May 6, Tabor, Loveland, and other directors signed a promissory note for $20,400 to the county, thereby completing the land purchase. This action elicited praise from the *Rocky Mountain News*, which called it a manifestation of confidence in the success of the project. With great pride the local press advertised the progress of various committees working to gather exhibits. Some trouble arose in neighboring New Mexico, when the governor appointed a commissioner after Tabor had already done so. The misunderstanding was soon resolved and the Territory moved ahead, gathering its specimens. Mutterings were also heard against the Eastern railroads' refusal to give lower excursion rates, but enough time still remained to work out a solution before the grand opening day.[15]

In theory, each Colorado county had its own local committee to secure exhibits and send them to Denver. Pitkin County was typical. The *Rocky Mountain Sun*, an Aspen paper, started in March to promote the Exposition, pointing out how much money Denver had pledged and that Leadville had offered $50,000, admonishing that Pitkin could not afford to be less generous. One J. P. Flynn, a leading citizen of Ashcroft, directed the county's operation, appointing agents to sell bonds and collect exhibits. The paper continued to publicize the Denver events, taking special care to point out that representatives were being sent to Europe to arrange visits of capitalists to the Exposition.

In April, Flynn warned that Pitkin County had no time to spare, and in May the Aspen Opera House hosted a countywide meeting to stimulate lagging response. Flynn's oratory at this meeting convinced the listeners, and the assembled citizenry voted to ask the county commissioners for $600 to cover shipping and building expenses for the exhibit. President Tabor and his associates had no money to help local groups. To promote the county further, it was decided to print a pamphlet for free distribution, necessitating more money, so special entertainments were staged and a general subscription list circulated. Flynn and the *Sun* hustled to meet the opening date and the latter fretted, "You can help and must," otherwise goodbye railroads, farewell smelters. The "good citizens" finally came through, and, when the Exposition opened, Pitkin County was represented by a handsome pavilion not quite completed. All was not as it might have been; a visitor wrote the *Sun* that it was really not as large as some others and was behind in printed matter and photographs, forcing Flynn and the others there to talk "as fast as auctioneers," describing the mining wonders of Aspen, Ashcroft, and the county.[16]

Back in Denver, Tabor, Loveland, and the rest of the management worked just as diligently as Flynn and his committee, ordering posters and folders from Omaha, contracting for water and sewer connections, working with commissioners from other states and territories, securing exhibits, whipping up enthusiasm, keeping the press furnished with publicity, trying to solve complaints over awarding exhibit space, and dealing with a hundred other little problems that surfaced. This multitude of tasks kept them busy as August 1 rapidly approached. Some county organizations failed completely, individual efforts being required to supplement them. After some haggling, the Denver and Rio Grande agreed to special rates for shipping exhibits to Denver; finally, special rates were even secured from New York to Denver. A chronic shortage of funds hampered operations, resulting in the Association's borrowing $40,000 from Denver banks on a ninety-day note, offering as security half of each day's gate receipts.

All these headaches receded as the opening approached. Praise was heaped upon Tabor and his co-workers — those men who had taken the enterprise in its feeble infancy, nourished it, and brought it to this promising fruition. Loveland had replaced Perky, who resigned his position to manage the Circle Real Estate and Railroad Corporation, which passed through one brief moment of prosperity because it connected with the exposition grounds. A little more than a week before the opening, Tabor gave his views as to why he had worked on and invested in what appeared for so long to be a shaky enterprise.

> The fact is, this enterprise has been one very dear to my heart, because I believed it was a project that, successfully carried out, would do more toward bringing Colorado and Denver to the attention of the world at large than any other scheme that could be devised.[17]

A downtown parade, passing through a city dressed in its holiday best, proclaimed the opening, after which the scene shifted to the fairgrounds, where Tabor presided over the inaugural ceremonies. The day's main speaker and one of the noted orators of his era, Pennsylvania congressman William D. "Pig Iron" Kelley, praised the region in oratorical flights of splendor, his remarks concerning making silver equal to gold drawing marked applause. Tabor then took the stage, giving a brief speech, calling the opening "undoubtedly the grandest event that has ever occurred in this great West." We will show here "to the world that the resources of the mines can produce the gold and silver necessary for a great part of the traffic of the world." On behalf of the association Horace then threw the switch, starting the machinery, signifying the exposition's opening. At the exposition baseball grounds, the powerful Leadville Blues blasted the Denver Browns 13–8; however, most people were too excited about visiting the exhibits to stay long at the game.

"Fancy has blossomed into fact, promise ripened into performance," cheered the *News* in praise of the first national mining show attempted in the United States. The Exposition building, its main hall 500 feet long, with four wings jutting out, was thronged with spectators that day. They found the exhibits incomplete, nor would they be completed until three weeks later; nonetheless, it was a worthy show. Some exhibitors were disgruntled over their sites, one Eastern iron firm finding its promised space situated in the middle of a large water tank. Such problems were ironed out, and the exposition went on with varied success until October 1.

Denver's reaction was one of pride in its own role and that of the richness of the surrounding country; much to local delight the respected *New York Times* agreed, in an editorial on August 8. While realizing that, except for New York and Boston, few Eastern manufacturers sent products, distance and cost being the problems, everyone agreed that the exposition still ought to help mining and mining methods. The *Times* pointed out that, while the whole country could not be expected to be stirred, the effect on the Rocky Mountains certainly would be beneficial. And they were absolutely right. The West was excited. Special newspaper editions commemorated the occasion, singing the praises of local resources. Excursion trains brought visitors from all over the region; Colorado counties were honored by special days and the local residents thronged in from each. From the heart of Denver it cost only 5 cents to reach the site by the Circle Railway. For those wishing to drive or ride, Broadway was "Denver's most fashionable driving street." Japanese fireworks brightened the night sky and band concerts, bicycle races, and Ute Indian dances filled the afternoons.

A few slip-ups marred the exposition. California was

unrepresented, thwarted by shipping costs. Nevada had somewhat better luck in its representation, although private citizens paid the expenses. Arizona got its exhibit there, then did not have the money to take it home. Colorado had the best exhibit, but even here the *Mining Record* warned on September 9 about the Freeman Mine exhibit — a property just sold under a miners' lien, without a record as a producer, yet having a very rich specimen on display.[18]

The exposition closed with formal ceremonies, including raffling off some of the mineral specimens, and foot and horse races. The management promised to protect exhibits left for next year's opening, and the Mining and Industrial Exposition of 1882 passed into history. To be honest, it was not an unqualified success, local press comments aside. Attendance increased slowly, errors were made because of inexperience, and complaints rained down on the management about such things as the location, ticket prices, and Sunday openings. Concessionaires were less than happy; one café proprietor lost almost half of his $10,000 investment, and even the ladies of the First Baptist Church, in charge of the ice cream pavilion, ended about a hundred dollars in the red.[19]

Tabor, whose main role had been to work with his numerous business associates to convince them to support the endeavor, received a great deal of praise for his efforts, as did Loveland. The *Leadville Daily Herald* agreed with the Central City *Register-Call* when it said Horace had given time, talent, and money, and more than this he could not do: "he is certainly entitled to great credit for the interest he has manifested in the exposition from the very inception of the great scheme. His is a self-sacrificing disposition, the noblest of all." During the actual operation he remained behind the scenes, taking part in only a few special events, such as planning for the National Institute of Mining Engineers, which held its convention in conjunction with the exposition in August.[20] In 1880 Tabor captured headlines with the Tabor Block, in 1881 with the Opera House, and in 1882 with the exposition; his name was now legendary.

CHAPTER 12

THE GREAT SENATE RACE

Politics are now nothing more than
a means of rising in the world.
Samuel Johnson, 1775

THE TABOR name was legendary, but the Tabor ambition
was not satiated, not with the eternal chase for the prestigious senate seat opening up again. As one wag put it,
as soon as a Colorado man strikes ore which runs over one
hundred ounces, he begins to dream of senatorial honors.
A good mill run was worth more than a good record.[1]

The next senate seat, up for election in January 1883,
belonged to Teller, who wanted another term; not yet having
attained his later eminence in the state, he was vulnerable,
especially with the Hill and Chaffee-Teller split. According
to press rumor, the starting line was getting crowded, with
Pitkin, Hamill, Routt, Thomas Bowen, Judge Moses Hallett,
ex-governor Samuel Elbert, and Tabor jockeying for favorable
starting positions. While the fight that unfolded was not
destined to rank with the greatest, the spectacle of all this
wealth battling for the position fascinated or sickened Coloradans as the stakes rose.

Notwithstanding his intention not to run again, Tabor
saw his name repeatedly mentioned as a prime candidate,
and there was no question that he was interested and willing.
One reason to keep his position strong in Leadville was the
fear, well grounded, that the outlying districts would never
let Denver elect both senators, and Hill already resided there.

Leadville also had more appeal because it was further south, giving Horace a more advantageous position in southern Colorado, which was miffed over not getting a fair share of the spoils. As early as January 1881 the *Leadville Daily Herald* ran a series of articles on possible candidates, saying, on the eighteenth, of one of its co-owners, "I know of no man who had a greater number of qualities entitled to respect. Governor Tabor is an earnest Republican, a careful, thorough worker in party ranks."

Nor did his numerous investments impede his progress, as he well realized, particularly the completion of the Tabor Grand Opera House. Even so, the press attacked, and one reason for his reluctance to commit himself was the realization that he would become a prime target, when and if he made a decision to run. Horace had learned from experience.

> I have made it a rule never to reply to newspaper attacks. While I respect the press and appreciate its power, I believe that the moment replies are made to charges that have no foundation, that moment a controversy arises that is of long duration, and harms more than an explanation does good.[2]

The Colorado situation changed upon the death of Garfield, with whom Hill seemingly had had more influence than Teller. Teller now swept to the forefront. The new president, genial Chester Arthur, did not know it, but he would be destined to play a major role in bringing about what contemporaries considered to be Colorado's greatest senatorial fight, the aftershocks of which would be felt for over a decade.

As 1882 opened, Tabor entered his last year as lieutenant governor, with no apparent ambition for the governor's chair. His chances for a senate seat, a long shot at best, depended on how many of his backers could be elected to the legislature. Now free of all state political desires, he could devote money and time to such a goal. Enough of each was spent to entice those twins of political humor and sarcasm, Dave Day and Eugene Field, into the arena to do battle. Field opened with "Tabor's silence on the political situation is what might be aptly termed tumultuous," while Day returned to an old theme that would not die, "libertine and prostitution."[3] Tabor's worsening matrimonial situation lent some credence to these latter insinuations, and rumors of affairs with other women must have been prevalent or these charges would long ago have been dismissed as fabrications.

The best-laid plans can misfire, and outside circumstances swiftly forced Tabor to plunge ahead faster than he had anticipated to gain the cherished position. President Arthur, after several months in office, decided to reconstruct his cabinet with men amenable to him and his program and offered to Teller the position of Secretary of the Interior, a distinct honor for a state as new as Colorado and for a man who had not yet served a full six-year term as senator.

Colorado Republican political circles were in a frenzy over the choice of his successor, while Teller momentarily hesitated about accepting. With the legislature in recess, the unenviable job of appointing a man to serve until the legislature reconvened fell to Governor Pitkin. Pitkin's choice would hold the office until he was confirmed or rejected by the next legislative session; regardless of this outcome, he would be in a good position to make a run at the full term. The Democratic *Rocky Mountain News* guessed that there were over 150 candidates, with Bowen, Hamill, Routt, Tabor, and Henry Wolcott in the lead and Chaffee, if his health improved, a dark horse. All this did little to console Pitkin, who had his own well-known senate aspirations. A rumor had Pitkin resigning to make Horace governor, who in turn would appoint him to the seat. This was quickly squelched by Tabor, who did not relish advancing a rival so advantageously.

Tabor's men did their best for their candidate, busily going to work creating a clamor for Tabor. The Leadville *Evening Chronicle* called him a man of sound judgment and hard common sense, who had built up Colorado, and petitions were quickly circulated. One massive petition had fifteen thousand signatures when it reached Pitkin's desk, or so Tabor claimed when interviewed. Pitkin remained noncommittal, while statewide pressure was brought to bear on the beleaguered governor by delegations of businessmen from Leadville and Denver. Denver rumors said Pitkin would never appoint Tabor, because he feared him. As if to show this to be baseless, on April 6 Tabor's boosters staged an impromptu carriage parade through Denver. April 6 was also the day that Teller's new appointment was confirmed by the senate, making the race now one of dead earnest.

Delegations from Leadville, headed by Lou Leonard, and other mining districts, one as far away as Rico, swarmed to Denver, all stopping at Tabor's Windsor headquarters to see the "old man" and push his candidacy. Maintaining an outward composure, Horace observed in an interview, "Whether I am appointed or not I shall feel that the hearty and disinterested support given me by my friends will more than compensate me for any disappointment I may suffer." Tabor, sensing his candidacy was not favored by Pitkin, still felt that he was the choice of the majority of the Republicans.

A Tabor reception held at the Windsor on the evening of April 8 climaxed the campaign, with Tabor being eulogized by the master of ceremonies, his old friend from Oro City days, Wolfe Londoner, now a Denver merchant. Tabor uttered a few remarks, boldly striking a new theme: if he failed to secure the appointment, he "[would] be compelled to be a candidate before the next legislature." Pitkin delayed two more days, then made a startling appointment — George Chilcott. Fringe party leader at best, Chilcott, a lawyer and rancher from Pueblo, had often been mentioned for office, only to find the prize eluding him, except for one term as territorial delegate to Congress. From Pitkin's point of view he had chosen wisely: Chilcott was not a real threat for the full-term nomination and the southern legislators would be more receptive to Pitkin's ambition after he had honored one of their own. Londoner snarled that Chilcott "is the weakest man in the state," while Leadville sat in stunned disbelief. Tabor played a cool hand, replying, when asked about taking his defeat so calmly, "Why not? My defeat has not disturbed me in the least and I expect that I could name some men

who feel mighty bad about this business."[4] His public statement notwithstanding, Horace neither forgave his one-time
running mate nor forgot what had happened. The campaign
for the full term commenced on that April 12, with all eyes
focused on the fall legislative election.

Tabor was not the only disappointed office-seeker; Del
Norte's Thomas Bowen, also a recent mining millionaire, had
worked hard with no success. William Byers ventured the
opinion that Tabor initially ran to keep Bowen out; considering
Horace's own genuine interest, this does not seem plausible.
He had just reason to fear this rival's aspirations, however.
The overt threat that the senate seat might become a plaything
of the "Bonanza Kings" aroused Denver's *Inter-Ocean* to warn
the state to be on guard: "Is Colorado to make these qualifications [ability and brains] a secondary consideration, and to
make bonanzas the standard of fitness?"[5]

Such attacks could be ignored; obviously money would
play a paramount role in any race. But Tabor's campaign
received a nearly mortal blow in mid-April when Augusta
sued her husband for "maintenance and support," charging
desertion. The fact that the husband had left the home could
be tolerated, if not accepted, by Victorian sensibilities, but
the charge of nonsupport went beyond the bounds of decency.
Friends of both jumped into the fray, which became a gossip-
monger's dream. Tabor's political fortunes dipped and stag-
gered, rallying just before completely falling.

Augusta demanded $50,000 per year "alimony," although
no suit for divorce was filed, alleging further that Tabor had
repeatedly offered her a portion of his fortune (Augusta
estimated it to be over $9 million), if she would grant a divorce.
This she steadfastly refused to do, though having "ample
cause" for action. Tabor countered, saying he had not refused
to pay her bills, and the court should not grant alimony or
support because no divorce decree had been asked. Following
these initial salvos, each cautiously eyed the other, while the
case dragged on all year, a time-bomb buried beneath Tabor's
political hopes. Both suffered. Augusta's image as the astute

businesswoman was hurt, when she lamely explained that she had invested more than half the money Horace had given her back in 1879 in profitless enterprises. Tabor, in his last answer to the suit, filed in November, denied emphatically that she was destitute, claiming she was worth at least $280,000. But he had transgressed the bounds of propriety in dealing with his wife and in having rumored mistresses, a fact not quickly forgotten, as the seamier side of this domestic squabble was aired.

A fleeting glimpse into this matter can be had in the Tabor vs. Tabor struggle over interests in the Windsor. In an unclear series of moves, Horace used Bush as a front to purchase Augusta's share of the hotel, which she had secured back in December 1880. Bush testified that Tabor wanted her out because she annoyed him; she also annoyed Bush, who wrote Horace, "I do not care a damn what anyone may say I will not stay in partnership with her and work myself to death for her benefit. . . . When I think of the concentrated venom of the woman in her fight against you I damn myself for what I have done for her." A few days later he again wrote, expressing his opinion just as emphatically about "that woman." Augusta, whose plight, regardless of the financial question, arouses sympathy, charged that Bush annoyed her about selling and finally "bulldozed" her into agreeing. Horace, meanwhile, took the best possible public stance when interviewed: "I am a man; Mrs. Tabor is a woman, and the sympathy that may arise out of the case — well, I would rather she received it."[6] More sympathy than the reader may imagine went to Tabor, if the newspaper accounts give an accurate indication of support, but none of this benefited an aspiring candidate.

Without looking back or weighing the significance of the whole affair, Tabor and his bandwagon moved forward. The opposition, with new ammunition to fire, awaited the next move. The summer passed pleasantly enough, except for minor wrestling for position. According to the *News*, Pitkin joined the Hill camp, which promised to support him for the seat. This group then planned to advance Henry Wolcott for governor. Field wielded his pen against the "old man," an increasingly-used nickname for the fifty-one-year-old Tabor, writing that he was in wonderfully fine condition, being able to "run five miles without once wheezing or complaining of his corns." This, the jovial Field reasoned, was of no small importance in the senatorial race. Behind the scenes the candidate moved to line up support on the local level, and he was joined by others. Hill, wanting a friend as junior senator and also realizing that he had to become involved to simplify his task in 1885 by electing a pro-Hill legislature and governor in 1883, jumped in. Chaffee returned to lead his and Teller's forces against the Wolcott bid for the governorship; the old pro managed to cut into Wolcott's early lead and keep him from gaining the necessary majority before the state convention opened.

Horace finally had to take a stand openly, and he joined the Teller-Chaffee crowd, known as the Windmills, originally a derisive term supposedly indicating that group's tendency toward boastfulness. The Argonauts, a term derived from the location of Hill's smelters at Argo near Denver, offered a tentative feeler to Horace, only to be spurned. Generally composed of the party's young bucks, this latter group started as the minority faction, making up for lack of numbers with some bitter infighting. Horace, weighing all the factors, pushed hard with both money and influence, taking a high tone at Ashcroft, stating that he did not want to be senator unless he could obtain the office honorably. Down in Denver, however, in the hard-pressed Windmill councils, his money and political power were pitted against the Wolcott thrust and its threat to his plans. He rushed to Lake County late in August to rally the forces, and Leadville remained loyal. Both sides resorted to bribery in the swing county of Arapahoe, with the Argonauts complaining that Londoner and Tabor visited many of the Denver "workshops and brickyards" buying votes. Despite a claimed expenditure of ten thousand dollars by Tabor, Arapahoe County was lost.

Eugene Field, whose *Denver Tribune* backed the Hill-Wolcott alliance, might have helped this outcome when he pulled off the joke of the campaign by placing this announcement in his paper:

> Hon. WOLFE LONDONER is the friend of the colored people —there's no doubt about that. As an evidence of it, he will to-day, between the hours of 10 a.m. and 5 p.m. distribute watermelons to the colored folks at his well-known place of business . . . All the *darkies* should be there.[7]

The startled Londoner protested heatedly, while at the same time scrambling to produce the watermelons or face an irate electorate.

The Windmills, with the advantages of money, Chaffee, and the staging of the convention in the Tabor Grand Opera House, whose owner distributed passes to pack the gallery, finally carried the convention. Emotion ran high, hisses and cheers intermingled on every speech. Tabor had earnestly supported the winning gubernatorial nominee, Lake County's Ernest Campbell, racing down the aisle when his nomination was assured, cheering "like a mad man." The Republicans, under party chairman Chaffee, now tried to pull everything together for the race. The defeated Argonauts held little hope for such a plan, the embittered *Denver Tribune* lashing out, "Gov. Tabor is so much pleased with himself as a statesman and politician, that he congratulates and shakes hands with himself every fifteen minutes." Tabor, always loyal, expressed the hope that "from now on we will have no 'Argonauts' and no 'Windmills.'"[8]

A united Republican party would have had a tough fight on its hands, because the Democrats nominated one of their strongest and most attractive candidates, Leadville smelterman James B. Grant. But the party was *not* united, a large majority of the Argonauts refusing to forgive and forget. To make matters worse, Campbell did not prove to be an attractive candidate, having a hard time putting down the charge that he was a renegade Democrat. Tabor, absent from Colorado in the first weeks in October, did not play an active role in the campaign until near the end, and then his main task was to keep Leadville in line and help out in Denver. He appeared at a few campaign rallies, contributed generously to the campaign chest, and gave an election-day holiday to his miners at the Tam O'Shanter. Initially predicting a Campbell victory in Lake County, Horace realized by November that the situation was less than rosy. He was correct — Lake County joined the rest of Colorado to produce a Grant victory. In spite of his efforts, which included a rumored fifty thousand dollars spent in Lake County, Tabor's hold on his former home territory slipped further, damaging his chances for the senatorship.[9]

The capture of the legislature by the Republicans was encouraging, although the party split widened as accusations of "scoundrelly and infamous" treachery and selfishness were hurled about with abandon. Dave Day was right when he concluded that the result was a slap at the bossism of Chaffee-Teller-Tabor. Chaffee, more than Tabor, took the brunt of the criticism, finally publishing an open letter justifying his position.[10]

Eugene Field again opened up on Horace, publishing a story which became somewhat standard with reference to Horace's supposed ignorance. According to the account, Pitkin alluded during a speech to meeting Tabor at Philippi, to which Tabor responded that there was not such a place in Colorado.[11] In his own sparkling fashion Field kept the story going throughout the entire campaign. While Philippi might be out, Horace had long since recrossed his senatorial Rubicon into a steadily deteriorating situation. His position in Lake had slipped and the Argonauts had a score to settle with him in Arapahoe County. Nor could he completely trust some of his fellow Windmills. Underneath it all the fuse still smoldered on the marital powder keg.

As the fateful January meeting of the Colorado legislature neared, he could count on his friends, although the Augusta embroilment had weakened some ties. And he had his wealth, a weapon no other candidate could match. Horace's activities widened to Fort Collins and Salida to meet with politicians; he used his rooms in the Windsor as general Denver headquarters. Bush acted throughout as his unofficial campaign manager, primarily responsible for contacting legislators. The *Leadville Daily Herald* editorially bolstered his campaign (he was, after all, one of the stockholders), but pitifully few other papers backed him.

The gaiety of the Christmas-New Year social season abated the anxiety somewhat, but did not stop his campaign. As of January 1, 1883, four major candidates had declared their interest in becoming junior senator. Tabor knew them all, since they were old party acquaintances. William Hamill, making his supreme bid for higher office, hoped for a deadlock, because the bitterness of the recent campaign prevented him from picking up many long overdue pledges of support. Frederick Pitkin, ending his second term as governor, was the choice of many party members and a large percentage of the Republican press. Del Norte's Iowa-born, forty-seven-year-old Thomas Bowen, millionaire from the San Juans, was the third candidate. This Union veteran was a cool operator under pressure. He and Tabor both felt they had a score to settle with Pitkin because of the Chilcott appointment. Pitkin was also the weakest financially, a decided handicap. If book had been placed on the four, Pitkin would have been the sentimental favorite, followed by Tabor, Bowen, and long-shot Hamill.

Behind these came others who hoped, by some miracle, to grab the brass ring after a deadlock eliminated the front runners. Ex-governor John Routt, also Leadville-enriched, led the Republican contingent, while the united Democrats loyally supported Thomas Patterson, whose ghost of a chance was based on a major break and betrayal in Republican ranks. Although far overshadowed by the full senatorial term, Teller's unexpired term of a few weeks still had to be filled, a lesser prize which in fairness should have been given to Chilcott.

In the far corners of the state rumblings of the coming

struggle were felt. Dave Day, with tongue in cheek, listed the going rate to bribe legislators, and, in the same issue of his paper, Day had Chaffee informing Tabor "that his repeated violations of the seventh commandment were against him in the senatorial struggle."[12] Horace should have known what to expect, especially when the long-simmering matrimonial spat exploded during the first week of January, a most unfortunate time.

The tipoff that something was drastically amiss came when Augusta did not receive callers on January 1; the next day she was granted a divorce on the grounds of desertion and nonsupport. In a matter of minutes it was all over for broken-hearted Augusta, who received $300,000 worth of property, although, as she sadly commented, the divorce was "not willingly asked for." Now the whole affair was in the open again, this time permanently settling the question but not silencing speculation, which was rampant. By Victorian standards it was shocking; separation could perhaps be accepted, but never divorce. Terms such as "vulgar" and a "nauseating scandal" were used by the press to describe it. The suddenness and finality caught the public unaware, doing nothing to further Horace's campaign. Tabor's loyal Leadville newspaper played it down and some of his friends even hinted the action was vindictive and revengeful. The timing was atrocious; Augusta had obviously made up her mind in November or early December to take the final action, because Horace was still filing answers to her April action in early November, indicating that the issue was still being debated. Apparently, through Bush, Tabor had desperately tried to persuade Augusta to hold off the suit one more month, even offering $5,000, which never materialized. And so Augusta moved ahead.

Though extremely reluctant to ask for a divorce, Augusta had plenty of justification. Her lawyer, Judge Amos Steck, claimed she knew enough to ruin Tabor forever, especially with regard to his practices with lewd women. The truth of that particular charge is now impossible to determine; probably he had been philandering since the Leadville bonanza days, providing the basis for the comments by Dave Day and others. The final choice, however, had been Augusta's; if she had meant to harm her husband in a way he would long remember, she could not have chosen a better opportunity. Her hurt was deep; no divorce action could remove the suffering Augusta had endured.[13]

During those wintry January days only a hint of the whole story was revealed. One name was linked on several occasions with Horace's, Elizabeth McCourt Doe; when asked if he would like to marry her, he cagily replied, "not saying I wouldn't like to she's a nice lady."[14] For the moment the public generally overlooked this mysterious Mrs. Doe.

Generally overlooked as well were rumors, appearing in late December in Denver, according to reports published in Chicago and New York newspapers, about a Tabor divorce that had been granted in Durango. Unaccountably, only a few Colorado papers picked it up in January, then it seemed to be shunted aside. When queried about it by a *Denver Republican* reporter, Tabor admitted a decree had been granted, but that when Mrs. Tabor objected to some portions of the proceedings and expressed willingness to bring suit herself in Arapahoe County, the matter had been allowed to rest. He flatly denied he had married Mrs. Doe the previous fall. Tabor's lawyer, Lou Rockwell, stated he told Tabor that the Durango divorce was "not worth the paper it was written upon."[15]

Tabor was fortunate that more investigation was not conducted at the moment and that the public did not know how much pressure had been exerted on Augusta to force her to concede. Bush had been busy in these arrangements, as the parties involved eventually admitted. Only a few scraps of paper remain hinting at what happened; in one, Bush wrote Horace, "Jesus Marie what a lucky thing she is so violently tempered."[16] Augusta's temper played into their hands on several occasions, but not before Bush took the full force of her wrath as a scapegoat for his boss.

Part of the reason the scandal faded was because of the political scene in Denver, highlighted by the upcoming inauguration and then the senate race. Tabor's stock was hurt, without question; how much was not yet known. He could consider himself lucky that other news items captured the front page. It is amazing, however, that somebody did not uncover the facts in time to completely sabotage the Tabor senatorial candidacy. Tabor's followers meanwhile looked to their leader for the stance to assume, and he continued as if nothing had happened, with his full attention focused on the legislative meeting.

> Sing a song of caucus,
>   Senatorial pie;
> Six or seven candidates
>   And none of them are high;
> While the caucus wrangles
>   O'er the precious prize,
> Along comes a dark horse
>   And nips it 'fore their eyes![17]

Thus wrote Eugene Field about what contemporaries thought to be the greatest political contest yet staged in Colorado. Political railbirds perched everywhere, offering their wisdom and hunches to all available listeners. Rumors were rampant: Bowen supports Tabor. Pitkin is being hurt by trying to keep Tabor's private affairs before the public. Hill has ordered his paper, the *Republican*, to magnify the Tabor scandal. Tabor's support is growing, shrinking, standing still. Hill is backing both Pitkin and Hamill to stop Tabor. Tabor's cause is hopeless; he is supported only by friends after his money. Tabor, Bowen, and Hamill have made a deal to defeat Pitkin. All signs point to Tabor's election. Tabor's men have been caught attempting to offer bribes for votes.[18] And so they went, through the inauguration, up to the first party caucus on Monday evening, January 15.

Tabor, concluding his last official duties as lieutenant governor, rode in Governor James Grant's inaugural parade. With mixed emotions he brought the legislative session to order; the final event of this phase of his political career took place appropriately enough in the Tabor Grand. The election question overshadowed all else, both for the legislators and the general public. When the fifty-three Republicans met, tension soared, only to come spiraling down with a deadlock; Tabor had sixteen votes, Pitkin twenty-one, Hamill ten, Bowen four, Willard Teller one, with one blank vote. Twenty-seven votes were needed for nomination. The last lap had begun. The next day all candidates were formally nominated in the regular session, with State Senator A. S. Weston, long-time Lake County resident, doing the honors for Horace. In the formal legislative balloting that followed, the caucus lines held. Tabor had to find swing votes from the Republican house members, since his senate votes came only from Lake County's two. In subsequent days the impasse continued, as secrecy cloaked the closed caucuses. After twenty-four ballots the Republicans remained deadlocked; the same was true after the forty-ninth. Speculation about deals and fights was rife, but nowhere could enough votes to elect be uncovered. The legislative situation, in the meantime, grew critical, since the number of days to introduce new bills was limited by statute. As the deadline approached, the fascinating senate scramble went on, no candidate willing to give an inch.

Horace's vote total ranged in the teens through the first few days, while Pitkin's remained in the low twenties. When Tabor's vote total dipped on January 19 and 20, Bowen's shot up, putting him in second place, lending credence to the charge that there had been some type of Tabor-Bowen deal, yet none of the other candidates conceded. The first break came on the twenty-third ballot, when Pitkin faltered and dropped into the teens. Bowen's votes went to Tabor, whose total came tantalizingly close, twenty-four, only to fall back again. No candidate seemed able to accomplish the feat or stampede the voters into a sudden change; the deadlock seemed permanent.[19]

Behind the scenes Tabor and his lieutenants worked furiously to gain the needed votes. To secure such a tempting prize seemed worth any cost. Political ethics and morals were discarded, apparently by all the candidates. Even before the caucus started, Tabor was accused of trying to bribe a Ouray representative, not directly but through a third party. A legislative committee was promptly appointed to look into the charge; it exonerated him. Bowen, who among all the candidates had a marked advantage because he was a legislative member, made the exoneration motion.

As the contest dragged on, the opportunity for outright victory faded, necessitating a shifting of Tabor's strategy to enlisting support as a second choice among some of the other candidates' supporters. Thus, if they dropped out, the votes would swing to the "old man." This might work, except that none of his rivals seemed inclined to remove himself, so possible alternatives were probed. The recent divorce hounded him, as he knew it would, and his support among the general public seemed to be slipping. Crusty Dave Day swore that Tabor's election would be an insult to virtue and intelligence, and he might have been echoing the sentiments of many others. There was simply no way that Tabor, Bush, Weston, and the rest could stop the stories nor measure their real impact. In the betting pools, Tabor became the odds-on favorite the first day, supplanting Pitkin, but there was little satisfaction in the accomplishment. Private betting was heavy throughout, with bets rising and falling on the backer's faith in his respective man in that day's voting.

Some of Tabor's supporters found themselves in hot water with the people back home for their stand. George Sample, representative from Arapahoe, was forced to justify his action by declaring in an open letter that he was not a tool of any faction and felt Tabor was the peer of any man in the running, a man who always proved himself a friend to his constituents. Sample's position is significant because he was a Black. In an election year the Black was important; fortunately, Tabor had been fairly consistent in his support, donating money, among other things. Saguache's Otto Mears, the little Russian-born Jew and San Juan road builder who helped rally Tabor votes in the House, was also in trouble at home but maintained his loyalty.

The informal Tabor-Bowen alliance started to crack by January 22, both sides suspicious that the other had not completely lived up to the bargain. Advocates of each accused the other side of breaking faith. With the alliance showing the strains of individual aspiration and mistrust, Bowen pulled even with Tabor in betting, and, according to "inside" sources, seemed likely to win. Bowen's hometown paper, the *Del Norte Prospector*, did nothing to engender good feeling when it remarked, "Tabor is the only man who shows greater strength in the caucus than open house. This shows that he has a purchased following." This fact of the two different vote totals continually worried Tabor, making him question why some did not have the courage to vote for him openly. Perhaps this reflected the divorce reaction as clearly as anything might.

Desperately, he looked to find new support; having played his cards well so far, Horace felt he could still win the prize, marital problems and all. His reliance on Bowen to stop Pitkin had worked, but now his erstwhile ally seemed bent on outfoxing him by fishing for Hamill support, something Tabor could not hope to gain because of the Hill faction's animosity. Southern Colorado also looked with more favor on Bowen, since, if the "old man" won, Denver would have both senators. In a much-discussed move, Bowen took the floor in a joint legislative session to deny a split with Tabor, protesting that he had given him all the votes he could and was not responsible for others not supporting the agreement. Bowen pointed out, fairly enough, that Tabor had not been able to deliver all his support either, through no fault of his own. Weston answered in a conciliatory manner, but the stories of bad faith and treachery persisted.[20]

Such sidelights failed to mask the fact that time was running out. Desperate men will do rash things, and Tabor had for some days apparently been offering money to secure votes. Bush admitted under oath that he paid out varied sums to undisclosed people to smooth the way. On the seventy-eighth ballot Horace forged ahead of Pitkin, maintaining the lead for the next seventeen ballots, nowhere, though, finding the combination to secure victory.

The end came suddenly. On January 26, after eleven days and ninety-six caucus votes, Bowen gained the needed twenty-seven votes to runner-up Tabor's thirteen. The race had been won, not necessarily by the swiftest, but by the coolest and shiftiest. Into Bowen's camp congratulations flowed, amid toasts and the exultation of victory. "So Fleet the Works of Men, Back to the Earth Again," philosophized the *News*, which saluted Tabor for a gallant fight. With a politician's resignation, the loser expressed himself pleased with Bowen's nomination and greeted pleasantly those people who came to his Windsor suite to offer condolences, though he told a reporter somewhat bitterly that, "This is the last political fight I will ever make for myself."[21] With the few visitors gone, the ex-candidate retired into his inner rooms, a saddened second-place finisher who had fought the hard fight and lost.

Postmortems do little to console losing candidates; nonetheless, they can give insights into the reasons for defeat. The final tally sheets showed that Tabor lost only two votes from the ninety-fifth ballot, while Bowen gained seventeen; Pitkin lost eleven, Hamill two, and Willard Teller and John Routt one each. Apparently, one of two things had happened: either Pitkin and Bowen made some kind of an agreement (rumored, never proven), or Pitkin's supporters, tiring of the protracted contest, decided Bowen was the least objectionable. The ever-faithful *Herald* claimed that the southern legislative members worked out an agreement, and this was indicated when Mears shifted his vote to Bowen, with the amazing comment that he had never been for Tabor entirely. The Argonauts, too, had a score to settle, and all these together apparently tipped the scales.

The charge of a bonanza grab hurt both men, and in the cutthroat battle it must be concluded that Bowen and his aides proved best at playing bluff and bargain. And, finally, there was that personal issue with its still unanswered questions, which haunted Tabor for the entire race.[22]

The primary reward taken, Horace was tendered the remaining thirty days of Teller's unexpired term, "like drawing for the capital prize and walking away with a Chromo," observed the *News*, disparagingly referring to the cheap prize of so many raffles. He could have turned it down, but that was not his nature. Not wanting to offend Tabor further and perhaps as a way to cancel past political debts cheaply, the party offered him the honor. Chilcott was sacrificed to a greater need, certainly indicating that any Bowen-Pitkin alliance had been rather weak. Senator-elect Bowen called for harmony in his acceptance speech, while Horace, in a personally revealing, short address, told the assembled legislators,

> You have seen fit to favor me with an election to the short term — the baby-term — which is for only thirty days. It is not always that one who goes in for the big prize is put off with one seventy-second part of it as I have been, yet I am very thankful, and am satisfied, especially as you have secured a very capable gentleman for the long term. As I will be in Washington but thirty days I will be able to be of but little service, but I shall do what I can and I shall take especial pains to commend the state to the kind consideration of the president.[23]

Though the assembled listeners could not have known it, those thirty days were going to be more newsworthy than Bowen's entire six years. The closing word on the past month's happenings came from Augusta, who wrote to her ex-husband on January 31, their twenty-sixth wedding anniversary. She sadly misjudged Horace here, as she had done earlier:

> Now you have had the honors of senateship which you deserted me for. And when your month is [up?] come home and let us live in harmony. As I will come to you. There is no need of having our case draged [sic] through court again. And as I am your wife I shall stand upon my rights. . . . Therefore I subscribe myself your loveing [sic] wife.[24]

Augusta would never have the chance to carry out her forlorn attempt at reconciliation.

CHAPTER 13

FOR THE LOVE OF BABY DOE

I do not like very much the office of senator but the
honors are great. They are next to the President.

Tabor to Elizabeth M. Doe, February 20, 1883

ON FEBRUARY 2, 1883, Senator Horace A. W. Tabor took
the oath and assumed his seat in the forty-seventh congress. Presiding over the session was Illinois' David
Davis, president *pro tem*, while in the White House Chester
Arthur was well into his second year of office. The senate's
membership, though not outstanding, included a few bright
lights, but Horace's brief term allowed only a speaking
acquaintance with a few of his senate colleagues.

Even with the briefness of the term, he was determined
to do his best for his state, and his attendance record reflected
this intention. Of the twenty-six days the senate met, Senator
Tabor was in his seat and answering roll call 80 percent of
the time. Senator Hill's percentage was just slightly better.
The junior Colorado senator filled vacancies on two committees, one on pensions and claims and the other a select committee to investigate and report on the best means of preventing the introduction and spread of epidemic disease. Regardless of appointments and attendance, a thirty-day senator
has no prestige or power on the floor and, consequently,
can do little but listen. The majority of the time, Tabor voted
the regular party stand on issues being debated during the
session's closing weeks. He could not have had the hours,
for example, to study the complex tariff measures, which
took up so much time and were so dull to all except interested

parties. On Tuesday, February 20, Horace presented his maiden resolution, a pension request from committee to the senate, which was granted, the first of several such actions. This was followed in the session's last week by his introduction of two bills, both of which were referred to the appropriations committee. One was of strictly local interest, the establishment of a military post in western Colorado, while the other was for the protection, promotion, preservation, and extension of the forests of the United States. The reason for the sudden interest in forests remains a mystery; in any case, the committee reported neither bill out during Tabor's term. Of more personal interest, Horace asked for government participation in the coming National Mining and Industrial Exposition; again, it was referred to committee. His last act was to present the credentials of his successor, Thomas Bowen.[1]

Socially, he had been more active, giving an elaborate dinner party for President Arthur and a few selected guests. In a room filled with flowers, Horace hosted the president with the best wine and food he could secure. He was completely satisfied, writing, "it was a grand, grand dinner." The *Washington Post* of February 26 described the dinner as one of the finest of the congressional session.

The results of his term proved meager, as he realized they would, but he had done all he could. He might have upheld Colorado's silver and lead interests, since the House at the time was having a running feud over the silver question, but the august senate refrained from such bickering, staying with the tariff. Worrying over a few patronage positions and mending a few local fences was about the extent of his efforts.[2]

While his abridged senatorial term winged past, Eugene Field beguiled the *Tribune* readers with hilarious accounts of the senator's "exploits." A few selections will suffice to show Field at his finest during his last months as associate editor. Many Coloradans enjoyed a hearty laugh at the bedeviled Tabor's expense, as Field's articles were picked up by newspapers throughout the state.

226

When Horace took his seat, the *Tribune* carried a very detailed account of the rare occasion, listing the prominent gentlemen and ladies who came to lionize the new senator, who promptly took the floor, delivering what was reported to be the most eloquent congressional speech since the days of Webster and Clay. On another occasion, the *Tribune* had Tabor holding the senate "at bay for three hours," while "gems of peroration flowed" with his "imagery and his fanciful flights of oratory, as well as his superb elocution, commanding breathless attention and eliciting the heartiest applause." When his term ended, flags were hung at half mast, and "it seemed as if the whole nation rose up as one man and bewailed the hour in which the patriot and statesman quitted the scenes of his labors and triumphs." One of Field's fabrications, Horace's "gorgeous velvet nightcap" and two hundred and fifty dollar ruffled nightshirt even attained the "distinguished" honor of being considered factual.[3]

Defense against this onslaught was useless, and Tabor rode out the storm in silence. Anyhow, he managed to upstage and outdo even Field's best by announcing his remarriage on March 1, amid circumstances even Field would have been hard pressed to conjure.

It was not just the fact that he remarried that stunned Coloradans, but she whom he took as his new wife. The love-struck senator of fifty-two married Elizabeth McCourt Doe, a twenty-eight-year-old grass widow. Born the year before Horace had traveled to Kansas, she came to Colorado with her first husband, William H. Doe, whom she divorced in 1880 after three years of marriage. In Central City, where they lived, she acquired the nickname "Baby Doe" and local fame as one of Colorado's most attractive women. Her devoted second husband later wrote, "My wife is blond and has a very fine profile." Add to this description youth, vivaciousness, and a flattering tongue, and one can imagine why Horace was smitten. Her pictures show the petite Baby Doe to have been slightly plump, as was stylish, with ringlets of blond hair framing an attractive face. This charmer had come west from Oshkosh, Wisconsin, trailing a hometown reputation of showing both a taste for masculine flattery and a trace of exhibitionism in flaunting her beauty and figure. Women did not like "Lizzie," even before the Tabor scandal.[4] After her divorce her activities are somewhat clouded. Eventually she met Horace, the two reached a mutual agreement, and an affair blossomed and deepened. This affair had been the one which pushed the infatuated suitor to pressure Augusta for a divorce. There had been other men in Baby Doe's life, though as far as is known she proved faithful to Horace once the two became permanently involved.

Horace had fallen head over heels in love. Revealingly, he showed his feelings in the letters sent to his "Darling Babe"; in truth, he sounded more like a gay, young blade in his first courtship than a mature mining man and senator.

> It is sweet my darling babe to write you but it would be very much pleasanter if I could be with you and be under the sweet influence of your smiles and loving self. . . . My darling I love you with all my heart and do so feel rejoiced that you love me as you do, you do love me I know. . . . Your loving boy With kisses (Feb. 18, 1883)
>
> My darling little girl I do so want to see you it seems an age since I saw you last. . . . What if we never had met? This world would have been a blank to me and I think it would have been cloudy to you. (Feb. 20)
>
> I love you to death and we will be so happy. Nothing shall mar our happiness for you are all my very own and I am yours from hair to toes and back again. I love you I love you Kiss Kiss for ever and ever . . . (Feb. 23)[5]

A love-struck youth could have done no better or worse. He signed the last quoted with love and kisses alternating at the bottom of the page. Infatuated, he did not fully consider the ramifications of the step he was about to take; he intended this marriage to be the crowning success of his career.

The wedding was the most lavish money could buy, far surpassing the elaborate Washington dinner party. They were married by a Catholic priest, with a star-studded congregation watching, in the magnificently decorated private parlors of the Willard Hotel, Washington's finest. The groom could have given his new bride little more. President Arthur was in attendance, along with Thomas Bowen, Jerome Chaffee, Henry Teller, the Colorado congressional delegation, Maxey Tabor, William Bush, and the McCourt family. Among the gifts the husband showered on his new wife was a $75,000 diamond necklace. President Arthur paid particular attention to the "vivacious and entertaining" bride and just before leaving, requested and received a rose from her bouquet. An "elegant" supper followed the ceremony. As Horace had written just a few days before:

> Now comes the crowning event of my life domestically and that is my marriage to the woman I love and love to death. Ah babe you are all mine mine forever. . . . It seems almost as if it is too much happiness for mortals but it belongs to us We give ourselves to one another and whose business is it We do not rob anybody of anything that belongs to them. . . . You say you will be happy to go when I go and come when I come well that shall be.[6]

Horace was wrong: it became many people's business, and the occasion proved to be national front-page gossip for weeks afterward.

Henry Teller, who had watched Tabor's political fortunes for the past four years, summed up his reaction frankly,

> Tabor has gone home, I thank God he was not elected for six years; Thirty days nearly killed us, I humiliated myself to attend his wedding because he was a senator from Colorado (but Mrs. Teller would not). I felt as if I could not afford to say that the State had sent a man to represent her in the Senate, that I would not recognize socially, but I could not have kept it up. . . . Tabor is an honest man in money affairs, and I believe he is truthful, but he has made a great fool of himself with reference to that woman, and he ought now to retire and attend to his private affairs.[7]

Horace had crossed his personal Rubicon; there could be no turning back, though the warm glow of the wedding masked such thoughts as the happy bride and groom bade their guests good night.

The newlyweds' marital tranquility was quickly shattered, as story after story rippled out from Washington and Denver, treating the whole country to one intriguing tidbit after another. The wedding, which had gained nationwide attention, only heightened interest in the new revelations emerging. From everywhere came comments about the senator and his bride, many of them sarcastic and moralizing, damning the Tabors and holding them up as examples to avoid. "Vulgar, shameful, distasteful, scandalous" were but a few of the epithets hurled at them in various Eastern newspapers. Stories Field wrote in jest were swallowed as "gospel truth," strengthening the growing anti-Tabor crowd's biased opinions.

At home his remarriage shunted other conversational topics aside, spurring the gossip hounds to renewed efforts. Augusta's friends rallied to her side and thousands of others sympathized with her plight. Indeed, from reading the press, one would conclude that Horace should never again seek political or any other honor from the state on which he had so generously bestowed his money. Few rallied to his defense. The faithful *Leadville Daily Herald* stood by him, concluding that it was a positive shame to break in so rudely upon the "honeymoon of a man who had done so many good things."[8]

The revelations which produced the adverse reaction left even his most loyal defenders hard-pressed. First came the announcement by the priest that he had been deceived about the Tabors' past marriages and was thus tricked into performing the ceremony. Obviously, someone had concealed the truth, since the Catholic Church would never have sanctioned such a union. Tabor feebly denied hiding his divorce, saying the topic had never been brought up and that his wife's father had arranged the wedding.

This complication paled, however, when the Durango divorce story finally was investigated. Durango, just about the most remote spot from Denver that Horace could choose still within Colorado, proved an ideal place from which to launch clandestine proceedings. Tabor owned property in the area, which provided perfect cover for traveling to and from without arousing undue comment. The facts of the case are these: the complaint was filed January 28, 1882; a summons served on Augusta was returned as "served on February 7" and a final decree was granted by County Judge John F. Hechtman on March 24. The plaintiff appeared in court but not the defendant or her lawyers. All this is on record in the La Plata County courthouse, except the actual complaint and other pertinent items, which are missing and were last heard to be in the possession of Tabor's attorney, Lewis Rockwell.[9]

Without question the entire proceedings were accomplished in the quietest possible manner. Tabor was definitely in Durango on March 24 and probably on January 28, since he was there in early February. Augusta, however, stoutly maintained that no summons was ever given her, while Bush wrote to Tabor, "I think she thought when the papers were served that you were trying to frighten her." This latter, unfortunately, is only an undated scrap of paper, seeming to indicate that some action was taken, because Tabor had very few papers served on his wife. As previously mentioned, Rockwell doubted the legality of the divorce. Bush later testified under oath that he lied about the summons, only to have Tabor testify that he did not employ Bush on the divorce matter and that Bush did not know about it. The grounds for these strange divorce proceedings were, according to Augusta, "every crime" except drunkenness, and according to rumor, adultery was one of them, too. No evidence supports this latter rumor, although it appears likely to have been one of the charges in the missing complaint.[10]

Augusta had filed for alimony in April 1882, a highly unusual move unless the Durango divorce was in the offing; in such a case, she would have been well within her rights; yet no mention was made of it by her lawyers. Tabor might never have intended this action as final, but rather as just a way to scare Augusta into action, because his desertion would have been better grounds than unfounded scandals involving adultery. It would be interesting to know when Rockwell warned that the divorce was fraudulent, when Bush swore the summons had been served, and why Augusta picked April 1882 and January 1883 to take action against her husband. Intriguing as the possibilities might be, they belong to the realm of speculation.

Denver was abuzz with stories, none more sensational than that Tabor had secretly married Baby Doe in September 1882 in St. Louis. The *Tribune* and *Rocky Mountain News* accused Tabor of this, while William Bush denied emphatically that a private wedding had been performed. Privately, he then reconsidered writing the senator that his uniform answer would be, "I don't know." The rest of the participants wisely remained in seclusion.

The facts were these, as gathered by the press: Tabor had been married to Elizabeth McCourt in St. Louis on September 30, by Justice of the Peace John Young in the law offices of D. P. Dyer, an old Tabor acquaintance. For obvious reasons the ceremony was kept secret. In the rush of events of 1883 this exposé was generally ignored or doubted, but it was true. They had taken out an "Application for License to Marry" and a marriage license, the latter returned signed by Young on September 30, after the wedding. Tabor perjured himself by signing on the application a statement reading, "that we are both single and unmarried, and may lawfully contract and be joined in marriage."[11]

This little affair raised a myriad of questions. If the Durango divorce was invalid, Horace was guilty of bigamy. One can only guess why these two took such a deadly gamble, considering what a revelation of it would do to Tabor's career. By waiting, they could have secured all they wanted and in the meantime would not have had to forgo the pleasure of each other's company. Several possible answers emerge. Looking ahead to a church wedding, they may have nonetheless deemed it prudent to have this safety factor (a civil marriage), just in case the Catholic Church discovered their previous marriages. This seems implausible. Perhaps Baby Doe thought herself pregnant, and Tabor felt he needed to legitimize the affair. If so, something went amiss. The most likely probability is that they thought the Durango divorce was legitimate and acted accordingly, although this leaves the question of the secrecy unanswered.

All these matters might not have been aired publicly, had it not been for the remarriage *and* the second Tabor sensation of the year, his split with his right-hand man, William Bush. Coloradans watched the dirty Tabor linen aired all over again, learning new sensational items all the while.

Affable, forty-two-year-old Bush had arrived in Colorado in 1871, quickly becoming a noted hotel operator. His rise to prominence came with his move to Leadville, where he hitched his star to Tabor's until April 1883, when the falling-out occurred. Many reasons were advanced for the split. Eugene Field blamed it on the fact that Bush would not allow his family to call on Baby Doe; Bush's brother Jim concurred to the point of stating that Mrs. Bush would not call. Another version was that Baby Doe had it in for him because of some slight from their Central City days, or perhaps she wanted to remove him to make room for her much-loved and handsome brother, Peter McCourt. McCourt, who would eventually become Tabor's trusted aide, complained that Bush threatened him to make Tabor let up or Bush would ruin his sister. Tabor accused Bush of embezzling $2,000 from the Tabor Grand, which he heatedly denied, telling Horace what he thought of this "in a pretty warm manner." Also, Bush owed Tabor money, which he apparently was slow in repaying. It is quite possible, too, that Horace was having second thoughts about Bush's handling of the divorce matters.[12]

During the spring and summer each principal participant sued for alleged sums owed. Some of Bush's accusations were startling: $5,000 to help Tabor become senator, $10,000 to search out testimony against Augusta, and $75,000 damages for malicious prosecution in the embezzlement case in which Bush had been found innocent. Tabor countered: $10,000 in stock losses, $10,000 in loans, plus other miscellaneous matters, for a total of $25,000 plus interest. Further excitement was generated when the senator asked for police protection against threats by Bush and his brother. Each new charge stimulated interest, finally moving even the *Tribune* to admonish street-corner gossips about "dragging in a woman."

The Tabor vs. Bush suit came to trial October 26, 1883, after Bush's lawyers failed in a move to discharge the case. High-powered lawyers sat in each corner, Lewis Rockwell and Thomas Patterson for Tabor and sarcastic Willard Teller and Edward Wolcott for Bush. The testimony provides one of the best glimpses of the Tabor business empire (it has been utilized repeatedly throughout past chapters); it was not to hear news of business transactions, though, that people crowded the courtroom. The listeners witnessed both humor and pathos in the days that followed.

Each side painted the other as black as possible, yet it was impossible to hide the fact that Bush and Tabor had worked closely together in many legitimate activities and were involved in some deals that morally, if not ethically, were questionable. Both contingents presented their cases, sometimes quite passionately, and it is hard at this late date to completely separate truth from mere accusation. Ed Wolcott observed that there was contradiction on nearly all points and that somebody was therefore guilty of perjury. The case continued to November 2, providing a fascinating peek at Tabor's personal life and business.

Augusta, taking the stand in an emotion-charged appearance, started to tell about the Tabor divorce, when Rockwell objected and the court upheld, refusing to let her testify as to what occurred between husband and wife before they were divorced. Horace walked in and Augusta "sat and looked" at him, while he turned his chair so as to face the jury and wall. She objected strongly to not being able to "tell the story" and then left.

Bush testified regarding numerous matters involving their transactions and the Tabor marital problems. In his estimation, the event which led to their final break had been the accusation of fraud, but it seems that the whole matter must certainly have been building before that. Tabor took the stand to agree on a few particulars, disagree on more occasions, and contradict Bush on numerous points, including refutation of the claim that Bush had been employed to contact Mrs. Tabor relative to a divorce. Each lawyer sought to strengthen his client's case. Owing to the amusement caused by some of the tilts between sides, it proved difficult to keep order. Even the fashion-conscious were fed tidbits, including that Tabor had not yet stopped wearing his low-cut summer shoes.

Tabor listened attentively to all testimony, often leaning over to confer with his lawyers on disputed points. He saw almost all his actions of the past four years reviewed in some form.[13] He and Bush both probably colored their testimony to suit their cases and each must have lied on certain points.

On November 2, lawyers for each side presented closing summations. Though the case revolved around money matters and business transactions, it was really Horace Tabor himself who stood on trial that day.

Don't you believe that Tabor would offer $10,000 for getting the divorce? Do you think a man who would go down to La Plata county and corrupt the judiciary; . . . who would manufacture evidence against an innocent woman he had lived with for twenty-five years, who had the desire he had to get that divorce . . . do you suppose such a man, and a man who was worth eight or nine millions of dollars would hesitate to pay the paltry sum of $10,000 to succeed in his purpose? (Teller)

So far as Mr. Tabor is concerned he is not my idea of what a man should be. . . . His faults are before the public. . . . Mr. Tabor, in place of being the black villain that he is painted — whilst he has weaknesses, whilst he has been guilty of error . . . he has always paid his debts, he has never been accused of lying, he has been liberal to a fault . . . he has built monuments in the capital city of our beautiful state, in which we all take pride. . . . The memory of Mr. Tabor himself will remain with his good works and his bad. (Patterson)[14]

The verdict now was in the hands of the jury — and the general public as well. An elated Tabor won a judgment of $19,958, which Bush hastily appealed. Several Denver newspapers hailed it as a popular verdict. The *Leadville Daily Herald* of November 4 said that this undercurrent of sympathy for Tabor was curious, because the people did not approve of his divorce or his senatorial aspirations. For some reason, though, they still wished him well and were always glad of his good luck. The long litigation finally was brought to an end in December 1885, when Horace agreed to settle for $19,000 and Bush, who had not been having much success in his appeal, conceded.

During the trial a *Denver Republican* reporter interviewed Augusta at home, publishing her comments under the somewhat misleading headline, "She Makes Some Spicy Revelations." Decidedly sentimental in approach, the article came out in the midst of the trial, despite the possibility of creating adverse publicity for Tabor. The scene and the theme were set when the reporter pictured the "general air of loneliness about the place which is not dispelled by the cordial greeting of the sad-faced woman who lives almost alone, a prey to silent reflections." Augusta rehashed some old points about the scandal and the fact that she had not received the summons, commenting that she had been in Leadville the day it was supposed to have been served in Denver. Drained emotionally and physically from all she had had to endure in the past ten months, Augusta stated that she did not consider herself divorced, repudiating her own Denver decree. Amazingly enough, she was contemplating trying to have it set aside; only the cost was holding her back. She was particularly worried about seeing that brood of "hungry cormorants feasting" on what rightfully belonged to Maxey and herself. This slashing attack on the McCourts indicated her bitterness.

Even if the divorce were annulled, Augusta had no illusions that her husband would live with her, but it would "be a great deal of satisfaction to me to know that the woman would be no more to him than she was before he gave her his name and mine." On the new Mrs. Tabor she unleashed her wrath. "She is a blonde, I understand, and paints [uses cosmetics]. Mr. Tabor has changed a great deal. He used to detest women of that kind." She only wanted his money, Augusta judged, and would stay with him as long as he "has got a nickel. . . . She don't want an old man." Her Mr. Tabor had changed a great deal, as Augusta pointedly observed; he was growing old and dyed his hair and moustache to give himself a rejuvenated appearance.[15]

Augusta's role in the Tabor story was completed; she had grown from a young New England woman to the tired, embittered divorcée of 1883. Much of the blame for what happened has to fall on her. Her austerity, coldness, and temper had driven the two far enough apart that new-found wealth snapped the bonds, as Horace climbed to unaccustomed heights, while she, sullenly disapproving, refused to accompany him. A disillusioned Augusta knew she had helped produce the wealth which had borne such bitter fruit. Writing about those long-ago days before the Little Pittsburg, she stated, with a touch of self-justification,

> I feel that in those years of self-sacrifice, hard labor and economy, I laid the foundation to Mr. Tabor's immense wealth; for, had I not staid [sic] with him and worked by his side, he would have been discouraged, returned to his trade, and so lost the opportunity which has since enriched him.

Tabor was also to blame, for he blindly overlooked in his faithful wife the virtues that so long had helped keep the family going, choosing rather to see only the faults. Heartbroken, she lived out the rest of her life in the loneliness of a broken home she had desperately wanted to save. Her friends stood loyally beside her but could offer no more than consolation. The last letter known to pass between the two reflected Augusta's feelings.

> Our son is to be married of Jan. the 17th [1884]. You have promised me that he should be well provided for financially. You also told Rockwell and Steck the same. Now something

237

> has to be done for him. You certainly cannot expect me to help
> him from the penurious mite that I received. So from your
> abundance I entreat you to help him. Your wife A. L. Tabor[16]

She had enough money and property to live well and did,
but all these proved small comfort. This dignified, simple
woman who had shared the long years of toil died in
Pasadena, California, in February 1895.

Between the father and son there was no particular love
in the 1880s, culminating in Horace's acrimonious remark,
"he is no son of mine." Even though Maxey appeared at
the wedding, he generally seems to have sided with his
mother, probably the underlying cause for the lack of rapport.
He never became one of his father's lieutenants, although
late in the seventies he worked closely with him on a few
projects. On his own he did not turn up any really profitable
business enterprises, perhaps indicating a lack of ability.

Out of the shambles of the divorce, remarriage, and the
Bush-Tabor legal wranglings came an amazing resurrection
of Tabor's political career. These events should have spelled
the end of his political ambitions or, at the least, the start
of a long hibernation period. His brother John offered some
sound advice which, unfortunately, went unheeded: "as you
have no very particular interest in this election as I see I
think if I were in your place I would keep away and let them
run it once without your money." The year 1883 was unusual,
full of surprises, none more startling than the Tabor-
for-President proclamation.

The Statesman, a radical independent paper edited by Cornell Jewett, who gained a measure of notoriety for his peace
advocacy during the Civil War, suggested Senator Tabor as
an 1884 presidential possibility for the Republican ticket. A
second George Washington, Jewett called him. "The champion of the working man, a new light for the ranks of the
People." This surprising nomination of "Colorado's honest
Citizen, Banker and Senator, of sterling talent and purity of
character," caught everyone off guard, even Tabor. Although
unembarrassed by consideration for such an honor, he forth-

rightly admitted, "Colorado is not ready yet to have a president . . ."[17] The only logical explanation for this astonishing action is the fact that Tabor and Jewett were connected in planning a national "anti-monopolistic" railroad, one of the latter's pet projects. Neither the presidential boom nor the railroad scheme ever materialized.

In the years that followed, a Tabor campaign banner unfurled almost annually, accompanied by little overt mention of his personal life. The "Grand Old Man," as he fondly became known to his followers, continued to carry some power within Colorado Republican circles, but his success did not improve. Obstinately, he refused to quit, thereby paving the way for one rejection after another.

As early as the fall campaign of 1883, Tabor was in harness, helping in the local elections. He also offered to defray delegate expenses to the 1884 Republican National Convention, if Denver were selected as the site; fortunately for his pocketbook, it was not. The *Leadville Daily Herald* displayed a "Tabor for Governor" banner and was joined by a few others, including A. H. Lacy, editor of Silver Cliff's *Wet Mountain Tribune*, who wrote the senator, "I think, without doubt that in Custer county, among the miners and the people outside of professional politicians that you will find many warm warm supporters . . ." Lacy had spotted the key to Tabor's hopes, which resided with the common people of the mining communities whom he had to carry solidly for any chance of success.

Horace's chances were furthered somewhat in 1884, when both presidential candidates (and particularly Democrat Grover Cleveland) were found to have skeletons in the closet. This made it hard for opponents to poke a finger at Tabor for his marital problems, and the scandals continued to recede. Tabor and his aides worked hard, canvassing county after county to pave the way for Tabor-committed delegates, and his campaign appeared to be generating momentum. Horace traversed much of the state, speaking at rallies in Central City, Pueblo, Denver, and Leadville. He wooed the Black voters by pointing out that they were allowed access to the Tabor Grand, thereby implying that a subtle discrimination existed elsewhere in Denver.[18]

The convention met in Colorado Springs in September, with stories of betrayals and rumors as favorite topics of conversation. Feeling himself in the lead, Horace jubilantly claimed 200 delegate votes, more than enough to win. Nominated as a man "whose heart is large, whose sympathies are universal . . . whose name cannot be disassociated from commercial grandeur and political consideration . . ." Tabor found reality depressing when he received only 104 votes on the first ballot. The victory went to another, "Honest Old Ben" Eaton, a Greeley farmer, on the nineteenth ballot.

The *Herald* wailed betrayal, bossism, and denial of popular will, while R. G. Dill wrote that a Tabor nomination so soon after 1883 was an impossibility. Eaton further represented the end of complete political control by mining interests and the emergence of the eventually dominant agrarian interest, which had long been overlooked in Colorado politics. Too many obstacles had been placed in the "old man's" path. The Republicans swept to victory that fall, limiting Democratic control of the governor's mansion to one term. According to ever-faithful Tabor, this was only natural. "The Republican party has a clean and honest record. It is for protection, for the people's rights and for free homesteads for rich or poor, who wish to become God's husbandmen."[19]

Two years later the state's biennial political excitement flourished again, this time with Horace not actively seeking any elective office. Rather he sought to become chairman of the convention; so did Henry Teller, and a battle was avoided, apparently, by the smooth hand of the master compromiser, William Hamill. Teller, full of honors, was made temporary chairman and Horace permanent chairman, as well as chairman of the Republican State Central Committee. The tempest passed, and Chairman Tabor was left with the responsibility of rallying the party to victory with a ticket headed by William Meyer, who was none too popular. Frank Hall averred that Meyer lacked "the indefinable elements of presence" a popular leader needed. The Hill and Wolcott factions were again at each other's throats, their eyes on Bowen's seat. The Democrats made the situation more difficult by selecting one of their best, Pueblo's young, energetic businessman, Alva Adams.

Horace's selection had been a popular one with the delegates and was generally approved in the Republican press. Lethargy replaced party enthusiasm once the convention hurrahs died away, leaving Tabor to marshal the victory. An example of the type of problem he faced was Boulder County, which felt itself aggrieved because of broken promises for party office. Calmly working to mend this rift, Chairman Tabor found his efforts undermined by a rumor that if county Republicans bolted from the regular ticket, university appropriations would be adversely affected, this institution being the pride of the city of Boulder. A vindictive Republican controlled legislature could do just that. It stirred a hornet's nest of antichairman and antiparty resentment, necessitating Tabor's answering the accusation in an open letter. "Any one knowing me knows that I endorse the liberal and proper use of public moneys toward the maintaining of all of our state institutions, especially those of an education nature." The Republican party, he continued, as one of its strongest platforms, was pledged to build up educational institutions.[20]

Appearing at rallies oozing confidence, coordinating speaking dates, keeping bolters in line, lining up newspapers, and finding money kept Tabor busy throughout the campaign. Money proved especially vexatious. Thomas Wiswall, party campaign treasurer, put the figure at $10,000 out of Tabor's own pocket; a number of people contributed nothing. For the party, it was all worthwhile, as only Meyer went down to defeat out of the thirteen major offices contested, and the Republicans won control of the legislature. Tabor had done well, running a well-managed campaign. Dill complimented him on earnest and thorough work, put in under discouraging circumstances. In Boulder County, where he had worked so hard, Adams won; his work there had succeeded only in keeping the total lower than it might otherwise have been. Several weeks later Horace commented that his sole desire had been for complete success of the Republican ticket, although, "I perhaps shall also always publicly expose those who ought to be grateful to a party and loyal to its cause, yet who secretly stabbed it in the back."[21] He was learning, though slowly, the strategy of a number of Colorado politicians whose only thought was personal advancement, not party, unless the two happened to coincide.

With only caretaker responsibilities until the next election, Chairman Tabor carried out routine responsibilities, picking convention dates and site and selecting delegates to attend the 1888 national convention. Again, however, the spark of ambition for elective office flickered brighter and Tabor set his cap for the governorship.

During the summer of 1888 his campaign jelled, a few papers lining up behind him, and by August the would-be candidate hit the campaign trail. Into the mining regions he went, speaking the words they wanted to hear on silver. "The Grand Old Man — Hon. H. A. W. Tabor — The People's Choice for Governor" was in the race to stay. The convention was held that year in the Tabor Grand Opera House. Tabor leaflets, banners, and campaign biographies bombarded the delegates, as the relentless fight for the nomination drew to a close with Tabor in the lead, trailed by Denver businessman Job Cooper; Tabor's earlier lieutenant, Wolfe Londoner; and Pitkin's one-time secretary of state, Norman Meldrum.

Outsiders thought it looked to be an exciting race, but astute, cynical Otto Mears remarked the nominations "are as good as made." Tabor's assistants, Thomas Wiswall and Peter McCourt, scrambled to round up uncommitted delegates and stimulate enthusiasm, while Tabor hospitably entertained a "constant stream" of visitors in his Windsor headquarters. It was 1878 all over again, though a decade had passed and the feature actor was older. Praised as a "man of the people, the friend of the people" in his nomination speech, Horace led the field on the first ballot with 186 votes, the mining counties producing the majority. With victory in reach, his friends tried to find the few more needed votes, but in vain. His total sank alarmingly on the second ballot and Cooper won on the fifth.[22] The third defeat and last was accomplished; no more cheers, no more campaigns.

The guilty party seems to have been Ed Wolcott, who was running hard for the senate and bargained successfully with Cooper. Wiswall felt that Tabor would have won early if the Wolcott-Cooper faction had not moved to stop him.[23] Ironically, the scene of his greatest triumph was also the site for his last bitter political defeat.

The Colorado Republican Party had selected virtual nonentities to run for governor — Campbell, Eaton, Meyer, and Cooper — who collectively had not done as much for the party or state as Tabor. Perhaps the "old man" carried too heavy a cross after his divorce, or perhaps he failed to realize that times were changing and party machines were the coming thing. Tabor's ambition had carried him far. Probably, if he had not divorced Augusta and remarried, the governorship would have been his. It seems quite likely that he was the people's choice, at least in the mining regions. The party professionals would have none of him; other men were more promising for their immediate plans. His long-time friend, Judge Wilbur Stone, in evaluating Tabor's political career, wrote that he had been "most outrageously and shamefully mistreated, part of the problem being his honesty and fidelity to friends, which had been taken advantage of by unscrupulous politicians."[24]

One more forlorn gesture was made. Tabor allowed his name to be submitted against Wolcott, but smooth Ed had the contest sewed up before Horace drew a deep breath. With the emergence of Wolcott, and Teller's reelection in 1885, an alliance emerged which kept control of the senate seats past the turn of the century. For ten years, Tabor had been a major figure in the Republican party. Now younger men took over. The old guard, except for redoubtable Teller and a bare handful of others, was gone. So were ten years of effort and hope and uncounted thousands of dollars. One wonders if he remembered that wise advice he uttered back in November 1879 but, regrettably, did not follow: "I desire no official position in or out of Colorado, and there is not one I seek or *would accept*. . . . If I go into politics I must spend money instead of making it, and this is what I am not going to do."

Not only was he not making money as he once had, but his investments were becoming more speculative, more marginal, and his operations more careless. For example, he purchased one hundred shares of the Denver Circle Real Estate Company, which intended to open a subdivision. He finally had to go to court to get his shares, testifying that he never attended a company meeting, nor even knew the company was struggling for existence. Equally foolish were his flyers in life and fire insurance. In the risky realm of fire insurance he organized the Tabor Fire Insurance Company in 1881 by purchasing the Colorado Fire Insurance Company. Tabor's knowledge of this intricate business was nil, except for a layman's comprehension of fire danger. Yet he served as president and on the board. Within a year the company faced several lawsuits and finally ceased doing business. According to newspaper accounts, the company, although well patronized (indeed, too well), dissolved because of the danger of a major conflagration in Denver, where nearly all of its policyholders resided. Such a catastrophe would bankrupt the company and "showed the directors that to continue taking risks would be to inspire a false confidence in property holders, with a prospect of final ruin. The chief mover in the dissolution was Governor Tabor."[25] This had been the first major organization bearing the Tabor name to fall by the wayside, one of the first real cracks to appear in the Tabor empire. Still, Tabor raced recklessly onward, trusting his own luck and providence to pull him through.

He became associated with the Great West Mutual Aid Association, which had a longer, though hardly more distinguished, career. Its plan was to insure "first class risks" in the "healthy belt," defined as the Great Plains (excluding unhealthy Texas and Oklahoma), the Rocky Mountains and the Pacific Coast states. Among the innovations it tried were hiring women agents and including miners in coverage without extra charge, an occupation most companies refused to consider for obvious reasons. Tabor's role in this apparently wonderful plan was to sit on the board of trustees, along with William Loveland and George Fryer. The Association struggled along without noticeable success; in at least one case a beneficiary's lawyer wrote Tabor urging him to see that the Great West Mutual paid its promised benefits.[26]

By the mid-1880s, Tabor had come face to face with the realization that success can breed disillusionment. Politically, financially, and even in mining, his initial achievements had been nearly or partially negated. Only in his personal life, and there only after scandal-ridden 1883, had he achieved the happiness and pleasure he sought.

Gov. Frederick Pitkin (front center), Tabor (front left), and State Officials, 1879. *State Historical Society of Colorado.*

Horace Tabor as Lt. Governor of Colorado. *Henry E. Huntington Library.*

Windsor Hotel, Denver's grandest in the 1880s, played many roles in the Tabor story. *State Historical Society of Colorado.*

The Tabor Block, the first of Tabor's Denver buildings. *State Historical Society of Colorado.*

Thomas Bowen, renowned poker player and winner of Colorado's nineteenth-century epic senatorial struggle. *State Historical Society of Colorado.*

Interior view of the main hall of the National Mining & Industrial Exposition, 1882. *State Historical Society of Colorado.*

David Moffat, banker, mine owner, and partner with Tabor on several ventures. *State Historical Society of Colorado.*

Henry Teller, Mr. Republican of Colorado. His appointment to the cabinet led to Tabor's greatest political fight. *State Historical Society of Colorado.*

Interior of the Tabor Grand, the scene of some of Tabor's finest moments and bitterest defeats. *State Historical Society of Colorado.*

Tabor Grand Opera House. *Henry E. Huntington Library.*

William Bush was as close to Tabor as any man. When they split, the public learned many titillating details. *State Historical Society of Colorado.*

Peter McCourt. Tabor's handsome brother-in-law. Pete came to prominence in the 1880s. *State Historical Society of Colorado.*

Lewis Rockwell, lawyer, represented Tabor in numerous cases and warned him about the Durango divorce. *State Historical Society of Colorado.*

Baby Doe Tabor. *State Historical Society of Colorado.*

Tabor's first daughter, Lily, nicknamed Cupid, gained national fame for her beauty and parents' wealth, 1886. *Denver Public Library Western Collection.*

Rose Mary (Honeymaid) knew fewer good times and more hardship than her older sister. *State Historical Society of Colorado.*

CHAPTER 14

THE TABORS AT HOME

I am happy and so I hope are you. . . . Lots of love
Dear Babe, I do love you so dearly [Postscript from Horace]
Cupid to Mama, April 16, 1893

FOLLOWING their marriage, Horace and Lizzie, or Babe, as he called her alternately, tried as hard as their millions and notoriety would allow them to assume the life of a normal, happily married couple. Although the aftereffects of the marriage and the Bush-Tabor trial lingered to hinder their course, they seemed content just to have each other and cared little for the opinions of the people around them, those whose standards they had so recently flouted.

If they planned to continue the social activities permitted to them by Tabor's money and position, they were in for a rude awakening. Denver's social elite turned its collective back on "that woman" and dashed any aspirations she might have had. Men were willing to do business with Horace, but the women generally supported Augusta against this threat to the morality and sanctity of marriage. Though some Denverites refused to receive the Tabors (they were, however, honored by several serenades), the outlying mining camps, where Tabor's name wove magic, were not so finicky. Leadville, Aspen, and Ashcroft, for example, did not let prejudices stand in the way of accepting the new Mrs. Tabor.

In spite of the snobs the Tabors remained socially newsworthy, particularly on their return from the wedding. On the opening night of Lawrence Barrett's April 1883 Denver appearance, the private box at the Tabor Grand was first used by the newly-married couple. The comments on the occupants were almost as long as the review of the performance. The standing-room-only audience was fascinated, and "there was a general leveling of opera glasses in the direction of the bride and groom." Perhaps symbolically, the new Mrs. Tabor held a lily in her hand throughout the performance.

All this receded in importance as the years passed, as a family grew and a happy home life blossomed. Gossips whispered that the infatuation would soon end and, after running through his money, she would leave him for greener fields. They, like Augusta, misjudged Baby Doe. Such speculation proved idle: their love deepened and they remained devoted to each other through the trials that were to come. Out of this union were born three children: two daughters — Elizabeth Bonduel Lily, July 13, 1884; Rose Mary Echo Silver Dollar, December 17, 1889 — and a son who died the day he was born, October 17, 1888.

The parents worried through the usual childhood ailments, joyfully observed the stumbling first steps, and excitedly heard the initial hesitant attempts to talk. Christmas, with all its excitement for the young, rekindled long-forgotten meaning for Horace, as he watched first Lily and then both of his daughters caught up in the season's anticipation and joy.

As a father and family man, Horace was devoted and loving, adoring his children. For a man in his late fifties, who had not contended with young children at home for over two decades, this took some adjusting, which he did in grand style. His love and concern for Lily, nicknamed Cupid, and Honeymaid (adding yet another name to the already overburdened second daughter), is shown most clearly in the letters he sent, which their mother faithfully saved, when the family was forced to spend time apart in the hectic 1890s:

[to Cupid]
1889: I want to hug you so badly I love you more than all the world.

1894: Be an awful good girl for mama has so much to do and you can make it easy for her by being a good girl. I shall not come to Mexico again without you, Honeymaid and mama.
[to Honeymaid]
1894: I love you my sweet little girl more than anyone can tell and Uncle Pete [McCourt] loves you too. Be an awful good girl don't cry or bother mama one little bit.
1898: I love you to death and it is so sweet of you to love your papa as you do but do not cry after papa but come to me in December.[1]

The daughters returned their father's affection and both grew into attractive young ladies, the apples of their father's eye.

The winsome, blue-eyed blonde, Lily, gained early renown as "Baby Tabor" and her picture, drawn by artist Thomas Nast, graced the cover of the January 8, 1887, *Harper's Bazaar*. Nast, who had visited the Tabors the previous fall, had been captivated by her beauty. The idol of her parents, she reigned supreme until her sister came along. According to stories current at the time, Lily had attended the opera since she was six weeks old, and her christening robes cost five hundred dollars. During these years little except happiness touched her life. The doting father wrote in February 1886, "I never wanted to have a lot of money as badly as I do now so that Our Baby will not have to buffet with the rough side of the world." One sadness to invade this idyllic scene was the disappearance of her dog, Lucky. The mystery of what happened to Lucky, half mastiff and half Newfoundland, was never resolved, except that his hide was found at a tannery.

The rough buffetings of the world hit the brunette Honeymaid harder, because her first real recollections were of the nineties. Her father was away more then, and his love was less lavishly bestowed, though no less heartfelt. Both girls received numerous letters telling them of his travels and discussing family activities they were engaged in or planning at home. He promised to bring them something, especially from his trips to Mexico, and his complete adoration of his two daughters was obvious.[2]

Horace's love for his "Darling Wife" never lessened after those romantic letters of his senate days. Soon after the wedding he wrote her from Leadville, "for you are all I have in this world that I especially prize. . . . I want you to love me to death for without your love I would be miserable." Three years later on a longer trip to New York he expressed his loneliness, "My darling wife I feel so bad every time I think of you being left for several weeks . . ." As late as 1893 he still signed his letters with kisses and pledged his eternal love. Not receiving a letter for what seemed endless weeks in 1894, the heartbroken husband dejectedly confessed, "Darling I love you beyond description and will be very happy when time comes to go to you. I do so want a letter from you." Occasionally, he could twit her just a little. "I do so hope you will not be annoyed and badly bothered by any admirer you well know that I know that you have many." In the same letter, however, he showed his deep appreciation, "The children through your teaching love me too much for me to be away."

She reciprocated his love, but unfortunately most of her letters have not survived. In a letter sent soon after Honeymaid's birth to "My own darling," she felt it was impossible for her to go to New York with him at present. Deeply regretting this, she displayed her affection for Horace in every line but especially in the last sentences, "I cannot live one day without seeing you my own true love, because I want you with me, I am not happy away from you not one hour. And to please you I would gladly sacrifice anything." In 1893, she admonished her "own darling" to "Take good care of yourself for I am all yours."[3]

Such devotion should have silenced the critics; unfortunately, the rumor-mongers had to have their pound of flesh. Eugene Field left Denver, but his parting blast appeared in an interview in the *Kansas City Evening Star*, which was more sarcastic than clever. No one with his talent came along to replace him, yet the stories continued, every so often penetrating to even this happiest of families and wounding the Tabors deeply. Even as late as 1898–1899 Horace heard comments about his wife and received letters both pro and con. Answering one, he angrily replied, "Mrs. Tabor needs no vindication for any act of hers in her whole life . . ." Writing in 1899 to his long-ago political foe, Edward Wolcott, Horace had this wise advice about the rumored separation of the Wolcotts:

> If possible make up this difference with Mrs. Wolcott. Do not let Senator Teller and Mr. Hill gloat over it. If possible go to her and make love anew and tell her it is all your fault (whether it is or not). If you feel that you can do this you will make us all happy.[4]

He also wrote Mrs. Wolcott a short note expressing his "sad regret" at the account of their troubles. To his wife he confided, "Well I have written both of the Wolcotts and kept copies I hope it will do no harm and I will be very glad if it does good." Probably more than anyone else in Denver, Tabor knew the political troubles and personal sadness the Wolcotts faced. While having no regrets for his own actions, he hoped to save them the pain. Whether his good intentions had much effect is debatable; however, the divorce did not go through and the Wolcotts reunited.

His own remarriage proved a sticky business for his many biographers. Hubert Howe Bancroft, the noted Western historian of the day, decided to handle it in this manner in his *Chronicles of the Builders*: "The data given by his wife [Augusta] must not be followed . . . [she] may be a little disgruntled and properly so, no doubt, being displaced by a younger woman. . . . With this question we have nothing to do. So we will steer clear of all these things." On writing to Bancroft about himself in 1889, Horace revealed his own inner feelings:

> In regard to my matrimonial life: It has been very unsatisfactory and I wish you would omit that entirely. I think it would be better. As to my son; he is no son of mine and I would rather you would omit this, but I suppose you are compelled to do it. I suppose in history, it is necessary really.[5]

Tabor's bitter reaction toward Maxey reflected their strained relations since the divorce, and a reconciliation would not come until the 1890s.

Bancroft, who once called the Tabors "very bad eggs," and said, "He put away his wife for some cause and married a disreputable woman. The least said about any of them the better," changed his mind when Tabor paid a fee to be included in the *Chronicles*. "Senator Tabor should be made to appear, so far as the facts will sustain him as being one of the most important factors in the development of Leadville." Continuing, Bancroft wrote that he should appear as the man, above all men, not only in Colorado, but in "that section of the country, who created an intellectual atmosphere."

As Horace grew older, his weight reached the 190s, topping 200 in the 1890s. Silver streaked his hair, his hairline crept back, and his shoulders stooped a little more, though behind his jaunty walrus mustache the eyes still glowed as they had in '59. As the years slipped by, he suffered from the ailments of advancing age; in New York in 1886, for example, he came down with what he described as malaria and suffered for three weeks. He visited the mineral baths at Glenwood Springs and Poncha Springs, Colorado, to seek relief and cheerfully wrote his wife that he felt much better. Just what his particular problems were he failed to mention; one hotel at which he stayed advertised its springs as "a sure cure for rheumatism and all blood diseases." Probably he suffered just aches and pains. Tabor refused to bow to such problems:

> I have always been very active; am physically very strong. Have never indulged in any athletic exercise. I have always been temperate. I take a drink once in a while. I never used tobacco in any form. As a partaker of wine, I am very moderate.

A return to active mining reconditioned Horace, who, despite what he claimed, had become physically soft from his desk duties and generally sedentary activities of the late 1870s and 1880s. Pete McCourt described him as a "joe dandy" and said, "You would think he wasn't over 40 years old . . . if he wasn't so damned truthful about his age nobody would know it." Horace pictured himself as in excellent health and losing a little weight. Tipping the scales at 200 pounds, he confessed, "is heavy enough." Still the rejuvenated sixty-three-year-old boasted, "I think I could walk a good race now."[6]

For recreation he enjoyed an evening of poker. It is hard to decide how good or bad he might have been at it, because stories support both contentions. According to legend, he lost thousands of dollars in some games and was supposedly an easy mark in rigged ones.

Tabor's personality did not change with the advent of wealth as much as some thought. Wilbur Stone, who knew him for years, characterized him as shrewd and far-seeing in business matters, with good judgment in politics, counterbalanced by his honesty and fidelity to his friends. The trust he placed in them was often betrayed, which hurt him in both business and politics. His reputation as an honest man stayed high, an "old-fashioned sort, without reservation or equivocations," wrote Bancroft. This statement must be evaluated in light of what the reader already knows of some of the inner workings of his mining deals.

He was still the friendly, outgoing fellow of Oro City, boasting one time, "I like people and they like me." Despite the experience gained in several campaigns, Horace was not a top-ranked orator, but he did improve and was certainly above average by the end of the decade. Changing styles in clothing "never occasioned much anxiety in [his] mind." There would be displays of wealth, or what people took to be displays, though generally no open ostentatiousness or flaunting of money. Of success he simply said (as near to being philosophical as he ever got), "In regard to success in life, I think that is to a great extent opportunity. We are all creatures of accident more than anything else." But concerning his own, he stated, "I do not know as there was much accident in my case."[7]

Of his brothers and sisters Horace was close to only two

in his later years, John, who worked with him, and Emily Moys. John had a rather sordid life, and on his death Emily lamented of him, "I wish he had lived a Christian life," and described him as a "poor broken down man." Tabor, who helped the Moys family, was probably closer to his sister, and she responded with equal affection.

Not only was he generous to his relatives but also offered charity open-handedly. In the Tabor collections are a series of letters from Father John Guida thanking Mrs. Tabor for their collective generosity to various individuals and causes. Emily admonished Horace, "you have done that too much [helped others]" and Guida praised, "May our Lord grant you again ample means to give full scope to your large hearted-ness." [8] Tabor's charitable nature was shown in many ways. Books were given to libraries. He donated the use of the Tabor Grand for many worthy causes and held free shows, especially at Christmastime, for the benefit of all children who could crowd into the auditorium. In 1893, when Colorado women were fighting for the right to vote, Baby Doe allocated two rooms in the opera house block to the woman suffrage campaign. Her sympathy proved well placed, as the ladies triumphed. Less publicly, the Tabors contributed to many churches in an ecumenical manner. As far back as his Leadville days, Horace had donated land and money, and to the Methodist Church he gave two chandeliers. He lent the Epis-copalians $3,000 and, when hard times hit the congregation, he agreed to cancel the debt on payment of $1,000. In Denver he and other public-spirited citizens helped support the Afri-can Methodist Church. To the Jewish residents of Leadville he presented land for a proposed synagogue, and to Denver's Sacred Heart Church he gave a special present to honor the visit of a bishop. For the Catholic church at Fond du Lac, Wisconsin, Tabor money purchased a stained glass window to honor his wife's father. In a host of individual matters, from small gifts to helping a man find work, Tabor generously shared his wealth and position with those less fortunate. [9] His acts were worthy of the finest Christian, even if he never regularly attended nor joined any church. His wife remained a Catholic throughout her life.

A familiar figure in Denver and throughout Colorado, the "old man" gradually regained the position he had lost in the bitterness and scandal of his marital problems. A few took advantage of him, like the woman who wanted to meet him in secret and whose letter was filed away with the simple notation, "Bad Woman." While Horace might have played the field before his second marriage, there was no hint of it afterward. Though he was still the easygoing and friendly Horace of old, few if any presumed to call him "Haw." Only extremely scattered references were found referring to him by this acronym. Apparently, it was not considered good taste, even by the multitude of people who criticized him and his activities. Certainly a Dave Day or Eugene Field would have made capital out of it, if they had been so inclined. For this historical misconception, twentieth-century Tabor biographers are to blame.

On returning to Colorado from Washington the Tabors lived in the Windsor, while speculation flourished as to where they might establish their home. It was rumored that they planned to build a residence in Washington, D.C., but they moved to Welton Street in Denver and then, two years later, in December 1886, to the corner of Olive Street (now Thirteenth Avenue) and Sherman, where they lived throughout the next decade. Their house cost $54,000, and more money was spent as Horace turned it into one of Denver's showplaces. It was here that the Tabors proudly watched their two daughters grow and faced the personal grief of the death of their only son at birth. Tragically, Tabor was out of town that day and had a difficult time getting back to his stricken wife. Lavishly furnishing his home and providing for his family, the father and husband saw to it that his loved ones lacked nothing. One young lady, who worked briefly for the Tabors in 1889, left a homey account of the household. Besides herself, she said, two men and two girls worked there. Mrs. Tabor was not hard to work for and was not an extravagant dresser, the opposite of what others said. She liked children very much and wanted to have hundreds, all dressed in white. The only hard part about the position was having to lie to callers when Mrs. Tabor did not want to see them.[10] Ever-generous Horace gave the help free tickets to the Tabor Grand Opera.

When the Denver and Suburban Street Railroad planned to build its track along Thirteenth Avenue, Tabor was one of three land owners to file separate suits against the company. He wanted an injunction, because the rails, poles, and wires would greatly interfere with "ingress and egress" and also injure or destroy valuable shade trees. One sympathizes with the harassed property owner, but progress proved, then as now, to be a hard taskmaster.

Wealth had its problems as well as its compensations. The Tabors were literally besieged by requests for contributions, running the gamut of almost every conceivable cause: help for "our daughter," or a "friend," free transportation, a loan to help through financial troubles, your patronage in establishing a new business, a little girl who wanted only a coat and hat — and so the stories went. One woman sent a chain letter, asking that Horace send money to a "consumptive lady" in Denver and make three copies to send to friends. There were requests for pictures, offers to tutor the girls, people wanting to work for them, complete strangers wishing to make calls to explain problems, and some who even asked for pieces of dresses to make a quilt.[11] The Tabors, generous with both time and money, found their reputation for benevolence attracting only those who sought to take advantage of them.

Just how rich the senator was during the 1880s cannot be ascertained, although the public seemed to think his treasure chest was bottomless. Augusta, in her suit for alimony in April 1882, estimated his fortune at $9,076,100. This is an invaluable reference to his property holdings, although it would seem it overestimates his worth, since she values the mines far too highly — except perhaps the Matchless. It was to her advantage in general to squeeze as much valuation out of his holdings as possible. The press placed his wealth at more than $10 million in some wild accounts, while Maxey more conservatively and realistically put it between $5 and $7.5 million.[12] Without quibbling about amounts, it can be said certainly that Tabor was one of Colorado's wealthiest residents during this decade. His fortune was slipping, behind the bold front, but on the surface he maintained both his financial standing and his reputation.

As the decade closed, Tabor could look back upon years that spanned the depths and heights of his life and career, from the bitterness of his divorce to the happiness of his remarriage and growing family. Honors had come his way in spite of setbacks. He had personally conducted ex-President Grant on his tour of Leadville and its mines, and had met other celebrities, including Oscar Wilde, who received a tour of the Matchless. He corresponded with political figures such as Illinois' John Logan and took great delight in inviting notables visiting Denver to the Tabor Grand. Either he had a strong feeling for "the boys in blue" or he vaguely regretted not having taken a more active role in the Civil War, because Horace eagerly supported Grand Army of the Republic activities. He gave flags to some Denver posts, donated the Tabor Grand for use by the veterans, and contributed money to help cover expenses of the national encampment held in Denver in July 1883. He became so involved in this event that one would have thought him a most dedicated member. Denver turned out the red carpet for the GAR. Tabor attracted attention by appearing in his new $3,000 coach, drawn by four "splendid" brown horses, wearing heavy gold-mounted harnesses, a display topped by a colored footman and coachman bedecked in crimson and old gold livery. Here was Horace at his gaudy worst, dressed in the "striking uniform" of the Tabor Light Cavalry.

The veterans responded to his generosity with a serenade and later made him an honorary member of the local Farragut Post Number 46. This gesture ended in a nasty little squabble over the merits of the honor, with Tabor finally renouncing it on the grounds that an honorary membership violated the rules of the GAR.[13] Here are shown clearly two effects of the second marriage. Undoubtedly, pressure was brought to bear on the post on just these grounds and, secondly, the display at the encampment came at the time the Tabors found that Denver society would have nothing to do with them.

With less objection Tabor continued his membership in the Pioneers of Colorado and attended the annual reunions, along with his wife and whatever McCourts happened to be living with or visiting them at the moment. He also helped organize the Denver Chamber of Commerce in 1884, served terms as vice-president and president, and finally was given a life membership in 1896.

His name graced two towns which appeared in the 1870s and 1880s. One, Tabor Station in Boulder County, was a coal town, better known as Canfield. The other, probably dearer to his heart, was Tabor City, located some twelve miles north of Leadville and seven miles south of Kokomo. He knew this area and his roots went deep here. The town, born in 1879 as Chalk Ranch, was renamed after the then lieutenant governor. Charles Thomas believed some of Horace's "friends" surveyed and incorporated it, while Tabor bankrolled the undertaking. Never amounting to much, although it acquired a post office and railroad connections, Tabor City at its peak probably had a dozen buildings and some reported "good lodes." The checkered career of this camp ended in June 1882, when fire destroyed what remained.[14]

Capitalizing on the name, several Tabor mines and mining companies appeared in which the namesake was not involved. Unwary investors might have assumed otherwise and been deluded. Other lesser-known and less significant Colorado individuals received greater tributes by having prominent landmarks, counties, or towns named after them; Tabor had none. His despairing lament in the last scene of *The Ballad of Baby Doe*, then, has special meaning:

> Oh God. Ain't there never no one
> Nothing
> Nohow
> Nowhere
> No time
> Not dust in the hands?

Although remaining newsworthy throughout these years, the Tabors received less attention as time passed. He had been in the public eye for almost a decade and the saturation point had probably been reached. No longer did he make a big impact, as he had when building the Tabor Grand or sponsoring a mining exposition. Politically, he was finished; socially, he was unacceptable, and in business, although he maintained his holdings, there was rarely a flash of the old daring. Only in mining had the Tabor name retained its mystique.

In 1889, some months before the birth of Honeymaid, the family took a tour of Europe and England, as did other wealthy families of that era. The Tabors came and went with little publicity, illustrating by contrast the public interest in Tabor between 1879 and 1889.

The closing years of the 1880s and the early 1890s were the happiest of those remaining to Tabor. Clouds were gathering on the horizon and troubles were brewing, but they could still be postponed for a time. Around him he had a devoted wife, who shared his life completely, and two pretty young daughters to brighten his advancing years. Wealth he still possessed, and it was reflected in his mode of living. What more could a man ask when approaching his sixties?

CHAPTER 15

ERODING EMPIRE

Satan deludes many in mines, making them think they see
great store of copper and silver where there is none.
Martin Luther, c 1530s

I N THE 1880s Tabor's money flitted hither and yon in
search of still greater financial bonanzas, like a flood
spreading thinly over the landscape and then slowly
receding.

In business and in mining a dangerous trend became
evident as the decade passed: investments in marginal operations and downright longshots. The gambles being taken
lengthened, speculations were indiscriminate, and fewer
transactions resembled the stable investments which once
characterized Tabor's activities. Indeed, some of his soundest
investments were sold and the money reinvested in shakier
propositions.

The First National Bank stock went to David Moffat in
February 1883, for $89,000, and Horace resigned as vice-
president and director. Not even a vote of thanks was
extended to the departing officer,[1] normally a common practice. No doubt ill-feeling existed, and he may have been forced
out following the divorce and senate contest.

The Leadville retrenchment mentioned earlier continued,
and finally the Tabor era drew to a close, except for mining
and the opera house. The Bank of Leadville, Tabor's first
venture of this sort, came to an ignominious end when it
failed in July 1883, triggering a panic that closed two other

Leadville banks. Fortunately for Horace, he had previously
sold his stock to George Fisher. Unfortunately, however, he
had deposited money in it, including the Tam O'Shanter
funds, and so had others who owed him money. Luckily
for his personal reputation, he had withdrawn just in time;
for some people, however, who thought his fortune backed
the enterprise, there was a rude awakening. His last construction project in the Carbonate Camp, the Tabor Grand Hotel,
which opened in 1885, had not initially been his project, nor
did he keep it long. Discussing it he said, "A committee of
Leadville citizens began [it] . . . were unable to carry the
finantial [*sic*] burden . . . I helped them a little in finishing
it." He helped by forming the Tabor Grand Hotel Furnishing
Company, which had sweeping plans, but ended up limiting
its operations to this project. The Tabor Opera House continued to exemplify the builder's civic-mindedness, though
1882 marked its last good year, highlighted by an appearance
by Emma Abbott. Shorter seasons of legitimate theater followed, reflecting the town's declining fortunes, which had
never really recovered from the disastrous year, 1880.[2] Tabor
correctly sensed this, becoming hesitant to invest in the town
proper.

No question remained now as to his main base of operation — it was and would be Denver, where the brightest
jewel in the Tabor empire still sparkled, the Tabor Grand
Opera House. A year after the memorable opening, the local
press commemorated the occasion with special praise for the
successful operation of the "Thespian temple of the city."
To recapture the original success, Emma Abbott opened the
second season, again bewitching Denver's opera patrons.

Just how profitable this investment turned out to be can
only be guessed at. The *Tribune* stated profits were $31,110
for the first year, with total receipts of $203,415, while Tabor
said that the profits amounted to only $20,000. The best
records available are for May 1882, which included the appearance of the then-famous Shakespearian actor, Lawrence Barrett, who received $2800 for seven performances. So large

were the crowds that the week netted $3333.67, the best since Abbott. Bush wrote Tabor, "so my venture for a certainty has been a grand success. We have worked like the devil to make it so." Included in the profits had been $28.25 for renting opera glasses so ladies could get a closer look at their idol, and $50.00 the Baptist Church paid for using the house on Sunday. Business was not always that good, Maxey commenting the next February that deep snow and cold weather cut the house so drastically that a week's performances showed only $138.00 profit.

Securing name performers continued to be a problem; regardless of what the press thought, Denver resembled a cultural oasis stranded in a theatrically unprofitable desert. To bring Barrett cost $656 in railroad fares and baggage fees alone. On another occasion Bush offered two well-known stage personalities $3,000 each plus round-trip railroad tickets from Kansas City. Bush, who worked hard during his tenure to line up attractions, found to his dismay the companies could not afford to come to Colorado to play a single week in Denver. To overcome this disadvantage he helped organize the Colorado Circuit, eventually known as the Silver Circuit. By the late eighties, with Bush long gone and Peter McCourt now in charge, it included Denver, Colorado Springs, Pueblo, Leadville, and Aspen in Colorado; Ogden and Salt Lake City in Utah; Cheyenne in Wyoming, and other smaller houses, for a total of fourteen. The Tabor Grand continued to be the prime attraction, and the co-owner of the Colorado Springs Opera House confessed that he was forced to take what was allotted to him, as the companies were usually booked by the Tabor for a week, spending another week on the Colorado part of the circuit.

Part of the problems which led up to the Tabor-Bush squabble originated with the operations of the opera house. Tabor admitted that "the business was kept in a more loose manner than men should," and each party contradicted the other's testimony about Bush's salary. The two also came to loggerheads at least once on booking plays. After Bush made a sixth contract for *Uncle Tom's Cabin*, Tabor told him to cancel, feeling they had had "enough of Uncle Tom and the mules . . . "³ Even for *Uncle Tom's Cabin*, which was undoubtedly one of the most popular plays during the eighties, six bookings in three years seemed a bit too much.

Into the 1890s the Tabor Grand reigned over Denver's theatrical world, a must for all visitors. One local enthusiast claimed it had but one rival in the world, the Paris Grand Opera; a more realistic estimate called it one of the finest theaters in America. Another publication stated, with only slight exaggeration, that the Tabor Grand had done much to make Denver known in all parts of the world. The greats of the theater performed on its boards: Lawrence Barrett, Edwin Booth, Sarah Bernhardt, Joseph Jefferson, Lillie (Lily) Langtry, and Helena Modjeska. Even Jack Langrishe took his bows, a well-deserved tribute.

Plays constituted the vast majority of the entertainments, trailed by operas and minstrel shows. Shakespeare apparently ranked number one, if the number of performances can be considered an index to popularity. *Othello, Hamlet, Julius Caesar*, and *Richard III* were the leaders. A fire, abetted by strong winds and below-zero temperatures, damaged the structure in 1884, but prompt action by the fire department saved the building. The year before part of a chimney had broken, giving some occupants a scare; the same year one of Denver's first artesian wells insured the opera house a steady water source. In 1886 the opera auditorium was renovated and repaired in time for the opening of the season.⁴ Tabor did well by his opera house, the best known of all the buildings he owned.

Twice Tabor found himself hauled into court because of implied discrimination in seating of Blacks in the Tabor Grand, contradicting those oft-spoken words of his about being the "friend of the colored man." The first incident involved one James Hawkins, who purchased dress-circle tickets, was refused admission, and sued for $5,000 damages. Tabor's lame defense was based on a "long-time rule" that tickets admitting them to the first floor would not be sold to "persons of color." Hawkins denied knowledge of such a rule and refused to have the tickets exchanged or take his money back. A jury found Tabor guilty, fining him four dollars and costs. Sarcastically, the *Rocky Mountain News*, February 13, 1886, commented that the jury evidently was convinced "that owing to the poor quality of shows given at the theater Hawkins was the gainer rather than loser by being kept out."

The second case involved James Mackey, one of the founders of the Denver Single Tax Association, which hired the opera house and brought in a speaker. Mackey had tickets for seats on the first floor, but was refused admission, on the same grounds as Hawkins. Being more aggressive, he went in and found the seats, whereupon the management called a police officer, who escorted him out and prevented his return. Mackey promptly sued for $10,000 and the case was argued to the state supreme court. Horace defended himself on the grounds that the Single Tax Association controlled both tickets and internal conduct of the house; consequently, it was not he who refused or neglected to admit the plaintiff.[5] To Tabor's discredit he overtly concurred with the discrimination practiced against his fellow citizens. That others of his time and place did likewise offers neither excuse nor justification.

An increasing problem and drain on the Tabor finances were the numerous lawsuits in which Horace found himself embroiled. One series of cases involved the orchestra at the Tabor Grand, which apparently was none too good, a fellow theater proprietor complaining to manager McCourt, "I am free to confess that your orchestra is the worst I have ever heard . . . get a proper orchestra (I don't give a damn whether it is a union or non-union . . .), but you have got to get good people capable of playing music. . . . " It had to be union, not scab, said the Denver Musical Protective Association when it went out on strike. As late as the fall of 1894, this issue was still being argued. Tabor was sued by a local Episcopal minister for presenting plays on the Sabbath, which "tended to corrupt the morals of young people of both sexes . . . " From almost every conceivable angle Tabor found himself sued or suing, keeping Lewis Rockwell and other attorneys constantly busy. Unpaid promissory notes, surety involving a crooked postmaster, stored books, a state bond issue, and unfulfilled contracts were just a few of the issues in question, right down to a case in 1893 when his dog bit the mailman; forty dollars was demanded because of the injuries received from this "vicious behavior."[6]

In one last typical Tabor move, he purchased the Fifteenth Street Theater and promised to remodel and make it into a first-class operation. He gave a $75,000 promissory note, which later brought him only grief. The building burned down and Tabor could never make the payments.

Aside from the Tabor Grand, few of his projects had been so cheered by the Denver press as the National Mining Exposition. Plans were laid for a second year, with Tabor reelected president. Pamphlets and speakers were dispatched to arouse lagging interest, as Loveland and Tabor again assumed control. This time some of the mountain communities dragged their feet noticeably, Dave Day bluntly calling the exposition a fraud. Tabor countered, charging that the counties had not purchased bonds last year, forcing management to pledge credit individually to keep the enterprise alive. Despite such bitterness, the exposition opened on July 17, 1883, in time to salute the national GAR encampment. Local support never reached expected levels, and generally the exhibits failed to match the previous year's. At the closing, September 30, it was obvious to most that the second annual National Mining Exposition had failed to arouse much enthusiasm. Tabor and his associates promptly decided not to attempt it again. A third one was tried under different management, and proved the correctness of Tabor's judgment. No exposition was held in 1885.[7]

Tabor and the others suffered losses and found themselves in court over nonpayment of bills, obviously indicating financial instability. Horace gave the demise of the National

Mining Exposition a fitting epitaph, "It done the State some good, but to us it was a good deal of a failure." In all, it cost him personally $30,484.[8] Shortly after the final 1884 closing, the grounds were sold and the building torn down.

Tabor was also having difficulty on another front, a long-festering fight over the Denver Post Office site. Back in 1881, Congress had authorized construction of the building, arousing immediate interest over the site, Tabor entering the scramble by offering a lot on Sixteenth and Arapahoe. The lot, valued at $125,000, was finally chosen in January 1883, although the government offered only $65,000. Senator Hill objected (he was not the only one), charging that a bribe had been given; with proof lacking, the issue died. To convince Horace to accept the offer, those owning nearby lots, who stood to gain from increased property values, pledged sums on a subscription basis to make up the difference. Tabor now was having a difficult time collecting those pledges. Such Colorado luminaries as ex-Governor John Evans and his son William were sued for nonpayment of $5,000. This case and others continued into the late 1880s before all were settled. Bush commented in 1883 that he suspected Tabor was sorry he ever made the government an offer of his Sixteenth Street property.[9] He was probably right.

A few honors came Tabor's way. He was made an honorary member of the Colorado Press Association — a deserved recognition, considering his efforts in the newspaper field. For a short time he owned an interest in the *Boulder News and Banner*, which helped heat the coals during the bitter little county Republican fight of 1886. Mainly, however, his interest was focused on the *Leadville Daily Herald*, the major paper under his control. Some confusion exists as to just when Tabor gained majority interest. R. G. Dill wrote that in April 1882 Tabor demanded the support of the paper for his senate campaign (the idea of which the other stockholders, including Dill, opposed). Tabor persisted and they finally "unloaded" their stock on him at a round premium. The paper itself listed Wallace and Dillon (perhaps just front men for

Tabor) as proprietors and publishers until October 1884, when Tabor was announced officially to have purchased the business. McCourt and the *Herald* both denied earlier that year that Tabor owned stock, but the previous Dill statement, the paper's loyal Tabor support, and a slander suit against it in August 1884, listing Tabor as a codefendant, all argue that he did own stock throughout these years. Tabor, whenever he took control, found himself in a newspaper fight with Carlyle Davis and his *Chronicle*. As an aid to furthering his gubernatorial ambitions, charged the unhappy Davis, it mattered little to Tabor whether the paper earned dividends or even paid expenses. According to Davis, the fight narrowed to a struggle between practical knowledge and experience vs. millions of dollars. In 1885, $150,000 later, Tabor lost his taste for such an expensive luxury and threw in the towel. In December 1885 the *Herald* was sold and became the *Herald-Democrat*.[10] Some of Davis's facts may be questioned, since he wrote the account years later, but the general story rings true.

During the 1880s and early 1890s, Horace continued to dabble in railroads with little success. His promotion of the Overland Broad Gauge Railroad Company was as abortive as his presidential campaign. Grandiose in conception (it included the laying of a trans-Atlantic cable), it was the brainchild of visionary Cornell Jewett, who dreamed of it as the "anti-monopoly" overland railroad. It was designed to run from New Jersey to San Francisco, independent of all existing monopolies. Horace probably did not invest money in this doomed plan and only served on the board. Why he would even associate himself with it is mystifying. In this same category was the Denver, Apex and Western Railroad, over which Tabor presided. Proposing to go from Denver to Idaho Springs, Georgetown, and Silver Plume, then through the mountains via tunnel to Leadville and beyond, the company completed some work, only to fall victim to the 1890s depression and Tabor's eroding fortunes. The railroad borrowed money and was unable to meet payments.

Somewhat more realistically, if also not profitably, Tabor became active in railroading in the Aspen area. This booming silver camp came into its own in the mid-1880s and Tabor, with his usual aplomb, turned there for investment. Rumors even had him building a business block. A planned Aspen City Railroad, to run within the city limits, was never put in operation, although the city council passed an ordinance allowing it to use the streets. By the spring of 1891 the council was discussing what to do with the company's "dead tracks." The Pitkin County Railroad hoped to have a line to Ashcroft, where Horace might at long last be able to tap the riches of the Tam O'Shanter. Final location surveys were reported to be in progress, but the reports must have been too discouraging and the project was dropped.[11] Even less is known of the stillborn Aspen and Southern Railroad, but it, like the others, drained some of the dwindling Tabor fortune.

Another long shot to recoup before it became too late was land speculation, and Horace tried here, as elsewhere, to plunge into the speculative frenzy of the 1880s. In 1881 he purchased an interest in the Las Animas or Vigil and St. Vrain Grant, which dated from the period of Mexican control and covered parts of Huerfano, Las Animas, Bent, and Pueblo counties. Long provocative and ill-favored, it gave Tabor only headaches. He purchased another share of it five years later, in the end controlling roughly half of the property. In the 1890s he was still futilely trying to have the grant confirmed and title cleared.

The Pueblo area fascinated him, believing as he did that the town had as good a chance as Denver to become a metropolis. Writing to Bancroft, he revealed, "I could say privately, that I think it has a little better [chance] but I would not want to say that openly." He purchased some land nearby and was interested in the Teller Ditch to irrigate land to the north and northeast. He never did as much for Pueblo, in spite of his private opinion, as he did for Denver. He regretted not having purchased more land in the capital city, as values jumped significantly after the completion of his two buildings and the influx of Leadville money. "I did not buy near enough land here in Denver. I should have bought a good deal of land before I commenced here."[12] A good thought, but it came too late.

For a fleeting moment, Tabor's "Elysium in the Tropics," Honduras, a "land flowing with milk and honey," promised lucrative prospects, a mirage of instant riches: uncounted mineral wealth, endless mahogany, maple and redwood forests, and acres of rich farm lands, all virtually virgin. It would make him "the richest man in America in ten years." Honduras, at this period just securing a stable government and being opened to foreign exploitation, was one of the poorest and most economically undeveloped of the Latin American nations. According to a promotional pamphlet of 1885, all this was to the country's credit, since labor was cheap, its wealth untapped, and the population "kindly disposed." Only "an infusion of Northern enterprise and energy" was needed. The Republic of Honduras–Campbell Reduction Company proposed to do just that, with the energetic Tabor as president and owner of 40 percent of the stock. Just for establishing a steamboat line on the Patuca River, the company was granted 360 square miles. The project looked promising for a while in 1884; then it collapsed. Baby Doe forlornly hung onto the shares after Horace's death. Even today the area remains primarily virgin country, with almost no roads or large villages.[13] Of all Tabor's ventures this ranks as one of the most speculative and intriguing. Whether this was just another stock-jobbing venture or a sincere attempt to tap Honduras's wealth is unclear.

Although these various enterprises kept Tabor before the newspaper public as an aggressive and progressive individual, disquieting doubts were rising as to his financial stability. As early as 1883, *Leslie's Illustrated* reported he was losing money rapidly and flatly predicted that in five years Tabor would be "as poor as he was when he went across the plains in a wagon." This was followed by other stories, scattered to be sure, of impending trouble. Stout denials, particularly supported by accounts of new Matchless strikes, were made, but were not always convincing. On paper everything continued to look good — the Tabor Block, operas, and various Tabor-named companies. The Dun Mercantile reference book, however, refused to give the senator or his companies a credit rating: "The absence of a rating indicates those whose business and investments render it difficult to rate satisfactorily to ourselves."[14]

To offset his declining fortunes, Horace was forced to borrow money. He had been doing this for years in financial emergencies on a short-term basis, usually in small amounts. These debts had been repaid; now, however, the amounts became bigger and the stakes higher. After trying to mortgage the Tabor Block and Grand Opera Block for $500,000, with no takers, he settled for a $350,000, five-year, 6 percent mortgage, with the two blocks as security.[15] If the loan remained unpaid after maturity, the interest jumped to 10 percent. Obviously, Tabor was in more trouble than the public realized. Having examined his futile attempts to recoup in real estate and business, one understands why he was sinking rapidly. Good money was going after bad. One hope remained: mining. Here Tabor's luck and optimism had not failed him since the discovery of the Little Pittsburg, and here he would cast his lot.

The Tabor Investment Company was begun in 1885 to buy and sell mines of "undoubted" merit. Within its framework he transacted many of the mining sales that took so much of his time as the nineties neared. He now bought mines he intended to sell rather than to work. Peter McCourt, who besides managing the Tabor Grand served as his brother-in-law's collection agent, was vice-president, and two relative newcomers, Thomas Wiswall and Lafayette Seaman, were secretary and general superintendent, respectively.

Through the Tabor Investment Company, the Poorman Mine at Caribou was sold to a Scottish syndicate. Caribou, Colorado's northernmost silver camp, was a decade past its peak when Tabor became interested in the Poorman, which finally came into its own in the 1880s after a slow start. Neil McKenzie, the owner, sold it on paper to the Tabor-controlled Poorman Mining Company in 1888, the Investment Company then peddling it in 1891. In the meantime, despite promises of active operation, Tabor did not sink much money into the mine. When the final sale was completed, involving $500,000, mostly in stock, McKenzie received the bulk of it and Tabor, who acted principally as a vendor, only a small percentage. This in no way equalled the sales of the late 1870s and did little to enrich Horace. The Tabor Investment Company also handled such smaller operations as the Niwot, the Colorado Central near Aspen, and the Silver Point, also located near Caribou. The Tabor name still cast its magic spell, for a local paper proclaimed that the appearance of the Tabor Investment Company heralded the coming into camp of the "heaviest and most successful" mining and developing organization in the state. The Niwot, located near the declining camp of Ward in Boulder County, once had been a gold producer; Tabor hoped to bring it back into production, then sell it. This would take money, as it had been closed since 1881; still he persisted, and a flurry of activity in 1888–1889 stimulated Ward's economy. But he failed to sell the Niwot.

As in the Leadville days, Senator Tabor also dabbled in numerous working mines, although the old spark was gone. Near Leadville he received congratulations in 1889 for new discoveries in the Lucy B. Hussey; it proved no new Little Pittsburg. He drove the shaft of the Experiment Mine down 340 feet before leasing the operation, a sure sign of declining interest. The Hunki-Dori Company made Horace its president, established a pool to sell stocks in the 1890s, then found the public not so gullible.[16] Times were changing on the mining market.

Nevertheless, there was always the tried and true to fall back upon, and this increasingly meant one mine, the Matchless. Though it had been a heavy producer, it continued to hold out remarkably well into 1884, under the management of Lou Leonard. These rich deposits repeatedly helped Horace shore up his other enterprises. Such affluence kept the owner in court to defend his interests. On one occasion, for example, an employee sued for damages after being injured.

The skilled and popular Leonard died in August 1884, leaving Tabor hard pressed to find someone to replace him. Col. A. V. Bohn, who had nearly been lynched by enraged miners during the Leadville strike, took over direction of the Matchless and several other operations. Three times in the remaining years of the 1880s the Matchless served as security for loans ranging from $10,000 to $25,000; each time, it was redeemed. New areas of the mine were opened, but, as normally happens, production leveled off, although it did continue, unlike other name mines which ceased operations. By the end of the decade older areas were being leased, indicating they were nearly mined out. A new era dawned in 1889, when for the first time stock was sold in the Matchless Mining Company. Bohn, still manager, issued encouraging reports periodically, sometimes most providentially, and the 1890s arrived with the Matchless ranking unchallenged as the foremost of Tabor's properties.[17] He still considered its profits his "pocket money," which he now allowed the public to enjoy with him. His obvious need for cash, however, was reflected in the stock-selling plan, something he would not have considered if the Matchless had continued producing up to her peak.

The Henriett and Maid of Erin, promising much, had as yet delivered little to their owners. The Henriett was returned to Moffat, Tabor, and their friends after a year's working by the English buyers, who had run into continual differences with the Americans, and who found only unpromising ore. The Maid was still locked in a dispute over claim sites. This case ended in the secretary of interior's office, where Henry Teller gained jurisdiction. While the case was undecided, the mine could not be profitably worked and the owners fretted. Oliver H. Harker, the mine manager, exploded when writing Moffat: "Am getting damned tired of only taking out expenses and I guess you are. Why in hell Teller don't do something is more than I can conjecture." The wait was worth the worry when Teller decided in favor of the Maid of Erin people, on the grounds that the Vanderbilt Mine claimants had no right to the Maid. In handing down his decision Teller established a precedent affecting all mining disputes of this nature — that ore found in a working shaft, as opposed to the original discovery shaft, gives valid claim to ownership over prior, albeit unworked, claims. That is, the discovery of mineral gave title to a claim regardless of first or other shafts sunk.[18]

With this question resolved and the Henriett back in Colorado control, the two mines were worked in conjunction, although still by two legally separate companies. Harker managed both, and his letters reveal the troubles of Leadville mining in the mid-1880s. Tabor occasionally visited the properties, but generally he, Moffat, and the others were absentee owners, necessitating frequent correspondence. All types of problems confronted Harker. For example, the Henriett owned nearly all the pumps keeping the water out of both properties; for a while, at least, the Maid did not pay her share of the expenses, which seemed unfair to the manager. The low price of silver and lead hurt operations, and Harker actually decreased output, hoping for better prices. As the companies moved into new grounds, the old were leased, necessitating varied agreements with the individuals or partners who thought they could make enough to warrant the expense and time of mining the older workings. Leasing under this situation produced as many headaches as royalties. Harker worried about selling ore to the smelters and, during one fight by a group of owners against what they considered low prices offered, actually accepted a higher price than was offered his striking colleagues. "As the matter stands as between the smelters and us the rules don't go. All they ask is that we keep silent." When Leadville banks started to fold, Harker worried, not only for fear of losing money, but because outside people were hesitant to accept local bank drafts. Just transporting ore to the smelters presented its problems; of the roads one spring he wrote, "They are hell." And finally there were always those court cases. On one case Tabor's lawyer Rockwell came to take testimony. Harker commented to Moffat that the testimony proved very good, but that he had "the witnesses all to pay and their expenses, board, whiskey, cigars, etc. Had to treat them very cleverly to get what was wanted."[19] To get whatever was wanted cost $195. Such little problems harassed Tabor, not only here, but in all his mines in varying degrees.

In May 1885, Eben Smith, a stockholder, replaced Harker as manager. Under his guidance the two mines finally reached their potential and were combined, with Tabor, Moffat, and Smith as directors, among others. These mines proved as valuable for lead as for silver and, despite the plunging price of both and continued water problems, were worked profitably into the 1890s. At least as late as 1898 dividends were still being declared, although, unfortunately for poor Horace, his shares had been given to the First National Bank as security on a loan, so he received no benefit.[20]

Leadville mining fluctuated in the later 1880s against a generally downward trend. Older mines declined, their deposits worked out, and few new ones replaced them. Hopes for a second contact or ore bed somewhere deeper in the earth pushed exploration, while costs skyrocketed and continued search for outside capital uncovered only minuscule amounts, nothing like 1878–1879. Horace tapped some St. Louis capitalists, even incorporating a Tabor Investment Company of St. Louis, but the scheme fell through, as did other projects. The *Engineering and Mining Journal* in December 1887 illustrated how sad the mines' plight was by publishing the last date they paid dividends: Little Pittsburg, 1880; R. E. Lee, 1882; Chrysolite, 1884; Little Chief, 1885. A dark cloud comprised of increased costs, decreasing profits, lower grade ore, depressed lead and silver prices, and few new deposits hung over them. Dumps now being reworked to salvage ore previously discarded as too low-grade indicated the plight. Tabor became involved in this with a process named the

Matchless concentrator, advertised as a "revolution" for mining.[21] It did not live up to its billing.

Elsewhere in Colorado, Horace's prospects shone little brighter. The once highly prized San Juans produced only leasing and a little outright work on the Alaska and Saxon. Nothing exciting was uncovered, and Tabor quietly ceased his efforts. More effort went into the Tam O'Shanter. First Eben Smith tried his skill for a year, accomplishing no wonders; he was replaced by John Tabor as superintendent. His success proved no better here than it had been with the Alaska. The Tam O'Shanter was worked through 1884, then leased, and it, too, finally fell silent. Even with the final confirmation of title in 1888, the mine remained idle except for ore reportedly shipped from the dump. Amazingly, this chronic nonproducer was still considered one of Tabor's major mines, and he used it as collateral for several loans. His share never came near to repaying what it had cost.

And in Ashcroft, the long-planned smelter was no godsend. The company that built it found Horace to be a hard man with whom to bargain, as he haggled over treatment costs, amount of ore furnished, and special railroad rates. Tabor finally shipped ore to Crested Butte instead, raising some local eyebrows. Eventually, he leased the smelter, indicating his actions might have been a freeze-out all along. The process, however, was inadequate, and soon ore was being shipped elsewhere. Tabor encountered more labor trouble at the Tam O'Shanter than at any other place since the 1880 Leadville strike. Non-Cornish miners struck against a Cornish foreman in the spring of 1883; the disagreement was finally settled peacefully. Conditions which led to Smith's dismissal, regrettably unstated, caused a second strike, bringing Lou Leonard racing over from Leadville with men to replace the strikers. Tabor also came to investigate the situation.[22]

A growing concern for Tabor and all silver miners was the increasingly unstable silver market, shown by the steadily declining price of that metal on the world market. The average price per ounce had slipped from $1.27 in 1874 to .94 by 1888. Increased production had helped bring this about, as had decreased demand and use. Westerners did more than just worry, as protests mounted steadily, backed by demands for government support of the silver price. Especially in those districts where the bonanza period had passed and production was based on low-grade ore were demands vociferous.

One way to save Colorado mining from permanent decline was to find some new process to treat low-grade ores profitably. While watching his Colorado properties produce less and less, Tabor busied himself with trying to find a solution, gamely looking for some way out of his strangling economic plight. An early attempt by the British-controlled Colorado Gold and Silver Extraction Company, a chlorination process, created a great deal of controversy. The *Engineering and Mining Journal* sneered at this process as worthless. Then Tabor thought he had found a process based on cyanide which might work. Edward Werner, Saguache rancher and miner, was the prime mover in introducing the MacArthur-Forrest process to Tabor and in interesting Scottish capital in organizing a company.

Werner had been corresponding with Leonard Gow, one of the principal investors in the Poorman, and by 1890 Gow was convinced of the possibilities of the process, if needed American capital could be found. Gow, a Glasgow ship-builder and industrialist, wrote to Werner in January, "We want it to be not merely a clever financial operation putting large sums of money [in] the pockets of the syndicate who underwrote it — but an *honest* and *highly* profitable investment for the shareholders." Tabor and Gow each wanted the other to put up the money, which gave Werner miseries trying to achieve a compromise. Finally, at a meeting, Tabor was granted the right to use the process at the Matchless and other properties in consideration "of services rendered and to be rendered to the company." Werner overcame the mutual distrust and pushed ahead; under the circumstances it was astonishing that the company ever got started. Gow thought Tabor was trying to unload his stock in the company, and Tabor uneasily worried about the money he was advancing. Each turn of events seemed only to produce more problems.[23]

Working through the Tabor Investment Company, Tabor found himself becoming more involved than he planned or than he had money to underwrite. The results proved discouraging, both in Colorado and in Oregon, where Werner went to set up a mill. Absentee owners on both sides of the Atlantic fretted and chafed about the declining stock value and Werner's failure in Oregon. Lafayette Seaman, on behalf of Tabor, wrote the harassed Werner that company shares could be sold in Denver for 5 cents, and the senator reluctantly furnished money needed for current expenses, saying he was short himself "just now." The Glasgow stockholders, now thoroughly disgusted, drew back, leaving only Tabor to support Werner.

Seaman, complaining to Werner that not one penny in aid had come from Glasgow, which "you know is not right," finally laid the situation on the line: "Unless we get money from some quarter pretty soon we will have to shut down. It is very hard to get money in Denver now." In the meantime everything went against the company: the Boulder mill was hampered by snow and lack of ore; the Ouray operation was slow getting started; the Denver mill was uncompleted; and a California mill was not in operation. The spring of 1891 was Tabor's last in the company. Seaman, on June 24, warned Werner again that "money is very tight here and hard to get at any price."[24] Other men would continue attempting to have the MacArthur-Forrest process accepted; not Tabor — he had matters much more pressing to attend to.

Regardless of whether the process would work (mounting evidence over two years appeared to say no), this proved to be the wrong time to launch another company. Tabor was strapped for surplus funds and the Scots would not open their purses without positive guarantees. Nor could investing money be found in Colorado to buy stock; money was tight, as Seaman testified. Too much had been tried too soon. Better one mill over the long haul, where the process had proved successful, than many where it was still untried. Werner blamed Glasgow for the troubles and hoped Tabor, with whom he remained "on most friendly footing," could carry it through. Horace could not, yet any glimmer appeared worth grabbing in his increasingly precarious financial situation. This one simply dragged him further down.

One of the concessions the senator received had been the exclusive right to use the process in Fremont County, Wyoming, without charge, in consideration for erecting a mill to speed its introduction in that state. No mill was built, nor did Tabor's Rose Mine there, though he thought it a good one, develop into anything. He also owned the Tabor Grand Lode Mining claim; both this and the Rose were near Atlantic City. Tabor's luck proved no better in neighboring Utah, though he had been interested in its potential much longer, having sent Lou Leonard to the southern part back in 1882 on an examination trip. His big Utah venture came in Uintah County in 1888; eventually he found himself in court after refusing to purchase claims the owners assumed he had promised to acquire. The trial revealed that the plaintiffs had found near Ashley a wondrous "asphaltum" bed, from which, after examination by a mining expert, Tabor, for once, backed off.

Similarly, but a little later in time, the Montana Mining & Investment Company proved no winner for Horace either. A dredging operation on the Jefferson River, southwest of Three Forks, it operated only during the summer of 1891 and ended with President Tabor and other stockholders being sued for nonpayment of debts. As he admitted to his wife, the big obstacle was how to save the gold. For most of the 1890s he toyed with placer claims in Idaho as well, mainly in Boise County. Some he purchased, others were filed in his name, with such titles as Honeymaid Tabor, Cupid Tabor, and Elizabeth McCourt. The only thing these did was drain money from his reserves, because they were almost entirely unworked or untested speculations. Indeed, if Tabor received any returns it would have been a minor miracle, because this whole area had been placered since the 1860s. It was unlikely that so many "valuable" claims would have been overlooked.

Texas, with its reputation for size and tall tales, inspired a story in 1883 that Tabor had purchased 170,000 acres of copper land. According to press releases, the confident owner exclaimed, "There is enough mineral under that tract to last a century. The supply is inexhaustible . . . " This wonder only awaited the coming of a railroad to tap it. The Colorado press liked to boost its local millionaire, but in this case, Tabor and a group of Easterners had actually obtained shaky title to some barren Texas land in Hardeman County and organized a company in which Tabor owned 16,000 shares out of 120,000. The old Civil War hero, General George McClellan, who died in 1885, was president of the organization, the Grand Belt Copper Company. Tabor hung onto his shares, even after the 1893 crash, probably because they were considered so worthless that no one wanted them, and long after his death his wife tried vainly to get something for them.[25] Another dream shattered and more money gone chasing the will-o'-the-wisp bonanza.

Tabor's wealth, once so strong on paper, was gutted by the end of the 1880s. His empire had eroded to the point where only a shell remained, and much of that was mortgaged. One risky investment followed another, the odds steadily becoming longer and the plunging greater. He had dreamed mightily and tried to fulfill those dreams. Overextended, Horace found himself caught in a spiral of borrowing to maintain his hold, while slipping deeper and deeper into debt. Worsening his plight was the fact that Colorado and silver mining suffered from their own economic woes and offered no solace. How much longer could he maintain himself? The answer lay in two mining areas still offering one more spin of fortune's wheel: his Mexican holdings and the well-named Vulture Mine in Arizona.

IV.
TWILIGHT OF
A LEGEND
1889-1899

CHAPTER 16

SO FLEET THE WORKS

Do not let it worry you if you fail, for if I can see
you happy I care not for brick or mortar
Tabor to wife, April 22, 1894

I N 1887, in an attempt to pull a financial rabbit out of the
hat and save his tottering, heavily mortgaged empire,
Tabor turned south to Arizona Territory, purchasing the
Vulture, once called "Arizona's Comstock" and the "richest
gold mine in the world," both exaggerations. However, it was
a gold mine and with the price of silver slipping dangerously
low, it beckoned as a more promising opportunity.

Situated in a setting appropriate for its name, a backdrop
of dry, jagged hills and cactus-strewn desert, the Vulture
had been through a checkered career since its discovery in
1863 by Henry Wickenburg. Isolation, distance from water
power, and the ever-lurking Indian menace added to the
inhospitable environment. It was profitably operated for a
few years, then went through several owners in a decade
before the Central Arizona Mining Company resumed operations there on a large scale in 1879. Ambitiously laying pipe
from the Hassayampa River, this group overcame the water
problem, only to falter and fail by 1885 amid lawsuits and
a collapsed stock price. Although only an estimate can be
made, the Vulture probably had produced $4 million in a
little over two decades since its discovery.[1]

Horace became interested in it soon after the Central
Arizona's demise and purchased the Vulture with promissory

281

notes in March 1887. What Arizona needed to develop its "vast mineral wealth," remarked an 1881 writer, was capital and men of enterprise. Here came Colorado's already legendary mining man to furnish just that and certainly he started off well, working the property and calling it another Matchless. He was careful to have the press know when he received a gold brick from its operation. But the murder of the Vulture's superintendent and two guards during a robbery of a Phoenix-bound gold shipment produced undesirable publicity. The bullion was later recovered but only one of the robbers was apprehended, although Tabor offered a $1,000 reward.[2] While giving the impression that he intended to work the Vulture, what he really had in mind was to sell it, and he had a hot prospect, the English-owned Kaiser Gold Mines Company.

Again, as he had done in the past, he baited the prize for European investors and appointed Lafayette H. De Friese, an attorney in New York and London, as his agent. De Friese quickly hooked the Kaiser Company; however, the cagey English agreed to buy only if given six months to work and examine the mine. If the mine did not prove as valuable as represented and they decided not to buy, Horace had to repay all outlays incurred. Ten years before he would not have agreed to such terms, but with the present situation what it was, he was forced to accept them. He felt confident that the transaction would be completed. The ever-watchful *Engineering and Mining Journal* observed that while the terms of the sale were very unusual, they presented a good basis for future transactions, when the vendor had faith in his property and was satisfied he was only asking a fair price.[3] The editors were aghast, however, that the only report on the mine was given by Tabor's engineers.

The English directors hired James Morrish, a Cornish-born mining engineer with worldwide experience, to take charge of the Vulture during the six-month exploratory period. In his subsequent letters and reports the story of the Vulture unfolds, and Tabor's methods come under scrutiny.

On arriving, Morrish was dismayed. "I have been connected with mining for upwards of twenty years, but I never in my life saw such a state of confusion and disorder at any mine as there is here, and I think it will be a rather heavy task to bring order out of this chaos." More specifically, in a coded telegram to London and a later letter, he described the mill as sadly out of repair and in a generally very bad state, while the mine was in "a most disreputable condition from top to bottom." Amazingly optimistic, he advanced his opinion that the property was fundamentally a very good one, although he honestly admitted it would take time and money to bring it to a dividend-paying status. He had conversed with Tabor in Denver before going to Arizona and agreed with him that they should rework the dump first, while the mine and mill were being put into good working order. Interestingly, his opinion of the mine itself appreciated in subsequent days, and he continued to be on the best of terms with Tabor. Horace reciprocated, saying, "I desire to do all in my power to carry you over any rough points and not, by being over particular, to hamper or fret you." In the same vein he wrote to the English board, thanking them for sending over a man who seemed to comprehend the situation and promising, for his part, to be prompt and fair.

Down at the Vulture, Morrish was learning the facts of Arizona mining. To the directors he wrote, "It requires care and firmness to deal with matters generally here and especially with the class of work people in this part of the country. They are like birds of passage. They start work and work a few days and then strike out for new fields and pastures green or otherwise." The longer he stayed, the more dejected and gloomy his communiqués became. Morrish had continual trouble with water in the mine, "more the appearance of an old disused quarry" than a mine, he thought, and the iron pipes bringing water from the Hassayampa were in such a bad state as to require constant attention and repair. Fuel for the mill and mine seemed extremely expensive to him at $8 per cord. Then came a severe rainstorm and flood, washing out the dam and portions of the waterrace and pipe line, stopping all work.

Now all kinds of harassments seemed to confront the

frustrated Morrish. Tabor was slow in sending him accounts, and when they finally arrived, several important vouchers were missing. The more he tested the mine and ore, the more he became convinced neither would pay for operation, and all he could see ahead was expensive dead work before any valuable deposits might be reached. Discouraging reports went to both Denver and London. Finally on February 2, 1889, Morrish advised against taking over the property. Desperate, because this sale was vital to his whole financial empire, Tabor wired Morrish that he was on his way to London to meet the directors. Morrish reiterated his position in a letter sent at the end of the month, "I see nothing now but a very poor mine before me. . . . I cannot recommend the Company to take over the property."[4]

Within a few weeks Morrish received a startling proposal from Peter McCourt:

> I have a very large contingent interest in the sale of that property all in stock and it is of sufficient interest to me that the sale goes through that I frankly say to you that if it does I will donate to you 5,000 shares of the stock which amounts to twenty five thousand and see that you have as good a position for the next two years with chances for the sales of other properties.

No one would know of the transaction, Peter confided, not even Tabor. This indicated how frantic the Tabor group had become, for without question Horace knew of the bribery offer. Morrish later testified under oath that in a conversation in Tabor's office on December 15 overtures had been made to induce a favorable report, and the amazed Morrish was promised a pecuniary reward.[5] He forthrightly turned it down and emerged a major witness in the case soon to be filed by the company.

The only concrete concession Tabor gained from his trip to London was a two-month extension, which proved to be too late. Morrish sent Kaiser his six-month report on March 4, showing that $32,000 had been expended and only $10,800 in bullion mined. He closed down all operations except pumping and awaited orders. They came quickly; in less than a month the directors informed Tabor that they had rescinded the agreement. Horace despairingly countered with a new proposal, only to have it flatly rejected. The end became almost a comic opera when Horace authorized his agent, William Farrish, to seize the property, which he did, backed by a small posse, from the startled Morrish. In a somewhat grandiose statement Tabor informed Farrish not to risk a life, for the mine was not worth sacrificing even one. Tabor's hopes in the Vulture evaporated in the desert sands.

It cost him even more before the affair was all over. Kaiser presented a bill for expenses and, following Tabor's refusal to pay, sued for $80,000 and won a verdict of $16,120 in 1892. The *Engineering and Mining Journal*, despite its earlier favorable attitude, charged that a deliberate fraud had been perpetrated and editorially castigated Horace. "The exposure of the infamy of his acts will probably lie lightly on one who is no novice in this kind of work. The disgrace and injury of such transactions fall heavily upon the whole American mining industry . . ."[6]

No paragon of virtue in some earlier mining deals, Tabor is displayed at his worst in the Vulture action — his hand forced by desperation, his methods sharpened by experience with the Chrysolite and Hibernia. The lessons learned there produced sad results here. Nor was he at his best in defending himself by denying everything, because the Kaiser people had kept good records and promptly pinned him to the wall. To be sure, there would be future attempts to operate the Vulture, but its real promise died with the withdrawal of the Kaiser Mines. The mine was nearly thirty years old and the vein had been lost, fractured by two faults, and would not be found again in Tabor's lifetime. Horace had purchased a property in wretched condition, even if one does not take Morrish's comments at face value since he may have been unused to American mining practices. Tabor hoped to make a quick profit; he failed, and more borrowed money vanished.

While the Vulture case dragged to its dismal close, Tabor

enjoyed the last days of his wealth and power in Denver. He regained some of the popularity and esteem he had lost earlier. As a fifty-niner, one of a vanishing species, he received a certain amount of respect and deference; and the "grand old man" had become something of an elder statesman in Colorado mining, one who spoke with the voice of experience and success. Walking on the streets of Denver, Tabor was a symbol of the old days, which, though only a decade or two removed, were irretrievably gone. His optimism never wavered, "In my opinion the mining industry will continue permanent in Colorado. There are going to be many valuable mines found yet in Colorado that are sleeping today; there is no question about that." In less than two years Cripple Creek was booming. Of the miner's life, he sagely replied to a starry-eyed interviewer that it was not very interesting. There was no romance in any kind of hard work. "The romance is always in results."[7] He knew that as well as anybody, better than most.

When in town, he took part in varied public functions, such as the cornerstone dedication ceremonies of the future capitol. And not only in the Queen City of the Plains, but in the whole state, his name still conjured the old enchantment. Leadville invited him to the opening of its ill-starred Ice Palace. In Durango, which once played such a pivotal role in his life, a local writer longingly awaited a Durango Tabor "to build himself an enduring monument in an opera house." In appreciation for all Horace had done for Denver a composer dedicated a march to him. And so it went, as the autumn years of his life passed into winter.

Beneath the façade, the scene was not so tranquil. Mortgaged to the hilt, unable to escape from the morass into which he was steadily sinking, Tabor found his time running short. It is not easy to reconstruct what happened, for one can never be sure that Horace even comprehended the total significance of every involvement.

On paper Tabor's position did not seem too precarious, since he owned mining properties and real estate. In Denver his Tabor Block, Opera Block, and home represented sound investments, although already a mortgage encumbered both blocks, one which he had been unable to meet. To pay off the $350,000 loan to the New England Mutual Life Company, Horace borrowed $400,000 from the Northwestern Mutual Loan Company at 6 percent for a five-year period. To secure this he gave the company a mortgage deed on the Tabor Grand and the Tabor Block in July 1891. Of this amount Horace received slightly over $40,000 in cash, the rest going to pay principal and interest.[8] In order to keep his financial empire afloat, he continually needed cash to pay taxes, assessment work on mines, insurance premiums, judgments in legal cases, and such smaller items as repairs, lawyers' fees, and heat and water bills, not to mention the salaries of his employees. Despite all this, he continued to invest and plunge; the result was only more money gone. These nickel-and-dime debts, so to speak, account for the increase of his borrowing in the $1,000 to $10,000 range, as he moved into the 1890s. At the moment these loans did not seem extravagant; however, principal and interest mounted steadily, putting a virtual mob of creditors on his trail.

From the Union National Bank of Denver various amounts totaling $171,625 were borrowed during 1892 and January 1893, some in forty- and ninety-day notes at a ruinous 10 percent, indicating clearly his precarious financial situation. To secure these loans, second and third mortgages were given on the Tabor Grand and Tabor Block. After fruitless negotiations, these unpaid notes were sold in February 1893 to the firm of Horace Bennett and Julius Myers, an action which made it the major Tabor creditor in Denver: Tabor had already borrowed $50,000 from this real estate and money brokerage partnership at 1 percent per month. They took as collateral more of his Denver property. Except for the latter amount, all the other deeds given were secondary to the mortgage held by Northwestern Mutual, an important fact to keep in mind. Indicating the depth of his problems, he secured the money from the Union National to pay off $130,000 borrowed from the First National in 1891. As the disastrous year 1892 neared its conclusion, Tabor borrowed another $36,000 from Denver attorney Augustus B. Sullivan, putting him over $657,000 in debt to these four creditors alone.[9] A staggering debt load, it was compounded by all the smaller debts and the relentless interest payments. Even his home had been mortgaged; the note was held by prominent Denver hardware man George Tritch in return for $30,000 at 12 percent annual interest.

Each note put him further in debt, failed to solve his problems, and provided only temporary relief while dragging him under. He needed clear money, but where was he to find it? His older mines were almost played out and he appeared to have lost the touch — the Tabor luck, as some chose to call it — to find more. Leadville, that once-dependable base, was trapped by dual troubles: the complete collapse of the silver price, down to the eighty-cents-an-ounce range, and decreasing lead production. Nor could a brighter picture be painted for other Colorado silver districts, which once had glittered so brightly. It is doubtful, even with a higher silver price, that many of his mines would have been returning a profit; some never had, and others had been mined for a decade or more with the high-grade ore long since gone. His Denver properties still were profitable; however, the generally retarded economic conditions of the mining regions were reflected here as elsewhere. The money gained from rents and theatre profits was not enough by itself to keep the heavily mortgaged properties above water, even under the best of circumstances. His wonderful plans for his Chicago, Honduras, and Texas properties and his host of companies had long since vanished, leaving behind only shattered dreams and valueless paper. Some of the Chicago property was given to the Catholic Church, and his 4 percent of the wondrous Calumet & Chicago Canal & Dock Company went for $6,000.

A desperate race to salvage what he could or at least wriggle out from under before the structure collapsed motivated a series of strategic moves. Horace tried to sell the Tabor Block, only to have the deal fall through. He offered to sell other property, but times were not auspicious and were worsening. Of more immediate importance was the organization of three companies: Tabor Mines and Mills, Tabor Real Estate, and Tabor Amusement. Into these he dumped his various holdings and on these companies borrowed still more money, leaving in his wake a confused financial picture and angry creditors. The companies were organized on March 16, 1892, with himself as president and his wife and Peter McCourt as officers and stockholders. Completely home-owned and operated, they were used by Tabor to wheel and deal endlessly. The real estate company received most of his Denver and Leadville properties. The Tabor Grand, Tabor Opera, and all leased interests of the Silver Circuit went into the amusement company, and into the Mines and Mills went the Matchless, Tam O'Shanter, Vulture, Mexican mines, and all other claims and mines he controlled.[10]

Of the three, the last played the most significant part and was the only one still active after the final debacle. On paper it looked like the other Tabor mining companies, since it could issue stock, locate, lease, purchase, and sell property and incur indebtedness; in truth it simply was a hand-maiden to serve his immediate needs. Tabor, as president, signed promissory notes, for example, on the Tam O'Shanter and Matchless, while the board of directors rubber-stamped its approval. Providing a convenient outlet for more borrowing and a front to transact financial negotiations, the idea of the company was not bad in itself; it might have helped a decade earlier to organize and coordinate his sprawling mining interests.

While these companies muddied the waters, with Horace borrowing money from unwary creditors on the paper worth of them or of company-owned properties, he and his wife shuffled property and money back and forth. Tabor deeded property to Baby Doe, then tried to get new loans in her name. She supposedly lent him money and they apparently endeavored to use the note as collateral. Meanwhile, McCourt and Tabor attempted to borrow from any likely person or company, even falsely withholding knowledge from the lenders, or so these people later charged.[11] It is incomprehensible that local people could have been duped in this manner. When Tabor went outside the state to secure funds, it was understandable that these lenders did too little investigation and placed too much faith in the Tabor name.

By mid-1892, faced with a confused and precarious situation, Tabor could redeem his fortune only with a longshot and he took it. The last chance was Mexico, with its legendary mineral wealth; Tabor's hope was the Santa Eduwiges Mine.

He had invested in this property just shortly before the ill-fated Michoacan Syndicate, the difference being that he maintained his interest in this legitimate enterprise. Located in the Sierra Madre above the small village of Jesus Maria in the state of Chihuahua, some 160 miles southwest of Chihuahua City, the mine had been worked during both the Spanish and Mexican periods. Once an important silver and gold producer in a recognized mining district, the Santa Eduwiges held out irresistible attractions to Tabor. He came in at a good time, with President Diaz's government encouraging foreign investment and establishing internal stability, thereby reducing the personal and financial risks. The bimetal standard of Mexico looked better and better when, throughout the world, the silver standard was being abandoned (a number of European nations had discontinued the use of silver currency), as it already had been for practical purposes in the United States. In 1873 Congress had passed a new coinage law dropping the silver dollar, thereby putting the country on the gold standard. This act, the infamous "Crime of 1873" to a generation of silver orators, took the government out of the silver purchasing market, which would not have been serious except that the price of silver declined and the mine owners suddenly found themselves at the mercy of the world market, rather than having the comfort of knowing the government would guarantee a price through its purchases for coinage. Add to this the attractions of low wages, the successful record of Mexican silver mining, and the belief, however naive, that previous operations had somehow failed to find the rich deposits, and it is easy to understand why Horace was only one of an increasing number of American investors to go south of the border.

As early as 1835, Josiah Gregg of Santa Fe trade fame had recorded a constant and often profitable business with Jesus Maria. He visited the village, describing the perilous trip into it and the difficult mining operations. His astute observations did not deter later Americans, and it was almost a foregone conclusion that someone would try to sell the mines to rich Yankees. One such enthusiastic visitor wrote in 1864, "I want to get you interested in what I believe to be, by all odds, the greatest mining district [Jesus Maria] in Mexico."[12] This particular attempt to do so proved premature, but in the 1880s the tempo picked up. On the report of the mining engineer J. C. Carrera, Horace and his friend A. S. Weston purchased the Santa Eduwiges and, following their lead, other Leadvilleites invested in the same area. Weston went down to act as general manager.

Tabor quickly found that absentee ownership in a foreign country was one nightmare after another. The property had to be refurbished — equipment, pipes, machinery, all having to be hauled over what generously could be called a road, more accurately merely a trail. Weston built a mill and tramway and supervised mining operations, while upholding his and Tabor's interests in two mining suits. Litigation finally shut down the mine in 1887. A Mexican court actually ousted the Tabor interests before an appeal to a higher court reversed the decision. The Americans owned 52 percent of the property, and the Mexican owners had filed their case on the grounds that legal conditions had not been fulfilled in developing the mine. Not until 1892 were all the issues settled and work resumed. By now Horace estimated he had $300,000 invested in the enterprise; he had little enough to show for it. Back in '84, however, he had boasted, "My Colorado mines are nothing as compared with this Mexican bonanza, as it seems to be practically inexhaustible." Now the time of testing was at hand; if he was correct, the Tabor empire was saved; if not, the last act was being played.

Tabor sent his brother John to Jesus Maria in 1892, and his report on Weston's troubles with the Mexicans helped end that gentleman's tenure. Tabor and Weston had a falling-out, and the former bought the latter's interest after Weston sued for his back wages. John also found the water supply low, hardly able to keep the mill going five minutes. Nor did he like the mill's condition; nevertheless, he buoyantly gushed that it was a "wonderful rich mine" with lots of ore. Peter McCourt and Tabor were down there by the end of the year, with the latter taking full charge. They were somewhat dismayed, as McCourt admitted. "We had every reason to believe Don Juan [Hart's] statements regarding the value of the ore, for he was the assayer and supposed to be our friend. The fact is he made very few assays and merely guessed at it." The exuberant Hart, the new general manager, had claimed it would pay over $1 million a year. "We would have been perfectly satisfied and wouldn't have got our ideas up where we had them." Despite this disappointment, McCourt, too, was carried away by the mine's potential. The Mexican debts incurred over the past years hung over the operation, yet so quickly was the mine placed in paying condition that McCourt wrote Baby Doe that they would be able to pay them off more quickly than anticipated.[13] This was encouraging, because then the money could be applied against those pressing Denver obligations.

Indeed, relief would come just in time; the flimsy Tabor financial structure had measurably deteriorated after the panic of 1893 hit Colorado and the whole country. Hard hit silver mines collapsed by the score, the Colorado labor commissioner listing 435 mines closed and 45,084 people out of work by the end of August. The state's population was only about 450,000. The number of profitably operating mines closed was somewhat less than 435, but the economic impact

of the unemployment was considerable. Railroads offered free
transportation East to help relieve Denver, since so many
had drifted there hoping to find some kind of work. Tabor,
just arriving home, had never seen its like. In one week twelve
Denver banks closed, and one worried Denverite wrote his
wife, "The stores and firms all over town are making assign-
ments and business is pretty nearly paralyzed." The same
man, Henry Wood, local assayer, summarized the mining
situation, "You cannot imagine how blue everybody in the
mining and smelting business is. Well we are all in the same
boat and will simply have to wait until the silver question
is settled on a new basis and commence on again." The *Rocky
Mountain News* of July 20 gave encouragement: "Shoulder
to shoulder men, while the war upon Colorado continues."
With the unemployed roaming about, banks and businesses
suspending, and mines ceasing work while a state economy
geared heavily to silver "petered out," it was not a pretty
picture that summer of '93, the third year of the "gay nineties."
Wood even noted that the number of tramway cars had been
reduced because so many people could not afford the money
to ride them.[14]

What this meant to Horace was obvious. Leadville was
finished as a silver camp and major producer, although continued gold production softened the blow. His silver mines,
there and elsewhere in the state, had no such cushion. The
hard times affected loans, person after person turning him
down while his creditors converged on him. McCourt hurried
to Chicago to try to get better terms on their notes; his attempts
failed and he sadly returned to his brother-in-law. Watching
the crash, Tabor realized nothing could be done from Denver;
he left his wife in charge and, with McCourt, raced back
down to Jesus Maria in the late summer. He knew now,
if not before, that his last hope rode on the outcome of mining
the Santa Eduwiges. For the first time a note of despair crept
into his correspondence and, in a moment of discouragement,
he wrote his "Babe" that they should leave Denver.

What a contrast was this Mexican venture to his first

mining experience thirty-four years before in the exciting days of '59! Now he was an alien in a foreign land, banking his experience and few remaining resources on the hope that a mine probably a hundred years old had extensive reserves left. Far from railroads or even a good-size settlement, in a mountainous desert terrain, Horace spun his last turn on the enigmatic wheel of fortune, which had played him such a fickle game.

Reports coming back to Baby Doe in Denver were encouraging. Horace literally bubbled in a letter on September 24, "This mine will give us money enough to enable us to disperse charity with a liberal hand as long as we may or can live and leave our children with lots of money. . . . It should give us net, longer than you will live, from $50,000 to $200,000 per month . . ." Such news certainly brightened Baby Doe's days, left as she was with the difficult job of fending off creditors and keeping the Denver situation on as even a keel as possible. McCourt, too, was impressed, especially with the mill's performance and the work of Don Juan Hart, who had been left in charge. The two Americans slept in the office adjoining the mill, the noise not bothering McCourt: "Oh! what beautiful music notes of gold and silver bars, grand opera isn't in it any longer . . ."

By December everything was still "OK in Chihuahua," except for one dark cloud, perpetually on the Tabor scene now, debt on the property. They were in debt to Enrique Creel, co-owner of Chihuahua's most powerful bank, a large landowner and political power. Even so, with the Santa Eduwiges producing (Tabor noted that $15,000 worth of bars were sent out January 2, 1894), it appeared that something could be salvaged. More encouraging reports came north in the next six weeks; $40,000 worth of ore was mined in January, while they were still getting the property in shape. McCourt, meanwhile, used his leisure time to learn Spanish, but not Horace: "The Senator don't care to learn spanish. I think the reason is he don't want to stay away from you any longer than possible." McCourt was also studying assaying, wrote

Tabor, who jokingly noted that he himself had not shaved in about seven weeks and whiskers did not become him. Such homey comments comforted the lonely wife, who was not at all convinced her sixty-three-year-old husband should be laboring so vigorously. Her brother reassured her that they both were in the prime of health.

Despite all their efforts, the Creel notes, totalling $44,929, could not be met and were extended at 1 percent interest per month. McCourt went to Chihuahua to try to resolve their problems, including the touchy issue of giving their Mexican partners their share of the proceeds. Pete candidly wrote a friend that they had had "hell with the Mexican owners since our bullion arrived" and were forced to give it to them. He also admitted they had been having trouble with the workers and even the other owners, whom he accused of trying to run the operation so as to pay only expenses and force the Tabors out. At the mine, Horace found himself faced with all types of problems. Americans were brought in to replace all the "head Mexicans"; the men wanted to draw wages nearly daily, as was the custom; and then someone broke into the amalgam room and stole $7,000. Tabor blamed it on the discharged group but could not prove it; fortunately, all the amalgam was recovered. John Tabor, who was still at the mine, wrote his sister-in-law that the senator had succeeded, by working quietly and systematically, in ousting the Mexicans from control. John never liked either them or their food, which would have "killed a decent american hog." The tramway cable broke, costing several days' work, and then a worker was killed and Horace found himself confronted by the technical aspects of Mexican law, all new to him. Then many of the timber supports had to be replaced, stopping mining for five more days.

Not until April did he really let his discouragement come to the front in writing his wife.

You say if this property is a failure sell it, it is not a failure but its not as good as we thought but it has had very rich ore and I am confident it will repeat itself many times, but

it is far from civilization and I want rest and love with you
and this is no place for you and the children.

To McCourt, who was in Chihuahua talking to Creel, he truthfully wrote that they had to sell the Vulture or this mine,
"not that this is not a good prospect but it is not good enough
for either of us to devote our lives to . . ." In June the last
letters came from Jesus Maria, with both McCourt and the
senator reporting everything arranged for the new manager;
thus, with little fanfare, Horace turned homeward.[15]

The Santa Eduwiges had failed. The reasons are not hard
to find. The expenses of opening and dead work had taken
a large chunk of the profits Tabor retained after sharing with
the other owners. Certainly the mine produced $40,000 some
months, but Tabor could not have kept much after deducting
expenses and then sharing the net. Not enough to save the
Tabor empire, obviously. Other problems dogged the operation, especially the apparent mutual distrust between the
Americans and Mexicans. John Tabor thought his brother
should have "taken a tumble" to their activities long before
he did, yet from McCourt's comment it sounded suspiciously
as if the Americans did not intend to share those early profits.
Word of Tabor's shaky financial condition reached Chihuahua
and did nothing to strengthen confidence. He and McCourt
endeavored to keep up a bold front, hesitating to ask for
further Mexican loans for fear of frightening creditors. The
Santa Eduwiges, with its pockets or ore shoots, and with
much barren rock in between, hurt Tabor's efforts; it was
so isolated that heavy transportation costs cut into profits.
Writing to Baby Doe, McCourt unintentionally gave the
epitaph for the Santa Eduwiges venture, "I only wish we
were out of debt, we then could have it all ourselves."[16]

On a smaller scale, Tabor and McCourt worked the
Bavicanora Mine, actually sixteen claims under this name,
in Sonora, about 150 miles northeast of the capital, Hermosillo.
A gold and silver property over a hundred years old, it had
been worked only spasmodically, primarily because of the
Apache danger. Horace had dabbled in Sonora mines as far

back as 1885; now intensity replaced speculation. The feverish demands of the hour caused him to be misled by James Stainburn, a smooth-tongued salesman. Several times in 1893 and 1894 McCourt and the senator visited the mine, the former feeling it was a good low-grade proposition, which needed a big outlay of money and development. Horace had neither the money nor the time, but took an option, positive "that we will find lots and lots of rich ore." Both finally quit "throwing away any more good money after bad," especially since it cost about $600 per month "to keep it alive." A mining engineer whom Tabor sent down had immediate second thoughts about accepting the position.

> . . . the great distance from civilization and god's country. The barrenness and scarcity of vegetation . . . , my associates of the lowest type of civilization nothing but cut-throat-greasers, yacca and apache Indians, who robbed a man for one dollar and stabbed him in the back . . .[17]

The Bavicanora was only one more step toward ruin.

So much rode on the outcome of these operations for hard-pressed Baby Doe, as she strove to maintain her husband's holdings in Denver and Colorado. She was his Denver eyes and ears: "I have no idea about our affairs there except by your telegrams . . ." She must be given a great deal of credit during those crucial years, 1893–1894, when she held the line, separated from her husband much of the time and under increasing creditor pressures. Tabor placed complete faith in his wife, giving her power of attorney to act on his behalf. His and McCourt's letters to her reveal much of what happened and the inner feelings of these two. The following are excerpts:

> The Senator thinks the only thing for you to do is to get some influence to induce Bennett and Myers to give us a year's extension. no matter what it costs for he cannot afford to lose the properties at any cost for reputation's sake. [McCourt, Jan. 17, 1893]
> The Senator and I have worried fearfully over the Denver affairs but your last letter has made us feel quite comfortable [Feb. 20, 1893]

Now my loving wife do not worry, we will do all in our power and we will surely pull out. [Tabor, Dec. 17, 1893]

Do nothing that will reflect in the least of unfairness   we had better lose our buildings than do wrong. I had rather have the money that it takes to clear our building than the building if it was not for the unpleasantness of it   do the best you can and if I have your love and our little angels I will be happy. [Feb. 11, 1894]

I hope you can do all you expect to but fear you have not measured Bennett & Myers. They are no doubt eager to get our blocks. I know you will do all in your power for us   none can do more and let the result be what it may . . . [Feb. 25, 1894]

I am feeling awfully well about the property here [Mexico] now, but I think you are in serious trouble in Denver. [April 8, 1894]

Now about this [mine] and the Vulture either one you can sell at whatever worth you can get if you can get an offer which will make us comfortable [April 29, 1894][18]

His main worry was for his wife, and he kidded her lightly, saying he hoped she would not be white-headed when he got back. Incredibly, his optimism never wavered, "You know all good mines are brought to me so if we want more mines we can get them very easily with money." Horace might just have been trying to keep up his wife's spirits, because the situation was extremely serious in Denver. By the time he returned it was out of his control and in the courts, through no fault of his "Babe." The poor woman showed the strain, putting her thoughts down in a note apparently intended only for herself:

. . . after-doing all I could I find I have done nothing   all I can bequeath to my little ones is my honor, my fidelity as a daughter-sister-mother-and wife   as such I have tried to be as near perfect as we poor mortals can be. I have made myself alone what I am but all my good work is forgotten but Lord thy will be done.[19]

Just after coming home from Jesus Maria the first time, in March 1893, Tabor gave a promissory note to Bennett and Myers for $250,000, payable in one year. This was the note that gave his wife such a difficult time. It was past due when he returned in 1894, the company already having filed to have the buildings put up for sale. This action spurred the Northwestern Insurance Company into activity on its note, the interest payments on which had not been maintained. Interest payments, taxes, insurance — Horace was in arrears everywhere he looked. Nor had the Colorado economy brightened since July 1893, and it would not for another year. Like a racing snowslide his troubles gained momentum and intensity, court cases multiplying, lawyers' fees mounting, and the Tabor silver fountain running dry. There was nothing he could do; the Tabor Amusement Company assigned its property in October for the benefit of all creditors, with Peter McCourt and Frank E. Edbrooke, the older brother of William, as trustees. The vultures now fought for the spoils.

The Northwestern people had the best claim, but Laura Smith, who purchased the Bennett and Myers note, would not give an inch and filed first on the scenery, furniture, and general furnishings of the Tabor Grand. The shrewd Bennett and Myers had gotten out from under the Tabor collapse just in time. Tabor might have encouraged Mrs. Smith to take the note, believing she would be easier to deal with; however, she proved just as intractable, and he confessed later, "She was very hard on me this morning and was very determined to get the buildings." Despite attempts by both the amusement and real estate companies to rescind the transaction, she legally had them and sued for a total of $271,000. About the only concession received was the dismissal of the attempt to force the property into a sheriff's sale.[20]

The major case, though, was that filed by the Northwestern Mutual in December over the $400,000 loan. It claimed that Tabor had not paid interest after March, failed to reinsure the property (part of the original agreement), and that the company had been forced to pay the taxes in September. In the event of such nonpayment, Northwestern had the right to declare the whole loan due and payable, which it did. Lamely, Horace countered with the argument that he did not have sufficient information on certain sections of the complaint and that the judgment should be against the Tabor Amusement and Real Estate Companies, which held title, not him. To no avail. Throughout 1895 testimony and records were collected and demurrers filed, as both sides maneuvered for the final hearing.

Still gamely trying, Tabor attempted to swing a $1 million loan in New York, finding no takers, although his correspondent thought he might be able to place it in Europe. Too late now, for by the time everything would have been ready, the case was in court. A few friends and even strangers wrote, wishing him success or assuring the family that it was just a matter of time before their fortunes improved; others dropped by to wish them well. Ultimately, it remained a lonely struggle.

After hearing all the evidence, the judge handed down his decision on April 20, 1896. The Tabor Block and Tabor Grand were to be sold to settle a judgment of $476,990. All other defendants, and it was quite a list, were forever "barred and foreclosed from all equity of redemption and claim of" those premises. A last-minute injunction to stop the sale was refused by the state supreme court and Northwestern Mutual submitted the highest bid at the sheriff's sale on June 23.[21] A few more legal maneuvers only forestalled the inevitable; Mrs. Smith got the opera house scenery, but little else for her troubles, and the others took what pickings they could find after Northwestern finished.

CHAPTER 17

BACK TO THE EARTH AGAIN

What Tabor did must be long remembered and will be
retold whenever the story of the upbuilding of Colorado,
is recounted.

Leadville Herald Democrat, April 11, 1899

ABOR had lost everything — at least everything his
creditors considered of any value. His home went to
Tritch, who had had a running argument for several
years because of Tabor's supposed neglect of the property.
This unpleasant bickering between creditor and debtor,
including court appearances, continued until November 1896,
when Tritch foreclosed, generously giving the late owner
forty-three days to raise the $62,500 to cover the first mortgage
he held. It was useless; the Tabors moved out by Christmas.
Tritch also got the horses, fancy carriage, and trappings that
had once so enlivened Denver's thoroughfares.[1] Gone, too,
was Leadville's Tabor Opera House, purchased three years
before by A. S. Weston for $32,000.

Tabor's mines were also lost. Some of the cases involving
them continued for several years. In Aspen the Tam O'Shanter
again went before the court, Tabor losing this round and
the mine — and so it was elsewhere. Only the proud Matchless, mortgaged to try to save the whole, was rescued. Baby
Doe, attempting to lease it, was advised by the few interested
parties that the present silver price was too low to warrant
the expense. Horace made some attempt to keep it open in
1895, until he finally leased it. McCourt, in Leadville in May

1895, concluded, "There is no way of running things up here much longer without money." Leadville merchants, perhaps remembering the old days, were patient with Horace when he only partially paid his bills. McCourt, meanwhile, worked to salvage what he could, while Tabor borrowed $18,000 from William Harp and two other men who held the Matchless lease, obligating the Tabor Mines and Mills to repay it in eighteen months. He was able to get another extension in the nick of time in 1898, but was unable to repay the note. By then even the Matchless was his in name only, Tabor receiving only one-eighth of any royalties.[2]

All this litigation required money, money that Tabor did not have to spare. His long-time legal adviser, Lewis Rockwell, finally gave notice regretfully that he could no longer represent him, because Horace owed him $2,500 and had no funds to pay. Lily, who was old enough to comprehend what was happening, wrote her Aunt Emily, "Papa and mamma have not the courage to tell you about it. They do not wish to write you until they can write good news."[3]

There was simply no good news to write. Baby Doe, displaying an increasingly religious nature over the past decade, desperately wrote her friend, the Mother Superior of the St. Clara Orphans' Home,

> We want your prayers & entreaties to God to save our properties and if they are saved we will build the new wing on your home and pay the debt — that is now on it and we will do as much as possible for your home every month.

Much more realistically, her lonely husband, again in Arizona in an attempt to straighten out Vulture legal matters, confided, "How I did hate to come away leaving you in the fire . . . and leaving so many complications. I do so hope and pray that one of our deals may go through, but in any case we have each other and the Children and all the love of each."[4] About all he had left was his family, their personal possessions, a few worthless mining claims and stock certificates — and memories. The sixty-six-year old man was going to have to start all over again, unless silver came back.

The cry of free silver evoked a ray of hope and Tabor grasped it. An old man in Denver, a young man on the Illinois prairies, and thousands more grasped it, too. The young man was the poet Vachel Lindsay, who captured the moment in verse, the moment when debtor West looked angrily at creditor East and fell back on free silver for its salvation.

> And all these in their helpless days
> By the dour East oppressed,
> Mean paternalism
> Making their mistakes for them,
> Crucifying half the West,
> Till the whole Atlantic coast
> Seemed a giant spider's nest.

The reader must not, from his present vantage point, think this was all logical. It was several parts sincere belief and a good dash of hope, mixed with much emotionalism. The man chosen to lead the crusade was William Jennings Bryan; "defender of the faith" he would be called. Thus, in the sixth year of the "gay nineties," America found itself in one of its most heated and emotional election campaigns.[5]

To Horace the subject was not new; he had been true to the silver issue since his rise to prominence eighteen years before. From his viewpoint it could be expressed in the simplest of terms. The silver price had declined steadily since the 1870s, the reason being the government's failure to maintain silver on parity with gold. The solution was to peg the silver price at a sixteen-to-one ratio in relation to gold, and restore the free and unlimited coinage of silver to provide a market. When the government had coined silver dollars, the ratio had been sixteen to one; however, since then the world price had gone steadily down, the ratio of silver to gold had gone up correspondingly. Now, if the miners could only get the government to return to the old sixteen to one ratio, they could sell their silver at a price well above the market price for bullion. Simplistic, yes, for it overlooked the decline of the mines (particularly relevant with regard to Tabor), increased costs, and the international decline in the use and price of silver, plus the overall increase in the

303

production of the metal throughout the West. He and other Western miners either overlooked or ignored logic in the accelerated free silver campaign of the 1880s and 1890s. Henry Teller emerged as silver's political champion, with Tabor not far behind as a silver spokesman.

To the eastern financier who desired a gold standard and considered silver coinage inflationary, this was heresy. Nor did the creditor East care to have the debtor West, whether farmer or miner, pay off its obligations with an inflated dollar. Further, silver was not acceptable in payment of international trade balances, and the continuing decline in the price of the metal made the coins less acceptable than other forms of currency. Thus were the battle lines drawn, fortified on both sides by misunderstanding and rhetoric.

The opening of the National Mining and Industrial Exposition back in 1882 had occasioned Tabor's praise of the role of silver and gold in the course of American development and a prediction that the exhibits would prove that the mines could produce the mineral necessary for a great part of the world's traffic. The next year, he declared more modestly that the only thing Colorado wanted was to have her silver and lead interests protected. The continuing price drop, however, led to stronger stands. In 1885 he served as a delegate to the National Silver Convention which met, fittingly enough, at the Tabor Grand. The delegates, responding to the conspicuous role he played and the use of his auditorium, gave him a standing ovation at the meeting's end. Horace became president of the state association and, as such, issued a stirring appeal to Coloradans, "Your interests are in Danger"; he urged them to rally to support a bill for the free and unlimited coinage of silver. Prompt response came, but not enough to push the bill through Congress in 1886. By 1889, his thinking and public utterances presaged Bryan's and those of other silver spokesmen.

> The United States being the greatest producer of silver I think it was very bad policy to allow a foreign government [England] to fix the price of it. . . . Give America an unlimited coinage

of silver and if Great Britain wants to buy any silver bullion, they have got to give her one hundred and twenty-nine for it. Then the miner of silver here, that has got silver could take it to the mint and get his silver dollars for it. . . . a large part of the East, particularly the American loaning interests would very much sooner adopt the one standard. The reason: you wipe out silver off from the face of the earth and you just double the value of gold and the gold securities and the debt securities, which have to be paid in gold. . . . A man that was in debt could never pay his debts. [Unlimited coinage would] commence a season of prosperity unparalleled in America that would continue for five, ten or fifteen years.[6]

Closing with an appeal to farmers, he showed that he, too, realized that a broader base than just mining was needed. Frankly admitting he did not know about all the ramifications, he studied the question, "without prejudice or partiality." This latter statement may be doubted, but not the fact that Tabor, like some other spokesmen, allowed an antiforeign bias to creep into his thinking. "Pretty near all you can see to admire over there [Europe] is old tumbled down buildings. That old muly country over there to set a price for us."

At the Colorado Silver Association the following year, Horace again foreshadowed Bryan: "Let silver drop to 75 cents per ounce and there would not be a silver mine worked in America, and all our western cities would be paralyzed; our railroads would cease to pay." At $1.29 "our farmers will never sell their products so cheap again." Lobbying for the cause, he visited President-elect Benjamin Harrison in a failing attempt to get a silver man as treasury secretary. In 1892 he journeyed to Washington, making a sentimental visit to the senate floor, and again saw Harrison, as well as Secretary of State Blaine. To Baby Doe he cheerfully wrote, "I am sure I have done good for the silver cause here. . . . My reception by them all was magnificent." Personal matters in the nineties increasingly forced the old warhorse to the sidelines, but he encouraged others, including Teller, to keep up the fight. Just before the 1896 election he had time for only token participation, and then, with the battle finally joined, he had no funds to contribute to this war, as he called it when writing to Teller. Believing his fate rode on the outcome, he bitterly accused,

> On account of my being such a strong advocate of *Free Coinage* it is at this time impossible for me to make a loan. I feel that the judges of this silver state should protect me until after the election for then there will be no trouble to make a loan.[7]

Bryan, the boy wonder who had espoused free silver, went down to defeat that November before candidate William McKinley and his Republican hordes. The silver bubble had burst.

As far as Tabor was concerned, Bryan's election and free coinage could not have ridden to his rescue in time. Those mines he still controlled, even with a higher silver price, would have needed capital to run, large outlays being necessary in many cases just to put them back in operation. Nor does it seem likely that a loan could have helped when, for all practical purposes, his property was on the sheriff's block. Yet he cannot be faulted for trying or for holding out a hope, regardless of how tenuous.

When the final collapse came, Tabor took it in stride and did his best to treat all concerned honorably. Writing McCourt in February 1897, he cautioned him to be honest and not react to others who had treated them badly, "that is no sign that we should rob him, then besides from my standpoint it is against your own honor and I hope you will go into court and say you were advised wrong." He himself tried to close up what business remained, commenting that "all I want is to keep what belongs to me and lead a quiet home life." He appeared always hopeful and no one remembered hearing him publicly complain of his reverses. What he did and where he went from late 1896 until the winter of 1897 is unclear. A story repeated years later by Joseph Smith, *Denver Post* reporter, places the family north of Golden for Christmas 1896, in impoverished circumstances.[8] Afterwards he spent some time in Denver, Leadville,

Colorado Springs, and Cripple Creek, before buying a home for ten dollars near Ward, in Boulder County. "Traveling," he jauntily wrote his wife, "always agrees with me." He now returned to Ward to mine again, where years before he had tried to revive the Niwot Mine. Here the search for gold was beginning again: it was 1859 once more, except that now Tabor was sixty-seven years old, with two young daughters and a wife to support.

Cripple Creek — the magic of gold rang in that name in the 1890s, because it replaced Leadville as the most prosperous Colorado camp. When silver shattered, Cripple Creek picked up the pieces, but they were gold. New millionaires appeared and a new age dawned as gold surged to the forefront. Tabor, interested in property in the district as early as 1893, missed out on the riches, as the Ben Eaton, Great Mogul, Free Coinage, and Phil Sheridan provided no bonanzas. He even organized the Consolidated Cripple Creek and West Creek Mining Company, but the old touch was gone; the money which was needed he simply did not have. Winfield Scott Stratton, who would make more money at Cripple Creek than Horace did from all his mines, came to the rescue with a $15,000 loan. Where this money went is not known, one source claiming it was used on Cripple Creek mines, on which Tabor gave up too early.[9] He never quit trying and still was seeking Cripple Creek's "Little Pittsburg" as late as January 1899.

He finally settled south of Ward, a locale which had the redeeming quality of being less expensive in all respects than booming Cripple Creek. Beyond that it was a declining gold camp, old and long since bypassed by the mining frontier. He and a small crew worked the Eclipse and several surrounding claims, trying to find paying ore. This was hard work for a man his age, but he now had few opportunities elsewhere. The mine had been abandoned for many years when Tabor saw some promise in it and started work. The money must have come either from Stratton or from the sale of Cripple Creek property, although Horace remained coy about the source. While here, Tabor received the most encouraging news in a long time, his selection as postmaster of Denver in January 1898. At the time, John Tabor was planning a trip to Alaska, the Klondike gold fields being the latest mining excitement, and had asked his brother to join him. The appointment changed Horace's plans.

Senator Ed Wolcott, in a magnanimous move, had nominated Tabor for the position and McKinley had approved it. The appointment caught most Coloradans by surprise, since Wolcott had not given any previous indication of favoring Horace, especially since his unrelenting silver view had put him outside the party in 1896. Ed apparently had some fence-mending to do with the silver interests, for he, unlike Teller, had remained loyal to the party, a stand which hurt him at home. Tabor's old nemesis, the *News*, announced the appointment on page one with pictures. Cards, letters, and telegrams flooded Tabor and the happy man asked his wife, "What do you think of that?" Among the multitude of congratulations was one from Teller: "I consider it a very handsome thing for Mr. Wolcott to do and I am sure the people of Colorado will heartily approve of it." Wolcott confided that nothing since being in public life had given him greater pleasure, for, even though they often disagreed on past political matters, he had "always cherished a regard for you, and in these later years when fortune has not dealt as kindly with you as you deserved, I have had great sympathy for you." Tabor, when interviewed, struck a harmonious chord, saying he and Wolcott had always been friends and confessing he expected to be appointed but would not say how long he had known it.[10]

The people of Colorado did approve, just as Teller foresaw. No longer did the image of 1883 project its shadow over all his activities. Purified by the fires of adversity and admired for his uncomplaining attitude, Tabor emerged as the Tabor of old, the fifty-niner, the patron of Leadville, Denver, and Colorado, and a man much beloved for all he had accomplished. The changed mood had been coming for years, this appointment serving as the catalyst to bring it into the open.

The postmastership, with its $3,700 salary, eased the Tabors' pressing financial burden and brought him back to Denver. Old friends rallied around on February 19, when he officially assumed the office, preventing him from spending much time on the job. Fortunately, the routine work went on regardless of who was postmaster. A host of people applied to him for jobs, but he took his time in gaining mastery of the new position, this post office being larger by far than the ones he had run two decades past (a lifetime ago now) in Buckskin Joe, Oro City, and Leadville. Seventy-six carriers and three men collecting mail served the thirty-two square miles covered by the various routes. He needed more men, but his patron, Wolcott, advised him that the Post Office Department had exhausted its appropriations. Wolcott did succeed in having two more clerks authorized for the Christmas holidays. Following the Christmas rush Tabor issued a public card of thanks to all his employees for their "able, energetic and thorough" handling of the mails. They responded with a petition praising his efforts.[11] As he entered his second year, Tabor was doing a good job and had settled down to the routine, with gratitude for this godsent opportunity.

For the first time in over a year, Tabor's name reappeared in the Denver city directory. The family was together again in the capital. Several separations still faced them; once, when Baby Doe and the girls were in Leadville, and again when they went East in the winter of 1898–1899. On the second occasion the heartsick postmaster wrote, "It is really terrible for you to be in New York and I here but if it is doing you and the children good I must stand it. I can stand anything that is for the good of all of you . . ." Nonetheless, their situation had become much more secure since the appointment and the future appeared rosy.

To be sure, old debts still hung over Tabor. He owed the First National Bank of Denver $55,452 for notes signed at various times since 1890. Throughout these last years he also carried on correspondence with Dumont Clarke, president of the American Exchange National Bank of New York. The debt here amounted to $53,000, secured by 41,901 shares of Breece Mining, the majority costing from $2.75 to $4.00 each, and Leadville Gas Co. stock. Tabor pleaded with Clarke not to sell the Breece stock until a better price than two dollars per share could be received. The long-patient Clarke admonished him, "my dear Governor, I am forced to the conclusion (reached long ago) that mining stocks are very uncertain. . . . the security for the loan so much below the amount of the loan for several years past, that now, as the value of the stock approaches the amount due us, we are fearful to let opportunity slip . . . " Finally, when the stock was sold in January 1899, liquidating all but $1,000-plus of the debt, the relieved Clarke said, "We know in your good heart it will cause you only satisfaction — for you are one of Nature's honest men . . . "

Horace, meanwhile, was busily trying to find a few overlooked sources of money. He found some 1879 Lake County warrants, somehow misplaced, and decided the government still owed him $3,869 for expenses of his Leadville postmastership days. Correspondence with the government failed to elicit any favorable response, bringing only the standard reply that the claims were not borne out by official records. Ed Wolcott later carried on the fight for Baby Doe, having no more luck against the rigid governmental position on vouchers. Tabor got no further in a suit against the receivers of the long defunct Bank of Leadville.[12] There were other, smaller debts and even a few notes owed him that remained unpaid or uncollected, although nothing like the multitude before 1896.

With a steady income and at least some surplus, the old miner started to reinvest in mines. Working through the Tabor Mines and Mills Company he secured a few "promising" lodes in Clear Creek, Gilpin, and El Paso counties and redeemed from tax liens several of his claims that none of his creditors had thought worthy of seizure. In a losing fight he had tried to retain control of the Vulture, which was finally sold at a sheriff's auction. Tabor visited the property several times in 1896, and John Tabor had managed it briefly. The latter's letters indicated in October 1896 that the property had not been worked for some time and had been leased in hopes of making some profit. Save this property, John cautioned, and you will be all right. Apparently, Horace wanted to retain it but did not have the money to pay off the debts; he tried to regain it after the sale. His case was continually hampered by lack of money, even his lawyer relentlessly pleading for payment and threatening to leave the case. The Arizona courts upheld the liens against the Vulture, and there the matter rested in the spring of 1899. Such setbacks dismayed but did not stop him. The ever-searching Tabor wrote his friend from the Chrysolite days, Dumont Clarke, about a gold mine reportedly opened near Port Deposit, Maryland. Disbelieving, Clarke replied, "I would say that I am not impressed with his statement [Tabor's informant], and can hardly believe it possible that a gold mine of any value could have been discovered in that section."[13] Emily wondered if it would not be better to forgo the costly prospecting and save money; her brother did not heed the admonition.

It was like old times again, as Tabor moved back into Republican party ranks, in gratitude, no doubt, for the appointment. Having been an open supporter of Bryan and a member of the National Silver Party, he returned with a few misgivings, but by November 1898 was loyally in the fold and even supporting Henry Wolcott's bid for the governorship. Reflecting his new allegiance, he told the electorate, "As far as free coinage is concerned, we will get it and at the hands of our friends, and not our enemies. The Republican party has met manfully all great issues and it will meet this." It was not like the old days, as far as results went, for the Republican party. His old friend and political opponent, Democrat Charles Thomas, won the governorship; the Republicans, even with Tabor, could not overcome the disastrous split of 1896. He cheered, though, when Teddy Roosevelt won in New York and was gladdened by other GOP successes throughout the country. The rejuvenated campaigner took to the local campaign trail in March 1899 to boost the regular party candidates in the city election. Come back, silver republicans, he advised, don't follow Teller, who is leading you into the Democratic camp. "Come home and be embraced by your first love, the Republican party." He again wooed the Black vote, reminding them in April, just before the election, of what the party had done, even referring to his own long-ago days in Kansas. But when the vote was counted, the party's candidate for mayor ran last.[14]

Some events painfully reminded him of past adversity. He was serving as president of the Colorado Mutual Fire Insurance Company until his reputation so hurt sales that the management asked him to resign. "Understand, Mr. Tabor, we have nothing but the interest of the Company at heart and nothing but the kindliest feeling toward you." However, the situation had come to the point that agents received nothing but complaints because the people lacked confidence. The public was notified that the resignation was voluntary because his "many" enterprises required his time. Somewhat soothing his feelings, a Chicago cigar company offered to use his name and picture for a new line of "high grade cigars," and he endorsed Paine's celery compound, to restore health and strength, which he used, "therefore know whereof I speak." His biographer, Hubert Bancroft, inquired if he would not like to establish a Tabor Institute of American History. It would be unique, Bancroft summarized, and immortalize the founder's name.[15] He did not know Tabor's current situation, obviously. Others remembered him, too; a few railroad passes and invitations to the dedication of new buildings at the University of Colorado and to mining tours were delivered to him. These reminded the senator of the days when such came by the dozens and his name headed the lists of dignitaries.

In the first part of April 1899, the family was reunited

after a separation which stretched back to October. He had sent his wife and children to New York to see if a change in climate could help Lily, who had suffered from respiratory illness for several years; her father called it catarrh and nervousness. The separation proved particularly painful. He faithfully wrote his family, worrying over the third-rate hotels they stayed in and their shortage of money, which continually bothered them and once forced the pawning of a ring and a banjo. Reassuring all that his health was the best, he fretted over how they were, since his wife suffered from neuralgia. It was an unhappy separation for the lonesome husband and father, who did not conceal it from his family.

Tell Mama that she and the children are my all in life. [October 24, 1898]

I am almost crazy with love for you all and I do hope this December will be our lucky month love, love. [November 21]

It is very lonesome for me with my three darlings away. Tell Mama that I think she might write me just one letter and that she ought to make it a real love letter such as she could write. [December 16]

I am very homesick for you Babe and for the joyous children. They are the dearest children in the world They are so honest, conscientious and affectionate. [March 8, 1899]

I was so delighted that you are coming home it will be so joyful to talk to you and love you all. [March 13]

Despite his pleading, his wife did not write, at least into February, when he lamented, "and from Babe I have not had one line to say nothing of the love letter wanted."[16] But all could be forgiven in the joyousness of meeting again. That last spring of the nineteenth century promised to be one of the brightest in many years for the Tabors.

With a steady income from the Denver postmastership, they found their immediate financial worries had abated. Their quarters in the Windsor were comfortable, if not equal to the style and elegance of previous times, at least adequate to their needs. Respected and admired again, Tabor basked in the esteem of his pioneering status and his contributions to Colorado. Indeed, he still retained his love of mining and had great hopes for his Eclipse Mine at Ward. Showing a friend rich ore samples from this property, Horace exclaimed, "That is all I've got now, and if that comes up I'll be on the top of the heap again." The old confidence was returning; with luck, maybe, he would climb to the top again.

Tabor could survey with pride the Denver he had done so much to modernize. It had been transformed from the crude little settlement of log cabins perched on the banks of Cherry Creek, where Tabor first visited four decades before, to a city of brick and steel, telephones and trolleycars, universities and parks, and nearly 133,000 people crowded together, more than had been in the whole Pike's Peak rush. It had more than fulfilled the forecast made back in the depressed days of 1867: "Denver is the great trading and outfitting station of the Rocky Mountain regions, and is destined to be the great central depot of the different railroads now building."[17] Tabor's faith and money had helped make this all possible.

Tuesday, April 4, 1899, was city election day and Horace went out to vote and work for the Republican candidates, even though not feeling his best. A few aches and pains were not unknown to a man of sixty-eight, but he tried not to worry about the years. A few days before, when his friend, Thomas Wiswall, had counseled him to think of his age, he quickly responded, "That's the least of my thoughts," and went on to describe his hopes in mining. The next day, however, he was worse and was forced to remain in bed. Thinking it only a "bilious attack," Tabor did not call the family doctor, but his worried wife did. Lily wrote her Aunt Emily that they were awfully worried about "our darling papa," and "We trust in our dear Lord for if we should lose papa how could we stand it." The trouble was diagnosed as appendicitis. Not until Friday did the situation worsen, with initial fears being expressed for his recovery. More doctors were called in for consultation, but, owing to Tabor's advanced years and the likely possibility it would prove useless, the decision was made not to operate.

On Sunday morning Tabor was baptized into the Catholic

faith, something he had been considering for some time privately; he had planned to join the Catholic Church later in the month. To Baby Doe, who was with him constantly, he reportedly turned and said, "This is the happiest moment of my life. I am at peace and resigned to the will of God." That evening the doctor advised the family that, with peritonitis rapidly setting in, Tabor probably had only twenty-four hours to live.

The next day, April 10, was cloudy and warm. From out of his window Horace viewed the mountains; it was for that reason he had chosen this suite. Far across Denver he could see the foothills, a mixture of brown, dark green, and patches of snow, topped by the white-crested Rockies beyond, a scene similar to his first view of the mountains on a spring day forty years before. Around his bed gathered his beloved wife and daughters, his son Maxey, and the physician, who could do nothing now. Death came peacefully. The dying husband, telling his wife that he suffered a little pain, closed his eyes and in a few minutes was gone.[18]

The evening papers announced it to Denver and Colorado. Pictures and a brief history were included, alongside eulogies for the man and his contributions. The quest of Horace Tabor was finished.

CHAPTER 18

THE MEASUREMENT OF A MAN

The memory of Mr. Tabor himself will remain,
with his good works and his bad.
Thomas Patterson, Nov. 2, 1883

IN THE last act of their *Ballad of Baby Doe*, John Latouche and Douglas Moore place an old and disillusioned Horace Tabor on the stage of the Tabor Grand where, in his imagination, his life passes in review. The triumphs portrayed were fleeting and a worried Tabor finally uttered these memorable lines in his own behalf:

How can a man measure himself.
The land was growing, and I grew with it.
In my brain rose buildings yearning towards the sky,
And my guts sank deep in the plunging mine shafts.
My feet kicked up gold dust wherever I danced
And whenever I shouted my name
I heard a silver echo roar in the wind.

The authors in this lament offer an intriguing key to the question of measurement: Tabor's grasp of the concept of a growing Denver and Colorado.

His awareness of Denver's destinies were shown when he said, "I thought that Denver was not building as good buildings as it ought to and I thought that I would do something towards setting them a good example." The Tabor Grand and the Tabor Block he correctly evaluated as the most important works of his life, whose construction "resulted in its [Denver's] growing up a city of fine buildings, which otherwise would have been of an inferior structure." Similarly, Denver historian Jerome Smiley stated, "It [Tabor Block] was the first really fine building planned in the city and its erection marked the beginning of a new era in Denver."[1]

All of Colorado gained from his investments in so many activities. At his financial height he feared neither cost nor obstacles and possessed the will to overcome any that appeared. Such faith encouraged others to try, and they did, going where Tabor went. His contemporary Coloradans appreciated his contributions. The *Rocky Mountain News* of April 11, 1899, eulogized Horace in these words: "Regarding him from the natural standpoint, he was one of Colorado's chiefest benefactors. He spent much of his money for that material development of Denver and Colorado that makes for prosperous communities." The *Leadville Herald Democrat* the same day reprimanded another attitude toward him: it was a shame, the editor wrote, that a man who valued friendships so much and gave so liberally received so little in return.

These contributions of his were apparent for all to see. The inner man presented more of an enigma. In April 1899 he was pictured as "a prince among the Colorado army of pioneers," and "a diamond in the rough who saw all sides of life." Tabor probably could not have wished to preserve a better memory of himself than this one of the "strong, rugged robust man" from Oro City:

> He used to be a great showshoe [skiis] man and no matter how deep were the drifts it would not deter him from starting for Denver when it came his time to visit this city. He was a great favorite here with the businessmen, and we enjoyed his visits. He was always good natured and full of life and energy . . . and he was always sanguine of making a big strike in California Gulch.[2]

There are certainly important insights herein; Horace was indeed full of life and energy and he did ooze optimism and faith. Yet this many-faceted man was not the simple pioneer described here.

A more complex evaluation was given by Samuel Leach,

who described good-natured Horace as an easygoing man, one who displayed the desire to make enough money to live comfortably, and who was given to periods of dreaming about it. Leach caught the Tabor who admitted he had to be "prodded just like the ox," whose wife did just that; the Tabor who, while a generous husband and father, did little on his own to help his wife in the store unless asked. Leach found the young Tabor to be naturally thrifty. He summarized: "each of them [Horace and Augusta] has fine qualities and they are good company."

One facet that stands out throughout Tabor's life was his restless pursuit of instant wealth. The coming of wealth magnified many of his youthful traits and brought others into sharp focus. That Tabor had native intelligence and the ability to grasp opportunity cannot be denied. He often showed that he was not averse to both physical and mental exertion. He undoubtedly proved to be too trusting, one might even say gullible, and his millions uncorked a speculative bent which was wholly undisciplined. Augusta and relative poverty had controlled this fault earlier. His business and mining operations ran the gamut from the well-run Matchless to the shoddy attempt to sell the Vulture, from the Tabor Grand to the Tabor Fire Insurance Company. Some of his investments were shrewd, others unbelievably naive, even approaching fantasy. This duality was accentuated by his changing investment philosophy, his fluctuating financial conditions, and his abounding faith in himself and Colorado. It also illustrated an inner conflict characterized, for example, by periods of boldness and resolution, followed by indecision and uneasiness. Here was a man who could sink to the level of deceiving stockholders, yet in the mid-1890s could rise to the occasion by trying to pay off his debts honestly and fairly. If he deceived others, he also trusted his fellow man to an almost limitless degree, from the days of the small grub-stakes to the manipulations of Republican politics. Generosity to both friend and foe and optimism towards himself and his endeavors, confidence that he could somehow muddle through, marked his whole career. Generally a kindhearted individual, he could be classified as an easy mark. Those highly admirable traits that were factors in his downfall were also endearments to his contemporaries.

In the end Thomas Patterson was right when he defended Tabor during the Bush trial:

> His faults are before the public and he has been denounced by the public and the press, but now they are combined and want justice done him. . . .
>
> Gentlemen of the jury, when the men who are following Mr. Tabor and their memories are forgotten, the memory of Mr. Tabor himself will remain, with his good works and his bad. I do not seek to hide the one nor extol the other, but with them all he will be known, and his memory will be pleasant to many a man and many a woman, and many a business project will flourish which he in his magnanimity and generosity and his lavish wealth has advanced with no stinted or sparing hand.[3]

His motivation to rise successfully in politics and the money spent to advance his interests made him little different from other contemporary mining men, such as Colorado's Nathaniel P. Hill and Thomas Bowen, Nevada's John Jones, and Montana's Marcus Daly and William Clark. Hard-fought campaigns, deals, and bribery typified the rise of the mining politicians. A notable example was the Montana fight between Clark and Daly.[4]

Entrepreneur Tabor was Colorado's answer to Eastern capitalists, such as Andrew Carnegie and John D. Rockefeller, or California's Collis Huntington, although he was not in their league with respect to wealth or national prominence. According to a recent historian of this period, the "Robber Baron," the unscrupulous, greedy industrial and financial magnate, "competed ruthlessly with his fellows, exploited his labor force, callously bilked investors, and corrupted legislators and other public officials without conscience, all the while masquerading behind a facade of unctuous respectability."[5] Tabor exhibited these traits, particularly in his mining endeavors. Overcapitalization; questionable use of inside information; shady if not downright fraudulent business methods; misleading, clever promotion; and a lack of responsibility toward the corporation's investors characterized some of Tabor's operations, as they did others of that day. Regrettably, he learned by the examples of those he came into contact with, and became as ruthless as any of them.

His name will always be remembered in mining; his career touched upon most aspects of it, from prospecting to ownership and speculation. From an all-around view he probably knew mining better than most of his contemporaries. Tabor was, however, not particularly an innovator in mining technology, although he did help through investment to pioneer the cyanide process. While the Matchless Mine received plaudits for sound mining practices, even here no innovations caught reporters' eyes. He did subsidize devices which inventors promised to be "revolutionary," such as the concentrator manufactured by the Matchless Concentrator Company. Whether he did this believing it was a technological advance or just one more economic speculation is not known.

Until the Cripple Creek discoveries, Horace was probably the single richest Colorado mining man of his generation, and by far the best known; he ranked with a handful of Western mining men as the most renowned nationally. His career spans the whole of nineteenth-century Colorado mining, from the placer days of '59 to the corporate operations of Leadville and Cripple Creek. Throughout the last two decades of that century Colorado remained the number one mining state in the United States. His fortunes provide ample testimonial to the vicissitudes of mining and the changing methods employed in the industry. His own methods evolved considerably. To be fair, he should be judged against the standards of his own time, a time which also saw the manipulations on the Comstock, the operations of men like George Roberts, and the copper struggles in Butte, Montana. Though these do not justify Tabor's maneuverings, they tend to put them in perspective.

The peak of his success came in 1878–1879: almost all his later endeavors were based upon profits made then or mines owned at that time which subsequently boomed. The Little Pittsburg and the Matchless were the most famous of his mines, with the latter producing for him, as he estimated in the late 1880s, perhaps half a million dollars profit.[6] Even Horace did not know exactly how much money it produced. The Little Pittsburg gave him a million dollars in the final sale, beyond two years profits from working it.

The only contemporary Colorado mining man who can be compared to Tabor, by virtue of his wealth and career, is Winfield Stratton, who unquestionably made more money, but did so late in his life. Consequently, he had much less impact over time on the state and the West. Hoarding his fortune, Stratton proved to be neither the plunger nor the investor that Tabor was. In consequence, he died a multimillionaire, endowing the Myron Stratton Home for poor children and old people as a fitting memorial. Before the discovery of their bonanzas, the lives of these men reflected typical mining frontier experiences. Tabor's career, however, had many more ramifications, and he showed a boldness and faith in himself and his endeavors which Stratton, except for his persistence in seeking a mining bonanza, displayed only to a lesser degree. Stratton felt his mines should be developed conservatively, the ore that remained unmined serving as a safe reserve for future constructive use. Tabor, except for the Matchless, exhibited an opposite speculative instinct. The two were completely different personalities, although similar in one striking aspect.

According to Stratton's biographer, Frank Waters, Stratton firmly held to the belief that any man who derived his wealth from natural resources should reinvest it to develop the home region.[7] Tabor demonstrated a corresponding idea, carrying it out at breakneck speed, to the detriment of his personal fortune. Much of his reinvestment helped further develop Colorado in the various phases of its economic growth after 1878. He could not concentrate in one area like a Carnegie or Rockefeller; Tabor and other western entrepreneurs had to diversify until development reached the point that specialization could appear. During Tabor's and Stratton's lifetimes, only mining offered this opportunity. Both of these men provided investment sources which helped Colorado break away from the bounds of financial colonialism that had so long guided its destiny. Tabor and Stratton, whose careers intersected occasionally, together epitomized Colorado mining, symbolized the lure of mining, and represented the zenith of individual success in mining in the nineteenth century.

Tabor had a sense of philanthropy, which Andrew Carnegie called the "Gospel of Wealth," although Horace never carried it as far as Carnegie did. It was with him long before he became a millionaire, somewhat like John D. Rockefeller, and Horace repeatedly shared what he could with those less fortunate. He also evidenced a desire to preserve his name in something cultural and intellectual, hence his interest in opera houses. Without doubt, this was one reason he built them, even though he claimed to have done it solely for profit. His drive, his desire for success ended with the loss of his wealth, but this made him no hapless entrepreneur. Nor does this failure or his actions justify the sarcastic attacks launched against him.

Intuitively, Tabor seemed to sense the needs of his time and people and tried to meet them. If a man's beliefs can be judged by his actions, then Tabor voted heartily for faith in the future. His failure does not at all lessen his significance.

By the time of his death, an entire generation had grown to manhood since he had come to Kansas and rushed to Pike's Peak. A new United States had emerged, based upon world power and prestige that could only have been dreamed about in the 1850s. On the day he died, the Denver papers were full of the news of this new era, with articles on the Philippine insurrection and the implications of the peace with Spain. Tabor had watched the brief Spanish-American War draw to a victorious close in 1898, undoubtedly little realizing its total significance. The old gave way to the new in the

1890s, and Tabor, along with those other survivors of his generation, was a relic of a bygone era. He had come West as a pioneer, to a land unsettled and untamed. His life had touched upon many of the major ingredients of settlement: transportation, mining, business, politics, and farming. Now there was no longer a definable frontier. In his own way, however small, Horace Tabor helped bring this about; what regrets he might have felt were minor compared to the sweep of change since 1855.

NOTES

PROLOGUE

1. *The Ballad of Baby Doe*. Copyright © (unpub.) 1956 by Douglas S. Moore and John Latouche. Copyright © 1957 & 1958 by Douglas S. Moore and Rosalind Rock, as Administratrix of the Estate of John Latouche, deceased. Chappell & Co., Inc., New York, N.Y., owner of publication and allied rights throughout the world.

CHAPTER 1

1. *Report of the Special Committee Appointed to Investigate the Troubles in Kansas* (Washington: Cornelius Wendell, 1856), pp. 831, 887, 889, & 893. *Herald of Freedom* (Lawrence), March 24, 1855. There is disagreement on the exact number of people who arrived.

2. Horace A. W. Tabor, "Autobiography" (Bancroft Library), p. 6. *Denver Times*, April 3, 1899.

3. *Herald of Freedom*, March 31 & July 14, 1855. See also *Report of the Special Committee . . . Kansas*, pp. 108, 831, & 892–93. Allan Nevins, *Ordeal of the Union* (New York: Charles Scribner's Sons, 1947), v. 2, pp. 301–02.

4. Francis A. Abbott, "Some Reminiscences of Early Days of Deep Creek, Riley County," *Collections of the Kansas State Historical Society*, v. 12, pp. 392–95. Alfred T. Andreas, *History of the State of Kansas* (Chicago: A. T. Andreas, 1883), p. 1301. H. Tabor, "Autobiography," pp. 5–6. *Herald of Freedom*, Dec. 22, 1855 & Jan. 12, 1856.

5. H. Tabor, "Autobiography," p. 8. *Herald of Freedom*, Jan. 12, 19 & March 1, 1856. *Report of the Special Committee . . . Kansas*, pp. 674–83, 713–39, & 786–87. Andreas, *History . . . Kansas*, p. 125.

6. *Herald of Freedom*, Dec. 22, 1855. "Journal of the House of Representatives of the State of Kansas," reprinted in the *Collections of the Kansas State Historical Society 1913–14* (Topeka: W. R. Smith, 1915), pp. 166, 190, 192, 199–200, 203–08, 210–12, 216–20, 223–35. See also *New York Times*, March 20, 1856; *Herald of Freedom*, March 8, 15, 22, 29, 1856.

7. *Herald of Freedom*, April 5, 1856.

8. "Journal . . . Kansas," p. 235. *New York Times*, July 17–19, 1856. H. Tabor, "Autobiography," p. 7. Charles Robinson, "Topeka and Her Constitution," *Transactions of the Kansas State Historical Society* (Topeka: W. Y. Morgan, 1900), v. 6, p. 299.

9. *Herald of Freedom*, Jan. 17 & 19, 1857. "Journal . . . Kansas," pp. 236–38. Andreas, *History . . . Kansas*, p. 155. There is some confusion as to when the House actually adjourned. *Squatter Sovereign*, Jan. 20, 1857.

10. "Journal . . . Kansas," p. 242–46. *Herald of Freedom*, June 20, 1857. See also issues of April 25, June 13, 27 & July 4, 1857. Alice Polk Hill, *Tales of the Colorado Pioneers* (Denver: Pierson & Gardner, 1884), p. 219. Albert Greene, "The Kansas River — Its Navigation," *Transactions of the Kansas State Historical Society*, 1905–06, v. 9, pp. 338–39. *Herald of Freedom*, April 11 & 18, 1857.

11. Hill, *Tales of the Colorado Pioneers*, p. 220.

12. *Herald of Freedom*, April 11, 1857. Andreas, *History . . . Kansas*, p. 1301. Richardson, *Beyond the Mississippi* (Hartford: American Publishing Co., 1867), p. 26.

13. *Portrait and Biographical Record of Denver and Vicinity, Colorado* (Chicago: Chapman Publishing Co., 1898), p. 137. See also Hill, *Tales of the Colorado Pioneers*, pp. 220–21. The exact date of Maxey's birth is October 9, 1857. His name was also spelled Maxie, Maxcey, and Maxcy, although Maxey was the correct one. *Denver Post*, Jan. 29, 1929.

14. *New York Times*, Sept. 20, 23, 28 & Oct. 15, 1858. *Daily California Express* (Marysville), July 21, 1858. See also LeRoy Hafen (ed.), *Pike's Peak Gold Rush Guidebooks of 1859*.

15. *Herald of Freedom*, April 2, 1859. See also Jan. 15, 22, March 12, 19 & 26, 1859.

16. H. Tabor, "Autobiography," p. 9.

17. H. Tabor, "Autobiography," pp. 8–9. *Rocky Mountain News* (Denver), Jan. 5, 1881. In the *News* Tabor said a man came along and asked him why he did not go; this set him to thinking about it.

18. *Rocky Mountain News*, Jan. 5, 1881. Moys to Tabor, March 19, 1887. Horace A. W. Tabor Manuscript Collection. Hereafter cited H. Tabor Manuscripts. The Lawrence lots eventually were given to Tabor's sister Emma, Emma Moys to Tabors, April 1, 1893.

19. "Journal of J. A. Wilkinson, Across the Plains in 1859," (Henry E. Huntington Library), pp. 40–44.

20. Hill, *Tales of the Colorado Pioneers*, pp. 221–22. Augusta Tabor, "Cabin Life," (Bancroft Library), discusses Kansas in two sentences, giving no specific dates.

CHAPTER 2

1. Horace Greeley, *An Overland Journey* (New York: Alfred Knopf, 1964 reprint), pp. 135–36.

2. *Rocky Mountain News* (Weekly), (Denver), May 14, 1859.

3. A. Tabor, "Cabin Life," p. 1. For a slightly different version by Augusta, see Hill, *Tales of the Colorado Pioneers*, pp. 222–23. This was supposedly written by Augusta and is more detailed than the same period of "Cabin Life." Dates are relative throughout the Tabor early years.

4. A. Tabor, "Cabin Life," p. 2. She must mean the whole trip took three weeks. Interestingly, Tabor skips over any mention of his problems at Idaho Springs, but says he made enough to pay the mortgage. H. Tabor, "Autobiography," p. 9.

5. *New York Times*, Nov. 18, 1859. Robert Bradford to William Waddell, Nov. 3, 1859, Robert B. Bradford Letters (Huntington Library), hereafter cited Bradford Letters; *Rocky Mountain News* (weekly), Nov. 3, 10, 24 & Dec. 1, 1859.

6. Bradford to Waddell, Nov. 29 & Dec. 15, 1859, and Jan. 18 & Feb. 1, 1860, Bradford Letters.

7. The sources for the section on Colorado City were H. Tabor, "Autobiography," p. 9; A. Tabor, "Cabin Life," p. 2. *Rocky Mountain News* (Weekly), Feb. 22 & March 14, 1860, and S. W. Burt & E. L. Berthoud, *The Rocky Mountain Gold Regions* (Denver: *Rocky Mountain News* 1861), p. 97. Comments on the Denver situation from Bradford to Waddell, Jan. 5, Feb. 3 & 21, 1860, Bradford Letters.

8. Sources for the preceding: A. Tabor, "Cabin Life," p. 3. Hill, *Tales of Colorado Pioneers*, pp. 224–26. H. Tabor, clipping found in the Dawson Scrapbooks (v. 23), State Historical Society of Colorado, taken from the *Great Divide*, Jan., 1892. This is the best account by Horace of this period. Ute Pass had been used in 1859 by miners to reach South Park.

9. Bradford to Waddell, March 15, 1860, Bradford Letters. *Rocky Mountain News* (weekly), March 28, April 25 and May 16, 1860. For a discussion of the discoverers and dates, see issues of May 23, July 25 and Aug. 15, 1860. *History of the Arkansas Valley, Colorado* (Chicago: O. L. Baskin, 1881), pp. 210–13, and Don & Jean Griswold, *The Carbonate Camp Called Leadville* (Denver: University of Denver Press, 1951), pp. 2–4.

10. A. Tabor, "Cabin Life," p. 3. See also H. Tabor, "Autobiography," p. 10, and Tabor clipping, Dawson Scrapbooks (footnote 8). Hill, *Tales of Colorado Pioneers*, pp. 227–28, has an elaborate discussion of this period. Ovando Hollister, *The Mines of Colorado* (Springfield: Samuel Bowles & Co., 1867), pp. 316–17.

11. Composite picture from the *Rocky Mountain News* (Weekly), June 13, 27 & July 4, 11, & 25, 1860. Hollister, *Mines of Colorado*, p. 115. Census 1860, Kansas Territory, Arapahoe County, California Gulch, pp. 267–320.

12. *Rocky Mountain News* (Weekly), Aug. 29, 1860. For further information see issues of Aug. 8, 22 & Oct. 10, 1860; Bradford to Waddell, July 4, 1860, Bradford Letters; Matthew Sheriff Diary, June 28–July 2, 1860, (State Historical Society) and Isaac Beardsley, *Echoes from*

Peak and Plain (Cincinnati: Curts & Jennings, 1898), pp. 254–56. Maxey Tabor Interview (State Historical Society), Hill, *Tales of Colorado Pioneers*, and the *Leadville Chronicle*, July 30, 1879, all state that Augusta went East.

13. *Rocky Mountain News* (Weekly), Nov. 28, 1860, and Horace Tabor, "Early Days," (Bancroft Library), p. 2. Augusta said later that Tabor went back East with her, but this is unlikely, considering other evidence. See the daily *Rocky Mountain News*, Nov. 23, and all issues Nov. 10–Dec. 15, 1860.

14. A. S. Weston, "A Fifty Niner Who Stayed," *Colorado Magazine* (Oct., 1959), p. 253.

15. *Rocky Mountain News* (Weekly), April 24, 1861, names a Mr. Tabor as part of the discovery party. Samuel F. Emmons, *Geology and Mining Industry of Leadville, Colorado* (Washington: Government Printing Office, 1886), pp. 8–9, also places Tabor in Iowa Gulch.

16. Wolfe Londoner, "Colorado Mining Camps" (Bancroft Library), pp. 7–8.

17. *Rocky Mountain News* (Weekly), July 17, 1861. See also issues May 2, 1860, June 12, and July 3, 1861; and the *Miners' Record* (Tarryall), July 13 & 27, 1861.

18. A. Tabor, "Cabin Life," p. 4. *Engineering and Mining Journal* (New York), March 30, 1878, p. 221. Frank Fossett, *Colorado* (Denver: Daily Tribune Steam Printing House, 1876), p. 118. Hereafter cited, Fossett, *Colorado* (1876).

19. *Rocky Mountain News* (Weekly), Jan. 18, 1862. See also issues of March 20, July 31, Sept. 4 & 11, 1861. *Miners' Record*, Aug. 10, 17, 31 & Sept. 7, 1861. *Leadville Democrat*, July 1, 1880. Fossett, *Colorado* (1876), pp. 54–57. Nolie Mumey, *History and Proceedings of Buckskin Joe* (Boulder: Johnson Publishing Co., 1961), pp. 1–14. John Evans, *Message to Legislative Assembly of Colorado, July 17, 1862* (Denver: Rocky Mountain News, 1862), pp. 10–11.

20. William Dutt to his sister, May 21, 1862, William S. Dutt Correspondence (Huntington). *Rocky Mountain News* (Weekly), March 1 & 8, 1862.

21. Eugene Parsons, "Tabor and Times," *The Trail*, Oct. 1921, p. 7. H. Tabor Clipping, Dawson Scrapbooks. W. W. Borden, *A Treatise on Leadville, Colorado* (New Albany, Ind.: Cannon Publisher, 1879), p. 29. *Denver Tribune*, June 25, 1879. *Inter-Ocean Mining Journal and Political Review* (Denver), Aug. 7, 1880, hereafter cited *Inter-Ocean*. Hubert H. Bancroft, *Chronicles of the Builders* (San Francisco: History Co., 1892), v. 4, p. 294. *Rocky Mountain News* (Weekly), April 26, May 24, July 5, July 31 & Sept. 25, 1862. For a record of his early mining activity see, Roy Davidson, "Some Early . . . , 1859–63," *Colorado Magazine*, Sept. 1941, p. 178.

22. *Reports of Territorial Officers of Colorado Territory* (Central City: David C. Collier, 1867), pp. 31–32. Horace Hale, *Education in Colorado, 1861–1885* (Denver: News Printing Co., 1885), pp. 21–23.

23. H. Tabor, "Autobiography," pp. 17–18.

24. *Rocky Mountain News*, June 23, 1866.

25. The Leach material is found in Samuel Leach, "Mosquito Mining District," *The Trail*, March 1926, pp. 10–13, and May 1926, pp. 7–10. These are reprints of letters sent by Leach, Oct. 1862, Jan., March & May 1863. See also Samuel Leach, "Early Day Reminiscences," *The Trail*, May 1911, pp. 5–9. Leach later went to Virginia City and Helena, Montana.

26. Nathan S. Hurd Interview, Dec. 11, 1921 (State Historical Society), p. 11.

27. A. Tabor, "Cabin Life," p. 4.

28. Fossett, *Colorado* (1876), pp. 54–57. *Rocky Mountain News* (weekly), May 28, June 28, Oct. 31, 1863, Feb. 3, & July 13, 1864.

29. F. J. Porter to Samuel Barlow, May 15, 1865, Barlow Collection, Huntington Library. *New York Times*, Jan. 6, 1863. Fossett, *Colorado* (1876), pp. 152–53. Rodman Paul, "Colorado as a Pioneer of Science in the Mining West," *Mississippi Valley Historical Review*, June, 1960, pp. 34–42.

30. Frank Fossett, *Colorado Its Gold and Silver Mines* (New York: Crawford, 1879), p. 147. Hereafter cited as Fossett, *Colorado* (1879).

31. Fossett, *Colorado* (1876), p. 57. Hollister, *The Mines of Colorado*, p. 299.

32. Isaac Ware Interview, *Western Miner and Financier*, April 19, 1899. *Rocky Mountain News*, July 13, & 29, 1868.

33. Bayard Taylor, *Colorado: A Summer Trip* (New York: G. P. Putnam & Son, 1867), pp. 119–21.

34. *Rocky Mountain News*, July 29, 1868, refers to Mr. Tabor of Oro City.

35. William H. Brewer, *Rocky Mountain Letters 1869* (Denver: Colorado Mountain Club, 1930), p. 43. Buckskin Joe revived briefly in 1879, but the Tabors by then were not considering returning.

CHAPTER 3

1. Taylor, *Colorado*, pp. 125–27. H. Tabor, "Early Days," p. 5. *Engineering and Mining Journal*, March 30, 1878, p. 221. Wolfe Londoner in his "Colorado Mining Camps" discussed the decline of Oro City in the 1860s while he was there. Hollister, *Mines of Colorado*, p. 317.

2. Hollister, *Mines of Colorado*, p. 318. Louis Simonin, *The Rocky Mountain West in 1867* (Lincoln: University of Nebraska Press, 1966), pp. 47–58.

3. Records pertaining to Tabor's postmastership in Oro City are found in H. Tabor Manuscripts. *Rocky Mountain News*, July 29, 1868

& Jan. 30, 1873. *Colorado Business Directory and Annual Register for 1876* (Denver: J. A. Blake, 1876), p. 38. A. Tabor, "Cabin Life," p. 4.

4. *United States v. Henry P. Farnum,* 199, 202, 203, & 210, First Judicial District Court Denver (1870). *United States v. William Beery*, 209, First Judicial District Court Denver (1872). *Rocky Mountain News*, June 26, July 7, 1869 & Aug. 1, 1871, P.H. Woodward, *Guarding the Mails or the Secret Service of the Post-Office Department* (Hartford: J. P. Fitch, 1881), pp. 191–93, 195, 227. Chapter 8 of this book deals with the case. A modern examination is Agnes W. Spring, "Who Stole Tabor's Gold?" *The 1966 Brand Book* (Denver). Copies of some of the postal forms Tabor filled out may be found in the National Archives.

5. A. Tabor, "Cabin Life," pp. 6–7.

6. A. Tabor, Cabin Life," p. 6.

7. The few remaining Tabor business records for this period are found in the John Harper Papers (Western Historical Collections, University of Colorado) and H. A. W. Tabor to Charles Nathrop, Sept. 24, 1870 & Sept. 26, 1871 (State Historical Society).

8. *Rocky Mountain News*, July 21, 1872 and weekly edition, July 24.

9. *History of the Arkansas Valley*, p. 216.

10. *Rocky Mountain News*, July 21, 1872, said Tabor had two stores, one at the upper and the other at the lower end of the gulch. This could have been the forerunner of the store at Malta. See also *History of the Arkansas Valley*, p. 220, and N. Maxey Tabor, "Interview."

11. A. Tabor, "Cabin Life," pp. 5–6. *Rocky Mountain News*, July 21, 1872 & April 11, 1899. Bancroft, *Chronicles of the Builders*, pp. 294–95. Wilbur F. Stone dictation found in the Tabor Material at the Bancroft Library gives a confused version of this same story. *Western Miner & Financier*, April 19, 1899, has a similar story, but with different names and ending.

12. A. Tabor, "Cabin Life," p. 5.

13. W. B. Vickers, *History of the City of Denver, Arapahoe County, and Colorado* (Chicago: O. L. Baskin & Co., 1880), p. 611. Ninth Census, Oro City, Lake County, Colorado, original returns. *Denver Tribune*, Jan. 28, 1883, states $35,000 in 1878. See also undated newspaper clipping, H. Tabor Manuscripts. Wilbur Stone, who knew the Tabors, said they were not poor. Stone, "Tabor," p. 4. While hard to read, by totaling up the personal property column, it is obvious Tabor had $5,000, not $3,000, as I stated in my *Rocky Mountain Mining Camps*.

14. H. Tabor, "Early Days," p. 4. Griswold, *Carbonate Camp*, p. 5.

15. Ninth Census 1870, Oro City, Lake County, Colorado, Original Returns, pp. 7–15. Tabor to Chas. Nathrop, Sept. 24, 1870 (State

Historical Society). Richard Carroll, "Mary Nash Mear, Pioneer," *Colorado Magazine*, Nov., 1934, p. 218.

16. Charles Kingsley, *South by West* (London: W. Isbister & Co., 1874), p. 120. Kingsley was in Colorado Springs, Nov. 1871–March 1872.

17. *Rocky Mountain News*, Aug. 1, 1870; July 21, 1872, Aug. 31, 1873 & May 13, 1874. *New York Times*, May 20, 1878. *Colorado Business Directory* (1876), p. 204. *Colorado Business Directory and Annual Register for 1875* (Denver: J. A. Blake, 1875), p. 197. *Colorado State Business Directory & Annual Register* (Denver: J. A. Blake, 1878), p. 208. Oro City was not directly involved in the so-called Lake County War. See Dyer, *Snow-Shoe Itinerant*, p. 291 and the *Rocky Mountain News*, Feb. 6, 1875.

18. Sewall Thomas, *Silhouettes of Charles S. Thomas* (Caldwell: Caxton Printers, 1959), p. 35. Tabor Manuscripts, Bancroft Library, Folder 5. Tabor Collection, First National Bank of Denver, has some canceled checks signed by Maxey. *City Directory of Leadville* (Denver: Daily Times Steam Printing House, 1879), p. 12. *Denver Tribune*, Dec. 1, 1878.

19. *Pueblo Daily Chieftain*, Feb. 18, 1876, has the letter and quotes the *Avalanche*. No further comment appeared in it concerning this incident.

20. H. Tabor, "Autobiography," p. 10. *History of the Arkansas Valley*, p. 380. See also, *Western Miner & Financier*, April 19, 1899. *Great Divide*, Jan. 1892, found in the Dawson Scrapbooks, vol. 23, State Historical Society.

21. *History of the Arkansas Valley*, pp. 216–217.

22. Rossiter Raymond, *Mines, Mills and Furnaces* (New York: J. B. Ford & Co., 1871), p. 332. Rossiter Raymond, *Statistics of the Mines and Mining in the States and Territories West of the Rocky Mountains* (Washington: Government Printing Office, 1873), pp. 364–65. Rossiter Raymond, *Mining Industry of the States and Territories of the Rocky Mountains* (New York: J. B. Ford & Co., 1874), pp. 299–300. Rossiter Raymond, *Mines and Mining in the States and Territories West of the Rocky Mountains* (Washington: Government Printing Office, 1874), pp. 308–09. Rossiter Raymond, *Statistics of Mines and Mining* (Washington: Government Printing Office, 1875), pp. 358, 374 & 383. *Rocky Mountain News*, July 21, 1872. Records of the California Mining District, California Gulch, Colorado Territory, 1867–1876, pp. 42–390.

23. Samuel H. Elbert, *Biennial Message* (Central City: Register Printing House, 1874), p. 21.

24. Frank Fossett, *Colorado Its Gold and Silver Mines* (New York: Crawford, 1880), pp. 407–08. Hereafter cited Fossett, *Colorado* (1880). *History of the Arkansas Valley*, pp. 217–18. Griswold, *Carbonate Camp*, pp. 22–24. Percy Fritz, *Colorado the Centennial State* (New York: Prentice-Hall, 1941), pp. 302–03.

25. The Oro City Territorial Assay Office, assay book is found in the Henry Ellsworth Wood Collection, Huntington Library. The name of the firm changed and it moved to Leadville in 1877. The book covers the period Sept. 1873 to Aug. 1878. *Rocky Mountain News*, Nov. 29, 1873.

26. Raymond, *Statistics* (1875), p. 383.

27. Oro City Territorial Assay Office, assay book, April, May, July 1876.

28. Dyer, *Snow-Shoe Itinerant*, pp. 279 & 320. Thomas Corbett, *The Colorado Directory of Mines* (Denver: Rocky Mountain News Printing Co., 1879), p. 270. *Rocky Mountain News*, March 20, 1879. *Engineering and Mining Journal*, Sept. 9, 1876, p. 172. *Leadville Democrat*, Feb. 10, 1880. The court appointed Tabor as the disinterested party in probating Dyer's will.

CHAPTER 4

1. Carlyle C. Davis, *Olden Times in Colorado* (Los Angeles: Phillips Publishing Co., 1916), p. 84. *Engineering and Mining Journal*, Sept. 9, 1876, p. 176, Jan. 27, p. 55, March 31, p. 205 and May 26, 1877, p. 353. *Rocky Mountain News* (Weekly), Oct. 31, 1877. *Harper's Weekly*, June 21, 1879, p. 475. Frank Hall, *History of the State of Colorado* (Chicago: Blakely Printing Co., 1890–91), v. 2, p. 435.

2. *History of the Arkansas Valley*, p. 219. *Engineering and Mining Journal*, Jan. 19, 1878, p. 41. *Rocky Mountain News* (Weekly), Jan. 2, 1878.

3. *Mining Record*, May 20, 1882, quoting the Oct. 25, 1877 issue. See also, *History of the Arkansas Valley*, pp. 220–23 & 218. *Rocky Mountain News*, Nov. 22, 1881.

4. Tabor letterheads are found in the Hamill and Teller papers at the Denver Public Library and in the Tabor Collection at the State Historical Society. The copy of the *Reveille* ad is found in the Tabor Collection. *Rocky Mountain News* (Weekly), June 12 & July 17, 1878. Griswold, *Carbonate Camp*, pp. 70–71.

5. A. R. Brown, quoted in Griswold, *Carbonate Camp*, pp. 73–74.

6. General Docket Book, Lake County, 1870–1880, pp. 105–13. *History of the Arkansas Valley*, p. 225. *Denver Tribune*, Feb. 19, 1878. *Engineering and Mining Journal*, March 30, 1878, p. 22. L. A. Kent, *Leadville* (Denver: Daily Times Steam Printing House, 1880), pp. 22–23.

7. *The Revised and General Ordinances of the City of Leadville* (Leadville: Chronicle, 1881), pp. 39, 62, 113–14. *History of the Arkansas Valley*, pp. 237–38. Leadville Book 1 (Minutes of the Board of Trustees), Feb. 1878–April 1879.

8. *The Revised . . . Leadville*, pp. 3–4.

9. *Rocky Mountain News* (Weekly), May 1, 15, 29, 1878. *Daily Chronicle*, Feb. 26, 28, March 1, 3 & May 9, 1879. Griswold, *Carbonate Camp*, 151–58. Martin Duggan, "Dictation," Bancroft Library. Leadville Book 1, pp. 206–07.

10. *Engineering and Mining Journal*, April 6, 1878, p. 240. *History of the Arkansas Valley*, p. 383. Bronson C. Keeler, *Leadville & its Silver Mines* (Chicago: E. L. Ayer, 1879), p. 7. *The Revised . . . Leadville*, p. 70. *Daily Chronicle*, Feb. 15, 1879. *Rocky Mountain News* (Weekly), May 15, 1878. Leadville Book 1, pp. 2–3, 50–54, and 162–67. *Denver Tribune*, Nov. 22, 1878.

11. *Denver Tribune*, Jan. 29 & March 16, 1879. *Rocky Mountain News* (Weekly), Feb. 19, 1879. *Daily Chronicle*, Feb. 7, 1879. Kent, *Leadville*, p. 167. H. Tabor, "Autobiography," p. 17. Vickers, *History of Denver*, p. 612. Leadville Book 1, pp. 62–63 & 190–91. Leadville Improvement Co., Incorporation Papers.

12. Composite picture of Leadville was taken from the following sources: *Denver Tribune*, Feb. 24, March 1, 3, May 18, 24, July 24, 25, & Dec. 22, 1878. *Rocky Mountain News* (Weekly), March 27, April 10, May 29, June 26, and July 17, 1878. *Engineering and Mining Journal*, April 6, 1878, p. 240. *History of the Arkansas Valley*, p. 268. John Loomis, *Leadville Colorado* (Colorado Springs: Gazette Publishing Co., 1879), pp. 15–17.

13. Mattie E. Stuthman, "High Altitude Memories," *Colorado Magazine* (Jan. 1952), p. 34. Carlyle C. Davis, "History of Colorado," Bancroft Dictation. Samuel Silver, "The Mines of Colorado," Bancroft Dictation.

14. H. H. (Jackson, Helen H.), "To Leadville," *Atlantic Monthly*, May 1879, pp. 567–79. See also *New York Times*, July 13, 1878, p. 2 and *The Engineering and Mining Journal*, Oct. 5, 1878, p. 243.

15. *Georgetown Miner*, no date, quoted in the *Denver Tribune*, Nov. 7, 1878.

16. Tabor to H. Teller, May 29, 1878, Teller Letters, Denver Public Library. *Rocky Mountain News* (Weekly), July 17, 1878. Davis, *Olden Times*, p. 120.

17. *Horace A. W. Tabor et al.* v. *Wert Dexter et al.*, District Court, Lake County, 154 (1878). H. Tabor, "Autobiography," pp. 10–11. *Engineering and Mining Journal*, June 15, 1878, p. 405. Samuel Emmons, *Geology and Mining Industry of Leadville, Colorado* (Washington: Government Printing Office, 1886), p. 468. *Denver Tribune*, June 12, 1878. *History of the Arkansas Valley*, p. 218. M. Tabor, "Interview." For an example of Tabor's earlier mining ventures, see Tabor to Edwin Harrison, Feb. 15, 1878, Harrison Papers, State Historical Society. The Little Pittsburg perhaps was named for Pittsburgh, Penn.; contemporary accounts are unclear.

18. H. Tabor "Autobiography," pp. 10–11. August Rische, "Interview," Bancroft Library. *Engineering and Mining Journal*, June 15, 1878, p. 405. Davis, *Olden Times*, pp. 203–04.

19. Sources for section on the Little Pittsburg: Fossett, *Colorado* (1880), pp. 452–53. H. Tabor, "Autobiography," p. 11; Rische, "Interview." *Horace A. W. Tabor, Jerome Chaffee, et al.* v. *Wirt Dexter et al.*, U. S. Circuit Court, Denver, 217 (1879). *Horace A. W. Tabor, Jerome Chaffee, et al.*, v. *Wert Dexter et al.*, District Court, Lake County, 149 & 154 (1878). Willis Sweet, *Carbonate Camps, Leadville and Ten Mile* (Kansas City: Ramsey, Millet & Hudson, 1879), pp. 54–59. *Denver Tribune*, July 25, Sept. 12, Oct. 2, 15, 26 & Nov. 7 & 23, 1878. *Denver Weekly Times*, Sept. 25, Oct. 23, 30 & Nov. 27, 1878. *Engineering and Mining Journal*, Oct. 12, 1878, pp. 260–61. Loomis, *Leadville*, pp. 12–13. *Rocky Mountain News* (Weekly), July 10, 1878. George Bishop, *Charles H. Dow and the Dow Theory* (New York: Appleton-Century-Crofts, 1960), p. 295. Deeds and Quit claims, L. C. Rockwell Collection. The spelling of the mine names varies, but I have chosen in all cases the one most commonly used at the time, hence Little Pittsburg, without an "h," and Winnemuck, rather than Winnemuc. All sale prices have to be considered an estimate, since the figures reported vary. For example, Rische's claim of $265,000 is refuted by the deed he signed with Chaffee, Nov. 5, 1878. See L. C. Rockwell Collection.

20. *Denver Tribune*, Nov. 28, Dec. 8, 1878 & Feb. 4, 1879. *Engineering and Mining Journal*, Feb. 8, p. 85 & Feb. 22, 1879, p. 124. *Horace Tabor, et al.* v. *Peter Finnerty et al.*, District Court, Lake County (1878), records found in H. Tabor Manuscripts.

21. *Denver Tribune*, Dec. 22, 1878. Fossett, *Colorado* (1880), p. 454.

22. H. Tabor, "Autobiography," p. 12. It is pronounced as if the "y" were a short "i".

23. *Denver Weekly Times*, Oct. 16, Nov. 23, 27 & Dec. 11, 1878.

24. *Reveille*, no date, quoted in the *New York Times*, May 20, 1878. *Pueblo Chieftain*, no date, quoted in the *Denver Weekly Times*, Oct. 23, 1878. *Engineering and Mining Journal*, Aug. 24, p. 135 & Dec. 14, 1878, p. 421. Fossett, *Colorado* (1880), p. 445.

25. *Denver Tribune*, Dec. 22, 1878. H. Tabor, "Autobiography," p. 17. *Denver Weekly Times*, Oct. 16 & Dec. 11, 1878.

26. *Denver Tribune*, March 5, 1879.

CHAPTER 5

1. Dill, *Political Campaigns*, p. 33. *Denver Tribune*, June 13, 1878.

2. Sources for the preceding section on the Republican party are as follows: Fossett, *Colorado* (1879), pp. 456–57. Walter Shelly, "The Colorado Republican Party: the Formative Years, 1861–1876," Unpublished Master's Thesis, University of Colorado, 1963, pp. 72–73 & 114–16. William Byers, *Encyclopedia of Biography of Colorado* (Chicago: Century Publishing Co., 1901), v. 1, pp. 101 & 198–99.

R. G. Dill, *The Political Campaigns of Colorado* (Denver: Arapahoe Publishing Co., 1895), p. 21. *Leadville Daily Herald*, June 6, 1884. *Rocky Mountain News* (Weekly), July 20, 1870. Fossett, *Colorado* (1876), pp. 336–39. *New York Times*, Dec. 13, 1878 & Jan. 4, 1883.

3. Hall, *History of Colorado*, v. 2, p. 471.

4. *Denver Tribune*, July 25, 31, Aug. 1, 6, 7 & 9, 1878. *Denver Daily Times*, Aug. 6 & 8, 1878. *Rocky Mountain News* (Weekly), July 17 & Aug. 7, 1878; (Daily), Aug. 9, 1878. See also Thomas Wiswall's comments on Tabor in 1878, Tabor Material, Bancroft Library.

5. *Rocky Mountain News*, Nov. 2, 1883. *Leadville Democrat*, Sept. 1, 1880. Dill, *Political Campaigns*, p. 36.

6. *Denver Tribune*, Aug. 9 & 11, 1878. *Rocky Mountain News*, Aug. 9, 1878. These papers published different versions of his acceptance speech; both agreed it was short.

7. Dill, *Political Campaigns*, pp. 29–30 & 38–39.

8. *Denver Weekly Times*, Aug. 21, 1878. *Denver Tribune*, Aug. 15 & 18, 1878. *Rocky Mountain News*, Oct. 31, 1883. D. E. Parks to Hamill, Aug. 11, 1878, Hamill Papers, Denver Public Library. For a Leadville Democrat's view see the *Rocky Mountain News*, Aug. 16, 1878.

9. *Rocky Mountain News*, Aug. 10, 11, 14, 16, 17, 21–23 & 27, 1878; (Weekly), Aug. 14 & 28, 1878. Dill, *Political Campaigns*, p. 37.

10. *Denver Tribune*, Aug. 11, 15 & 24, 1878. *Silver World* (Lake City), Aug. 31, 1878. *Daily Register-Call* (Central City), Aug. 16 & 24, 1878. *Boulder County News*, Aug. 16, 23 & 30, 1878. *Denver Daily Times*, Aug. 12 & 14, 1878.

11. George Shaw to Hamill, Aug. 23, 1878, Hamill Papers. *Reveille*, no date, quoted in the *Boulder County News*, Aug. 30, 1878.

12. Tabor to Hamill, Aug. 19, 22 & Sept. 5, 1878; Charles Lavender to Hamill, Aug. 29, 1878; and Parks to Hamill, Aug. 11 & 29, 1878, Hamill Papers. *History of the Arkansas Valley*, p. 238.

13. *Pitkin & Belford Campaign of 1878* (Denver: Republican State Central Comm., 1878), pp. 1–4.

14. *Rocky Mountain News*, Sept. 3, 5–7 & 10, 1878.

15. Tabor to Hamill, Aug. 22, 1878; Parks to Hamill, Sept. 11, 1878, Hamill Papers. *Daily Register-Call*, Aug. 15, 1878. *Denver Tribune*, Aug. 21, 29, Sept. 13 & 18, 1878. *Denver Weekly Times*, Sept. 18, 1878. *Georgetown Courier*, Sept. 19, 1878. *Saguache Chronicle*, Sept. 7, 1878. *Boulder County News*, Sept. 6, 1878. *Rocky Mountain News* (Weekly), Aug. 28 & Sept. 4, 1878; (Daily), Sept. 14, 1878.

16. *Rocky Mountain News*, Sept. 17, 21, 26 & 27, 1878. *Denver Tribune*, Sept. 19, 22 & 29, 1878.

17. *Denver Daily Times*, Sept. 25 & Oct. 1, 1878. *Rocky Mountain News*, Oct. 1, 1878. Dill, *Political Campaigns*, p. 45. *Leadville Daily Herald*, April 1, 1881. *Rocky Mountain News* (Weekly), Jan. 8, 1879. *Senate Journal of the General Assembly of the State of Colorado, Second*

Session, Convened at the City of Denver, Jan. 1, 1879 (Denver Times Steam Printing House, 1879), pp. 16–17.

18. *Rocky Mountain News*, Oct. 4–5, 1878.

19. H. Tabor, "Autobiography," p. 19. *Denver Tribune*, Sept. 19, 1878.

20. *Rocky Mountain News* (Weekly), April 9, 1879.

CHAPTER 6

1. Chaffee to Teller, June 16, 1878, Teller Papers, Denver Public Library. Dill, *Political Campaigns*, pp. 29–38.

2. Hall, *History of Colorado*, v. 3, pp. 22 & 37. Dill, *Political Campaigns*, pp. 32, 37, 40–41. Thomas F. Dawson, *Life and Character of Edward Oliver Wolcott* (New York: Knickerbocker Press, 1911), pp. 117–22 & 148. Elmer Ellis, *Henry Moore Teller Defender of the West* (Caldwell: Caxton Printers, 1941), p. 119.

3. *Rocky Mountain News* (Weekly), Nov. 13, 20, 27, Dec. 18, 1878; Jan. 1 & 8, 1879; (Daily), Jan. 3, 7 & 8, Feb. 11, 1879. *Denver Tribune*, Dec. 27, 1878; Jan. 8–10, 1879.

4. Ellis, *Teller*, p. 119. Dawson, *Wolcott*, pp. 122 & 148–49. Thomas, *Silhouettes*, p. 52. *Rocky Mountain News*, Feb. 11, 1879.

5. *Senate Journal* (1879). *Denver Tribune*, Jan. 16–Feb. 8, 1879. *Rocky Mountain News*, Jan. 16 & 23, 1879.

6. *Daily Chronicle* (Leadville), Jan. 30, Feb. 6, 8 & 11, 1879. *Rocky Mountain News*, Jan. 16 & 23, 1879. *Denver Tribune*, Feb. 8 & 11, 1879.

7. H. Tabor, "Autobiography," p. 18.

8. *Rocky Mountain News* (Weekly), Nov. 12, 1879. See also issue Aug. 27, 1879.

9. Stock Ledger No. 1, First National Bank, p. 48. Minutes of the Board of Directors and Stock Holders Meetings, First National Bank, 1865–67, 1879–81. Certificates of Stock, First National Bank. Bank Statements, Book 1, May 1875–Feb. 1889. All found in the archives of the First National Bank. *Denver Tribune*, Jan. 16, 1879. *Rocky Mountain News*, Jan. 14, Oct. 10, 1880 & Jan. 12, 1881. Hall, *History of Colorado*, v. 2, p. 456.

10. "Bank of Leadville Records," Colorado State Historical Society. *History of the Arkansas Valley*, pp. 256–57. *Rocky Mountain News* (Weekly), Sept. 4, 1878. *Denver Weekly Times*, Sept. 18 & Dec. 4, 1878. Keeler, *Leadville*, pp. 5–6. *Denver Tribune*, Feb. 9, 1879. *Daily Chronicle*, Feb. 6, 1879. *New York Tribune*, July 2, 1879. *Engineering & Mining Journal*, April 6, 1878, p. 240. *Rocky Mountain News*, Aug. 16, 1878.

11. *Leadville Daily Herald*, Jan. 1 & March 2, 1882. *Democrat*, July 30, 1880. A. Tabor Scrapbook, v. 2, p. 19. Griswold, *Carbonate Camp*,

pp. 121–22. *History of the Arkansas Valley*, p. 258. Leadville Telephone Company, Incorporation Papers.

12. *Leadville Illuminating Gas Co.* v. *H.A.W. Tabor*, Denver District Court, 8138 (1886). *Daily Chronicle*, June 5, 1879. *Leadville Weekly Herald*, Nov. 8, 1879. *Democrat*, Aug. 5, 1880. *Leadville Daily Herald*, Jan. 1, 1881. *History of the Arkansas Valley*, pp. 257–58. *Terms, Rules and Regulations . . . Citizens with Gas* (Leadville: Herald Steam Printing Co., 1879), pp. 1–8.

13. *Daily Chronicle*, Jan. 29, Feb. 6, 10, 12, 14 & 21, 1879. *Rocky Mountain News*, Feb. 15, Sept. 16, 1879; Jan. 1 & July 13, 1880. *Democrat*, April 6, May 22 & June 14, 1880. *Leadville Daily Herald*, Jan. 1, April 7, 1881 & Jan. 1, 1882. *Inter-Ocean*, July 10, 1880, p. 386. "Tabor Hose Running Team Account Book," H. Tabor Manuscripts. H. A. W. Tabor Hose Company, No. 1, Incorporation Papers.

14. *Daily Chronicle*, March 5–6, 1879. *History of the Arkansas Valley*, p. 383. H. Tabor Manuscripts, Scrapbook 4, p. 1. *Leadville Weekly Herald*, Dec. 27, 1879, Sept. 4, 1880. *Leadville Daily Herald*, Jan. 1, 1881 & Jan. 1, 1882. *Democrat*, Aug. 26, 28 & Sept. 1, 1880. *The Southwest* (Durango), July 28, 1883. A. Tabor, Scrapbook, v. 2, p. 20.

15. *History of the Arkansas Valley*, p. 383.

16. Kent, *Leadville*, pp. 24–25.

17. *Denver Tribune*, March 7, 1879. *History of the Arkansas Valley*, p. 380. See also the *Leadville Daily Herald*, Jan. 1, 1881. *Rocky Mountain News*, Oct. 16, 1878.

18. *Denver Tribune*, April 17, 1879. *Rocky Mountain News*, Nov. 16, 1879. *Leadville Weekly Herald*, Nov. 15, 22 & 29, 1879. *Leadville Daily Herald*, Jan. 1, 1881. *Democrat*, Jan. 4 & April 4, 1880. Dorothy M. Degitz, "History of the Tabor Opera House, Leadville, Colorado, from 1879–1905," unpublished Master's Thesis, Western State College, 1935, pp. 11–21. Robert Strahorn, *To the Rockies & Beyond* (Omaha: The New West Publishing Co., 1879), p. 216. Tabor letter (1888), Bancroft Library. Griswold, *Carbonate Camp*, pp. 269–72. *History of the Arkansas Valley*, p. 383. The building cost an estimated $30,000 to $31,000.

19. *Rocky Mountain News* (Weekly), May 21, 1879; (Daily), April 30 & May 14, 1879. *Daily Chronicle*, April 30, May 14, June 27 & July 11, 1879. *Democrat*, March 3, April 10, 16, 23; May 28–29 & Aug. 10, 1880. *Leadville Daily Herald*, April 1, 17 & Nov. 22, 1881.

CHAPTER 7

1. Fossett, *Colorado* (1880), p. 454. *Denver Tribune*, Feb. 11, 1879. *New York Tribune*, April 14, 1879. The Little Pittsburg profited heavily from its lead sales, lead being needed as flux in smelting.

2. James R. Keene to James Hague, March 27, 1879, and James

Hague to James Keene, April 16, 1879. Hague's Little Pittsburg notebook and other Little Pittsburg records are found in the James D. Hague Collection, Huntington Library.

3. Hague to Keene, April 16, 1879, Hague Collection. The original telegram read in part, "Turbid cart or by liberal estimate deal hunter taper pigeon." Turbid was code for "there is now in actual sight," cart meaning "three," and so forth.

4. Balance sheet Little Pittsburg, April 1, 1879, Hague Collection. Tabor himself did not know how much he made per day, but admitted to $51,700 for one month, *Rocky Mountain News*, March 28, 1879.

5. *Denver Tribune*, March 18 & April 1, 1879. *New York Tribune*, April 5, 1879. *Rocky Mountain News* (Weekly), April 9, 1879. *Leadville and Oro* (New York: Denver & Rio Grande, 1878), discussed the feasibility of building a railroad.

6. *Rocky Mountain News*, April 5, 1879. *Denver Tribune*, April 11, 16, & 17, 1879.

7. *Engineering and Mining Journal*, June 14, 1879, p. 438. *Rocky Mountain News* (Weekly), May 14, 1879; (Daily), June 5, 1879. *Daily Chronicle*, May 15, 1879.

8. The Dow articles are found in the appendix of Bishop, *Dow Theory*, pp. 289–343. *Engineering and Mining Journal*, May 24, p. 380, June 14, p. 438, and June 28, 1879, pp. 462–63. *Rocky Mountain News* (Weekly), May 28, 1879, (Daily), April 27, 1879. Dow lists those who went to Leadville.

9. Stock quotations, *Engineering and Mining Journal*, Nov.–Dec. 1879.

10. *Engineering and Mining Journal*, June 28, p. 461, July 5, p. 8, July 12, p. 25 & Aug. 16, 1879, p. 131. *Rocky Mountain News*, May 13, July 24, Aug. 2, 1879.

11. *Rocky Mountain News*, Sept. 5 & 8, 1879. *Denver Times*, Sept. 9, quoted in the *Mining Record*, Sept. 20, 1879, p. 231.

12. Chrysolite Silver Mining Notebook, Hague Collection. See also *Rocky Mountain News* (Weekly), Oct. 29, 1879. Kent, *Leadville*, p. 34. Fossett, *Colorado* (1879), p. 459. *John Borden et al. v. A. D. Searl*, District Court, Lake County, 436 (1879). *Rocky Mountain News*, Sept. 4, 12 & 24, 1879. *Engineering and Mining Journal*, April 13, p. 257, & 27, 1878, p. 293. See also *New York Times*, May 20, 1878.

13. Raymond and Keyes reports are found in *Chrysolite Silver Mining Company* (New York: David H. Gildersleeve, 1880), pp. 20–21 & 26–27.

14. Hague to Colehoun(?), Aug. 31, 1879, Hague Collection. *Leadville Democrat*, Feb. 28, 1880. See also *Leadville Weekly Herald*, Nov. 8, 1879 and *Engineering and Mining Journal*, Nov. 22, p. 383 & Dec. 20, 1879, p. 459. Fossett, *Colorado* (1880) p. 477. *Mining Record*, Jan. 17, 1880, p. 50. *Rocky Mountain News*, Sept. 12, 1879.

15. *Chrysolite Silver Mining Company*, pp. 2–4. Chrysolite stationery

found in the Hague Collection. Fossett, *Colorado* (1880), p. 477. There were three Bordens involved in the Chrysolite and Little Pittsburg including William and John. They were apparently related as father, son and uncle. William was a Chrysolite trustee.

16. *Rocky Mountain Sun*, Aug. 19, 1882. *Denver Tribune*, April 20, 1879.

17. *Denver Tribune*, April 17, 1879. See also issues of Jan. 31, March 2, April 1, 11 & 16, 1879. *Daily Chronicle*, Feb. 22, 1879. *La Plata Miner*, April 12, 1879. Abstract of title Alaska Mine, found in Tabor Manuscripts. For 1878 see the *Engineering and Mining Journal*, April 20, p. 277 & Sept. 14, 1878, p. 190. *Denver Tribune*, Sept. 4 & Nov. 23, 1878. Alaska Consolidated Mining co., Incorporation Papers.

18. *Engineering and Mining Journal*, June 14, p. 433 & Aug. 23, 1879, p. 131. *Daily Chronicle*, July 3, 1879. *Rocky Mountain News* (Weekly), July 9 & Aug. 27, 1879; (Daily), April 19 & July 15, 1879. *Solid Muldoon* (Ouray), Sept. 19, Oct. 3, 1879 & Jan. 9, 1880. *Mining Record*, July 26, p. 68, Aug. 2, p. 87, Aug. 23, p. 148 & Dec. 27, 1879, pp. 540–41. Morgan Draper wrote several letters to the *Mining Record*, the one quoted was August 23. See the *Daily Chronicle*, April 21, 1879, for information on the Betcher and Grand Central Mining Company.

19. Hall, *History of Colorado*, v. 2, p. 444. *Denver Tribune*, Aug. 18, 1878. *Daily Chronicle*, Feb. 13, 1879. Original plat of the Matchless and abstract of title are found in Tabor Manuscripts. Document signed by Lou Leonard, June 30, 1881, Tabor Manuscripts. Emmons, *Geology*, pp. 480–81. *History of the Arkansas Valley*, p. 290. *Rocky Mountain News* (Weekly), Aug. 27, Sept. 10 & Dec. 10, 1879. *Leadville Weekly Herald*, Nov. 8, 1879. *Dennis Sullivan & Peter Finerty* v. *Horace A. W. Tabor*, District Court, Lake County, 1777 (1881). *H. A. W. Tabor* v. *Denniss Sullivan et al.*, District Court, Lake County, 1791 (1881).

20. *Denver Tribune*, April 17 & 19, 1879. Jones apparently was involved at Leadville with Roberts. They both had common Comstock backgrounds and were involved in several schemes together including the American Mining Stock Exchange.

21. *Harper's Weekly*, Aug. 23, 1879, p. 663. *Frank Leslie's Illustrated Newspaper*, April 12, 1879, p. 12. *Daily Chronicle*, March 26, 1879.

CHAPTER 8

1. *Engineering and Mining Journal*, Jan. 17, p. 53, Jan. 24, p. 63; Feb. 21, p. 140, Feb. 28, p. 156, March 6, p. 176, March 13, 1880, p. 191. See also stock quotations in all Jan.–Feb. issues. *New York Tribune*, Jan. 31, 1880. *Mining Record*, Feb. 21, pp. 179 & 189, Feb. 28, 1880, p. 215. *Leadville Democrat*, Jan. 15 & Feb. 19, 1880. See

Henderson, *Mining in Colorado*, pp. 89–92 for Lake County ore production.

2. *Leadville Democrat*, Feb. 25, 29, March 5, 6, 8, 9, & 14, 1880. *Mining Record*, Feb. 21, p. 189, Feb. 28, p. 215, March 6, 1880, pp. 220 & 237. *Engineering and Mining Journal*, Feb. 28, p. 156 & March 6, 1880, pp. 176–78. *Rocky Mountain News*, Feb. 27, 1880.

3. *Leadville Democrat*, March 11 & 14, 1880. *Rocky Mountain News*, March 10, 1880. *Leadville Democrat*, April 1, 1880, reprints the interview. See also issues March 7, 10 and April 7, 1880. *Rocky Mountain News*, March 25, 1880. *Inter-Ocean* (Denver), April 4, 1880, pp. 67–68. *Mining Record*, March 27, 1880, p. 290. The controversy received nation-wide attention as all of these papers quoted comments from other sources.

4. *Inter-Ocean*, June 13, 1880, p. 313. *Leadville Democrat*, April 7, 1880.

5. *Leadville Democrat*, March 23 & April 1, 1880. *Rocky Mountain News*, March 18, 1880. *Inter-Ocean*, April 4, 1880, pp. 61 & 67. *Denver Weekly Times*, March 17, 1880. Unidentified newspaper articles, Augusta Tabor Scrapbook, v. 2, Denver Public Library, p. 72.

6. Laidlaw & Co. to Hague, Feb. 20, 1880, Hague Collection. *Leadville Democrat*, March 17, 30, April 18, 1880. *History of the Arkansas Valley*, p. 233. *Chronicle*, no date, quoted in the *Engineering and Mining Journal*, May 21, 1881, p. 356. Hall, *History of Colorado*, v. 2, p. 458. *Solid Muldoon*, March 28, 1880. G. Thomas Ingham, *Digging Gold Among the Rockies* (Chicago: Cottage Library Publishing House, 1881), pp. 389–90. *Engineering and Mining Journal*, March 20, p. 207 & March 27, 1880, p. 224.

7. *Solid Muldoon*, March 28, 1880. *Leadville Democrat*, April 18, 1880. Hall, *History of Colorado*, v. 2, pp. 458–59.

8. *Leadville Democrat*, May 27, 1880. See also issues of April 13, 16 & May 5. Fossett, *Colorado* (1880), pp. 454–55. Hall, *History of Colorado*, v. 2, pp. 455–58. *History of the Arkansas Valley*, pp. 233–34. *Inter-Ocean*, April 4, 1880, p. 67. *Engineering and Mining Journal*, May 15, 1880, p. 335.

9. *Leadville Democrat*, May 11, 1880. *Engineering and Mining Journal*, Dec. 25, 1880, p. 417. *Mining Record*, May 8, p. 434 & May 15, 1880, p. 459. *Engineering and Mining Journal*, April 24, 1880, p. 290. *Leadville Democrat*, April 16, 1880. Stretch to Hague, Feb. 24, 1880, Hague Collection.

10. *Mining Record*, March 6, 1880, p. 220. *New York Mail*, March 15, quoted in the *Leadville Democrat*, March 16, 1880. See also issues Jan. 17, Feb. 3–7, 19 & March 4, 1880. *Engineering and Mining Journal*, Jan. 24, p. 62 & Feb. 28, 1880, p. 156.

11. *Engineering and Mining Journal*, March 27, p. 220, April 10, p. 262, April 17, pp. 267, 269 & 276, April 24, p. 294, May 15, p. 343 & June 5, 1880, pp. 383–84. See also stock quotations April–June. *Leadville Democrat*, April 11 & 24, 1880.

12. *Mining Record*, May 22, p. 482 & May 29, 1880, p. 525.

13. *Leadville Democrat*, May 27, 1880. See issues from May 27–June 1. Charles M. Hough, "Leadville, Colorado, 1878–98, A Study in Unionism," unpublished Master's Thesis, University of Colorado, 1958, pp. 24–31 & 37–49. Joseph R. Buchanan, *The Story of a Labor Agitator* (New York: Outlook Co., 1903), pp. 11–15. *A Report on Labor Disturbances in the State of Colorado from 1880–1904* (Washington: Government Printing Office, 1905), pp. 35, 69, & 72–74.

14. *Engineering and Mining Journal*, June 12, 1880, p. 410. *Leadville Democrat*, May 30–June 4, 9, 1880. *Mining Record*, June 12, 1880, p. 550. *Rocky Mountain News*, May 27–June 11, 1880.

15. *Leadville Weekly Herald*, June 19, 1880. *Leadville Daily Herald*, Jan. 1, 1881. *Leadville Democrat*, June 5–19, 1880. *Engineering and Mining Journal*, June 12, 1880, p. 412. Hough, "Leadville . . . Unionism," p. 56. Vernon Jensen, *Heritage of Conflict* (Ithaca: Cornell Univ. Press, 1950), p. 23. Buchanan, *Labor Agitator*, pp. 19–24 & 33–34. *Rocky Mountain News*, June 13, 1880. Davis, *Olden Times*, pp. 250–55.

16. Hall, *History of Colorado*, v. 2, pp. 460–63. *Leadville Democrat*, June 11–14, 1880. *New York Tribune*, June 14, 1880. Executive Record, v. 4, pp. 523–25. *Senate Journal of the General Assembly of the State of Colorado, Third Session, Convened at the City of Denver*, Jan. 5, 1881 (Denver: Tribune Publishing Co., 1881), pp. 40–42. *Leadville Daily Herald*, Jan. 1, 1881. Tabor did not declare martial law in Pitkin's place as some writers have claimed, but Pitkin almost made him a brigadier general to command the militia in quelling the trouble. Frederick Pitkin Letterpress Book, State Historical Society, pp. 311–12 & 325.

17. *Leadville Circular*, July 3, 1880, Hague Collection. *Leadville Weekly Herald*, June 19, 1880. *Leadville Democrat*, June 18, 1880. *Engineering and Mining Journal*, Aug. 28, 1880, p. 139. *Rocky Mountain News*, July 4, 1880. The story of Tabor's regretting his actions was told to Joseph Smith, quoted in Peryl Parson's "H. A. W. Tabor's Bittersweet Christmas," *Denver Post*, Dec. 24, 1961.

18. *Rocky Mountain News*, June 13–23, 1880 & Jan. 6, 1881. *Leadville Democrat*, July 22, Sept. 7–8, 1880.

19. *Leadville Democrat*, May 28 & June 11, 1880. *History of the Arkansas Valley*, p. 239. Hough, "Leadville . . . Unionism," p. 51. *Rocky Mountain News*, June 17, 1880.

20. *Mining Record*, May 29, p. 507 & June 19, 1880, p. 579. *Inter-Ocean*, July 31, 1880, p. 425. Davis, *Olden Times*, pp. 248–49. Dill, *Political Campaigns*, p. 50.

21. *Mining Record*, Jan.–March, 1880. *Engineering and Mining Journal*, June–Aug., 1880, Jan. 1, 1881, p. 1. *New York Times*, June 2, 1880. Balch, *The Mines*, p. 482. *Leadville Democrat*, Feb. 8, 17, 27, March 5, 6, & April 16, 1880. *Leslie's Illustrated*, June 19, 1880, p. 258. *Rocky Mountain News*, March 5, June 6, 1880.

22. *Commercial Bulletin* (New York), July 18, 1880, quoted in the *Leadville Democrat*, July 20, 1880. See also July 8. *Mining Record*, July 10, 1880, p. 27. *Engineering and Mining Journal,* July 3, p. 13 & July 17, 1880, p. 37. See also weekly stock quotations.

23. *New York Tribune*, July 29, 1880. *Engineering and Mining Journal,* July 24, pp. 53 & 61, & July 31, 1880, p. 77. *Rocky Mountain News*, July 17, 1880.

24. *Inter-Ocean*, July 31, 1880, pp. 424 & 429. *Rocky Mountain News,* July 31, 1880.

25. *Leadville Democrat*, Sept. 8, 1880. *Engineering and Mining Journal,* Sept. 18, p. 185 & Oct. 9, 1880, p. 233. *Mining Record*, Sept. 25, 1880, p. 289. *Leadville Weekly Herald*, Oct. 2, 1880. See also *Leadville Democrat*, Aug. 4, 10, 24, 29, Sept. 2 & 8, 1880. *Denver Weekly Times*, Aug. 4, 1880. *Engineering and Mining Journal*, Aug.–Sept., 1880.

26. *Engineering and Mining Journal*, Oct. 16, p. 49 & Nov. 6, 1880, pp. 297 & 304.

27. *Chrysolite Silver Mining Company* (New York: np, 1880), pp. 1–2.

28. *Inter-Ocean*, Aug. 7, p. 441 & Aug. 21, 1880, p. 474. *Leadville Democrat*, Aug. 10, 1880. *Mining Record*, April 2, 1881, p. 314.

29. *Engineering and Mining Journal*, Nov. 6, 1880, pp. 297 & 304. See also issues July 31, p. 77, Aug. 7, pp. 85 & 97 & Oct. 16, 1880, p. 264. *Mining Record*, July 31, p. 97 & Aug. 7, 1880, p. 127. *Rocky Mountain News*, Dec. 2, 1881.

30. *Mining and Scientific Press* (San Francisco), Aug. 28, 1880, p. 134.

31. *Rocky Mountain News*, Aug. 1, 1883. *Mining Record*, April 2, 1881, p. 314.

32. S. C. Shaeffer to Tabor, Dec. 15, 1881, Tabor Collection, First National Bank. *Engineering and Mining Journal*, Sept. 13, p. 190, Nov. 29, p. 400 & Dec. 6, 1879, p. 422. *Mining Record*, Sept. 13, p. 206, 211, Nov. 1, p. 352, Nov. 8, p. 372 & Nov. 22, 1879, p. 420. *Rocky Mountain News*, Jan. 11 & March 20, 1880.

33. Corbett, *Colorado Directory of Mines*, p. 271. *Leadville Democrat*, Jan. 4 & 23, 1880. The cases involving the Lickscumdidrick are found in the Lake County District Court, civil cases, numbers 1447, 1448, 1449, 1455, 1456 & 3476. *Leadville Weekly Herald*, Dec. 6, 1879 & Jan. 24, 1880. Tabor to Lou Leonard, Feb. 4, 1881, Tabor Manuscripts.

CHAPTER 9

1. Rezin Constant, "Colorado as Seen by a Visitor of 1880," *Colorado Magazine* (May 1935), p. 112. Contracts, Bills and some Letters relating to the Tabor Block construction are found in the Tabor

Collection, First National Bank. *Rocky Mountain News*, Feb. 1, 3, Oct. 3, 1879, Jan. 1 & March 7, 1880. *Denver Tribune*, Feb. 2, 16, & April 1, 1879. *Denver Weekly Times*, March 17, 1880.

2. *Leadville Weekly Herald*, March 13, 1880. *Inter-Ocean*, March 14, 1880, p. 2 & April 8, 1882, p. 216. *Denver Weekly Times*, March 17, 1880. Bancroft, *Chronicles of the Builders*, v. 4, p. 308. Elmer Crowley, "The History of the Tabor Grand Opera House, Denver, Colorado," unpublished Master's Thesis, University of Denver, 1940, pp. 7–13.

3. *Rocky Mountain News*, June 23 & Dec. 15, 1880. M. Tabor Interview. *History of the Arkansas Valley*, p. 383.

4. E. J. Moys to Tabor, April 25, (1882), H. Tabor Manuscripts. *A. Tabor v. H. Tabor*, District Court, Denver 6035 (1882). *Rocky Mountain News*, April 20 & 28, 1882. *Denver Tribune*, April 19 & 27, 1882. *Daily Register-Call*, April 20–24, 1882.

5. *George F. Wanless v. William Bush, H. A. W. Tabor et al.*, Denver District Court, 6461 (1882). *Leadville Democrat*, Jan. 8–9, Feb. 7–15 & June 12, 1880. *Rocky Mountain News*, (Weekly), Oct. 29, 1879, (Daily), Feb. 19, 1880, Feb. 19 & June 16, 1881. A. Tabor Scrapbook, v. 2, p. 56. Griswold, *Carbonate Camp*, p. 88.

6. Alice S. Spencer, "Newspapers in Gunnison County; 1879–1900," unpublished Master's Thesis, Western State College, 1932, pp. 103–110. Tabor quote on the *Circular* found in the July 3, 1880, issue. Examination of the few remaining copies of the *Elk Mountain Bonanza* did not identify the owner. *Gunnison Review*, April 9, 1881.

7. *Rocky Mountain News*, March 25 & April 25, 1880. *Mining Record*, Sept. 17, 1881, p. 273. *Gunnison Daily Review*, Oct. 26, 1881 & March 13, 1882. *Gunnison Review*, May 15, 1880 & Aug. 6 & 13, 1881.

8. Clarence Mayo to his sister, Aug. 7, 1882, Clarence H. Mayo Letters, 1879–82, Huntington Library.

9. Marshall Field to Tabor, Aug. 4, 1883. F. T. Osgood to Tabor, July 20, 1883, S.V. White to Tabor, Sept. 2, 1881. H. Tabor Manuscripts. *Rocky Mountain News* (Weekly), April 2 & Nov. 12, 1879. *Leslie's Illustrated*, Nov. 29, 1879, p. 223. A. Tabor Scrapbooks have several references to Tabor's Chicago property. Kent, *Leadville*, p. 168, says Tabor had controlling interest in the Calumet . . . Co., as early as 1880. Records of the Calumet & Chicago Canal & Dock Co., Illinois State Archives.

10. Agreement between Tabor and H. Henove, May 11, 1880. Tabor to S. V. White, May 12, 1880. Balance Sheet, S. V. White & Co., Jan.–Feb., 1883, H. Tabor Manuscripts. *Rocky Mountain News*, Oct. 30–Nov. 2, 1883. *Horace A. W. Tabor v. William Bush*, Denver District Court, 6748 (1883).

11. *Leadville Democrat*, July 9, 1880. *Rocky Mountain News*, July 17, 1880. *Leadville Weekly Herald*, Dec. 6, 20, 1879 & Jan. 17, 1880. For the previous paragraph on Tabor's Leadville business see *Leadville Democrat*, Jan. 22 & April 22, 1880. *Leadville Weekly Herald*, Nov.

22, 1881 & May 3, 1882. *Rocky Mountain Sun,* May 7, 1882. Robert Ormes, *Railroads and the Rockies* (Denver: Sage, 1963), p. 317. Evergreen Lakes . . . Company, Incorporation Papers.

12. *Leadville Circular,* July 3, 1880. *Inter-Ocean,* July 10, 1880, p. 382. *Leadville Democrat,* April 3, 13 & Aug. 4, 1880. *Rocky Mountain News,* April 13, 1880. A. Tabor Scrapbooks, v. 2, p. 6. Ormes, *Railroads,* pp. 282 & 284. See also Robert G. Athearn, *Rebel of the Rockies.* Tabor had earlier been interested in the Mosquito Pass wagon road. See the Company Incorporation Papers.

13. *Rocky Mountain News,* July 29 & Dec. 15, 1880, Jan. 1, July 1, 1881 & Feb. 8, 1882. *Leadville Weekly Herald,* April 13, 1882. Stock Denver, Utah & Pacific Railroad found in the Tabor collection, State Historical Society. *Inter-Ocean,* July 31, 1880, p. 423. *Denver Weekly Times,* Aug. 4, 1880. A. Tabor Scrapbooks, v. 2, pp. 6 & 32. Ormes, *Railroads,* pp. 241–42.

14. A. Tabor Scrapbooks, v. 1, has several references to the stage line. *Dolores News* (Rico), May 28, 1881. *Durango Record,* April 28, May 3 & 21, 1881. *Mining Record,* Aug. 20, 1881, p. 177. *Edward Kneezell* v. *Sewall & Tabor,* La Plata County Court, 157 (1882). *J. H. Pinkerton* v. *Tabor & Wasson,* La Plata District Court, 111 (1881). *Thomas Stanton* v. *H. A. W. Tabor's Pioneer Stage & Express Line Co.,* La Plata County Court, 200 (1882). *The Southwest,* Oct. 7, 1882. *Durango Weekly Record,* Dec. 1, 1881 & Jan. 20, 1882.

15. *Solid Muldoon,* April 16, 1880. *Leadville Democrat,* March 26–April 15, 1880. Robert Perkin, *The First Hundred Years* (Garden City: Doubleday & Co., 1959), p. 347. *Leadville Weekly Herald,* March 27, April 3 & 10, 1880.

16. Dill, *Political Campaigns,* pp. 48–49. Dawson, *Wolcott,* pp. 150–51. *Leadville Democrat,* Jan. 24, March 30, May 27 & June 27, 1880. *Leadville Weekly Herald,* March 27, April 3 & May 29, 1880. *Rocky Mountain News,* Oct. 31, 1880.

17. *Leadville Democrat,* Jan. 2, 8, 11, 17, Feb. 19, 29, Aug. 8, 24, 27, 1880. *Solid Muldoon,* Jan. 16, 1880. *New York Times,* Aug. 27, 1880. *Leadville Weekly Herald,* Aug. 28, 1880. *Denver Weekly Times,* Sept. 1, 1880. *Rocky Mountain News,* July 16–Oct. 19, 1880.

18. Hall, *History of Colorado,* v. 3, p. 31, v. 2, pp. 469–70. *History of the Arkansas Valley,* p. 409. *Denver Weekly Times,* Dec. 1 & 8, 1880. *Rocky Mountain News,* Jan. 5–23, 1881. *Leadville Daily Herald,* Jan. 8 & 18, 1881. *Denver Tribune,* Jan. 12, 1881. Hubert H. Bancroft, *History of Nevada, Colorado and Wyoming, 1540–1888* (San Francisco: The History Co., 1890), p. 448. Corbett, *Legislative Manual,* p. 76.

19. "Executive Record," v. 4, pp. 120–27. *Solid Muldoon,* Dec. 22, 1882. *Democrat* quoted in *Leadville Weekly Herald,* Dec. 21, 1882. *The Southwest,* Dec. 23 & 30, 1882. *Denver Tribune,* Dec. 16, 19, 1882. "Executive Record," v. 3, pp. 463–64. *Rocky Mountain News,* Dec. 15, 1880.

20. "Executive Record," v. 4, pp. 11–19. *Rocky Mountain News,* Sept. 3, 15 & 22, 1881. *Denver Tribune,* Sept. 10, 1881. *Leadville Daily Herald*, Dec. 13 & 24, 1882.

CHAPTER 10

1. Stone remembrances found in the Tabor Material, Bancroft Library. *Rocky Mountain News,* Sept. 11, 1880 & Jan. 1, 1881. Expense accounts for construction are found in the archives of the First National Bank. *Denver Weekly Times,* Oct. 13, 1880.

2. *Denver Tribune,* Sept. 2, 1881. *Rocky Mountain News,* Jan. 14–18, Aug. 21–Sept. 4, 1881. See also *Denver Tribune,* Aug. 13–Sept. 6, 1881. The price of tickets ran from one to two dollars. Chicago-born Emma Abbott was thirty-two years old and had her operatic debut in Covent Garden theater in 1876.

3. *Rocky Mountain News,* Sept. 6, 1881.

4. A. Tabor to H. Tabor, Sept. 3, 1881, H. Tabor Manuscripts.

5. *Rocky Mountain News,* Oct. 30–31, 1883. *Denver Times,* Oct. 29, 1883. *Leadville Daily Herald*, Oct. 30, 1883.

6. *Rocky Mountain News,* Sept. 8, 1881. See issues Sept. 6–8. *Denver Tribune,* Sept. 6–8, 1881. "Maritana" was first produced in London in 1844.

7. Eugene Field, *A Little Book of Tribune Verse* (New York: Grosset & Dunlap, 1901), p. 196, prints the entire poem. For humorous stories on Tabor check the *Tribune* throughout this entire period. The story of Tabor and Shakespeare has appeared too many times to cite, but most certainly is apocryphal since Tabor was not illiterate.

8. Frances Kingsley (ed), *Charles Kingsley his Letters and Memories of his Life* (London: Henry S. King & Co., 1877), v. II. pp. 441–42. Robert Martin (ed), *Charles Kingsley's American Notes* (Princeton: Princeton University Library, 1958), pp. 51–55. Crowley, "History of the Tabor Grand Opera House," pp. 39–45.

9. W. H. Bergtold, "Denver Fifty Years Ago," *Colorado Magazine* (March, 1931), p. 71. *Rocky Mountain News,* Sept. 6–18, 1881. *Denver Tribune,* Sept. 6–18, 1881. Bancroft, *Chronicles of the Builders,* v. 4, p. 311. Thomas, "An Old Timer," p. 5.

10. *Rocky Mountain News,* Jan. 16, Feb. 19, 23, March 16, 24, July 13, 1881 & April 23, 1882.

11. *H. A. W. Tabor* v. *Chrysolite Silver Mining Co.,* U.S. Circuit Court, 692 (1881). *H. A. W. Tabor* v. *the Little Chief Mining Co.,* Lake County, District Court, 1690 (1881). *Engineering and Mining Journal,* 1881. *Leadville Daily Herald*, Feb. 1, 25, March 2, 1881. *Mining Record,* June 18, p. 578 & July 9, 1881, p. 33 & Aug. 13–Sept. 1881. *Rocky Mountain Sun,* Feb. 18, 1882.

12. R. E. Lee sources: *Leadville Democrat*, Jan. 16, 1880. *Engineering and Mining Journal*, Jan. 24, 1880, p. 68. *Leadville Daily Herald*, March 5, 1881 & Jan. 1, 1882. *Mining Record*, June 4, 1881, p. 539. Emmons, *Geology*, p. 483. It was rumored in July 1879 that the Little Pittsburg people purchased it. Big Chief sources: Robert Corregan & David Lingane, *Colorado Mining Directory* (Denver: Colorado Mining Directory Co., 1883), p. 400. Big Chief Records, H. Tabor Manuscripts. Leadville Insurance Co. Collection, Western History Collections, University of Colorado. Glass-Pendery sources: *History of the Arkansas Valley*, p. 284. *Rocky Mountain News*, Feb. 8, 1880. *Leadville Weekly Herald*, Feb. 14, March 6 & 27, 1880. *Leadville Daily Herald*, Jan. 23, 1881 & Jan. 1, 1882. *Engineering and Mining Journal*, Aug. 27, 1881, p. 140.

13. *H. A. W. Tabor v. the Big Pittsburg Consolidated Silver Mining Co.*, U.S. Circuit Court, 1024 (1882). Rockwell to Leonard, July 20, 1881, Leonard to Rockwell, July 25, 1881. H. Tabor Manuscripts. *Mining Record*, July 2, p. 12, Aug. 13, p. 153 & Oct. 29, 1881, p. 420. *Leadville Daily Herald*, Oct. 21 & Nov. 16, 1881. *Rocky Mountain News*, July 3 & Oct. 22, 1881.

14. Sources on the Matchless: *Leadville Democrat*, July 14, Aug. 14, 25 & Sept. 2, 1880. *Leadville Weekly Herald*, Aug. 7, 14, Sept. 25 & Oct. 9, 1880. *Leadville Daily Herald*, Jan. 1, Feb. 19, March 4, 29, April 10, Nov. 2, Dec. 1, 1881, Jan. 29, 31, Aug. 25, 1882 & Jan. 1, 1883. *Engineering and Mining Journal*, 1880–81. *Mining Record*, 1881–82. *Rocky Mountain News*, Jan. 15, 1882. Sources on Lou Leonard: *History of the Arkansas Valley*, pp. 350 & 353. *Leadville Democrat*, Aug. 8, 1880. *Leadville Daily Herald*, Aug. 26, 1884.

15. *Mining Record*, Aug. 20, 1881, p. 180. See also issues March 13, p. 250, May 15, p. 468, Nov. 6, 1880, p. 444, March 4, p. 200, April 1, 1882, p. 297. *Solid Muldoon*, Jan. 25 & Aug. 13, 1880. *Engineering and Mining Journal*, Aug. 28, 1880, pp. 138–39.

16. *Leadville Daily Herald*, Jan. 1, 17, Nov. 12 & Dec. 1, 1881; Jan. 1, April 11, 21 & Oct. 11, 1882. *Mining Record*, Feb. 26, p. 205, April 30, 1881, p. 420; March 25, pp. 275–76, Oct. 21, p. 395 & Dec. 2, 1882, p. 514. *Denver Tribune*, Oct. 13 & 20, 1882. *Weekly Republican*, Oct. 19, 1882. *Rocky Mountain News*, April 8, 1882. *John Riley, et al. v. H. A. W. Tabor*, Lake County, District Court, 876 (1880). *Chester Bullock et al. v. H. A. W. Tabor*, Lake County, District Court, 1110 (1880). The Henriett is misspelled in several ways, but the version used here was that used by the company, which should have known the correct spelling.

17. *Mining Record*, March 5–May 14, 1881. For the early history of the Hibernia see *History of the Arkansas Valley*, p. 294. *Leadville Democrat*, April 15, 1880. *Leadville Weekly Herald*, April 17, 1880. Hibernia Consolidated material, H. Tabor Manuscripts. *Rocky Mountain News*, March 3, 1880; Feb. 3, 17, 19, 1881. Sources of the Scooper trouble: *Leadville Daily Herald*, Oct. 11 & 15, 1882. *Mining Record*, Jan. 17, 1880, p. 59. *Lake City Mining Register*, Oct. 20, 1882.

18. *Leadville Daily Herald*, March 12, 27, April 10, 20, Oct. 26, Nov. 26, Dec. 1 & 13, 1881. *Mining Record*, 1881. *Engineering and Mining Journal*, Jan. 22, p. 61, Feb. 5, p. 96, Sept. 10, p. 172, Sept. 24, p. 205 & Dec. 24, 1881, p. 419. *Rocky Mountain News*, March 11, 1881.

19. *Rocky Mountain News*, June 8, 25, Dec. 2, 1881 & Oct. 30, 1883. *Engineering and Mining Journal*, Sept. 24, 1881, p. 205. *Leadville Daily Herald*, March 27, Oct. 25 & 26, 1881.

20. *Leadville Daily Herald*, Jan. 1, 7, 20, 25, March 23, April 14, May 25, June 17, Aug. 8 & Sept. 8, 1882. *Engineering and Mining Journal*, Feb. 4, p. 64, May 20, p. 265 & July 22, 1882, p. 47. *Mining Record*, April 8, p. 315 & Sept. 23, 1882, p. 299. *Weekly Republican*, Dec. 14, 1882. Leonard to Tabor, March 23, 1882, Tabor Collections, First National Bank.

21. *Leadville Democrat*, Jan. 14, March 3, 5, 9, Sept. 4 & 30, 1880. *Denver Tribune*, Oct. 19, 1882. Thomas, "An Old Timer," p. 3. *Rocky Mountain News*, April 1, 25, June 6, Oct. 20, 1880; Feb. 16 & March 11, 1881. *Denver Republican*, Jan. 8, 1883. *Colorado Miner*, Oct. 21, quoted in the *Mining Record*, Oct. 28, 1882. Balch, *Mines*, p. 1174. *The Del Monte Consolidated* (c1880). Ballarat Mining Co. Stock, H. Tabor Manuscripts. Como Iron, Coal & Land Co. Records, H. Tabor Manuscripts. *The Como Iron, Coal and Land Company* (Denver: Collier & Cleaveland, 1881). Tabor came to dislike coal lands, see "Autobiography," p. 20. Daisy Consolidated Records, H. Tabor Manuscripts. *Edward T. Bradford et al. v. Henry S. Kearny, et al.*, U. S. Circuit Court, 1170 (1883). *Jacob Sanders & H. A. W. Tabor v. Jacob Cypher & William Mendenhall*, Lake County, District Court, 1323 (1880).

CHAPTER 11

1. *Rocky Mountain Sun*, July 16, 23, Aug. 13, 27, Sept. 3, 10, Oct. 29, Nov. 5 & Dec. 3, 1881. Sources on his other Aspen Mines: *Leadville Democrat*, Aug. 13, 1880. *Rocky Mountain Sun*, July 7 & Dec. 22, 1883. Sources for the Wheel of Fortune: *Engineering and Mining Journal*, Feb. 22, p. 132 & Dec. 20, 1879, p. 457. *History of the Arkansas Valley*, p. 393. *Leadville Daily Herald*, Jan. 1 & April 15, 1882. *Jacob Hecht & John Still v. S. H. Foss, H. A. W. Tabor et al.*, Lake County, District Court, 1008 (1880).

2. *Rocky Mountain Sun*, July 16, 1881, Feb. 18 & Aug. 26, 1882. *Mining Record*, July 1, 1882, p. 7. *Denver Tribune*, Aug. 12 & Sept. 6, 1881.

3. *H. A. W. Tabor v. Nicholas N. Atkinson et al.*, U. S. Circuit Court, 782 (1881). Tabor took over this case from Bruckman. Bruckman's name is spelled several different ways. *Rocky Mountain Sun*, Jan. 7, Feb. 18, 25, March 11, 18, 1882. *Leadville Daily Herald*, Feb. 4, 18, June 21, Dec. 29, 1882. *Rocky Mountain News*, March 6–7, 1882 & Jan. 8, 1883. *Denver Tribune*, March 6–7, Dec. 29, 1882; April 22,

1883. *Engineering and Mining Journal*, May 5, 1888, p. 329. H. A. W. *Tabor et al.* v. *J. F. Chaney et al.*, Lake County, District Court, 1925 (1881).

4. *Leadville Daily Herald*, Jan. 1, Aug. 23, 31 & Oct. 22, 1882. *Rocky Mountain Sun*, Feb. 4, Aug. 12, 23, 26, Sept. 2, Oct. 21 & Dec. 2, 1882. *Rocky Mountain News*, Jan. 7, 1882. *Denver Tribune*, Jan. 31, 1882.

5. Balch, *Mines*, pp. 1167–68. H. R. Whitehill, *Biennial Report of the State Mineralogist of the State of Nevada* (San Francisco: A. L. Bancroft & Co., 1879), pp. 76–77. *History of Nevada* (Oakland: Thompson & West, 1881), pp. 491–92. Kinkead, *Second Biennial Message*, p. 23. *Engineering and Mining Journal*, Oct. 4, p. 255, Dec. 20, 1879, pp. 460–61. *Mining & Scientific Press*, July 17, 1880, p. 37. *Mining Record*, May 21, 1881, p. 493 & Nov. 4, 1882, p. 444.

6. Lew Wallace, *Report of the Governor . . . for the Year 1879* (Washington: Government Printing Office, 1879), pp. 5–7. Lionel Sheldon, *Report of the Governor of New Mexico . . . for the Year 1883* (Washington: Government Printing Office, 1883), pp. 4–5.

7. G. W. Miller to Tabor, Feb. 26 & 29, 1884, H. Tabor Manuscripts. *Horace A. W. Tabor & John E. Wurtzebach* v. *the Sierra Grande Mining Co.*, 3rd Judicial District, New Mexico, 692 (1883). Hubert H. Bancroft, *History of Arizona and New Mexico 1530–1888* (San Francisco: History Co., 1889), pp. 753–55. Waldemar Lindgren et al., *The Ore Deposits of New Mexico* (Washington: Government Printing Office, 1910), pp. 18, 268–81. Benjamin Silliman, *The Mineral Regions of Southern New Mexico* (1882), pp. 4–6, 12. *Leadville Daily Herald*, May 6, June 9, Sept. 12 & Oct. 7, 1882. *Denver Tribune*, June 9, Sept. 23, Nov. 1, 4, 18, 1882. *Rocky Mountain Sun*, July 1, Sept. 26, 1882. *Engineering and Mining Journal*, Nov. 11, p. 253 & Nov. 25, 1882, p. 285.

8. *Mining Record*, Nov. 11, p. 458 & Nov. 25, 1882, p. 503. *Engineering and Mining Journal*, Oct. 3, 1885, p. 245.

9. *Michoacan Syndicate* (New York: David H. Gildersleeve, 1881–82), pp. 4–25. Balch, *Mines*, p. 1159. *Mining Record*, Nov. 12, p. 471, Dec. 24, 1881, p. 603; Jan. 14, p. 38, Jan. 28, p. 96, Feb. 4, p. 102 & March 11, 1882, p. 230. *Engineering and Mining Journal*, March 25, 1882, p. 159. *Leadville Daily Herald*, Feb. 11, March 4, 1882. *New York Times*, Nov. 20, 1881.

10. *Leadville Weekly Herald*, Jan. 24, Feb. 14, May 15, 1880. *Leadville Democrat*, May 25, June 6, July 16, Sept. 17, 1880. *Inter-Ocean*, July 24, 1880, p. 410. *Leadville Daily Herald*, Nov. 25 & Dec. 4, 1880. Sources for the Supply Company: *Mining Record*, Dec. 6, 1879, p. 468. Kent, *Leadville*, p. 156. A. Tabor Scrapbook, v. 2, p. 32.

11. *Leadville Daily Herald*, Jan. 1, Dec. 31, 1881, June 3, July 19, Dec. 31, 1882 & Jan. 1, 1884. *Mining Record*, Sept. 30, 1882, p. 323. *Engineering and Mining Journal*, June 2, p. 321, Aug. 4, 1883, p. 61. Emmons, *Geology*, pp. 626–28. *The Arkansas Valley Smelting Co. et al.* v. *The Tabor Milling Co. et al.*, Lake County, District Court, 2528

(1883). *H. A. W. Tabor* v. *P. McCann*, Lake County, District Court, 2600 (1883). *Patrick McCann & Charles Fish* v. *H. A. W. Tabor*, records in H. Tabor Manuscripts. Bill to Tabor, Dec. 18, 1882, H. Tabor Manuscripts.

12. *Leadville Daily Herald*, Feb. 23, 1881. Tabor Mine Co., Records, H. Tabor Manuscripts. *Engineering and Mining Journal*, June–Oct. 1881.

13. *Denver Tribune*, Aug. 1, 1882. *Rocky Mountain News*, Jan. 12, March 25, May 8, 1881 & May 3, 1882. *Engineering and Mining Journal*, Jan. 15, p. 46 & April 16, 1881, p. 263. Simley, *History of Denver*, p. 476.

14. *Park County Bulletin*, no date, quoted in *Inter-Ocean*, March 11, 1882, p. 138. *Programme for the First Annual Exhibition of the National Mining and Industrial Exposition at Denver* (Denver: Tribune Publishing Co., 1882), pp. 2–18. *Mining Record*, April 15, 1882, p. 341. *Rocky Mountain News*, July 30, 1882. *Inter-Ocean*, Feb. 11, 1882, p. 85. *Denver Republican*, April 3, 1882. *Denver Tribune*, Jan. 22, 28, Feb. 7, 8, 11, 12, March 2 & April 1, 1882. *New York Times*, April 26, 1882. National Mining . . . Association, Incorporation Papers.

15. *Rocky Mountain News*, May 3, 7, 9, 29 & June 2, 1882. *Denver Tribune*, May 4, 28 & 31, 1882. *Board of County Commissioners of the County of Arapahoe* v. *The National Mining and Industrial Exposition Association et al.*, Denver District Court, 6774 (1883). *Mining Record*, May 13, 1882, p. 442.

16. *Rocky Mountain Sun*, March 18–Aug. 12, 1882.

17. *Leadville Daily Herald*, July 20, 1882. See also issue July 19. Association meeting minutes July 20, 1882, H. Tabor Manuscripts. *Rocky Mountain News*, June 2, 3, 20, 21 & July 30, 1882. *Denver Tribune*, June 3, 19, 28, July 3, 7, 19 & Aug. 1, 1882. *Leslie's Illustrated*, July 22, 1882. *Solid Muldoon*, July 14 & 21, 1882. *Henry Gibson* v. *The National Mining and Industrial Exposition Association et al.*, U. S. Circuit Court, 1959 (1886). *Thomas P. Hughes* v. *The National Mining and Industrial Exposition et al.*, Denver District Court, 6430 (1882). The Denver Circle Railroad Company was eventually absorbed by the Santa Fe.

18. W. B. Ewer, "Report on the National Mining and Industrial Exposition," *Appendix to the Journal of the Senate and Assembly of the 25th Session of the State of California* (Sacramento: State Printing Office, 1883), pp. 5–9. *Mining and Scientific Press*, Aug. 5, p. 88 & Aug. 12, 1882, p. 104. John Kinkead, *Second Biennial Message* (Carson City: J. C. Harlow, 1883), p. 24. Frederick Tritle, *Biennial Message of the Governor of Arizona Territory* (Prescott: n.p., 1885), pp. 19–20. *Rocky Mountain News*, July 30–Oct. 2, 1882. *Denver Tribune*, Aug. 1–Oct. 2, 1882. *New York Times*, Aug. 7–8, 1882. *Frank Leslie's Illustrated*, Aug. 19–26, 1882. *Harper's Weekly*, Sept. 16, 1882, p. 581. Both *Harper's* and *Leslie's* include illustrations. *Daily Enterprise* (Bonanza, Colorado), special edition, Aug. 1882. *Engineering and Mining Journal*, Aug.–.Sept. 1882. *Mining Record*, Aug.–Sept. 1882. *Solid Muldoon*,

Aug. 18 & 25, 1882. *Denver Republican*, Oct. 7, 1882. Flora Stevens, "Molecules from the Denver Mining Exposition," *Kansas City Review of Science* (Aug. 1882), pp. 249–52.

19. *Denver Tribune*, Sept. 27 & Oct. 2, 1882. *Rocky Mountain News*, Sept. 29–Oct. 2, 1882. *Solid Muldoon*, Sept. 29, 1882.

20. *Leadville Daily Herald*, Aug. 1, 1882. *Denver Tribune*, Aug. 11, 1882, *Rocky Mountain News*, July 30 & Aug. 20, 1882.

CHAPTER 12

1. *Inter-Ocean*, Aug. 7, 1880, p. 439. For Tabor as president of the Colorado Senate see, *Senate Journal . . . Third Session*, Jan. 5–Feb. 13, 1881.

2. *Leadville Daily Herald*, March 27, 1881. See also issues of Jan. 18, 23 & April 3, 1881. *Rocky Mountain News*, Sept. 2, 3, 7, 14, 15, 18, 1880, July 26, 30, Sept. 7, 9, 10, 16 & 18, 1881. *Leadville Democrat*, Sept. 3, 11, 1880. *Denver Weekly Times*, Nov. 17, 24, Dec. 15, 1880. *Solid Muldoon*, Sept. 30 & Oct. 14, 1881.

3. *Solid Muldoon*, Jan. 27, 1882. *Denver Tribune*, Jan. 19, 1882.

4. *Rocky Mountain News*, April 12, 1882. For sources of the 1882 senatorial race see Dill, *Political Campaigns*, pp. 66–67. Hall, *History of Colorado*, v. 3, pp. 30–32. *Rocky Mountain News*, March 27, April 12, 1882. *Leadville Daily Herald*, March 29–April 12, 1882. *Denver Tribune*, March 23–April 12, 1882. *Denver Republican*, April 2–12, 1882. For an anti-Tabor paper see the *Daily Register-Call*, March 30–April 6, 1882. *Rocky Mountain Sun*, April 1, 1882. On Chilcott see *New York Times*, Dec. 12, 1878. *Legislative, Historical and Biographical Compendium of Colorado* (Denver: C. F. Coleman, 1887), p. 34.

5. *Inter-Ocean*, April 15, p. 229 & April 22, 1882, pp. 249 & 252. See also *Rocky Mountain News*, April 12, 1882 for Byer's interview.

6. *Leadville Daily Herald*, April 21, 1882. Bush to Tabor, May 8 & 19, 1882, H. Tabor Manuscripts. *Denver Tribune*, April 19 & 27, 1882; Oct. 31, 1883. *Rocky Mountain News*, Dec. 15, 1880; April 20 & 28, 1882; Oct. 31, 1883. *A. Tabor* v. *H. Tabor.*

7. *Denver Tribune*, Sept. 5, 1882. See also issues June 26, 30, Aug. 26–Sept. 9. *Rocky Mountain News*, April 23, 25, 28, June 19, 21, Aug. 15–Sept. 11 & 29, 1882. *Denver Republican*, Aug. 29, 1882. *Denver Times*, Sept. 2–8, 1882. *Inter-Ocean*, April 29, p. 269 & May 13, 1882, p. 310. *Leadville Daily Herald*, April 13–15, 19–30, July 29, Aug. 1–2, 18, 22, 29 & Sept. 10–13, 1882. Dill, *Political Campaigns*, pp. 56–58 & 64–69. The *News* claimed $100,000 was spent by both sides. There were 1,046 Negroes in Denver proper and a total of 2,435 in the state.

8. *Denver Times*, Sept. 12, 1882. *Rocky Mountain News*, Sept. 11–17, 1882. *Denver Tribune*, Sept. 12–18, 1882. *Leadville Daily Herald*, Sept. 20, 1882.

9. Dill, *Political Campaigns*, pp. 68–69 & 63–64. Hall, *History of Colorado*, v. 3, pp. 36–37. Wilbur F. Stone, *History of Colorado* (Chicago: S. J. Clarke Publishing Co., 1918), v. 1, p. 432. Dawson, *Wolcott*, pp. 167–69. *Denver Tribune*, Nov. 7, 1882. See also issues Oct. 4–Nov. 8, 1882. *Leadville Daily Herald*, Oct. 11–Nov. 6, 1882.

10. *Leadville Daily Herald*, Nov. 18, 1882. See also issues Nov. 6–11, 1882. *Solid Muldoon*, Nov. 8, 1882. *Weekly Republican*, Nov. 16, 1883. *Rocky Mountain News*, Nov. 9, 1882. *Denver Tribune*, Nov. 9, 1882. *Rocky Mountain Sun*, Nov. 11, 1882.

11. *Denver Tribune*, Aug. 17, Oct. 31, Nov. 1 & 10, 1882. See also Eddie Foy and Alvin Harlow, *Clowning Through Life* (New York: E. P. Dutton & Co., 1928). Field revived it after Tabor saw "Julius Caesar" in April 1883; see the *Denver Tribune*, April 19, 1883.

12. *Solid Muldoon*, Dec. 15 & 19, 1882. *Leadville Daily Herald*, Nov. 26, Dec. 12–16, 1882. *Weekly Republican*, Dec. 21, 1882. *Denver Tribune*, Dec. 18, 1882. *Tabor v. Bush*. See also Dill, *Political Campaigns*, p. 80. Ellis, *Teller*, p. 154. Bancroft, *History . . . Wyoming*, p. 451.

13. *Denver Tribune*, Dec. 31, 1882 & Jan. 4, 1883. *Denver Republican*, Jan. 3, 1883. *Leadville Daily Herald*, Jan. 4 & Oct. 30, 1883. *Daily Register Call*, Jan. 3, 1883. *New York Times*, Dec. 24, 29, 1882 & Jan. 4, 1883. See also A. Tabor Scrapbooks. A copy of the final divorce decree is in the H. Tabor Manuscripts, as well as a document of transfer for "La Veta Place."

14. *Denver Republican*, Jan. 3, 1883. *Leadville Daily Herald*, April 21, 1882 & Oct. 30, 1883. Gossip of Tabor's affairs had been drifting around openly for at least a month before the final divorce.

15. *Denver Republican*, Jan. 3, 1883. *Daily Register Call*, Jan. 3, 1883. *New York Times*, Dec. 29, 1882, p. 9.

16. Bush to Tabor (?), undated, H. Tabor Manuscripts.

17. Field, *A Little Book of Tribune Verse*, p. 240.

18. *Leadville Daily Herald*, Jan. 1–15, 1883. *Denver Republican*, Jan. 2–15, 1883. *Denver Tribune*, Jan. 4–16, 1883. *Rocky Mountain News*, Jan. 4–16, 1883. *The Southwest* (Durango), Jan. 6 & 13, 1883. *Solid Muldoon*, Jan. 12, 1883. *Denver Journal of Commerce*, Jan. 13, 1883. *New York Times*, Jan. 14, 1883.

19. *Rocky Mountain News*, Jan. 15–24, 1883. *Denver Republican*, Jan. 15–24, 1883. *Denver Tribune*, Jan. 16–24, 1883. *Leadville Daily Herald*, Jan. 16–24, 1883.

20. *Leadville Daily Herald*, Jan. 16–27, 1883. *Rocky Mountain News*, Jan. 16–27, 1883. *Denver Tribune*, Jan. 16–27, 1883. *Denver Republican*, Jan. 16–27, 1883. *Boulder County Herald*, Jan. 17, 1883. *Solid Muldoon*, Jan. 19, 1883. *The Southwest*, Jan. 20, 1883 has a good account of the first bribery charges. *Daily Register-Call*, Jan. 3–27, 1883.

21. *Rocky Mountain News*, Jan. 27, 1883. *Denver Tribune*, Jan. 27–28, 1883. Charges of Tabor bribery come from the testimony of Bush in his case against Tabor. Bush might have been lying, but the odds strongly seem to favor the use of bribes, probably by several can-

didates. *Denver Republican*, May 23, 1883. *Tabor v. Bush. Leadville Daily Herald*, Oct. 31, 1883. *Solid Muldoon*, Feb. 9, 1883, accused Tabor of spending $200,000. *Leadville Daily Herald*, Jan. 20, 1883, answered some charges.

22. *Leadville Daily Herald*, Jan. 27, 28 & 30, 1883. *Denver Republican*, Jan. 27, 1883. *Denver Tribune*, Jan. 27–28, 1883. *Rocky Mountain News*, Jan. 27–28, 1883. *Solid Muldoon*, Feb. 23, 1883. *New York Tribune*, Jan. 28, 1883. *The Southwest*, Jan. 27, 1883. Stone, "Tabor." *Gunnison Daily Review-Press*, Jan. 24–28, 1883. *Lake City Mining Register*, Feb. 2, 1883. *Fairplay Flume*, Feb. 1, 1883. *Georgetown Miner*, Jan. 20 & Feb. 3, 1883. The vote totals vary somewhat; I have used those given by the *Tribune*.

23. *Leadville Daily Herald*, Jan. 28, 1883. *Denver Tribune*, Jan. 28, 1883, has a slightly different version. See also the issue of Jan. 30. *Rocky Mountain News*, Jan. 28, 1883; Hall, *History of Colorado*, v. 3, pp. 38–9; *Leadville Daily Herald*, Feb. 1, 1883; *Gunnison Daily Review-Press*, Jan. 25, 1883. For the Pitkin view, see Irving Howbert, *Memories of a Lifetime in the Pike's Peak Region* (New York: G. P. Putnam's, 1925), pp. 261–62.

24. A. Tabor to H. Tabor, Jan. 31, 1883.

CHAPTER 13

1. *Congressional Record 47th Congress, 2nd Session* (Washington: Government Printing Office, 1882), v. 14, pp. 1961–3707. *Journal of the Senate of the United States of America, Being the Second Session of the Forty Seventh Congress* (Washington: Government Printing Office, 1882), pp. 277–519. *Congressional Directory 47th Congress, 2nd Session* (Washington: Government Printing Office, 1883), p. 10, has a fairly accurate account of Tabor's career to 1883.

2. Tabor to Frank (?), Feb. 24, 1883, Tabor letters, Denver Public Library. *Denver Tribune*, Feb. 14, 19, 22 & 28, 1883. *Rocky Mountain News*, Feb. 28, 1883. *Denver Republican*, Feb. 5, 1883. *Leadville Daily Herald*, Feb. 14, 16, 23 & 24, 1883. *The Washington Post*, Feb. 3 & 5, 1883. The *Post* did not think much of the 47th Congress, see Feb. 7 & March 4, 1883.

3. *Denver Tribune*, Feb. 2, 3, 5, 6, 8, 9, 10, 12, 14, 15, 16, 21 & March 5, 9, & 10, 1883. Field claimed the *Congressional Record's* treatment of "our distinguished and venerated representative" aroused a storm of protest in Colorado, there being no mention of his faithful service in that journal. Dave Day, Field's only serious rival, ran a poor second on this particular issue. See *Solid Muldoon*, Feb. 2, 9, & 23, 1883.

4. The following records or copies were found in H. Tabor Manuscripts: Elizabeth McCourt certificate of baptism, marriage to William Doe, divorce from William Doe, and letters to her from Jake Sands

and a folder of eight love letters written from 1873–83. *Leadville Daily Herald*, March 4, 1883. *Daily Register-Call*, March 1, 1883, called her a woman of many strong and worthy qualities. H. Tabor, "Autobiography," p. 22. The best modern story of Baby Doe's early years is Caroline Bancroft, "The Belle of Oshkosh," *The Denver Westerners 1953 Brand Book*, pp. 113–30.

5. Tabor to Elizabeth McCourt Doe, Feb. 18, 20 & 23, 1883, H. Tabor Manuscripts.

6. Tabor to Elizabeth McCourt Doe, Feb. 24, 1883. The lack of punctuation is original. See also letters Feb. 20, 23 & 24, for comments on the dinner party he gave. The Tabor wedding was well covered in the local and national press. Sources used were *New York Times*, March 2, 1883; *The Washington Post*, March 2 & 3, 1883; *Leadville Daily Herald*, March 1–6, 1883; *Daily Register-Call*, March 2–6, 1883; and *Denver Tribune*, March 2–3, 1883. *Leslie's Illustrated*, March 10, 1883, p. 43, has an account of the earlier banquet.

7. Teller to Thomas Dawson, March 8, 1883, Teller Collection, State Historical Society. Bancroft, *Chronicles of the Builders*, v. 4, pp. 324–25, summarizes the senate term favorably.

8. *Leadville Daily Herald*, March 7, 1883. For the reaction to the marriage see the following papers, all of which carry other newspaper comments: *Weekly Republican*, March 8 & 15, 1883. *Denver Tribune*, March 1–17, 1883. *Boulder County Herald*, March 7, 1883. *Denver Republican*, March 7–10, 1883. *Solid Muldoon*, March 9, 1883. *The Southwest*, March 10, 1883. A. Tabor Scrapbook, v. 1.

9. *Horace A. W. Tabor* v. *Augusta L. Tabor*, District Court, La Plata County, 141 (1882). Judgment Book I, p. 65. Register of Action, i, p. 38.

10. *Durango Record*, Feb. 4 & March 24, 1882. *New York Times*, Dec. 29, 1882. *Rocky Mountain News*, Oct. 30, 1883. *Weekly Republican*, March 15, 1883. *Leadville Daily Herald*, Nov. 1–2, 1883. *Denver Tribune*, Oct. 31, 1883. Bush, undated scrap. Tabor Manuscripts.

11. Tabor-McCourt application for License & Marriage License, Sept. 30, 1883, Recorder of Deeds, St. Louis. Bush to Tabor, March 12, 1883, H. Tabor Manuscripts. *Denver Tribune*, March 10, 1883. *Rocky Mountain News*, March 5, 1883. For further on the St. Louis wedding see: *Denver Tribune*, March 5, 1883; *Weekly Republican*, March 8, 1883; *New York Times*, March 5, 1883. For the issue of the deception of the priest see: *New York Times*, March 4 & 21, 1883; *Denver Tribune*, March 3 & 9, 1883; *New York Tribune*, March 5, 1883. Baby Doe listed her age as 23 on the marriage application; Tabor was honest.

12. *The Southwest*, May 12 & Aug. 18, 1883. *Solid Muldoon*, April 27, 1883. *Denver Tribune*, April 21–24, 1883. *Denver Republican*, May 23, 1883. *Rocky Mountain News*, April 21, 23 & Nov. 2, 1883. Forbes Parkhill, *Wildest of the West* (New York: Henry Holt & Co., 1951), p. 161.

13. *Denver Republican*, May 23, 1883. *Denver Tribune*, May 23, 1883.

New York Times, May 25 & July 20, 1883. *New York Tribune*, July 21, 1883. *Rocky Mountain News*, Sept. 6, 1883. *Horace A. W. Tabor v. William Bush*, District Court, Denver, 6748 (1883). Court record of the trial, Denver Public Library. *Leadville Daily Herald*, Oct. 27–Nov. 3, 1883. *Denver Times*, Oct. 29–Nov. 2, 1883. *Rocky Mountain News*, Oct. 27–Nov. 3, 1883. In the H. Tabor Manuscripts are several letters from people offering aid to Tabor to defeat Bush, one writer calling him "that rascal."

14. *Rocky Mountain News*, Nov. 2, 1883. *Leadville Daily Herald*, Nov. 2–3, 1883. Bush miscellaneous material, H. Tabor Manuscripts.

15. *Denver Tribune*, Oct. 31, 1883. A letter from Augusta to Horace was dated May 27, 1883, formally asked "Mr. Tabor, Dear Sir," for a box at the Opera. For the aftermath of *Tabor* v. *Bush* see: *New York Times*, Nov. 3, 1883. *Rocky Mountain News*, Nov. 3, 1883 & Jan. 22, 1884. *Leadville Daily Herald*, Dec. 20, 1883. *The Southwest*, Jan. 20, 1884. *Silver Standard* (Silver Plume), Dec. 12, 1885. *Denver Tribune-Republican*, Dec. 9, 1885.

16. Augusta to Tabor, Dec. 20, 1883, H. Tabor Manuscripts. For loyal Augusta comments see: Parsons, "Tabor and Times," p. 7. Stone "Dictation" and Davis "Dictation," Bancroft Library. *Western Miner & Financier*, April 19, 1899.

17. *The Statesman*, Oct. 17, Nov. 12 & Dec. 15, 1883. *Leadville Daily Herald*, Oct. 28, 30, 1883. John Tabor to Tabor, March 22, 1883. H. Tabor Manuscripts, Scrapbooks, v. 5, p. 17 & 24, v. 6, p. 18. *Rocky Mountain Herald*, Dec. 1, 1883.

18. Dill, *Political Campaigns*, p. 87. Wiswall, "Dictation," p. 2. Bancroft, *Chronicles*, v. 4, p. 325. *Leadville Daily Herald*, April 29, May 6 & Aug. 7, 1884. H. Tabor Manuscripts, Scrapbooks, v. 10, p. 7. For the early 1884 campaign see: *Leadville Daily Herald*, Jan.–June 1884. *Solid Muldoon*, Jan. 4, 1884. A. H. Lucy to Tabor, Feb. 25, 1884. *Rocky Mountain News*, March 11, 1884. *Rocky Mountain Sun*, May 31, 1884. Hall, *History of Colorado*, v. 3, p. 44.

19. Dill, *Political Campaigns*, pp. 94–5. *Leadville Daily Herald*, Aug. 20, Sept. 10–16 & 24, 1884. *Rocky Mountain News*, Aug. 6, Sept. 3–9 & 13, 1884. *Solid Muldoon*, Sept. 5, 12 & 19, 1884. *Georgetown Courier*, Sept. 18, 1884. *Weekly Tribune-Republican*, Aug. 28, 1884. Tabor to wife, no date, 1884, H. Tabor Manuscripts. See also *Leadville Daily Herald*, Sept. 14–Oct. 16, 1884.

20. *Boulder County Herald*, Oct. 20, 1886. *Boulder News & Banner*, Oct. 12, 1886. *Weekly Tribune-Republican*, Oct. 28, 1886. Hall, *History of Colorado*, v. 3, pp. 45 & 49. Dill, *Political Campaigns*, pp. 104–05. *Leadville Evening Chronicle*, Sept. 22 & 30, 1886. *Silver Standard*, Oct. 2, 1886. *Rocky Mountain News*, Sept. 28–30, 1886. Wiswall, "Dictation," p. 2 says Tabor accepted reluctantly the chairmanship of the state committee.

21. For the 1886 campaign see: *Leadville Evening Chronicle*, Oct. 2–20, 1886. *Denver Tribune-Republican*, Sept. 30–Oct. 29, 1886. *Boulder*

County Herald, Oct. 6–27, 1886. *Georgetown Courier*, Oct. 7–28, 1886. *The Daily Advertiser* (Trinidad), Oct. 1–12 & 22–Nov. 5, 1886. *Silver Standard*, Oct. 2–30, 1886. Dill, *Political Campaigns*, pp. 109–13. H. Tabor Manuscripts, Scrapbooks, v. 6, pp. 17 & 126. Estimates of his expenses in this campaign range as high as $75,000.

22. *Denver Republican*, Sept. 5–6, 1888. For the campaign see: *Silver Standard*, March 10, May 19, Aug. 11 & 25, 1888. *Weekly Republican*, March 15, May 17, July 5, Aug. 23, 1888. *Colorado Graphic*, June 9, Aug. 4–Sept. 1, 1888. *Solid Muldoon*, June 15, 22, July 6, 20 & Aug. 3–31, 1888. *Rocky Mountain Sun*, July 7, 1888. *Denver Republican*, Aug. 5–Sept. 5, 1888. *Leadville Evening Chronicle*, Aug. 6, 1888. *Daily Denver Times*, Sept. 4, 1888. *Rocky Mountain News*, May 16 & Sept. 4–6, 1888. Harrison to Tabor, July 2, 1888, H. Tabor Manuscripts.

23. Wiswall, "Dictation," pp. 3–4. Dill, *Political Campaigns*, pp. 120–22. *Denver Republican*, Sept. 6, 1888, said Wolcott joined Cooper because he wanted to be with a winner. Bancroft, *Chronicles*, v. 4, pp. 326–27. *Colorado Graphic*, Sept. 8, 1888. *Solid Muldoon*, Sept. 7 & 14, 1888. Dill said Wolcott could have nominated Cooper on the first ballot but let him grow gradually so long as no danger of a Tabor boom emerged. M. Quay to Tabor, no date, 1888 & Nov. 5, 1888, H. Tabor Manuscripts.

24. Stone, "Tabor." See also Fitz-Mac (James MacCarty), *Political Portraits* (Colorado Springs: Gazette Printing Co., 1888), pp. 31–32 & 39.

25. *H. A. W. Tabor v. Rufus Clark, John Hanna, Denver Circle Real Estate Co. et al.*, Denver District Court, 7864 (1886). *Universal Fire Insurance Co. v. Tabor Fire Insurance Co.*, Denver District Court, 16079 (1892). *Universal Fire Insurance Co. v. Tabor Fire Insurance Co.*, Denver District Court, 7335 (1883). *Colorado Fire Insurance Co. v. Tabor Fire Insurance Co.*, Denver District Court, 5929 (1882). *Rocky Mountain News*, July 14, 16, Sept. 1, Nov. 27 & Dec. 28, 1881. *Denver Tribune*, March 4, 1882. *Rocky Mountain Sun*, March 11, 1882. It was first incorporated as the Tabor Fire Insurance Co. of Leadville.

26. J. B. Webster and J. T. Summerville to Tabor, undated, H. Tabor Manuscripts. H. Tabor Manuscripts, Scrapbooks, v. 6, p. 23. *Rocky Mountain News*, Aug. 22, 25, Nov. 5, Dec. 10, 1880; July 19, 1881; Jan. 12, 22, 1882; Aug. 28, 1883; Jan. 3, 1884 & July 1, 1885.

CHAPTER 14

1. Tabor to Lily, Aug. 31, 1889 & Jan. 3, 1894. Tabor to Honeymaid, Feb. 25, 1894 & Nov. 19, 1898. For letters to Tabor, see Lily to father, Nov. 23, 1898, and Silver to father, Dec. 22, 1898. H. Tabor Manuscripts. See Stone, "Interview," Bancroft Library, for an opinion of "that woman."

2. Tabor to wife, Feb. 4, 1886. Tabor to Lily, Sept. 24, 1893, H. Tabor Manuscripts. *New York Times*, Jan. 21, 1887. *Colorado Graphic*, Nov. 12, 1887. *Harper's Bazaar*, Jan. 8, 1887. The picture was also in *Harper's Weekly*.

3. Horace to My Darling Wife, June 6, 1883, Feb. 4, 1886, Oct. 9, Dec. 17, 1893; Feb. 18 & March 18, 1894. Babe to Horace, undated (probably 1890) & Jan. 12, 18(93), H. Tabor Manuscripts.

4. Tabor to E. Wolcott, March 19, 1899. Tabor to Mrs. E. Wolcott, March 13, 1899. Tabor to wife, March 13, 1899, H. Tabor Manuscripts. On the question of Baby Doe's activity, see Tabor to E. F. McCourt, Jan. 20, 1899. For the Eugene Field interview see *The Southwest*, Aug. 18, 1883.

5. H. Tabor, "Autobiography," pp. 21–22. H. H. Bancroft, "Instructions for writing the biography of HAW Tabor," pp. 3–4, Bancroft Library.

6. Tabor to wife, March 18, 1894. For his health see P. McCourt to Lizzie, Sept. 15 & 23, 1893. Tabor to wife, Feb. 4, 1886; Sept. 13, 1888; June 15, 1889, H. Tabor Manuscripts. H. Tabor, "Autobiography," p. 22. For instruction of Tabor biography see "Instructions," p. 1. H. Bancroft, "Colorado Notes," pp. 2–3. John Caughey, *Hubert Howe Bancroft* (Berkeley: Univ. of California Press, 1946), p. 316.

7. H. Tabor, "Autobiography," p. 2. Stone, "Interview." He claimed to have known Tabor for thirty years. Parsons, "Tabor's Bittersweet Christmas." Bancroft, *Chronicles of the Builders*, v. 4, pp. 337–38. "Great Divide" clipping, Dawson Scrapbooks, v. 23. John Tabor to Baby Doe, March 9, 1894, H. Tabor Manuscripts.

8. E. J. Moys to Tabor, Nov. 30, 1897. J. Guida to Tabor, April 22, 1897. E. J. Moys to Tabor, Nov. 8, 1898, discusses their brother's death. Tabor was close to his sister, as mentioned, and there is a whole series of letters in the H. Tabor Manuscripts. See also Guida letters.

9. Tabor to Pete, Oct. 17 (two telegrams) and to wife, Oct. 18, 1888. The Guida letters are full of his charitable activities. E. Beck to Tabor, Jan. 19, 1890. N. McKenzie to M. Page, Dec. 13, 1890. L. Schreiber to Tabor, July 23, 1884. Rev. Joseph Keenan to Mrs. Tabor, Aug. 30, 1889. Mary L. Lathrop to Mrs. Tabor, Jan. 8, 1894. H. Tabor Manuscripts. A. Tabor Scrapbooks, v. 2, p. 35. Susan B. Anthony, et al., *The History of Woman Suffrage* (Indianapolis: Hollenbeck Press, 1904), pp. 515 & 518. *Denver Tribune*, Feb. 23, 1882. *Rocky Mountain News*, May 15, 1880; Aug. 30, 1881 & Dec. 12, 1886. *Leadville Weekly Herald*, Jan. 3, 1880. Bancroft, *History of Nevada, Colorado and Wyoming*, pp. 508–09, says Tabor annually gave $10,000 to schools and charity.

10. Jennie Sandelin, *Steamboat Pilot*, April 6, 1939, Tabor clippings, State Historical Society. On the Washington home see *Leadville Daily Herald*, Dec. 2, 1883. On the Denver homes see the *Denver Times*,

Dec. 16, 1886. *Weekly Tribune Republican*, Dec. 16, 1886. C. E. N. to Tabor, Feb. 25, 1898, is the letter from the "bad woman."

11. The H. Tabor Manuscripts have many requests, too numerous to list here. *Horace A. W. Tabor* v. *Denver and Suburban Railway Co.*, District Court, Denver, 14280 (1891). One bill gives an uncompleted total of food purchased for the Tabor household in May–June, 1887, as $195.55.

12. Numerous sources estimate Tabor's wealth. No individual, including Horace, knew the exact amount. See for example: *Rocky Mountain News*, April 20, 1882. *New York Tribune*, Jan. 28, 1883. Maxey Tabor, "Interview." *New York Times*, Jan. 4, 1883. *Leadville Daily Herald*, April 21, 1882. *Weekly Tribune Republican*, Nov. 4, 1886. *Western Miner & Financier*, April 19, 1899.

13. *Rocky Mountain News*, July 15, 19, 25, 27, 29, Aug. 23, 1883 & Jan. 19, 1884. *Leslie's Illustrated*, July 23, p. 371 & Aug. 11, 1883, p. 403. *Denver Tribune*, Jan. 19, 1884. For the Grant visit see *Leadville Democrat*, July 23–24, 1880. *Leadville Weekly Herald*, July 31, 1880. Horace never gave up his support of the veterans and in 1889 was advocating a National Soldiers' home to be built in Colorado. John Logan to Tabor, May 28, 1885. Phil Sheridan to Tabor, March 22, 1887. H. Tabor Manuscripts.

14. *Daily Chronicle*, April 16, 26, 1879. *Rocky Mountain News* (Weekly), July 9, 1879. Thomas, "An Old Timer," pp. 5–6. *Leadville Daily Herald*, Nov. 27, 1880. *Denver Tribune*, June 27, 1882. George Crofutt, *Crofutt's Grip-Sack Guide to Colorado* (Omaha: Overland Publishing Co., 1885), p. 147. "Place Names in Colorado," *Colorado Magazine* (Jan. 1943), pp. 127–28.

CHAPTER 15

1. Stock Ledger, no. 1, p. 48 and Minutes of the Board of Directors, Jan. 30, 1883. First National Bank Records.

2. H. Tabor, "Autobiography," p. 22. Tabor Grand Hotel Furnishing Co., Incorporation Papers. *Leadville Daily Herald*, May 28–29, 1884. *Leadville Daily Chronicle*, July 19 & Oct. 22, 1886. Sandra Dallas, in *No More Than Five in a Bed*, pp. 91–94, has a brief history of the hotel. Tabor earlier might have owned the Clarendon, see *Streeter* v. *Tabor*. Sources on the opera house: *Leadville Daily Herald*, Jan. 1, 1882. Degitz, "History of the Tabor Opera House," pp. 13–14. Sources on the Bank of Leadville: *H. A. W. Tabor* v. *Bank of Leadville*, District Court, Denver, 11269 (1889). *Rocky Mountain News*, July 27, 1883. Davis, *Olden Times*, pp. 262–63. *Leadville Daily Herald*, Jan. 1, April 21, 1882 & Nov. 1, 1883.

3. *Rocky Mountain News*, Oct. 30, 1883. See also issues of Oct. 31 & Nov. 1, 1883. *Denver Tribune*, Sept. 5 & 19, 1882. *Leadville Daily*

Herald, Sept. 26–29, 1882. Tabor Opera Records, H. Tabor Manuscripts. Bush to Tabor, May 18, 20, 22, 1882. Maxey Tabor to Tabor, Feb. 11, 1883. Pete to Lizzie, May 20, 1890, H. Tabor Manuscripts. Howbert, *Memories*, p. 254. The names of the theatres in the Silver Circuit are found on a letterhead of the Tabor Grand. According to the *Denver Tribune*, April 8, 1883, Tabor at one time dreamed of a nationwide chain of opera houses.

4. Material for the preceding section on the Tabor Grand Opera is found in: Emily Faithful, *Three Visits to America* (Edinburgh: David Douglass, 1884), p. 129. *Tourists' Handbook of Colorado, New Mexico and Utah* (Denver: 1885), p. 4. W. G. M. Stone, *The Colorado Hand-Book: Denver and Its Outings* (Denver: Barkhausen & Lester, 1892), pp. 47 & 51. "Tabor Grand Opera House Publication," pp. 7–8. Crowley, "History of the Tabor Grand Opera House," pp. 86–105, 108, 137, 141–42, 147 & 190–91. *Rocky Mountain News*, Jan. 5, 1884. *Silver Standard*, July 24, 1886. *Denver Tribune*, Feb. 6, 1883. *The Artesian Wells of Denver* (Denver: News Printing Co., 1884), pp. 5 & 19.

5. *James Hawkins* v. *H. A. W. Tabor*, District Court, Denver 7435 (1885). *James Mackey* v. *Horace A. W. Tabor*, District Court, Denver 12557 (1890). *Rocky Mountain News*, Feb. 13, 1886 & Jan. 27, 1890. Mackey's appeal was dismissed on the grounds Tabor was not responsible for the actions of the arresting persons. Mackey's right to occupy the seat was not denied.

6. A. Hayman to McCourt, Dec. 18, 1893. Sperry to Tabor, Aug. 29, 1894. See also Henderson to McCourt, Dec. 18, 1893, H. Tabor Manuscripts. *The National Mohawk Valley Bank* v. *Horace A. W. Tabor et al.*, U.S. Circuit Court, 1895 (1886). *D. D. Mallory* v. *Howard Chapin & H. A. W. Tabor*, U.S. Circuit Court, 1536 (1884). *United States* v. *George Hazen & Horace A. W. Tabor*, U.S. District Court, 540 & 541 (1887). *Sarah Clifford* v. *Horace Tabor et al.*, U.S. Circuit Court, 3017 (1893). *Leopold B. Weil* v. *Horace A. W. Tabor et al.*, District Court, Denver 7592 (1886). H. Tabor Scrapbooks, v. 6, pp. 24–25. Horace Phelps to Tabor, Nov. 20, 1893. H. Tabor Manuscripts. *H. Hart* v. *H. A. W. Tabor & Peter McCourt*, District Court, Denver, 17171 (1892). *Tabor Amusement Co. & Peter McCourt* v. *David Henderson*, Circuit Court, Denver, 20474 (1894). *Ferdinand Stark* v. *Tabor Amusement Co., et al.*, District Court, Denver, 20145 (1893). *New York Times, Feb. 28, 1888.*

7. *Frank Leslie's Illustrated*, July 28, 1883, p. 371. *Mining Record*, Dec. 23, 1882, p. 574. *Rocky Mountain News*, Feb. 1, March 2, July 17, 18, Aug. 1, Oct. 1, 1883; Aug. 31 & Sept. 1, 1884. *Denver Tribune*, Feb. 11, March 2 & Aug. 15, 1883. *Denver Republican*, Jan 5 & Feb. 5, 1883. *Solid Muldoon*, March 2, 1883. *Engineering and Mining Journal*, Sept. 13, 1884, p. 171 & April 11, 1885, p. 250. Tritle, "Biennial Message," pp. 20–22. *Grand Army Magazine*, April 1883, pp. 209–14. For the Fifteenth Street Theater, see *H. A. W. Tabor et al.* v. *Charles Clinton et al.*, District Court, Denver, 22679 (1895). *Rocky Mountain News*, Dec. 3, 1890.

8. National Mining Exposition statement, H. Tabor Collection. H. Tabor, "Autobiography," p. 19. Smiley, *History of Denver*, pp. 476–77. *Leadville Daily Herald*, May 1–2, 1884. *Weekly Tribune-Republican*, Oct. 2, 1886. *Denver Republican*, Jan. 27, 1883. For court cases see: *Thomas P. Hughes* v. *National Mining and Industrial Exposition et al.*, District Court, Denver, 6430 (1882); *Gibson* v. *the National . . . Exposition*; and *Board of County Commissioners* v. *the National . . . Exposition*.

9. *Rocky Mountain News*, Jan. 16–18 & May 13, 1881, Jan. 8–9, July 10, Oct. 7, Dec. 1, 1883 & Oct. 21, 1884. *Denver Tribune*, March 30, 1883. *Boulder County Herald*, Jan. 10, 1883. *Leadville Daily Herald*, April 8, 1883 & Oct. 21, 1884. *H. A. W. Tabor* v. *J. Evans*, Denver District Court, 7437 (1886). *H. A. W. Tabor* v. *John Good*, District Court, Denver, 9152 (1888).

10. *Leadville Daily Herald*, Jan. 5, 1883, March 28, June 18, July 11 & Oct. 21, 1884. *Boulder County Herald*, Oct. 20, 1886. David, *Olden Times*, pp. 179–82. Dill, *Political Campaigns*, p. 67. *Silver Standard*, Dec. 12, 1885. *James Lannan* v. *J. W. Wallace, T. Dillon . . . , H. A. W. Tabor*, District Court, Lake County, 2979 (1884). Augusta in 1883 said Horace was trying to buy the *Denver Tribune*; nothing came of it, however.

11. *Leadville Daily Herald*, Oct. 27, 30 & Dec. 16, 1883. *The Statesman*, Oct. 17, Nov. 12 & Dec. 15, 1883. W. C. Jewett to Tabor, Jan. 11, 1884 [?]; Aspen City railroad records & Pitkin County railroad records, H. Tabor Manuscripts. Aspen City Railroad Company & the Pitkin County Railroad Company Incorporation Papers. Tabor was president of the Pitkin County railroad. *Engineering and Mining Journal*, July 6, p. 13 & July 20, p. 56, Aug.24, 1889, p. 167. *Rocky Mountain Sun*, Aug. 3, Sept. 7, 1889 & May 30, 1891. For the Denver, Apex & Western see: H. Tabor scrapbooks, v. 5, p. 23, and the following court cases: *Adams* v. *Denver Apex, Baker* v. *Tabor*, and *Colorado River Irrigation* v. *Denver Apex*. Denver Apex & Western Incorporation Papers & Amended Articles. *Weekly Register-Call*, April 24 & May 22, 1891. *Denver Republican*, April 20 & 25, 1892. *Northwestern Financier*, Nov. 1891. *Denver Times*, Dec. 10, 1898.

12. H. Tabor, "Autobiography," pp. 18–19. Vigil and St. Vrain Grant records, H. Tabor Manuscripts. Vigil and St. Vrain Grant records, Rockwell Collection. *Colorado Chieftain*, March 23, 1871. *Weekly Republican*, May 17, 1888. *Pueblo Daily Chieftain*, March 6, 10 & April 4, 1889.

13. Norman Rue to author, March 18, 1969. A. T. Byrne, *Honduras, a Brief Sketch of its Resources* (San Francisco: Francis, Valentine & Co., 1885), pp. 2–9. Vincent Checchi, *Honduras: A Problem in Economic Development* (New York: Twentieth Century Fund, 1959), pp. 2, 58 & 71–72. *Denver Tribune*, Feb. 20, 1884. *Leadville Daily Herald*, April 29, May 7, 29 & June 19, 1884. *Engineering and Mining Journal*, June 28, 1884, p. 486. Republic of Honduras-Campbell Reduction records, H. Tabor Manuscripts.

14. *The Mercantile Agency Reference Book (and key)* . . . (San Francisco: R. G. Dun & Co., 1887), pp. 516, 548–54. *Frank Leslie's Illustrated*, July 28, 1883, p. 371. *Rocky Mountain News*, Feb. 28, 1884. *Daily Register-Call*, Feb. 4, 1886. *Leadville Daily Chronicle*, Jan. 8, 1886. *Weekly Republican*, Feb. 2, 1888. See also *Denver City Directories*, 1886–1890.

15. *Northwestern Mutual Life* v. *Horace A. W. Tabor et al.*, District Court, Denver, 21840 (1894). *Daily Register-Call*, Feb. 4, 1886. The H. Tabor manuscripts have numerous records of his borrowing money during these years. H. Reed to Tabor, March 6 & April 21, 1885, H. Tabor Manuscripts. Reed tried to swing a $500,000 mortgage.

16. Poorman Mine records. Tabor Investment Records, H. Tabor Manuscripts. *Mining Record*, Feb. 21, 1885, p. 119. Silver Point records, H. Tabor Manuscripts. *Engineering and Mining Journal*, Aug. 10, p. 122, Aug. 24, p. 166 & Dec. 14, 1889, p. 528. *Weekly Republican*, July 25, 1889 & Jan. 9, 1890. Experiment mines records, H. Tabor Manuscripts. *Weekly Tribune-Republican*, April 8, 1886. Hunki-Dori records, H. Tabor Manuscripts. *Leadville Daily Herald*, July 4, 1884. *Rocky Mountain Sun*, March 8 & 29, 1890. *Boulder News*, Oct. 4 & Dec. 6, 1888; Jan. 10, March 28, May 30 & June 27, 1889.

17. Matchless records, H. Tabor Manuscripts. *Leadville Daily Herald*, Jan. 1, April 14, Nov. 14, 1883; March 11 & April 5, 1884. Harker to Moffat, June 1, 1884, Maid of Erin records, First National Bank. *Engineering and Mining Journal*, 1883–1890. *Weekly Tribune-Republican*, April 2, 1885. *Mining Record*, 1883–1885. *Leadville Evening Chronicle*, March 30 & Sept. 4, 18, 1886. *Weekly Republican*, Nov. 24, 1887; Feb. 2, May 24, 1888; July 25, Aug. 22 & Nov. 14, 1889. Matchless Mining Company, Incorporation Papers. It was stocked at 500,000 shares, par value $1. Forbes Parkhill, in his "How Tabor Lost his Millions," raised questions about the validity of the Matchless reports. There is doubt in this author's mind as well, but proof is lacking.

18. Harker to Moffat, Feb. 5, 1884. Henriett Mining records, First National Bank. *Leadville Daily Herald*, Feb. 20, March 2, April 23 & Oct. 10, 1884. Clark Spence, *British Investments . . . 1860–1901*, p. 75 has the Moffat-Henriett sales and return.

19. These letters, Harker to Moffat, sent in 1884 and 1885, are found in the Maid of Erin and Henriett records, First National Bank.

20. Tabor Collection, First National Bank. Henriett and Maid of Erin records, H. Tabor Manuscripts. *Engineering and Mining Journal*, 1884–1891. Harker to Moffat, May 17, 1885, Maid of Erin Records, First National Bank. Eben Smith called the Maid the "wettest hole in camp." *Rocky Mountain News*, Feb. 13, 1886.

21. Matchless Concentrator Co. records, H. Tabor Manuscripts. Matchless Concentrator Company, Incorporation Papers. *Mining Record*, May 23, 1885, p. 321. *Weekly Tribune-Republican*, July 15, 1886. For general mining conditions see: *Engineering and Mining Journal*, Oct. 9, 1886, p. 262; Sept. 17, p. 210, Dec. 31, 1887, p.

496 & Nov. 10, 1888, p. 399. *Leadville Daily Chronicle*, Jan. 8, 1886. *Leadville Herald Democrat*, July 14 & Aug. 11, 1889. Tabor Investment Company of St. Louis Incorporation Papers.

22. Tam O'Shanter material is found in: *Rocky Mountain Sun*, 1882–90. The *Rocky Mountain Sun*, Sept. 22, 1883, called the story of the second strike false. *Denver Republican*, Sept. 13, 1883. *Leadville Daily Herald*, Aug. 31, Oct. 22, 1882; Feb. 18, 1883 & June 10, 1884. *Engineering and Mining Journal*, 1883–90. *Rocky Mountain News*, Sept. 17, 1883. San Juan material is found in: *Solid Muldoon*, Aug. 1, 22, Sept. 19, 1884 & July 22, 1887. *Mining Record*, May 16, 1885, p. 308. Alaska Mine records, H. Tabor Manuscripts. Tabor eventually lost these mines because of failure to pay taxes. According to legend Tabor also attempted to purchase the Lone Wolf Mine, one of the San Juan's lost bonanzas. See Marshall & Cornelius, *Golden Treasures of the San Juan*, pp. 15–17.

23. Werner to Seaman, Feb. 18, 1891. Gold and Silver Extraction Mining & Milling Company papers, State Historical Society. See the following letters: Gow to Werner, Jan. 11, May 2, June 4, 19, 28, Nov. 15, Dec. 19, 1890. H. A. Jones to Werner, May 27 & June 4, 1890. T. L. Wiswall to Werner, July 21, 1890. Seaman to Werner, Dec. 24, 1890 & Feb. 12, 1891. Agreement of May 15, 1890, between Tabor and the Company. See the *Engineering and Mining Journal*, 1888–89, for comments on the Colorado Gold and Silver Extraction Co. Werner's full name was Max Edward Werner von Wernshuysen.

24. Werner to T. Bowen, April 20, 1891. Seaman to Werner, Feb. 12, April 20, May 4, June 24 & Aug. 26, 1891. Werner to Gow, May 7, 1891. *Engineering and Mining Journal*, May–June, 1892. Eben Smith papers, Denver Public Library, has letters from the company until 1894. The MacArthur-Forrest process eventually proved to be a good one.

25. Grand Belt Copper Co. records, H. Tabor Manuscripts. *Leadville Daily Herald*, Oct. 21 & 27, 1883. *Engineering and Mining Journal*, Sept. 5, p. 170, Oct. 31, p. 303 & Dec. 19, 1885, p. 427. Utah mining references: *Leadville Daily Herald*, Feb. 16, 1882. *Robert Brown & Thomas A. Walley* v. *Horace A. W. Tabor et al*; District Court, Denver, 10415 (1890). Ashley became the town of Vernal. Wyoming mine records, H. Tabor Manuscripts. Montana mining records: *The Commercial National Bank of Cleveland* v. *Horace A. W. Tabor*, U. S. Circuit Court, 2817 (1893). Tabor to wife, July 22, 1891. Idaho mine records, H. Tabor Manuscripts. Montana Mining Land & Investment Company, Incorporation Records. Fremont County, Wyoming, Miscellaneous Record Book B, Mining Record Book H, Quit Claim Deed Book C, and Mining Record Book D. Tabor held the Rose and Tabor Grand as late as Dec. 1897.

CHAPTER 16

1. James B. Tenney, "History of Mining in Arizona," p. 399. Unpublished manuscript, Special Collections, University of Arizona Library. Richard Hinton, *The Hand-Book to Arizona* (San Francisco: Payot, Upham & Co., 1878), pp. 144–45. *Arizona Miner*, March 14, 1886 & Dec. 21, 1867. *Mining and Scientific Press*, 1867–1880. Richard McCormick, "Message to Fifth Legislative Assembly," *Journals of the Fifth Legislative Assembly* (Tucson: Tucson Publishing Co., 1869), p. 35. Rossiter Raymond, *Mines, Mills and Furnaces*, pp. 257–60. *Engineering and Mining Journal*, 1880–86. Sexton to Ord, Sept. 8, 1869, *Report of the Secretary of War* (Washington: Government Printing Office, 1869), pp. 133–34. *Weekly Arizona Miner*, Feb. 18, 1871 & March 14, 1879. Raymond, *Statistics* (1875), p. 394.

2. *Prescott Morning Courier*, March 21–31, 1888. Vulture Records, H. Tabor Manuscripts. *Weekly Republican*, May 24, 1888. *Denver Republican*, Oct. 26, 1887. Patrick Hamilton, *The Resources of Arizona* (Prescott: 1881), p. 118. The Vulture price was $265,000.

3. Contracts found in the Vulture Mining Records entered as evidence in the case of *Kaiser Gold* v. *Tabor*. Hereafter cited Vulture Records. *Engineering and Mining Journal*, Oct. 20, 1888, pp. 322 & 330.

4. Morrish to Kaiser Gold, Feb. 23, 1889. See also letters of Nov. 1, 6, Dec. 4, 6, 8, 29, 1888; Jan. 17, 29 & Feb. 2, 1889. Tabor to Morrish, Nov. 17, 20, 22, Dec. 6, 1888 & Feb. 16, 1889. Tabor to Board of Directors, Nov. 23, 1888. Morrish Deposition, Feb. 24, 1891. Vulture Records.

5. McCourt to Morrish, March 18, 1889. Morrish Deposition, Feb. 24, 1891. Vulture Records.

6. *Engineering and Mining Journal*, Feb. 6, 1892, p. 176. See also issues Aug. 31, p. 187 & Nov. 9, 1889, p. 404; Feb. 27, 1892, p. 247. Morrish Deposition, Feb. 24, 1891. Morrish to Kaiser, March 4, 1889. Tabor to Directors, April 27, 1889. Kaiser to Tabor, May 2, 1889. Vulture Records. Tabor to Alfred Bates (1889), Bancroft Library. *The Kaiser Gold Mines Company, Limited* v. *Horace A. W. Tabor*, U.S. Circuit Court, 2450 (1889). Tabor to William Farrish, May 9, 1889, and Vulture Records, H. Tabor Manuscripts.

7. H. Tabor, "Autobiography," p. 14. Tabor interview in the *Great Divide*, Jan. 1892, Dawson Scrapbooks, v. 23.

8. *Northwestern Mutual Life* v. *H. A. W. Tabor et al.*

9. Union National Bank and Bennett & Myers, Records, H. Tabor Manuscripts. *Tabor Amusement Company, Tabor Real Estate Company* v. *Horace W. Bennett and Julius Myer*, District Court, Denver, 20856 (1894). *The Tabor Real Estate Company and Horace A. W. Tabor* v. *A. B. Sullivan et al.*, District Court, Denver, 21270 (1894). Tritch material, H. Tabor Manuscripts. *George Tritch, Jr.* v. *Horace A. W. Tabor & E. B. Tabor*, District Court, Denver, 19149 (1893). R. W. Woodbury to Tabor, Feb. 27, 1893, H. Tabor Manuscripts.

10. Tabor Mines and Mills Records, H. Tabor Manuscripts. *James W. Newell, et al.*, v. *Tabor Mines and Mills Co. et al*; District Court, Lake County, 4860 (1895). Tabor Real Estate Company Records & Tabor Amusement Company Records, H. Tabor Manuscripts. *Tabor Amusement* v. *Bennett*. Thomas Wiswall was in all these companies for a short time, but resigned before the crash. Horace & E. B. Tabor to the Calumet . . . Co., Feb. 6, 1895. Horace and E. B. Tabor to the Catholic Bishop of Chicago, May 10, 1894. H. Tabor Manuscripts. Tabor Mines & Mills, Tabor Amusement & Tabor Real Estate Companies, Incorporation Papers, Colorado State Archives.

11. *The Provident Trust Co.* v. *Tabor Investment Co. & H. A. W. Tabor*, U.S. Circuit Court, 2975 (1893). For other Tabor dealings see warranty deed, H. Tabor to E. Tabor, Jan. 30, 1892. Quit Claim Deed, March 17, 1892. E. Tabor promissory note to H. Tabor, March 7, 1892, Tabor Real Estate and Tabor Amusement Co. promissory note to H. Tabor, July 15, 1893, H. Tabor Manuscripts. Also check all the court cases cited in this chapter.

12. Charles Botts to Henry Bacon, Dec. 17, 1864, Henry Bacon Papers, Huntington Library. J. C. Carrera, *Report on the Santa Eduwiges Mine in the State of Chihuahua, Mexico* (Chicago: Rand, McNally & Co., 1883), pp. 5–16. W. L. Cooper's Report on the Santa Eduwiges Mine, H. Tabor Manuscripts. Florence & Robert Lister, *Chihuahua Storehouse of Storms* (Albuquerque: University of New Mexico Press, 1966), pp. 91–92 & 163–80. Marvin Berstein, *The Mexican Mining Industry 1890–1950* (Albany: State University of New York, 1964), pp. 19, 27 & 29. Josiah Gregg, *Commerce of the Prairies* (New York: Henry Langley, 1844), v. 2, pp. 105–11. Jesus Maria is today called Ocampo.

13. John Tabor to E. Tabor, June 15, 1892. Pete to Lizzie, Jan. 9, 17, Feb. 7 & 20, 1893, H. Tabor Manuscripts. For other Santa Eduwiges history see: *Leadville Daily Herald*, Dec. 21, 1883; April 12, May 7 & 28, 1884. *Engineering and Mining Journal*, 1881–89. *H. A. W. Tabor* v. *Lewis Herefort*, District Court, Denver, 17184 (1892). *A. S. Weston* v. *H. A. W. Tabor*, District Court, Lake County, 4358 & 4359 (1892). *Mining Record*, May 16, 1885, p. 309. *Leadville Herald-Democrat*, July 6, 1889. A.S. Weston to Tabor, March 5, 1884, Ignacio Maemanus to Tabor, Nov. 19, 1891, and Weston receipt of Tabor payment, July 22, 1892, H. Tabor Manuscripts. The mine's name was spelled in several ways; the one used was that on the letterhead of the company.

14. Wood to wife, July 24, 1893, Wood Collection. See also letters June 26, July 19, 22 and Nov. 23, 1893. Ellis; *Teller*, p. 216. *Weekly Republican*, Jan. 4, May 25, June 29, July 20 & Sept. 14, 1893. *Rocky Mountain News*, July 16–20, 1893. Jerome Smiley, *Semi-Centennial History of the State of Colorado* (Chicago: Lewis Publishing Co., 1913), v. 1, pp. 710–712. *Silver Standard*, July 22, 1893. *Engineering and Mining Journal*, Aug. 5, 1893, p. 131, thought Colorado was taking the silver crash too hard. For Tabor's problems getting loans, see Fred Bulkley

to Tabor, Aug. 14, 1893 and C. Hunn to E. Tabor, Dec. 5, 1893. The *Rocky Mountain News*, July 22, 1953, has a letter from a man who remembered having trouble collecting money from Tabor.

15. Tabor to wife, Sept. 15, 22, 24, Nov. 20, Dec. 2, 4, 1893; Jan. 3, 9, 17, 24, Feb. 1, 4, 11, 18, 25, March 4, 9, 11, 14, 18, 25, April 1, 8, 11, 22, 25 & June 7, 1894. Pete to Lizzie, Sept. 3, 15, 23, Dec. 4, 18, 21, 23, 1893; Feb. 20, March 9, 12 & June 7, 1894. Tabor to Pete, March 14 & April 18, 1894. W. Cooper to Tabor, March 13, 1894. Creel to Tabor, June 7, 1894. John Tabor to E. Tabor, March 9, 1894. Pete to Arthur Bondwell, March 15, 1894. H. Tabor Manuscripts. Lister, *Chihuahua*, pp. 153, 178, 182 & 205, discusses Creel.

16. Pete to Lizzie, March 9, 1894. See also John Tabor to E. Tabor, March 9, 1894. Pete to Bondwell, March 15, 1894. H. Tabor Manuscripts. The geologic structure of the mine was explained to the author by T. Clendenin, a mining engineer who examined it. Clendenin to author, April 23, 1968. For general comments on problems and results of Mexican mining, see David Pletcher, *Rails, Mines and Progress*; John Hammond, *Autobiography*, v. 1; and Berstein, *The Mexican Mining Industry*.

17. W. L. Cooper to Tabors, March 24, 1893. See also Jan. 9, 1893. J. Stainburn to Tabor, Feb. 9, 1893. Stainburn to E. Tabor, Feb. 13, 1893. W. L. Cooper Report, April 25, 1893. Tabor to wife, Dec. 17 & 21, 1893. Pete to Lizzie, Dec. 18, 1893 & March 9, 1894. E. Reed to Tabor, April 21, 1885. H. Tabor Manuscripts. Stainburn proved a complete failure, dying of "excessive dissipation" while in charge of the property. Tabor, in 1895, sold whatever rights he still had to the New Jersey-based Bavicanora Gold and Silver Mining Co.

18. Pete to Lizzie, Jan. 17 & Feb. 20, 1893. Tabor to wife, Sept. 24, Dec. 17, 1893; Feb. 11, 25, April 8 & 29, 1894, H. Tabor Manuscripts.

19. Part of a long note dated Monday, the 19th, 1894 (probably November), H. Tabor Manuscripts. See also Tabor to wife, Feb. 11, March 18, April 22 & 29, 1894.

20. *Tabor Real Estate Co. & Tabor Amusement Co.* v. *Laura D. Swickhimer et al*; District Court, Denver, 21588 (1894). *Tabor Amusement Co. & Tabor Real Estate Co.* v. *Bennett & Myers. L. D. Smith* v. *Tabor Amusement Co., F. E. Edbrooke and Peter McCourt*, District Court, Denver, 21611 (1894), *Northwestern Mutual* v. *Tabor*. Tabor to H. Teller, Aug. 29, 1896, Teller Papers, State Historical Society. Laura Smith (nee Swickhimer) claimed Tabor's agents asked her to purchase the claim; Tabor's defense was based on the premise that the companies were forced against their free will to accept dictated terms. Under her terms, the note was extended eighteen months. See the *Denver Republican*, April 20, 1894, for the earliest attachment. Smiley, *History of Colorado*, pp. 711–12 & 745–46.

21. *Northwestern Mutual* v. *Tabor*. H. Tabor Scrapbooks, v. 1, pp.

23 & 45, v. 2, p. 56. On the loan attempt, see O. Geer to Tabor, Oct. 2, 1895. H. Teller thought it was good security for a million dollars, "even in the present period of depression and low prices," Teller to A. Gunnell, Nov. 5, 1895, H. Tabor Manuscripts. Tabor to Teller, Aug. 29, 1896, Teller Papers. Although ruled insolvent, Tabor never declared bankruptcy.

CHAPTER 17

1. George Tritch to Tabor, June 9, 1893 & Sept. 6, 1894. Rising, Brown & Malone to Mr. and Mrs. Tabor, May 18, 1895. Tritch to E. Tabor, Sept. 19, 1894. Tabor-Tritch agreements, April 30, 1895 & Nov. 10, 1896. Tritch acquired a $30,000 mortgage held by the Northwestern Mutual. *Pueblo Daily Chieftain*, March 21, 1893.

2. Matchless records. Minutes of the Directors of the Tabor Mines & Mills, July 10, 1895, Aug. 11, 12, 1896 & March 26, 1898. R. Hughes to E. Tabor, May 20, 1894, Pete to Tabor, May 27 & Sept. 13, 1895. W. Page to Tabor, June 9, 1895. W. Harp to P. McCourt, May 7, 1895. H. Tabor Manuscripts. *W. R. Harp* v. *Tabor Mines & Mills*, District Court, Lake County, 4768 (1895).

3. Lily to Aunt Emma, June 1896. Rockwell to Tabor, Dec. 18, 1896. H. Tabor Manuscripts. *Mason B. Carpenter & William McBird* v. *Tabor Mines & Mills Co.*, District Court, Denver, 22834 (1895). *Tabor Mines & Mills Co.* v. *Fred Bulkley et al.*, District Court, Denver, 23541 (1895).

4. Tabor to wife, Nov. 10, 1896. E. Tabor to Mother Superior, July 20, 1896. H. Tabor Manuscripts.

5. Wayland Parrish and M. Hochmuth, *American Speeches* (New York: Longmans, Green & Co., 1954), pp. 492–500. Paul W. Glad, *McKinley, Bryan and the People* (New York: J. B. Lippincott, Co., 1967), pp. 113–88. Vachel Lindsay, *Collected Poems* (New York: MacMillan Co., 1967), p. 99.

6. H. Tabor, "Autobiography," pp. 14–16. See also: *Denver Tribune*, Aug. 2, 1882 & Feb. 12, 1883. *Weekly-Tribune Republican*, Feb. 5 & Sept. 5, 1885. *The Idea*, Feb. 7, 1885. *Silver Standard*, Feb. 20 & March 6, 1886. *Denver Republican*, Sept. 5, 1888.

7. Tabor to Teller, Aug. 29, 1896, Teller Papers. Teller to Tabor, Feb. 15, 1892, Tabor to Wife, Feb. 17, 1892. Speech before the Colorado Silver Association, Jan. 30, 1890, H. Tabor Manuscripts. H. Tabor Scrapbooks, v. 5, pp. 11 & 23, v. 10, pp. 81 & 100. *New York Times*, Feb. 21, 1889, called his first visit to Harrison "low comedy."

8. Parsons, "Tabor's Bittersweet Christmas." Tabor to Pete, Feb. 22, March 12, 1897, Pete to Tabor, March 14, 1897. H. Tabor Manuscripts. Tabor to Teller, Aug. 29, 1896. Teller Papers. *Rocky Mountain*

News, Jan. 14, 1898. I do not believe he worked at a Leadville smelter, see Davis, *Olden Times*, p. 313.

9. Records of the Ben Eaton, Free Coinage, Consolidated Cripple Creek & West Creek Mining Co., H. Tabor Manuscripts. *Carpenter v. Tabor Mines & Mills. The United News* (London) to Tabor, Nov. 5, 1897. Tabor to Wife, Jan. 25, 1896 & Sept. 22, 1897. Louis Swift to Tabor, Jan. 29, 1899, H. Tabor Manuscripts. Stratton Loan: Check to Tabor Mines & Mills, July 15, 1895, H. Tabor Manuscripts. David Strickler, "The Fight for the Stratton Millions," *Brand Book of the Denver Westerners* (Boulder: Johnson Publishing Co., 1963), p. 85. Various accounts say Tabor used the money in Cripple Creek, Ward, and to save the Matchless.

10. *Rocky Mountain News*, Jan. 14, 1898. *Durango Evening Herald*, Jan. 13, 1898. *Denver Republican*, Jan. 14 & Feb. 19, 1898. *Denver Times*, Jan. 13, 1898, *Silver Standard*, Jan. 15, 1898. John Tabor to Tabor, Jan. 11 & 13, 1898. Tabor to wife, Jan. 24, 1898. Teller to Tabor, Jan. 14, 1898 & E. Wolcott to Tabor, Jan. 28, 1898. H. Tabor Manuscripts. Information on Ward is found in: Hart Cabin Deed, Nov. 24, 1897. Eclipse Records. J. Hartley to Tabor, May 31, 1898. H. Tabor Manuscripts. *Rocky Mountain News*, Jan. 14, 1898.

11. E. Wolcott to Tabor, Dec. 21, 1898. Employees petition and general postoffice material, H. Tabor Manuscripts. *Rocky Mountain News*, Feb. 20, 1898. *Denver Times*, Dec. 28, 1898. S. Purdy, "Weighing the Mail," *Illustrated Sentinel*, April 20, 1898, copy at the State Historical Society.

12. Dumont Clarke to Tabor, Feb. 11, 1891; Aug. 27, Nov. 22, 1894; Nov. 27, 1897; Oct. 14, 26, 1898 & Jan. 13, 1899. Tabor to Clarke, Nov. 27, 1897 & Sept. 7, 1898. E. Rollins & Sons to Tabor, Dec. 20, 1898. Tabor to Lyman Gage, July 25, 1898. A. Lousche to Wolcott, Sept. 10, 1898. W. Cochran to Wolcott, April 24, 1900. Leadville Post Office Material, H. Tabor Manuscripts. *Denver Times*, July 4, 1898 & March 20, 1899. Tabor Notes, Tabor Collection, First National Bank. Tabor to Wife, March 8, 1899, H. Tabor Collection. *Leadville Democrat*, March 9, 1880.

13. Dumont Clarke to Tabor, Oct. 26, 1898. W. W. Davis to Tabor, Sept. 21, 1898. Vulture Mine Records, H. Tabor Material. *Phoenix Daily Herald*, May 19, 1896 & Jan. 12, 1897. *Arizona Daily Citizen*, Nov. 12, 1896. Thomas Armstrong to Tabor, May 17, 25, Oct. 9, 1897, June 23, Nov. 15, Dec. 27, 30, 1898 & Jan. 21, 1899. Tabor to wife, Feb. 9, 1899. H. Tabor Manuscripts. *Thomas L. Wiswall et al. v. Tabor Mines & Mills Co. et al.*, Third Judicial District Court, Territory of Arizona, 2646 (1896). *Wiswall et al. v. Tabor Mines et al.*, Supreme Court, Territory of Arizona, 630 (1898). Tabor Mines & Mills records. Tabor to John Jenkins, May 16, 1898. Emma to Baby Doe, Sept. 25, 1898. John Tabor to Tabor, Oct. 24 & 28, 1898. H. Tabor Manuscripts.

14. *Rocky Mountain News*, Jan. 14, & Nov. 8, 1898. *Denver Times*,

Nov. 3, 1898; March 8, 30, April 3 & 5, 1899. H. Tabor Scrapbooks, v. 5, p. 9. Tabor to Darlings, Nov. 12, 1898. H. Tabor Manuscripts.

15. H. Bancroft to Tabor, July 10, 1898. O. Linch to Tabor, Oct. 18 & 20, 1898. H. Tabor Scrapbooks, v. 2, p. 23. Baxter Cigar Co. to Tabor, Feb. 9, 1898. Invitation to University of Colorado Dedication, April 16, 1898. Invitation to a mining tour of Boulder County, Feb. 9, 1898, H. Tabor Manuscripts. *Durango Evening Herald*, Nov. 26, 1898.

16. Tabor to Lily and Honeymaid, Oct. 24, 1898. Tabor to Darlings, Oct. 26, Nov. 4, 10, 12, 17, Dec. 7, 16, 20, 1898; Jan. 11, Feb. 10, March 8 & 13, 1899. Letters from Emma to Tabor, Oct. 22, 1896 & to Baby Doe, Sept. 25, 1898, mention Lily's illness. H. Tabor Manuscripts. He signed most of his letters "Horace" or "Papa," but at least once used "Hod."

17. James P. Whitney, *Colorado, in the United States of America* (London: Cassell, Petter & Galpin, 1867), p. 35. Eclipse Mine material: *Denver Evening Post*, April 10, 1899. Joe [Hartley] to Tabor, May 31, 1898, H. Tabor Manuscripts.

18. Accounts of his last days differ on minor points. The events were reconstructed from the following sources: Lily to Aunt Emily, April 8, 1899, H. Tabor Manuscripts. *Rocky Mountain News*, April 10–15, 1899. *Denver Evening Post*, April 10–11, 1899. *Leadville Herald Democrat*, April 11–15, 1899. *Durango Evening Herald*, April 10 & 14, 1899. *Denver Republican*, April 10–12, 1899. *Weekly Republican*, April 13, 1899. *Denver Times*, April 10, 1899. *Boulder County Herald*, April 10–11, 1899. *The Engineering and Mining Journal*, April 15, 1899, p. 44, has a confused account. A copy of his will is in the H. Tabor Manuscripts. No mention was made of Tabor's telling his wife to hang onto the Matchless Mine.

CHAPTER 18

1. Smiley, *History of Denver*, pp. 481 & 965. H. Tabor, "Autobiography," pp. 18–19. His contemporaries agreed in general. For example, see comments by N. P. Hill, Charles Thomas, Walter Cheesman, and Thomas Wiswall, in the *Rocky Mountain News*, April 11; *Denver Evening Post*, April 10; and *Weekly Republican*, April 13, 1899. See also Rowell, "Dictation"; Stone, "Tabor," p. 18; and Maxey Tabor, "Interview."

2. *Weekly Republican*, April 13, 1899. See also the *Denver Times*, April 10, 1899, and the other papers cited in the last two footnotes of the preceding chapter. For earlier comments examine the *Denver Tribune*, Jan. 17, 1882, *Inter-Ocean*, Aug. 7, 1880 and *Leadville Daily Herald*, Jan. 18, 1884.

3. *Rocky Mountain News*, Nov. 2, 1883. Tabor was one of thirty-nine

Colorado millionaires in 1892, six of whom found their wealth mainly in gold and silver mining.

4. For a discussion of western politics and these men see: Earl Pomeroy, "Toward a Reorientation of Western History: Continuity and Environment," *Mississippi Valley Historical Reivew* (March, 1955), pp. 586–88. Rodman Paul, *Mining Frontiers of the Far West*. C. B. Glasscock, *The War of the Copper Kings*. Lewis Gould, *Wyoming: a Political History* gives an interpretative look at neighboring Wyoming at the same time.

5. John Garraty, *The New Commonwealth 1877–1890* (New York: Harper, 1968), p. 13. For a longer discussion see Matthew Josephson, *The Robber Barons*; Ray Ginger, *Age of Excess*, Chapters 2 & 3; and John Tipple, "The Robber Baron in the Gilded Age," *The Gilded Age*, Chapter 2. Thomas Cochran and William Miller, *The Age of Enterprise* (New York: Harper, 1961), p. 153. Tipple, "The Robber Baron," pp. 18, 33 & 36. Tipple argues it was the corporation not the man which gave the image. This was not true in Tabor's case. Garraty, *New Commonwealth*, p. 25. H. Tabor, "Autobiography," p. 21.

6. H. Tabor, "Autobiography," pp. 11 & 14. Paul, *Mining Frontiers*, and Wiliam Greever, *The Bonanza West*, are two excellent sources to read about other mining men and the industry.

7. Frank Waters, *Midas of the Rockies* (Denver: University of Denver Press, 1949), pp. 237–38, 267 & 389. H. Tabor, "Autobiography," p. 20. A new biography of Stratton is needed; the best available is Frank Waters, *Midas of the Rockies*.

BIBLIOGRAPHICAL ESSAY

THE researcher into the Tabor story must be watchful for bias on the part of many authors. Nineteenth-century writers were often highly laudatory or extremely critical. Twentieth-century writers managed to produce a Tabor that was as much fiction as fact. Regrettably, the failure to research, the reliance on folklore and legend, and the utilization of earlier historically unsound efforts have left the researcher with few secondary Tabor sources that can be relied upon. They rest upon bookshelves more as examples of biographical assassination than contributions to scholarship.

The researcher then must return to the original sources. It is here that the life, spirit, and significance of the Tabor era can be captured, insofar as is possible at this late date.

For the serious researcher, by far the most outstanding collection is the Horace Tabor Papers (referred to by the older name, "Tabor Manuscripts," in the footnotes) in the State Historical Society of Colorado (Denver). These have recently been organized and a five-volume calendar prepared, which will be invaluable to future researchers. The vast majority of these papers were saved by Baby Doe, thus the emphasis is on the 1880s and 1890s; included, however, are many others pertaining to her activities after her husband's death. Because of Tabor's investments and position, these papers touch upon a variety of topics not limited to Colorado. The Denver Public Library has the best holdings of Augusta's papers, although regrettably she was not the "saver" the second Mrs. Tabor was. The First National Bank archives offer a surprising array of Colorado and Tabor records which have been little utilized.

Outside of Colorado, the Bancroft Library at Berkeley contains the best Tabor collection, especially his autobiography, gathered by the staff of Hubert H. Bancroft in the

1880s. It also has other interviews and records which touch upon aspects of Tabor's life. To work at the Huntington Library, in San Marino, California, was not only a pleasure but extremely rewarding. The James D. Hague collection there holds unsurpassed pertinent papers relating to Leadville, Tabor, and his mines.

An exceedingly valuable source was the records of the lawsuits. Tabor was sued over manifold matters, and each case gave some insight into the man, his activities, and the times. Like mines, some records proved more valuable than others. How many cases he was involved in will probably never be known, but I examined over 170 dated almost entirely after 1878. Incorporation papers give information, but far too often are just standardized forms.

Along with primary unpublished material, the newspapers and journals gave the most help. With expected reservations for editorializing, omissions, and biased reporting, these sources proved a bonanza on all aspects of Tabor's life. The two New York papers, *The Engineering and Mining Journal* and *The Mining Record*, are indispensable for mining matters; the San Francisco *Mining and Scientific Press* is not particularly helpful on Rocky Mountain mining. The *Rocky Mountain News* is the best overall Colorado paper of that time, and the researcher is aided by the index at the Western History Department of the Denver Public Library, although it is neither error-proof nor completely comprehensive. The *Denver Tribune* is newsy as long as Eugene Field and his staff cavorted, but the reader must remember to be alert. The *New York Times* is helpful and particularly useful with its index. With most of the papers, however, the researcher must dig it out on his own; it is time-consuming but eminently worthwhile and can be an adventure. The Leadville and Denver papers obviously are the best sources, although hardly a Colorado paper in the late 1870s and 1880s does not carry Tabor stories.

An amazing number of nineteenth-century publications discuss Tabor or his activities. To make comments on them all would be redundant. The reader is referred to the list which follows. Outstanding among the mining studies are Raymond's many reports, Emmons, and Henderson. Frank Hall, Frank Fossett, and R. G. Dill (the latter wrote the section on Lake County in *History of the Arkansas Valley, Colorado*) have made major contributions to Colorado history.

More recent histories have suffered from some of the same problems already mentioned about the Tabor biographies. The best study on Leadville is the Griswolds' *Carbonate Camp*. The *Colorado Magazine* and *The Trail* offer varied articles, from old-timers' reminiscences to recent scholarship. Mining has produced some good monographs and general examinations, spearheaded by the works of Rodman Paul, William Greever, and Clark Spence, but much of the rest of Colorado history still needs scholarly study. Regrettably, too many men and events have been ignored or only glossed over in favor of what seem to be more exciting and interesting subjects. The result has been distortion and lack of interpretation.

Tabor, the most renowned nineteenth-century Colorado figure, the individual most readily identified by visitors and residents alike, has been the victim of sensationalism and a bad press. In a way he is not much better known than his contemporaries Jerome Chaffee, David Moffat, or Thomas Bowen. Much still needs to be done to illuminate the 1859–1899 period in Colorado history, as those who research into this fascinating era will find out.

The following list of sources includes only those quoted in the text. It serves as a guide to the type of material utilized and, it is hoped, will be of help to others who work in this same area.

UNPUBLISHED MATERIAL

Bacon, Henry Douglas.   Papers.   Huntington Library.
Bancroft, Hubert H.   Colorado Notes, Dec. 1884.   Bancroft Library.
Bank of Leadville Records.   State Historical Society of Colorado.
Bradford, Robert B.   Letters.   Huntington Library.
California Mining District, California Gulch, Colorado Territory.   Records, 1860–76.   State Historical Society of Colorado.

California Gulch. Original Census Returns 1860.

Chaffee, Jerome B. Papers. First National Bank, Denver.

Como Iron, Coal and Sand Co. Report. State Historical Society of Colorado.

Court Records:

Colorado Reports. Cases Adjudged in the Supreme Court of Colorado, 1864–1899.

Lake County. Probate Court Record of Estates, 1869–1880.

———. Probate Court Accounts of Executors & Administrators, 1870–79.

———. General Indexes Defendants & Plaintiffs, 1879–1899.

———. General Docket Book, 1870–1880.

La Plata County. General Index to Defendants, 1877–97.

Maricopa County, Territory of Arizona: Docket Fee Book, 1887–1898.

Ouray County. General Indexes to Defendants and Plaintiffs, 1878–1898.

San Juan County. General Indexes to Defendants and Plaintiffs, 1891–99.

———. Index to Court Records.

United States. First District Colorado. General Docket, May, 1862–July, 1876.

———. Circuit Court District of Colorado Registers, 1876–1899.

Crowley, Elmer, "The History of the Tabor Grand Opera House, Denver, Colorado." Unpublished Master's Thesis, University of Denver, 1940.

Davis, Carlyle. "History of Colorado." Bancroft Library.

Dawson, T. F. Scrapbooks. State Historical Society of Colorado.

Degitz, Dorothy M. "History of the Tabor Opera House, Leadville, Colorado, from 1879–1905." Unpublished Master's Thesis, Western State College, 1935.

Duggan, Martin. Dictation. Bancroft Library.

Dutt, William S. Correspondence, 1859–64. Huntington Library.

Elders, Martin. Testimony. Arizona Library and Archives.

Executive Record. Territory and State of Colorado, 1875–1885. Colorado State Archives.

First National Bank of Denver. Bank Statements, 1875–89. Certificates of Stock. Minutes of the Board of Directors and Stockholders meetings, 1865–1883. Stock Ledger, First National Bank.

Fremont County Records. Wyoming State Archives.

Gold & Silver Extraction Company of America. Records. Bancroft Library.

Gold and Silver Extraction Mining and Milling Co. Records. State Historical Society of Colorado.

Hague, James D. Mining Collection. Huntington Library.

Hamill, William. Papers. Western History Department, Denver Public Library.

Harper, John. Papers. Western History Collections, University of Colorado.

Harrison, Edwin. Letters. State Historical Society of Colorado.

Henriett Mine Records. First National Bank.

Hough, Charles M. "Leadville, Colorado, 1878–1898: A Study in Unionism." Unpublished Master's Thesis, University of Colorado, 1958.

Huntington, Daniel J.W. Collection. Arizona Pioneer Historical Society.

Hurd, Nathan. Interview. State Historical Society of Colorado.

Incorporation Papers. (Unless otherwise stated, all are found in Colorado State Archives.)

> The Alaska Consolidated Mining Company.
>
> The Aspen City Railroad Company.
>
> The Bank of Leadville.
>
> Calumet and Chicago Canal and Dock Co. Illinois State Archives.
>
> Chrysolite Consolidated Mining Company. New York Archives.
>
> The Denver, Apex and Western Railway Company.
>
> Denver Water Supply Company.
>
> Evergreen Lakes and Mineral Springs Company.
>
> The Gold and Silver Extraction Company of America. Bancroft Library.
>
> Leadville Telephone Company.
>
> Little Pittsburg Consolidated Mining Company. New York Archives.
>
> The Matchless Concentrator Company.
>
> The Matchless Mining Company.
>
> Michoacan Syndicate. New York Archives.
>
> Montana Mining Land and Investment Company.
>
> The National Mining and Industrial Exposition Association.
>
> The Pitkin County Railroad Company.
>
> Republic of Honduras Campbell Reduction Company. New York Archives.
>
> Tabor Amusement Company.
>
> Tabor Fire Insurance Company.
>
> Tabor Fire Insurance Company of Leadville.
>
> The Tabor Grand Hotel Furnishing Company.
>
> The H. A. W. Tabor Hose Company, No. 1.
>
> The Tabor Investment Company.
>
> The Tabor Investment Company of St. Louis.
>
> Tabor Mines and Mills Company.
>
> The Tabor Prospecting and Mining Company.
>
> Tabor Real Estate Company.

Law Cases

> *Frank Adams, Receiver Commercial National Bank* v. *The Denver Apex & Western Railway Co. et al*. U.S. District Court, 1272 (1896).

The Arkansas Valley Smelting Co. et al. v. *The Tabor Milling Co. et al.* District Court, Lake County, 2528 (1883).

Nathan A. Baker v. *H. A. W. Tabor et al.* District Court, Denver, 26420 (1898).

The Board of County Commissioners of the County of Arapahoe v. *The National Mining and Industrial Exposition Association et al.* District Court, Denver, 6774 (1883).

John Borden, Horace A. W. Tabor et al. v. *A. D. Searl.* District Court, Lake County, 432 (1879).

Edward Bradford et al. v. *Henry S. Kearny et al.* U.S. Circuit Court, 1170 (1883).

Robert Brown et al. v. *Horace A. W. Tabor et al.* District Court, Denver, 10415 (1889).

Chester Bullock et al. v. *H. A. W. Tabor et al.* District Court, Lake County, 1110 (1880).

Mason B. Carpenter et al. v. *The Tabor Mines and Mills Co.* District Court, Denver, 22834 (1895).

Sarah Clifford v. *James Carlile et al.* U.S. Circuit Court, 3017 (1893).

The Colorado Fire Insurance Co. v. *The Tabor Fire Insurance Co.*, District Court, Denver, 5929 (1882).

Colorado River Irrigation Co. v. *The Denver Apex & Western Railway Co. et al.* U.S. Circuit Court, 2959 (1893).

The Commercial National Bank of Cleveland v. *Horace A. W. Tabor.* U.S. Circuit Court, 2817 (1893).

The Denver City Consolidated Silver Mining Co. v. *Charles Hall et al.* District Court, Lake County, 1455, 1456 (1880).

Henry Gibson v. *the National Mining and Industrial Exposition Association et al.* U.S. Circuit Court, 1959 (1886).

Charles Hall, H. A. W. Tabor et al. v. *Jacob Rupp et al.* District Court, Lake County, 3476 (1887).

W. R. Harp v. *Tabor Mines & Mills.* District Court, Lake County, 4768 (1895).

H. Martyn Hart v. *H. A. W. Tabor & Peter McCourt.* District Court, Denver, 17171 (1892).

James Hawkins v. *Horace A. W. Tabor.* District Court, Denver, 7435 (1885).

Jacob Hecht et al. v. *S. H. Foss et al.* District Court, Lake County, 1008 (1880).

Thomas P. Hughes v. *The National Mining and Industrial Exposition* *et al.* District Court, Denver, 6430 (1882).

The Kaiser Gold Mines Company, Limited v. *Horace A. W. Tabor.* U.S. Circuit Court, 2450 (1889).

Edward Kneezell v. *Sewell & Tabor.* County Court, La Plata, 157 (1882).

James Lannan v. *J. A. Wallace et al.* District Court, Lake County, 2979 (1884).

Leadville Illuminating Gas Co. v. *H. A. W. Tabor.* District Court, Denver, 8138 (1886).

James Mackey v. *Horace A. W. Tabor.* District Court, Denver, 12557 (1890).

D. D. Mallory v. *Howard C. Chapin et al.* U.S. Circuit Court, 1536 (1884).

The National Mohawk Valley Bank v. *Horace A. W. Tabor et al.* U.S. Circuit Court, 1895 & 2116 (1886 & 1887).

James W. Newell et al. v. *The Tabor Mines & Mills Co. et al.* District Court, Lake County, 4860 (1895).

Northwestern Mutual Life v. *Horace A. W. Tabor et al.* District Court, Denver, 21840 (1894).

J. H. Pinkerton v. *Horace Tabor et al.* District Court, La Plata County 111 (1881).

The Provident Trust Co. v. *The Tabor Investment Co. et al.* U.S. Circuit Court, 2975 (1893).

John Riley et al. v. *H. A. W. Tabor et al.* District Court, Lake County 876 (1880).

Jacob Sanders & H. A. W. Tabor v. *Jacob Cypher et al.* District Court, Lake County, 1323 (1880).

L. D. Smith v. *Tabor Amusement Co. et al.* District Court, Denver, 21611 (1894).

Thomas Stanton v. *H. A. W. Tabor's Pioneer Stage & Express Line Co.* County Court, La Plata, 200 (1882).

Ferdinand Stark v. *Tabor Amusement Co. et al.* District Court, Denver 20145 (1893).

Josephine F. Streeter v. *Horace A. W. Tabor.* U.S. Circuit Court, 2096 (1887).

Dennis Sullivan et al. v. *Horace A. W. Tabor.* District Court, Lake County, 1777 (1881).

Augusta Tabor v. *Horace Tabor.* District Court, Denver, 6035 (1882).

H. A. W. Tabor v. *Nicholas N. Atkinson et al.* U.S. Circuit Court, 782 (1881).

—— v. *Bank of Leadville.* District Court, Denver, 11269 (1889).

—— v. *the Big Pittsburg Consolidated Silver Mining Co.,* U.S. Circuit Court, 1024 (1882).

—— v. *William Bush.* District Court, Denver, 6748 (1883).

—— *et al.* v. *J. F. Chaney et al.* District Court, Lake County, 1925 (1881).

—— v. *Chrysolite Silver Mining Co.* U.S. Circuit Court, 692 (1881).

—— v. *Rufus Clark et al.* District Court, Denver, 7864 (1886).

—— *et al.* v. *Charles M. Clinton et al.* District Court, Denver, 22679 (1895).

—— v. *Denver & Suburban Railway Co.* District Court, Denver, 14280 (1891).

—— *et al.* v. *Wert Dexter et al.* District Court, Lake County, 149 & 154 (1878).

—— *et al.* v. *Wirt Dexter et al.* U.S. Circuit Court, 217 (1879).

—— v. *John Evans.* District Court, Denver, 7437 (1886).

———— *et al.* v. *Peter Finnerty et al.* Records in State Historical Society of Colorado.

———— v. *John Good.* District Court, Denver, 9152 (1888).

———— v. *Lewis Herefort.* District Court, Denver, 17184 (1892).

———— v. *Little Chief Mining Co.* District Court, Lake County, 1690 (1881).

———— v. *Patrick McCann.* District Court, Lake County, 2600 (1883).

———— v. *Dennis Sullivan et al.* District Court, Lake County, 1791 (1881).

———— v. *Augusta L. Tabor.* County Court, La Plata, 141 (1882).

———— *et al.* v. *Sierra Grande Mining Company.* Third Judicial District Court of New Mexico, 692 (1883).

Tabor Amusement Co. et al. v. *Horace W. Bennett et al.* District Court, Denver, 20856 (1894).

Tabor Amusement Co. et al. v. *David Henderson.* Circuit Court, Denver, 20474 (1894).

Tabor Mines and Mills Co. v. *Frank Bulkley et al.* District Court, Denver, 23541 (1895).

Tabor Real Estate Co. et al. v. *Laura D. Swickhimer et al.* District Court, Denver, 21588 (1894).

Tabor Real Estate Co. et al. v. *A. B. Sullivan et al.* District Court, Denver, 21270 (1894).

George Tritch, Jr. v. *Horace A. W. Tabor & E. B. Tabor.* District Court, Denver, 19149 (1893).

United States v. *William H. Beery.* First Judicial District, 209 (1872).

United States v. *Henry P. Farnum.* First Judicial District, 199, 202, 203, 210 (1870).

United States v. *George Hazen et al.* U.S. District Court, 540 (1887).

Universal Fire Insurance Co. v. *The Tabor Fire Insurance Co.*, District Court, Denver, 7335, 16079 (1883, 1892).

George Wanless v. *William Bush et al.* District Court, Denver, 6461 (1882).

Ward Consolidated Mining Co. v. *Chas. Hall et al.* District Court, Lake County, 1447, 1448, 1449 (1880).

Leopold Weil v. *Horace A. W. Tabor et al.* District Court, Denver, 7592 (1886).

A. S. Weston v. *H. A. W. Tabor.* District Court, Lake County, 4358, 4359 (1892).

Thomas Wiswall et al. v. *Tabor Mines and Mills Co. et al.* Third Judicial District Court, Maricopa County, Arizona, 2646 (1896).

Thomas Wiswall et al. v. *Tabor Mines and Mills Co. et al.* Supreme Court of the Territory of Arizona, 630 (1898).

Leadville. Minutes Board of Trustees, Feb. 1878–April 11, 1879.

Leadville Insurance Co. Collection. Western History Collections. University of Colorado.

Londoner, Wolfe. "Colorado Mining Camps." Bancroft Library.

Maid of Erin Mine Records. First National Bank.

Mayo, Clarence H. Letters, 1879–82. Huntington Library.

Oro City. Original Returns, Ninth Census, 1870.

Oro City Territorial Assay Office, Assay Book. Henry Wood Collection, Huntington Library.

Pitkin, Frederick. Letterpress Book, 1879–1881. State Historical Society of Colorado.

Rische, August. Interview. Bancroft Library.

Rockwell, L. C. Collection. Xeroxed copies in author's possession.

Rowell, Charles. Dictation. Bancroft Library.

Shelly, Walter. "The Colorado Republican Party: The Formative Years, 1861–1876." Unpublished Master's Thesis, University of Colorado, 1963.

Sheriff, Matthew. Diary. State Historical Society of Colorado.

Silver, Samuel. "The Mines of Colorado." Bancroft Library.

Spencer, Alice S. "Newspapers in Gunnison County; 1879–1900." Unpublished Master's Thesis, Western State College, 1932.

Stone, Wilbur. "Tabor." Bancroft Library.

Tabor, Augusta. "Cabin Life in Colorado." Bancroft Library (published in the *Colorado Magazine*, 1927 & 1959).

———. Copy of one page of her Diary. State Historical Society of Colorado.

———. Scrapbooks. Western History Department, Denver Public Library.

Tabor, Elizabeth B. Miscellanea. Western History Department, Denver Public Library.

———. Papers. State Historical Society of Colorado.

Tabor, Horace A. W. "Autobiography." Bancroft Library.

———. Clippings. Western History Department, Denver Public Library.

———. Collection. First National Bank.

———. "Early Days." Bancroft Library.

———. "Life of H. A. W. Tabor." Bancroft Library.

———. Letters. Denver Public Library.

———. Papers [manuscripts]. State Historical Society of Colorado.

———. Tabor-McCourt Marriage Records. Recorder of Deeds, St. Louis.

Tabor, Nathaniel M. Interview. State Historical Society of Colorado.

Teller, Henry. Letters. Western History Department, Denver Public Library.

———. Collection. State Historical Society of Colorado.

Tenney, James. "History of Mining in Arizona." Special Collections, University of Arizona, Library.

Thomas, Charles. Papers. State Historical Society of Colorado.

Vulture Mining Records. *Kaiser Gold Mines* v. *Horace Tabor.* Archival Division, Denver Federal Center.
Wilkinson, J. A. Journal. Huntington Library.
Wood, Henry E. Collection. Huntington Library.
Wiswall, Thomas. "Tabor." Bancroft Library.

NEWSPAPERS AND JOURNALS

Arizona Journal-Miner (Prescott, Arizona), scattered issues 1887.
Bonanza Daily Enterprise (Bonanza, Colorado), Exposition edition, August 1882.
Boulder County Herald (Boulder, Colorado), Dec. 27, 1882–April 4, 1883; scattered issues 1886.
The Boulder County News (Boulder, Colorado), Aug. 9–Oct. 11, 1878.
The Boulder News (Boulder, Colorado), Aug. 28, 1888–Aug. 29, 1889.
Boulder News and Banner (Boulder, Colorado), scattered issues 1886 & 1887.
Carbonate Chronicle (Leadville, Colorado), Aug. 2–Sept. 20, 1884.
Carbonate Weekly Chronicle (Leadville, Colorado), Nov. 15, 1879 & Jan. 3, 1880.
Colorado Graphic (Denver, Colorado), Jan. 29, 1887; Feb. 19, Aug. 2–Sept. 15, 1888.
The Colorado Transcript (Golden, Colorado), Aug. 7–Nov. 13, 1878.
Congressional Record (Washington, D.C.), Feb. 3–March 3, 1883.
Daily Advertiser (Trinidad, Colorado), Sept. 29–Oct. 12, Oct. 22–Nov. 5, 1886.
Daily Chronicle (Leadville, Colorado), Jan. 29–July 31, Oct. 11, 1879.
Daily Register-Call (Central City, Colorado), Aug. 13–24, 1878; scattered issues 1881–83; 1886.
Denver Daily Times (Denver, Colorado), July 27–Aug. 20, Sept. 2–9, Sept. 24–Oct. 9, 1878; Aug. 28–Sept. 15, 1882; Oct. 29–Nov. 2, 1883; scattered issues 1897–1901.
Denver Exchange Journal (Denver, Colorado), Dec. 10, 1887–Jan. 7, 1888.
Denver Field and Stream (Denver, Colorado), Feb. 5, 1898.
Denver Journal of Commerce (Denver, Colorado), Jan. 13, 1883.
Denver Post (Denver, Colorado), Jan. 22, 1929.
Denver Republican (Denver, Colorado), scattered issues 1882, 1883, 1888, 1892, 1894, 1898.
Denver Tribune (Denver, Colorado), Feb. 13, 1878–May 14, 1879; Aug. 12–Sept. 18, Dec. 19, 1881–March 30, 1883.
Denver Tribune-Republican (Denver, Colorado), Sept. 29–Oct. 8, Oct. 20–29, 1886.
Denver Weekly Times (Denver, Colorado), Aug. 7–Dec. 25, 1878; March 17, Aug. 4–Dec. 29, 1880.
Dolores News (Rico, Colorado), May 28, 1881.
Durango Evening Herald (Durango, Colorado), Sept. 7, 1898–Aug. 31, 1899.
Durango Record (Durango, Colorado), April 28–Dec. 18, 1881.

Durango Semi-Weekly Herald (Durango, Colorado), April 13, 1899.
Engineering and Mining Journal (New York, New York), July 1876–June 1894.
Fairplay Flume (Fairplay, Colorado), Jan. 11–Feb. 1, 1883.
Frank Leslie's Illustrated Newspaper (New York, New York), Aug. 10–Oct. 19, 1878; Jan. 4, 1879–Aug. 28, 1880; scattered issues 1881–83.
Georgetown Courier (Georgetown, Colorado), scattered issues 1884, 1886, 1888.
Georgetown Miner (Georgetown, Colorado), Jan. 20–Feb. 2, 1883.
Grand Army Magazine (Denver, Colorado), April 1883.
Gunnison Daily Review (Gunnison, Colorado), Dec. 29, 1881–Jan. 9, 1882.
Gunnison Daily Review-Press (Gunnison, Colorado), Jan. 23–29, 1883.
Gunnison Review (Gunnison, Colorado), May 15–Oct. 9, 1880; March 19–April 9, June 15, Nov. 15, 1881.
Harper's Bazar (New York, New York), Jan. 8, 1887.
Harper's Weekly (New York, New York), June–Sept. 1879; July–Oct. 1882; Feb.–March 1883.
Herald of Freedom (Lawrence, Kansas), scattered issues 1855–57, 1859.
The Idea (Durango, Colorado), Aug. 2, 1884–March 27, 1886.
Inter-Ocean (Denver, Colorado), March 14–Sept. 4, 1880; Jan. 7–July 1, 1882.
Kansas Free State (Lawrence, Kansas), Sept. 24, 1855.
Kansas Tribune (Topeka, Kansas), Nov. 28, 1857.
Lake City Mining Register (Lake City, Colorado), Jan. 5–Feb. 2, 1883.
La Plata Miner (Silverton, Colorado), April 12, 1879.
The Leadville Circular (Leadville, Colorado), July 3, 1880.
Leadville Daily Chronicle (Leadville, Colorado), Jan. 6–Feb. 1, March 30–31, July 16–Oct. 20, 1886.
Leadville Daily Herald (Leadville, Colorado), Oct. 21, 1880–Oct. 21, 1884.
Leadville Democrat (Leadville, Colorado), Jan. 1–Sept. 30, 1880.
Leadville Evening Chronicle (Leadville, Colorado), Aug. 4–22, 1888.
Leadville Herald Democrat (Leadville, Colorado), July 6–Aug. 16, Sept. 29–Oct. 15, 1889; April 11–15, 1899.
Leadville Weekly Herald (Leadville, Colorado), Nov. 1, 1879–Oct. 23, 1880.
Miners' Record (Tarryall, Colorado), July 4–Sept. 14, 1861.
The Mining Industry and Tradesman (Denver, Colorado), March 1891.
The Mining Record (New York, New York), July 5, 1879–June 30, 1883; Jan. 3–June 27, 1885.
Mining and Scientific Press (San Francisco), Jan. 4, 1879–June 25, 1881; July 9, 1882–June 30, 1883; Jan. 1887–June 1888.
New York Herald-Tribune (New York, New York), 1879–1890.
New York Times (New York, New York), 1851–1893.
The Northwestern Financier (Denver, Colorado), Nov. 1891.
Prescott Morning Courier (Prescott, Arizona), March 20–31, 1881.

Pueblo Daily Chieftain (Pueblo, Colorado), Feb. 18, 1876; March 6, 10, April 4, 1889.

Rocky Mountain Herald (Denver, Colorado), Dec. 1, 1883; Oct. 17, 1891.

Rocky Mountain News (Denver, Colorado), scattered issues 1866–1899.

Rocky Mountain News (Weekly), April 23, 1859–Dec. 28, 1870; Jan. 3, 1877–Dec. 24, 1879.

Rocky Mountain Sun (Aspen, Colorado), July 9, 1881–Jan. 3, 1885; Dec. 3, 1887–Oct. 6, 1888; scattered issues 1889–1891.

The San Juan Prospector (Del Norte, Colorado), July 5–Sept. 27, 1884.

The Semi-Weekly Inter-Ocean (Chicago, Illinois), March 13, 1879.

Silver Standard (Silver Plume, Colorado), Sept. 10, 1885–Dec. 29, 1888; Jan. 2, 1892–April 28, 1894; scattered issues 1889, 1897, 1898.

Solid Muldoon (Ouray, Colorado), Sept. 5, 1879–May 11, 1883; scattered issues 1884, 1887, 1888.

The Southwest (Durango, Colorado), Oct. 7, 1882–July 19, 1884.

Squatter Sovereign (Atchison, Kansas), scattered issues 1855–57.

The Statesman (Bayonne, New Jersey), Oct. 17, Nov. 12, Dec. 15, 1883.

Territorial Expositor (Phoenix, Arizona), May 6, 1881.

Tombstone Daily Prospector (Tombstone, Arizona), March 22, April 12, 1888.

The Washington Post (Washington, D.C.), Jan. 28–March 8, 1883.

Weekly Democrat (Leadville, Colorado), Jan. 1, 1881.

Weekly Phoenix Herald (Phoenix, Arizona), May 20, 1881; March 17–24, 1887; April 9, 1891.

Weekly Register Call (Central City, Colorado), April 24, May 22, 1891.

Weekly Tribune-Republican (Denver, Colorado), Oct. 23, 1884–Dec. 23, 1886.

Weekly Republican (Denver, Colorado), Sept. 7, 1882–April 19, 1883; Jan. 6, 1887–Oct. 16, 1890; April 17, 1892–Jan. 11, 1894.

The Western Miner and Financier (Denver, Colorado), April 19, 1899.

The Western Mountaineer (Golden, Colorado), Nov. 1–Dec. 20, 1860.

White Pine Cone (White Pine, Colorado), Aug. 8–Sept. 19, 1884.

ARTICLES AND BOOKS

Abbott, Francis A. "Some Reminiscences of Early Days of Deep Creek, Riley County." *Collections of the Kansas State Historical Society, 1911–12.* Vol. 12, pp. 392–96.

An Address to the People of the United States and of Kansas Territory, by the Free State Topeka Convention. Leavenworth: Leavenworth Times Office, 1857.

Andreas, Alfred. *History of the State of Kansas.* Chicago: A. T. Andreas, 1883.

Anthony, Susan, *et al. The History of Woman Suffrage.* Vol. 4. Indianapolis: Hollenbeck Press, 1904.

Arrington, Leonard. "The Changing Economic Structure of the

Mountain West, 1850–1890," Utah State University Press, Monograph Series (June 1963), Bobbs-Merrill Reprint Series.

The Artesian Wells of Denver. Denver: News Printing Co., 1884.

Balch, William. *The Mines, Miners and Mining Interests of the United States in 1882.* Philadelphia: Mining Industrial Publishing Bureau, 1882.

Bancroft, Caroline. "The Belle of Oshkosh," *The Denver Westerners 1953 Brand Book.* Denver: The Westerners, 1954.

Bancroft, Hubert H. *Chronicles of the Builders.* Vol. 4. San Francisco: History Co., 1892.

———. *History of Arizona and New Mexico 1530–1888.* San Francisco: History Co., 1889.

———. *History of Nevada, Colorado and Wyoming 1540–1888.* San Francisco: History Co. Publishers, 1890.

Beardsley, Isaac. *Echoes from Peak and Plain.* Cincinnati: Curts & Jennings, 1898.

Beebe, Lucius. *The Big Spenders.* New York: Doubleday & Co., 1966.

Bergtold, W. H. "Denver Fifty Years Ago," *Colorado Magazine* (March 1931), pp. 67–73.

Bernstein, Marvin. *The Mexican Mining Industry 1890–1950.* Albany: State University of New York, 1964.

Bishop, George W. *Charles H. Dow and the Dow Theory.* New York: Appleton-Century-Crofts, 1960.

Blake, J.A. *Colorado Business Directory and Annual Register for 1876.* Denver: J. A. Blake, 1876.

Borden, W. W. *A Treatise on Leadville, Colorado.* New Albany, Ind.: Cannon Publisher, 1879.

Brewer, William H. *Rocky Mountain Letters 1869.* Denver: Colorado Mountain Club, 1930.

Buchanan, Joseph R. *The Story of a Labor Agitator.* New York: Outlook Co., 1903.

Burt, S. W. & Berthoud, E. L. *The Rocky Mountain Gold Regions.* Denver: Rocky Mountain News, 1861.

Byrne, A. T. *Honduras, a Brief Sketch of its Resources.* San Francisco: Francis, Valentine & Co., 1885.

Carrera, J. C. *Report on Santa Eduwiges Mine in the State of Chihuahua, Mexico.* Chicago: Rand, McNally & Co., 1883.

Carroll, Richard. "Mary Nash Mear, Pioneer," *Colorado Magazine* (Nov. 1934), pp. 215–18.

Caughey, John. *Hubert Howe Bancroft.* Berkeley: Univ. of California Press, 1946.

Checchi, Vincent. *Honduras, a Problem in Economic Development.* New York: Twentieth Century Fund, 1959.

Chrysolite Silver Mining Company (Annual Reports). New York: Chrysolite Co., 1880, 1881, 1883.

Chrysolite Silver Mining Company. New York: David H. Gildersleeve, 1880.

City Directory of Leadville. Denver: Daily Times Steam Printing House, 1879.

Cochran, Thomas C. and Miller, William. *The Age of Enterprise.* New York: Harper, 1961.

Colorado Business Directory and Annual Register for 1875. Denver: J. A. Blake, 1875.

Colorado State Business Directory and Annual Register. Denver: J. A. Blake, 1878.

The Como Iron, Coal and Land Company Colorado. Denver: Collier & Cleaveland, 1881.

Constant, Rezin. "Colorado as Seen by a Visitor of 1880," *Colorado Magazine* (May 1935), pp. 103–17.

Corbett, Thomas *The Colorado Directory of Mines.* Denver: Rocky Mountain News Printing Co., 1879.

————, (ed.). *The Legislative Manual of the State of Colorado.* Denver: Denver Times, 1877.

Corregan, Robert. & Lingane, David. *Colorado Mining Directory.* Denver: Colorado Mining Directory Co., 1883.

Crofutt, George. *Crofutt's Grip-Sack Guide to Colorado.* Omaha: Overland Publishing Co., 1885.

Dallas, Sandra. *No More Than Five in a Bed.* Norman: University of Oklahoma Press, 1967.

Davidson, Roy A. "Some Early Manuscript Records of Park County, Colorado, 1859–63," *Colorado Magazine* (Sept. 1941), pp. 168–79.

Davis, Carlyle. *Olden Times in Colorado.* Los Angeles: Phillips Publishing Co., 1916.

Dawson, Thomas F. *Life and Character of Edward O. Wolcott.* New York: Knickerbocker Press, 1911.

Degitz, Dorothy. "History of the Tabor Opera House at Leadville," *Colorado Magazine* (May 1936), pp. 81–89.

The Del Monte Consolidated Mining Company of Leadville. Del Monte Consolidated, c 1880.

Denver City Directory. Denver: Ballenger & Richards, 1886–93, 1895–99.

Dill, R. G. *The Political Campaigns of Colorado.* Denver: Arapahoe Publishing Co., 1895.

Dyer, John L. *The Snow-Shoe Itinerant.* Cincinnati: Cranston & Stowe, 1890.

Elbert, Samuel H. *Biennial Message.* Central City: Register Printing House, 1874.

Ellis, Elmer. *Henry Moore Teller Defender of the West.* Caldwell: Caxton Printers, 1941.

Emmons, Samuel F. *Geology and Mining Industry of Leadville, Colorado.* Washington: Government Printing Office, 1886.

Evans, John. *Message to Legislative Assembly of Colorado, July 17, 1862.* Denver: Rocky Mountain News, 1862.

Ewer, Warren. "Report on the National Mining and Industrial

Exposition, Held at Denver, Colorado, August 1882," *Appendix to the Journals of the Senate and Assembly . . . of the State of California.* Vol. 5. Sacramento: State Printing Office, 1883.

Faithful, Emily. *Three Visits to America.* Edinburgh: David Douglass, 1884.

Field, Eugene. *A Little Book of Tribune Verse.* New York: Grosset & Dunlap, 1901.

Fitz-Mac [MacCarthy, James] *Political Portraits.* Colorado Springs: Gazette Printing Co., 1888.

Fossett, Frank. *Colorado.* Denver: Daily Tribune Steam Printing House, 1876.

————. *Colorado its Gold and Silver Mines . . . Resorts.* New York: C. G. Crawford, 1879.

————. *Colorado Its Gold and Silver Mines.* New York: Crawford, Printer, 1880.

Foy, Eddie and Harlow, Alvin. *Clowning through Life.* New York: E. P. Dutton & Co., 1928.

Gaeddert, Gustave R. *The Birth of Kansas.* Lawrence: University of Kansas, 1940.

Garraty, John A. *The New Commonwealth 1877–1890.* New York: Harper, 1968.

Ginger, Ray. *Age of Excess: The United States from 1877 to 1914.* New York: Macmillan, 1965.

Glad, Paul. *McKinley, Bryan, and the People.* New York: J. B. Lippincott Co., 1964.

Glasscock, C. B. *The War of the Copper Kings.* New York: Bobbs-Merrill, 1935.

Gould, Lewis. *Wyoming, a Political History, 1868–1896.* New Haven: Yale University, 1968.

Greene, Albert. "The Kansas River—Its Navigation," *Transactions of the Kansas Historical Society, 1905–06.* Vol. 9, pp. 317–58.

Greever, William. *The Bonanza West.* Norman: University of Oklahoma Press, 1963.

Gregg, Josiah. *Commerce of the Prairies.* New York: Henry G. Langley, 1844.

Griswold, Don & Jean. *The Carbonate Camp Called Leadville.* Denver: University of Denver Press, 1951.

H. H. (Jackson, Helen H.) "To Leadville," *Atlantic Monthly* (May 1879), pp. 567–79.

Hale, Edward E. *Memories of a Hundred Years.* Vol. 2. New York: Macmillan Co., 1902.

Hale, Horace M. *Education in Colorado, 1861–1885.* Denver: News Printing Co., 1885.

Hall, Frank. *History of the State of Colorado.* Vols. 2 & 3. Chicago: Blakely Printing Co., 1890–91.

Hamilton, Patrick. *The Resources of Arizona.* Prescott: A. L. Bancroft & Co., 1881.

Hammond, John Hays. *The Autobiography of John Hays Hammond.* New York: Farrar & Rinehart, 1935.

Henderson, Charles. *Mining in Colorado.* Washington: Government Printing Office, 1926.

Hill, Alice Polk. *Tales of the Colorado Pioneers.* Denver: Pierson & Gardner, 1884.

Hinton, Richard J. *The Hand-Book to Arizona.* San Francisco: Payot, Upham & Co., 1878.

Historical Statistics of the United States Colonial Times to 1957. Washington: Government Printing Office, 1960.

History of the Arkansas Valley, Colorado. Chicago: O. L. Baskin & Co., 1881.

History of Nevada. Oakland: Thompson & West, 1881.

Hollister, Ovando. *The Mines of Colorado.* Springfield: Samuel Bowles & Co., 1867.

Howbert, Irving. *Memories of a Lifetime in the Pike's Peak Region.* New York: G. P. Putnam's, 1925.

Ingham, G. Thomas. *Digging Gold Among the Rockies.* Chicago: Cottage Library Publishing House, 1881.

Jensen, Vernon. *Heritage of Conflict.* Ithaca: Cornell University Press, 1950.

Johnson, Samuel A. *The Battle Cry of Freedom.* Lawrence: University of Kansas Press, 1954.

Josephson, Matthew. *The Robber Barons.* New York: Harcourt, Brace & World, 1962 (reprint).

Journal of the Senate of the United States of America . . . Forty-Seventh Congress. Washington: Government Printing Office, 1882.

"Journal of the House of Representatives of the State of Kansas," *Collections of the Kansas State Historical Society 1913–14.* Vol. 13. Topeka: W. R. Smith, 1915.

Keeler, Bronson. *Leadville and its Silver Mines.* Chicago: E. L. Ayer, 1879.

Kent, L. A. *Leadville.* Denver: Daily Times Steam Printing House, 1880.

Kingsley, Charles. (Frances Kingsley, ed.) *Charles Kingsley, His Letters and Memories of his Life.* Vol. 2. London: Henry S. King & Co., 1877.

————. (Martin, Robert, ed.) *Charles Kingsley's American Notes.* Princeton: Princeton University Press, 1958.

————. *South by West.* London: W. Isbister & Co., 1874.

Kinkead, John. *Second Biennial Message.* Carson City: J. C. Harlow, 1883.

Leach, Samuel. "Early Day Reminiscences," *The Trail* (May 1911), pp. 5–9.

————. "Mosquito Mining District," *The Trail* (March, May 1926), pp. 10–13, 7–10.

Leadville and Oro. New York: Denver & Rio Grande, 1878.

Legislative, Historical and Biographical Compendium of Colorado. Denver: C. F. Coleman, 1887.

Lindgren, Waldemar, *et al.* *The Ore Deposits of New Mexico.* Washington: Government Printing Office, 1910.

Lindsay, Vachel. *Collected Poems.* New York: Macmillan Co., 1967 (reprint).

Lister, Florence & Robert. *Chihuahua Storehouse of Storms.* Albuquerque: University of New Mexico Press, 1966.

Loomis, John. *Leadville Colorado.* Colorado Springs: Gazette Publishing Co., 1879.

McCormick, Richard. "Message to Fifth Legislative Assembly," *Journals of the Fifth Legislative Assembly.* Tucson: Tucson Publishing Co., 1869.

Marshall, John & Cornelius, Temple. *Golden Treasures of the San Juan.* Denver: Sage Books, 1961.

The Mercantile Agency Reference Book (and Key) for the Within Pacific States and Territories. San Francisco: R. G. Dun & Co., 1887.

Michoacan Syndicate. New York: David H. Gildersleeve, 1881–82.

Morgan, H. Wayne (ed.). *The Gilded Age.* Syracuse: Syracuse University Press, 1963.

Mumey, Nolie. *History and Proceedings of Buckskin Joe.* Boulder: Johnson Publishing Co., 1961.

Nevins, Allan. *Ordeal of the Union.* Vol. 2. New York: Charles Scribner's Sons, 1947.

Nichols, Alice. *Bleeding Kansas.* New York: Oxford University Press, 1954.

Ormes, Robert. *Railroads and the Rockies.* Denver: Sage Books, 1963.

Parkhill, Forbes. *The Wildest of the West.* New York: Henry Holt & Co., 1951.

Parrish, Wayland & Hochmuth, Marie (ed.). *American Speeches,* New York: Longmans, Green & Co., 1954.

Parsons, Eugene. "Tabor & Times," *The Trail* (Oct. 1921), pp. 3–9.

Paul, Rodman W. "Colorado as a Pioneer of Science in the Mining West," *Mississippi Valley Historical Review* (June 1960), pp. 34–50.

———. *Mining Frontiers of the Far West, 1848–1880.* New York: Holt Rinehart & Winston, 1963.

Perkin, Robert. *The First Hundred Years.* Garden City: Doubleday & Co., 1959.

Pitkin and Belford, Campaign of 1878. Denver: Republican State Central Committee, 1878.

"Place Names in Colorado, T." *Colorado Magazine* (Jan. 1943), pp. 26–36.

Pletcher, David. *Rails, Mines and Progress: Seven American Promoters in Mexico, 1867–1911.* Ithaca: Cornell University Press, 1958.

Pomeroy, Earl. "The Age of Enterprise," *Mississippi Valley Historical Review* (March 1955), pp. 579–600.

Portrait and Biographical Record of Denver and Vicinity, Colorado. Chicago: Chapman Publishing Co., 1898.

Programme for the First Annual Exhibition of the National Mining and Industrial Exposition at Denver. Denver: Tribune Pub. Co., 1882.

Prospectus of the Leadville and Pennsylvania Consolidated Mining Company. Leadville & Pennsylvania Mining Co., n.d.

Purdy, S. R. "Weighing the Mail," *Illustrated Sentinel*, April 20, 1898.

Raymond, Rossiter. *Mining Industry of the States and Territories of the Rocky Mountains.* New York: J. B. Ford & Co., 1874.

————. *Mines, Mills and Furnaces.* New York: J. B. Ford & Co., 1871.

————. *Mines and Mining in the States and Territories West of the Rocky Mountains.* Washington: Government Printing Office, 1874.

————. *Statistics of Mines and Mining.* Washington: Government Printing Office, 1875.

————. *Statistics of the Mines and Mining in the States and Territories West of the Rocky Mountains.* Washington: Government Printing Office, 1873.

A Report of Labor Disturbances in the State of Colorado from 1880 to 1904. Washington: Government Printing Office, 1905.

Report of the Secretary of War. Vol. 1. Washington: Government Printing Office, 1869.

Report of the Special Committee Appointed to Investigate the Troubles in Kansas. Washington: Cornelius Wendell, 1856.

Report of the Social Statistics of Cities: Part 2, *The Southern and the Western Cities.* Washington: Government Printing Office, 1887.

Reports of Territorial Officers of Colorado Territory. Central City: David Collier, 1867.

The Revised and General Ordinances of the City of Leadville. Leadville: Chronicle, 1881.

Richardson, Albert. *Beyond the Mississippi.* Hartford: American Publishing Co., 1867.

Robinson, Charles. "Topeka and Her Constitution," *Transactions of the Kansas State Historical Society.* Vol. 6. Topeka: W. Y. Morgan, 1900.

Senate Journal of the General Assembly of the State of Colorado (1879). Denver: Times Steam Printing House, 1879.

———— (1881). Denver: Tribune Publishing Co., 1881.

Sheldon, Lionel. *Report of the Governor of New Mexico . . . for the Year 1883.* Washington: Government Printing Office, 1883.

Sherman, John. *John Sherman's Recollections of Forty Years in the House, Senate and Cabinet.* Vol. 1. Chicago: Werner Co., 1895.

Silliman, Benjamin. *The Mineral Regions of Southern New Mexico.* 1882.

Simonin, Louis (Clough, Wilson, translator). *The Rocky Mountain West in 1867.* Lincoln: University of Nebraska Press, 1966.

Smiley, Jerome. *History of Denver.* Denver: J. Williamson & Co., 1903.

————. *Semi-Centennial History of the State of Colorado.* Vol. 1. Chicago: Lewis Publishing Co., 1913.

Smith, Joseph (Parsons, Peryl, ed.). "H. A. W. Tabor's Bittersweet Christmas," *Denver Post,* Dec. 24, 1961.

Spence, Clark C. *British Investments and the American Mining Frontier 1860–1901.* Ithaca: Cornell University Press, 1958.

Spring, Agnes W. "Who Stole Tabor's Gold?" *The 1966 Brand Book.* Boulder: Johnson Publishing Co., 1967.

Statistics of the Population of the United States at the Tenth Census. Vol. 1. Washington: Government Printing Office, 1883.

Stone, W. *The Colorado Hand-Book: Denver and Its Outings.* Denver: Barkhausen & Lester, 1892.

Stevens, Flora. "Molecules from the Denver Mining Exposition," *Kansas City Review of Science* (Aug. 1882), pp. 249–52.

Stone, Wilbur. *History of Colorado.* Vol. 1. Chicago: S. J. Clarke Publishing Co., 1918.

Strahorn, Robert. *To the Rockies and Beyond.* Omaha: The New West Publishing Co., 1879.

Strickler, David. "The Fight for the Stratton Millions," *Brand Book of the Denver Westerners.* Boulder: Johnson Publishing Co., 1963.

Stuthman, Mattie. "High Altitude Memories," *Colorado Magazine* (Jan. 1952), pp. 33–37.

Sweet, Willis. *Carbonate Camps, Leadville and Ten Mile.* Kansas City: Ramsey, Millett & Hudson, 1879.

Tabor Grand Opera House. Denver: Dove & Temple, 1883.

Taylor, Bayard. *Colorado: A Summer Trip.* New York: G. P. Putnam & Son, 1867.

Terms, Rules & Regulations upon which the Leadville Illuminating Gas Co. . . . Leadville: Herald Steam Printing Co., 1879.

Thomas, Sewell. *Silhouettes of Charles S. Thomas.* Caldwell: Caxton, 1959.

Tourists' Handbook of Colorado, New Mexico and Utah. Denver: 1885.

Tritle, Frederick. *Biennial Message of the Governor of Arizona Territory.* Prescott: 1885.

Vickers, W. B. *History of the City of Denver, Arapahoe County and Colorado.* Chicago: O. L. Baskin & Co., 1880.

Wallace, Lew. *Report of the Governor of New Mexico . . . for the Year 1879.* Washington: Government Printing Office, 1879.

Waters, Frank. *Midas of the Rockies.* Denver: University of Denver Press, 1949.

Weston, A. S. "A Fifty-Niner Who Stayed," *Colorado Magazine* (Oct. 1959), pp. 249–53.

Whitehill, H. *Biennial Report of the State Mineralogist of the State of Nevada.* San Francisco: A. L. Bancroft & Co., 1879.

Whitney, James. *Colorado in the United States of America.* London: Cassell, Petter, & Galpin, 1867.

Woodward, P. H. *Guarding the Mails or the Secret Service of the Post-Office Department.* Hartford: J. P. Fitch, 1881.

INDEX

Abbott, Emma, 172, 174, 177, 260, 345 n2
Adams, Alva, 241, 242
Alaska Mine: Tabor buys half, 112; works, 120–22, 181–82, 274
Alaskite, 182
Amelung, Frederick, 181
American Mining Stock Exchange (New York), 140–41
Arthur, Chester: 208–209; Tabor entertains, 226, 229
Ashcroft, Colo., 190–91
Aspen, Colo., 190, 246, 261
Atkinson, Nicholas, 192–93

The Ballad of Baby Doe: xiii; quoted, xiv, 179, 257, 316
Bancroft, Caroline, xiii
Bancroft, Hubert H.: 312; discusses Tabors, 250–51
Bank of Leadville: Tabor helps organize, 100; fails, 259–60, 310
Banking: Tabor involvement, 98–100, 155, 259
Bankruptcy: Tabor never declares, 364 n21
Bavicanora Mine, 296–97
Beery, William, 39, 45
Belford, James, 83, 86
Big Chief Mine, 180
Blacks: politically, 4, 214, 239–40, 350 n7; discrimination against, 262–63
Blaine, James: Colorado investments, 183
Blood, James, 8
Bohn, A. V., 271
Borden, John, 117, 338 n15
Borden, William, 73, 338 n15
Boulder, Colo.: political fight, 241
Bowen, Thomas: 73; senatorial aspirations, 211, 216; senatorial race 1883, 220–24
Breece Mining Co., 188, 310
Bruckman, Samuel, 192
Bryan, William J., 303

Buckskin Joe, Colo.: discovered, 26–27; Tabor's life in, 30–32; declines, 33–35; revives 1879, 329 n35
Bull-Domingo Mine, 147
Bush, William: 101–02, 151, 158, 159, 178, 187, 191, 199, 217, 218; operates Clarendon, 107; stock speculations, 157; Leadville politics, 162; Tabor Grand, 172, 261–62; Tabor divorce, 175, 231; on Augusta, 212; helps in senatorial race, 216, 222; Tabor sues, 233–36
Byers, William: 211; describes Denver, 15–16

California Gulch: gold discovery, 21; declining, 36–37; discovery of silver, 53–54
Calumet and Chicago Canal and Dock Co.: Tabor invests in, 156; Tabor gives up on, 288
Campbell, Ernest, 214
Caribou, Colo., 52, 269
Caribou Mine, 74, 131
Carnegie, Andrew, 319, 321, 322
Chaffee, Jerome: 89, 98, 116, 185, 191; Little Pittsburg Mine, 74, 111, 112–15, 128–31; politician, 80–81, 93, 96, 213–14
Charity: Tabor's activities, 104, 253–54
Chicago, Ill.: Tabor investments, 155–56, 288
Chilcott, George: 224; appointed senator, 210
Chinese: not welcomed in Leadville, 69; campaign issue 1878, 87
Chrysolite Mine: 179; Tabor buys into, 76, 117–19; consolidation, 116–17; declines, 132–34; miners strike, 134–35, 139, 146; collapse, 141–46
Civil War: Tabor reaction to, 29
Clarendon (hotel), 106–07
Clarke, Dumont, 310–11
Colorado: panic 1893, 292–93, 363 n14

Colorado City, Colo., 18–19

Colorado Edison Telephone Co.: Tabor president of, 99

Como Iron, Coal and Land Co., 188

Cook, Charles, 149

Cooper, Job, 242–43

Creel, Enrique, 294–96

Cripple Creek, Colo.: 286; Tabor investments, 307

Daly, George, 135

Davis, Carlyle, 69, 72, 266

Day, Dave: 163, 166, 208–09, 215, 217, 221; Tabor satires, xii; on Little Pittsburg, 130

Day Silver Mining Company, 193

De Friese, Lafayette, 282

DeKay, Drake, 199

Denton, William, 196

Denver, Colo.: described, 15; Tabors winter 1859–60, 17–18; Tabors move to, 93, 96; changing, 97–98, 314; Tabor's business activities, 149–51, 171–76, 177–78, 244, 260–62, 289; Tabor's contributions, 316–17

Denver Apex and Western Railroad, 266

Denver Chamber of Commerce, 257

Denver Circle Railroad Co., 204, 349 n17

Denver Circle Real Estate Company, 244

Denver City Chariot Omnibus Company, 160

Denver and Rio Grande Railroad, 158–59, 191, 201

Denver Stock Exchange, 178–79

Denver, Utah and Pacific Railroad, 159–60

Dill, R. G., xii, 50, 60, 83, 85, 104, 130, 139, 151, 240

Dow, Charles, 114, 115

Dow, Louis, 22

Draper, Morgan, 121

Duggan, Martin, 65

Dun, Robert G., 131

Durango, Colo.: 160, 286; Tabor secures divorce, 230–31

Dutt, William, 27

Dyer, John: 27, 54; Tabor probates son's will, 332 n28

Dyer Mine, 54

Eaton, Ben, 240

Eclipse Mine, 307, 314

Edbrooke, Frank, 299

Edbrooke, William, 112, 149, 151, 173, 201

Elbert, Samuel, 52

Elk Mountain Bonanza: Tabor part owner, 154–55

Evans, John, 27, 80, 265

Evergreen Lakes and Mineral Springs Co., 158

Excelsior Mine, 147–48

Family: Tabor's first marriage, 9–10, 29–33, 42, 46–48; marital problems, 151–52, 175, 211–12, 217–18; remarriage, 227–29; scandals, 230–33; affection for wife and daughters, 247–50, 302, 309, 312–13. See Augusta Tabor, Elizabeth Tabor, Maxey Tabor.

Farnum, Henry, 38

Field, Eugene: 208, 219, 233; Tabor satires, xii, 213, 215, 226–27, 352 n3; creates Tabor legends, 176; political joke, 214; leaves Denver, 249

Field, Marshall: 117, 156, 171; owns share Chrysolite, 76

Fire Companies: Tabor supports, 102–03

First National Bank of Denver: 116, 309–10; Tabor invests in, 98–99; Tabor sells stock, 259

Fisher, George, 100, 102

Flynn, J. P., 203

Fossett, Frank, xii, 33, 53, 75, 110, 118

Freeman Mine, 206

Fryer, George, 71–72, 73, 245

Gandy, Lewis: *The Tabors*, xiii

Garfield, James, 166

Geary, John, 8

Gilpin, William, 25

Glass-Pendery Consolidated Mining Co., 180

Gothic, Colo., 154–55

Gow, Leonard, 275–76

Grand Army of the Republic, 256

Grand Belt Copper Co., 278

Granite, Colo., 188

Grant, James: 191, 198; wins governorship, 214–15
Grant, Ulysses: Tabor takes on tour, 256
Grant, Ulysses Jr., 119
Great West Mutual Aid Association, 244–45
Greeley, Horace: describes Denver, 15
Green, J. P., 43
Gregg, Josiah, 291
Gunnison, Colo.: Tabor's investments in, 155

H. A. W. Tabor Pioneer Stage and Express Line, 160–61
Hague, James: 110–11; examines Chrysolite, 117, 118
Hall, Frank, xii, 81, 94, 137, 164, 240–41
Hamill, William: 81, 94, 240; campaign 1878, 84, 87, 88; senatorial aspirations, 216, 220–23
Harker, Oliver, 182, 271–72
Harp, William, 302
Harrison, Benjamin, 305, 365 n7
Harrison Hook and Ladder, 102
Hawkins, James, 262–63
Henriett Mine: 183; mining problems, 271–73
Hibernia Mine: 148; Tabor troubles, 184–88
Hill, Nathaniel: 225; senator, 94–96, 207–08; campaign 1882, 213–14
Holland, Vermont, 5
Hollister, Ovando: comments on California Gulch, 37
Honduras: Tabor invests in, 268
Hook, George: discovers Little Pittsburg, 71–72; sells out, 73
Hunki-Dori Company, 270
Hurd, Nathan, 32

Idaho: Tabor investments, 277–78

Jackson, Helen H.: visits Leadville, 70
Jamestown, Colo., 189
Jefferson Territory: Tabor elected to legislature, 25
Jesus Maria (Ocampo), Mexico, 291, 363 n12

Jewett, Cornel, 238, 266
Jones, John: 119, 124–25; background, 339 n20

Kaiser Gold Mines Company: works Vulture Mine, 282–85
Kansas: Tabor goes to, 3; involved politics, 6–9; farms, 10–11
Karsner, David: *Silver Dollar*, xiii
Kelley, William D., 204
Kellogg, Samuel, 20
Keyes, Winfield: 159; Chrysolite, 118–19, 132–33, 142; examines Little Pittsburg, 115; miners' strike, 135; reputation hurt, 146
Kingsley, Charles, 46, 177

Labor troubles: Leadville 1880, 134–39; Tam O'Shanter, 274
Lacy, A. H., 239
Land Grants: Tabor dabbles in, 267
Langhorne, James, 184, 187
Langrishe, Jack, 107, 262
Lauret City, see Buckskin Joe
Lawrence, Kansas, 3, 4, 326 n18
Leach, Samuel: discusses Tabors, 30–32; evaluates Tabor, 317–18; goes to Montana, 329 n25
Leadville, Colo.: boom 1877–78, 60; city government problems, 63–67; grows, 67–70; arouses jealousy, 70; role in Colorado politics, 81–82; Tabor's business activities in, 100–02, 106–08, 158, 259–60; criminal problems, 104–06; miners' strike 1880, 134–39; hurt by 1880 events, 139–40, 145; Tabor's political base, 162; Tabor era ends, 259–60; mining declines, 273, 293
Leadville Daily Herald: Tabor part owner, 153–54; Tabor controls, 265–66
Leadville Evening Times: Tabor part owner, 154
Leadville and Great Eastern Broadgauge Railroad, 159
Leadville Illuminating Gas Company, 101, 107, 310
Leadville Military Companies, 103–04, 135
Leadville Mining Railroad, 159
Leadville Omnibus and Toll-Road Co., 102

Leadville and Roaring Fork Mining and Prospecting Co., 190
Leadville Stock Exchange, 108
Leadville Telephone Co., 100–101
Leadville, Ten Mile and Breckenridge Railroad, 159
Legends: growth of Tabor, xi–xii, 112, 125, 206
Leonard, Lou: 182, 193, 194, 274, 277; Tabor's bookkeeper, 74; Hibernia, 186; backs Tabor, 210; manages Matchless, 180–81, 270–71; death, 271
Lickscumdidrick Lode, 148
Little Pittsburg Mine: 321; discovered, 72; Tabor involvement with, 72–75; production, 75; development, 109–10; for sale, 111–15; prospers, 116; collapse, 127–132, 145–46; name spelling, 334 n19; lead sales, 337 n1
Londoner, Wolfe: 26, 242; backs Tabor, 210; campaign 1882, 213–14
Loveland, William: 84, 88–89, 159, 245; political foe of Tabor, 162; National Mining and Industrial Exposition, 200–06
Lovell, William "Chicken Bill": sells Chrysolite to Tabor, 76
Lucy B. Hussey Mine, 270

MacArthur-Forrest Process, 275–76, 361 n24
Mackey, James: 263; appeal dismissed, 358 n5
Maid of Erin Mine, 183, 360 n20. See Henriett Mine
Malta, Colo., 52, 55
Marriages. See Family.
Matchless Concentrator Co., 273–74, 320
Matchless Mine: 289, 321; Tabor acquires, 122–23; bonanza, 180–81; in the 1880s, 270–71; Tabor tries to keep, 301–02; validity of production, 360 n17; "hang onto" legend, 367 n18
Mater, Charles, 59
Maxey, Nathaniel, 14, 19
McCann, Peter, 198–99
McCourt, Peter: 242, 269, 270; brother of Baby Doe, 233; Silver Circuit, 261; offers bribe, 284; in Mexico, 292, 293–96; appointed trustee, 299; Tabor advises, 306
McMachen, Edgar: *The Tabor Story*, xiii
Mears, Otto, 221–22, 223, 242
Mexico: Tabor invests in mining, 196–97, 290–97
Meyer, William, 240–41
Michoacan Syndicate, 196–97
Mines: sale prices vary, 334 n19; spelling of names, 334 n19. See individual names.
Mining: early Colorado silver, 52–53; problems of, 122; code used, 338 n3. Tabor's activities in: early experiences, 16–17, 20–21, 22–24, 35; Nevada and New Mexico investments, 193–96; Mexican investments, 196–97, 290–97; grubstaking, 49; small mining operations, 50, 54–55, 77, 120–22, 179–82, 188–89, 190, 270–74, 277–78, 307–08, 313–14; philosophy, 109; how selected mines, 123–24; selected mine managers, 182–83; mining sales not in cash, 183–84; mill and smelter investments, 198–99, 275–77; on miner's life, 286. See individual mines.
Mining Record (New York): muckrakes Tabor, 184–87
Moffat, David: 98, 183, 185; partner of Chaffee, 74; sells Little Pittsburg stock, 113–15; buys Tabor's Little Pittsburg stock, 116; role in Little Pittsburg collapse, 128–31; Denver, Utah and Pacific Railroad, 159–60
Montana: Tabor investments, 277
Mooney, Michael, 134
Morrish, James: Vulture mining engineer, 282–85
Mosquito Pass wagon road: Tabor interested in, 344 n12
National Mining and Industrial Exposition, 200–06, 264–65
New Discovery Mine, 71–72, 73, 74, 110, 111
New England Emigrant Aid Company, 3
Newspapers: Tabor's activities, 153–55, 265–66
Nicknames: Tabor called "Grand

Old Man," 239; not called Haw, 254, 367 n16

Niwot Mine, 270

Northwestern Mutual Insurance Co., 287, 299–300

Oro City, Colo. (No. 1): Augusta's reaction to, 23–24; Tabors return to, 35

Oro City, Colo. (No. 2): camp moved, 45; description of, 45–47; declines, 59

Patterson, Thomas: 87, 216; defends Tabor, 234–35; on Tabor, 319

Payne's Bar (Idaho Springs), Colo.: Tabor mines, 16–18

Perky, H. D., 200, 201, 204

Phillips Mine, 27

Pierce, Franklin, 7–8

Pike's Peak: rumors of gold, 11–12, 13

Pioneer Association: Tabor member, 29, 257

Pitkin, Frederick: 90, 212; candidate for governor, 81; nominated governor, 83, 164; Leadville miners' strike, 136–37; senatorial issue, 209–10, 216, 220–23

Pitkin County Colo.: involvement in National Mining Exposition, 202–03

Politics, Tabor's involvement: in Kansas, 6–9; pre-1876, 25, 48; mayor of Leadville, 62–67, 104–06; lieutenant governor, 80, 82–83, 95, 96, 165; acting governor, 165–67; senatorial aspirations, 95, 207–08, 209–11, 219–24, 351 n21; senator, 224, 225–27; campaigns: 1878, 83–90; 1880, 162–65; 1882, 213–15; 1884–88, 239–44; 354 n21; 1898–99, 311, 314; delegate to Republican State Central Committee, 79; on politics, 91; presidential boom, 238–39; Republican party chairman, 240–42; silver issue, 303–06; rejoins Republicans, 311–12; did not declare martial law 1880, 341 n16

Poorman Mine: 124; Tabor buys, sells, 269–70

Postmaster: Buckskin Joe, 28; Oro City, 37; Leadville, 70–71; Denver, 308–09

Printer Boy Mine: Oro City's best, 37, 49–50, 51

Prostitutes, 23, 68

Pueblo, Canon City and Leadville Railroad, 158–59

Pueblo, Colo.: Tabor considers investments, 97; Tabor invests in area, 267

Railroads: Tabor speculates, 158–60, 266–67

Raymond, Rossiter: 50–51, 54; examines Little Pittsburg, 114–15; role in Little Pittsburg collapse, 128, 129; Chrysolite Mine, 117, 133, 142–45; reputation hurt, 146

Republican Party: in Colorado, 80–82; senatorship, 94–95. See Politics.

Reveille: 68; Tabor invests in, 98; Tabor merges, 153

Rische, August: 100; discovers Little Pittsburg, 71–72; partner with Tabor in Little Pittsburg, 73–74; Alaska Mine, 112

Robert E. Lee Mine, 137, 179–80

Roberts, George: 140, 157, 320; Chrysolite involvement, 118–19; Chrysolite collapse, 144–45; New Mexico investments, 194

Robinson, George, 165

Rockefeller, John, 319, 322

Rockwell, Lewis: 218, 264, 273; Tabor's lawyer, 180–81; on Durango divorce, 231–32; defends Tabor, 234; Tabor owes money, 302

Rocky Mountain News: attacks Tabor 1878, 84–90; regrets Tabor attack, 91–92

Routt, John: 97, 216, 223; supports Grant, 163

Rowell, Charles: Tabor's Leadville agent, 158

St. Louis, Missouri: Tabor secretly married, 232

Sample, George, 221

San Juan mining region: Tabor investments in, 120–22; Tabor criticized for lack of support, 181–82

Santa Eduwiges Mine: Tabor's last hope, 290–96
Scooper Mine, 184
Seaman, Lafayette, 269, 276
Sewell, Arthur, 119
Silver Circuit, 261
Silver issue, 290, 303–04
Silver price: declining, 274–75
Slavery: Tabor's attitude toward, 4
Smiley, Jerome, 317
Smith, Eben: 98, 182, 273, 274; at Tam O'Shanter, 193
Smith, Laura: troubles with Tabor, 299–300, 364 n20
Solitaire Mine, 194–95
Stainburn, James, 297, 364 n17
Steck, Amos, 217
Stevens, William, 53
Stock Exchanges: Leadville, 180; American, 140–41; Denver, 178–79
Stone, Wilbur: 172, 243; comments on Tabor, 252
Stratton, Winfield: lends money to Tabor, 307; compared to Tabor, 321–22
Sullivan, Augustus, 288
Sumner, Edwin V.: dismisses Free Soil Legislature, 7

Tabor, Augusta Pierce: marriage and divorce, 9, 78, 92, 151–53, 175, 211–12, 217–18, 224, 231–32; frontier experiences, 10, 14, 16, 20–21, 32–33, 39–40, 40–44; goes to Maine 1860, 24; first Leadville Christmas, 62; hurt by political attacks, 87; affluence bothers, 96–97; significance of, 179, 237–38, 318; involved in Bush trial, 234; interviewed, 236–37
Tabor, Elizabeth Bonduel (Cupid), 247–48, 302, 311, 314
Tabor, Elizabeth McCourt (Baby Doe): 218, 352 n4; marriage to Tabor, 227–29, 246–47; business responsibilities 1890s, 289–90, 293–98; increasingly religious, 302; husband's last days, 314–15
Tabor, Emily (Moys): 302, 314; Tabor's sister, 5; on Tabor's matrimonial problems, 152; Tabor helps, 253

Tabor, John: 253, 274, 311; Tabor's brother, 5; Alaska Mine, 122, 181–82; advises brother, 238; goes to Mexico, 292, 295–96; planned to go to Alaska, 308
Tabor, Maxey: 14, 24, 30, 40, 100, 250–51, 315; Tabor's son, 11, 326 n13; helps father, 47, 48, 59; sides with mother, 151, 238; Scooper Mine, 184; father comments about, 250–51; spelling of name, 326 n13
Tabor, Rose Mary (Honeymaid): Tabor's daughter, 247–48
Tabor Amusement Co., 289
Tabor Block, 149–50, 161, 287, 300, 316, 317
Tabor City, 257
Tabor Fire Insurance Company, 244
Tabor Grand Hotel, 260
Tabor Grand Opera House (Denver): 260–61, 262, 287, 299–300, 316; construction, 150–51, 171–73; opens, 173–76
Tabor Hose Co. No. 1 (Leadville), 102–103
Tabor Hose Co. No. 5 (Denver), 99
Tabor Investment Company, 269–70
Tabor Milling Co.: Tabor's involvement, 198–99
Tabor Mine Co., 199–200
Tabor Mines and Mills Co., 289, 310
Tabor Opera House (Leadville): 106–08, 260; cost, 337 n18
Tabor Real Estate Co., 289
Tabor Station, 257
Tam O'Shanter Mine: 124; Tabor's investment in, 190–93; never produces, 274
Taylor, Bayard: visits Buckskin Joe, 34–35; visits Oro City, 36
Teller, Henry: 240; senator, 80–81; opposed Hill, 94–96; appointed Secretary of Interior, 208–10; on Tabor, 229; silver spokesman, 304–06; congratulates Tabor, 308
Teller, Willard: 192; senatorial race 1883, 220–23; Bush's lawyer, 234–35
Thomas, Charles, 311
Topeka, Kansas: Free Soil capital, 6
Tritch, George, 288, 301

Utah: Tabor investments, 277
Ute Pass: in 1859, 327 n8

Vulture Mine (Arizona): 124; Tabor owns, 281–85; Tabor tries to regain, 302, 311; price of, 362 n2
Vulture Mine (Colorado), 145

Wallace, Lew, 193
Wanless, George, 154
Ward, Colorado: 270; Tabor mines near, 307–08
Ware, Isaac, 34
Wealth: Tabor's, 44–45, 330 n13; estimated, 255–56; declining, 268–69
Werner, Edward, 275–77
Weston, Algernon S.: 165, 182, 220, 291–92; describes Oro City, 25; buys Tabor Opera House, 301

Weston, William, 122
Wheel of Fortune Mine, 124, 189
Wilde, Oscar: tours Matchless, 256
Windsor Hotel: Tabor invests in, 151; Tabor fight over, 212
Wiswall, Thomas, 241, 242, 269, 314
Wolcott, Edward: 81, 83; supports Hill, 94; Bush's lawyer, 234; wins senatorship, 243–44; Tabor advises, 250; appoints Tabor postmaster, 308
Wolcott, Henry: 81, 159, 213; Tabor thwarts, 165, 167
Wood, Alvinus, 53
Wurtzebach, John, 194, 195, 198
Wyoming: Tabor investments, 277
Young, John, 232

Zeandale, Kansas: Tabor settles near, 3–4; growing, 10